# THE NEW ENCYCLOPEDIA OF
# AQUATIC LIFE

# THE NEW ENCYCLOPEDIA OF
# AQUATIC LIFE

## VOLUME II

### FISHES AND AQUATIC MAMMALS

EDITED BY

ANDREW CAMPBELL
AND JOHN DAWES

☑®

Facts On File, Inc.

*Published in North America by:*
Facts On File, Inc.
132 West 31st Street,
New York NY 10001

**THE BROWN REFERENCE GROUP PLC**
(incorporating Andromeda Oxford Limited)
8 Chapel Place,
Rivington Street,
London EC2A 3DQ
www.brownreference.com

*Editorial Director*  Lindsey Lowe
*Project Manager*  Peter Lewis
*Art Directors*  Martin Anderson, Chris Munday
*Editor*  Rita Demetriou
*Cartographic Editor*  Tim Williams
*Picture Managers*  Claire Turner, Helen Sim
*Picture Researchers*  Alison Floyd, Becky Cox
*Production Director*  Alastair Gourlay
*Production Controller*  Maggie Copeland
*Editorial Consultant*  Graham Bateman
*Indexer*  Ann Barrett

**Library of Congress Cataloging in Publication Data**
available from Facts On File

Vol ISBN: 0-8160-6200-5
Set  ISBN: 0-8160-5119-4

Facts On File books are available at special discounts
when purchased in bulk quantities for businesses,
associations, institutions or sales promotions. Please
call our Special Sales Department in New York at
(212) 967-8800 or (800) 322-8755.

You can find Facts On File on the World Wide Web at
http://www.factsonfile.com

Cover design by Cathy Rincon

Printed in China

10 9 8 7 6 5 4 3 2 1

**Photo** page ii: *West Indian manatees* Doug Perrine/Planet
Earth Pictures.

# Advisory Editors

**Dr. W. Nigel Bonner,**
British Antarctic Survey,
Cambridge, England

**Professor Fu-Shiang Chia,**
University of Alberta,
Edmonton, Canada

**Dr. Richard Connor,**
University of Massachusetts at
Dartmouth, North Dartmouth,
Massachusetts

**Dr. Peter Evans,**
University of Oxford,
England

**Dr. John Harwood,**
Gatty Marine Laboratory,
University of St. Andrews
Scotland

**Dr. David Macdonald,**
University of Oxford,
England

**Dr. John E. McCosker**
Steinhart Aquarium
California Academy of Sciences
San Francisco, California

**Dr R. M. McDowall**
Ministry of Agriculture and
Fisheries
Christchurch
New Zealand

**Dr. Bernd Würsig**
Texas A&M University
College Station
Texas

# Artwork Panels

Mick Loates
Denys Ovenden
Colin Newman
Priscilla Barrett
S. S. Driver
Roger Gorringe
Richard Lewington
Kevin Maddison
Malcolm McGregor
Norman Weaver

# Contributors

**PKA**  Paul K. Anderson, University of Calgary,
Canada

**SSA**  Sheila S. Anderson, British Antarctic
Survey, England

**RGB**  Roland G. Bailey, University of London,
England

**GJB**  Gerald J. Bakus, University of Southern
California, Los Angeles

**CCB**  Carole C. Baldwin, National Museum of
Natural History, Washington, D.C.

**KEB**  Keith E. Banister, (formerly) British
Museum, London, England

**RB**  Robin Best, Instituto Nacional de
Pequisas de Amazonia, Brazil

**RCB**  Robin C. Brace, University of
Nottingham, England

**BB**  Bernice Brewster, British Museum,
London, England

**PB**  Paul Brodie, Bedford Institute of
Oceanography, Dartmouth, Nova Scotia,
Canada

**AC**  Andrew Campbell, Queen Mary College,
University of London, England

**JEC**  June E. Chatfield, Gilbert White
Museum, Selborne, Hampshire, England

**JD**  Jim Darling, West Coast Whale
Research, Fairbanks, Alaska

**JD**  John Dawes, Manilva, Málaga, Spain

**GD**  Gordon Dickerson, (formerly) Wellcome
Research Laboratory, Beckenham,
England

Characins and catfishes
see page 214–19

| | | | | | | |
|---|---|---|---|---|---|---|
| **GDi** | Guido Dingerkus, American Museum of Natural History, New York | **CL** | Christina Lockyer, British Antarctic Survey, England | **LW** | Lindy Weilgart, Dalhousie University, Canada |
| **DPD** | Daryl Domning, Howard University, Washington, D.C. | **HM** | Helene Marsh, James Cook University, Australia | **RSW** | Randall S. Wells, Moss Landing Marine Laboratories, Moss Landing, California |
| **AWE** | Albert W. Erickson, University of Seattle, Seattle, Washington | **AM** | Tony Martin, NERC Sea Mammal Research Unit, St. Andrews, Scotland | **HW** | Hal Whitehead, Dalhousie University, Canada |
| **PGHE** | Peter G.H. Evans, University of Oxford, England | **JMcC** | John E. McCosker, California Academy of Sciences, San Francisco, California | **IW** | Ian J. Winfield, Centre for Ecology and Hydrology, Cumbria, England |
| **SAF** | Svein A. Fosså, Akvariekonsulenten, Grimstad, Norway | **RMcD** | Bob McDowall, Ministry of Agriculture and Fisheries, Christchurch, New Zealand | **BW** | Bernd Würsig, Texas A&M University, College Station, Texas |

**GDi** Guido Dingerkus, American Museum of Natural History, New York

**DPD** Daryl Domning, Howard University, Washington, D.C.

**AWE** Albert W. Erickson, University of Seattle, Seattle, Washington

**PGHE** Peter G.H. Evans, University of Oxford, England

**SAF** Svein A. Fosså, Akvariekonsulenten, Grimstad, Norway

**RG** Ray Gambell, International Whaling Commission, England

**PRG** Peter R. Garwood, University of Newcastle upon Tyne, England

**DEG** David E. Gaskin, University of Guelph, Canada

**CG** John Craighead George, North Slope Borough Dept. of Wildlife Management, Barrow, Alaska

**JG** Jonathan Gordon, WildCRU, University of Oxford, England

**JH** John Harwood, NERC Sea Mammal Research Unit, St. Andrews, Scotland

**GJH** Gordon J. Howes, British Museum, London, England

**JJ** Jack Jackson, Woking, Surrey, England

**SDK** Scott D. Kraus, New England Aquarium, Boston, Massachusetts

**J-LP** Johanna Laybourn-Parry, University of Lancaster, England

**CL** Christina Lockyer, British Antarctic Survey, England

**HM** Helene Marsh, James Cook University, Australia

**AM** Tony Martin, NERC Sea Mammal Research Unit, St. Andrews, Scotland

**JMcC** John E. McCosker, California Academy of Sciences, San Francisco, California

**RMcD** Bob McDowall, Ministry of Agriculture and Fisheries, Christchurch, New Zealand

**JMP** Jane M. Packard, University of Florida, Gainesville, Florida

**VP** Vassili Papastavrou, University of Bristol, England

**LP** Lynne R. Parenti, Smithsonian Institution, Washington, D.C.

**TP** Theodore W. Pietsch, University of Washington, Seattle, Washington State

**PSR** Philip S. Rainbow, Queen Mary College, University of London, England

**GBR** Galen B. Rathbun, California Academy of Sciences, Cambria, California

**RR** Randall Reeves, University of Quebec, Canada

**AT** Andrew Taber, Wildlife Conservation Society, New York, New York

**PLT** Peter L. Tyack, Northeast Fisheries Science Center, Woods Hole, Massachusetts

**LW** Lindy Weilgart, Dalhousie University, Canada

**RSW** Randall S. Wells, Moss Landing Marine Laboratories, Moss Landing, California

**HW** Hal Whitehead, Dalhousie University, Canada

**IW** Ian J. Winfield, Centre for Ecology and Hydrology, Cumbria, England

**BW** Bernd Würsig, Texas A&M University, College Station, Texas

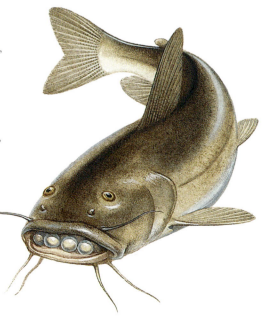

# CONTENTS

## IUCN CATEGORIES

**Ex** Extinct, when there is no reasonable doubt that the last individual of a taxon has died.

**EW** Extinct in the Wild, when a taxon is known only to survive in captivity, or as a naturalized population well outside the past range.

**Cr** Critically Endangered, when a taxon is facing an extremely high risk of extinction in the wild in the immediate future.

**En** Endangered, when a taxon faces a very high risk of extinction in the wild in the near future.

**Vu** Vulnerable, when a taxon faces a high risk of extinction in the wild in the medium-term future.

**LR** Lower Risk, when a taxon has been evaluated and does not satisfy the criteria for CR, EN or VU.

Note: The Lower Risk (LR) category is further divided into three subcategories: Conservation Dependent (cd) – taxa which are the focus of a continuing taxon-specific or habitat-specific conservation program targeted toward the taxon, the cessation of which would result in the taxon qualifying for one of the threatened categories within a period of five years; Near Threatened (nt) – taxa which do not qualify for Conservation Dependent but which are close to qualifying for VU; and Least Concern (lc) – taxa which do not qualify for the two previous categories.

Rorquals
*see pages 336–37*

# PREFACE

**ALL LIFE ON EARTH ORIGINATED IN THE PRIMEVAL** seas some 4,000 million years ago. After eons of evolution, the waters that cover over two-thirds of our planet are home to a bewildering array of creatures, from tiny single-celled animals to giant squid and monstrous sharks, and from beautiful and delicate sea anemones, corals, and sponges to grotesque angler fishes and other denizens of the deep.

The aim of the *New Encyclopedia of Aquatic Life* is – to hazard an obvious pun – to give the reader an "in-depth" insight into this largely hidden underwater world and reveal the secrets of its diverse inhabitants. Organized into two volumes, the *New Encyclopedia* proceeds from the microscopic to the gargantuan: Volume 1 treats the aquatic invertebrates and begins a comprehensive review of fishes, while Volume 2 completes the fishes section and covers the aquatic mammals. The common denominator of all the taxonomic groupings described is that they lead an entirely aquatic lifestyle.

**Aquatic invertebrates** are invertebrate animals that live in the sea, fresh water, or moist terrestrial habitats; they also include many parasites whose "aquatic" environment is that of the bodies of their hosts. The term "invertebrates" refers to the fact that none of these animals has a bony or cartilaginous backbone.

Some invertebrate phyla, while overwhelmingly aquatic in habits, contain groups that have terrestrial forms. For example, although segmented worms are mainly marine, the earthworms live in damp soil; also, slugs and snails are terrestrial variations of the mainly aquatic mollusks. For completeness, such terrestrial forms are also considered here. The diversities of form and biology are immense – a salmon and an elephant have more in common with one another than do many apparently related members of invertebrate phyla.

Thanks to the prominent part they play in our lives, birds and mammals are hugely popular subjects of study and amateur interest. By contrast, aquatic invertebrates are seen by some people as the poor relations of the animal kingdom. This is far from the case. For sheer beauty, the microscopic architecture of the diatoms and the sea anemones is not easily surpassed. For their capacity to cause devastating disease in humans, the malaria and bilharzia parasites are without equal. And, for complexity of structure and intelligence, the squids and octopuses rival fishes in their mastery of the water and in their fascinating behavior.

Molecular analysis has resulted in a major revision of invertebrate systematics, and our text endeavors to reflect the latest findings. However, some chapter groupings remain mere "flags of convenience" and should not be taken as indicating taxonomic affinities between the different groups described.

With over 24,000 species known to science, **Fishes** are found almost everywhere: from the cold lightless waters of the deepest oceans to lakes high in the Andes mountains, on land, in mud, underground, in the air, even in trees. There are luminous fishes, transparent fishes, and electric fishes. The size range is colossal, from species that are fully grown at 9mm (0.4in) to species reaching 12.5m (41ft) in length. Some species are represented by countless millions of individuals, while others just manage to survive precariously with a handful of individuals.

Fish classification continues to be a matter of great debate among ichthyologists; as with the invertebrates, DNA studies have radically altered our understanding of relationships. While the present survey broadly adopts the scheme proposed by Joseph S. Nelson's authoritative volume *Fishes of the World* (3rd edn., 1994), we have given compilers of the individual accounts free rein to follow their preferred classifications. The meticulously compiled web resource FishBase (www.fishbase.org) has also been of invaluable help to the authors and editors of the current work, not least by supplying a standard set of common English species names.

Finally, the section on **Aquatic mammals** surveys two totally unrelated orders whose members are adapted to life at sea: the whales and dolphins (order Cetacea) and the dugong and manatees (order Sirenia). From a distance, the torpedo-shaped uniformity of marine mammals masks the character of each species; the illusion may be of animals with less individuality than some of the more familiar terrestrial mammals. But with closer study, that illusion is banished, and the ways of whale and dolphin spring intimately to life, and in so doing emphasize the subtlety and frailty of the natural web, and the dependence of the monumental upon the minute.

The bulk of the *New Encyclopedia* comprises general entries describing the biology, distribution, diet, breeding, and conservation status of particular groups; these groups are treated variously at the level of phyla (invertebrates), orders (fishes) or families (sea mammals). Each such entry incorporates a fact panel providing a digest of key data, and often including outline drawings to help the reader visualize the creatures in question. For large groups this information is consolidated in a separate table. In addition, special features focus in detail on subjects as diverse as the origin of malaria, Sockeye salmon breeding runs, and Dugong seagrass grazing.

As well as the outline drawings there are many color illustrations by highly gifted wildlife artists that vividly bring their subjects to life (because fishes vary widely in size, it is not possible to show them to scale in the plates). Throughout, color photographs from diverse sources complement and enhance the text and artwork.

We are much indebted to the contributors who updated the text of the original 1985 edition by Banister and Campbell; sadly, Keith Banister, who died in 1999, could not be among them. Thanks are also due to the design, editorial, and production team who have seen the *Encyclopedia* through to publication. For all involved in this undertaking, a major reward is in knowing that the work will help raise awareness about the fragility of life in our oceans, lakes, and rivers, and the pressing need to conserve it at all costs.

**ANDREW CAMPBELL**
QUEEN MARY COLLEGE, UNIVERSITY OF LONDON

**JOHN DAWES**
MANILVA, SPAIN

# Pike, Salmon, Argentines, and Allies

**m**EMBERS OF THE ORDERS INCLUDING *pike, smelts, salmon and their allies are of great interest to many people. They contain prize angling fishes, important food fishes, and fishes of great interest to biologists for their migratory habits. The last include many examples of diadromy – the phenomenon of migration between fresh and salt water. Diadromous species that spawn in fresh waters are said to be anadromous, while those spawning in the sea are said to be catadromous.*

The superorder Protacanthopterygii was originally created to contain primitive teleostean fishes such as pike, salmon, lantern fishes, whale fishes, and galaxiids. However, research has shown that this is an artificial grouping united largely on primitive characters which do not indicate true relationships. Consequently the superorder and its orders and families have often been revised and continue to be unstable. The classification currently most widely accepted comprises three orders, the Esociformes, Osmeriformes, and Salmoniformes (see Salmon, Pike, and Related Families).

## Pike
### FAMILY ESOCIDAE

The pike are renowned sport fishes, some of which grow to a very large size and are known for their fighting abilities once hooked. They are powerful and aggressive predators, mostly on other fish, and generally lead solitary lives. In many fish communities their feeding has a major impact on the abundance and behavior of smaller species.

The distribution of pike is basically circumpolar. Of the five species, the Northern pike is widespread in North America, Europe and Asia, but the others are more local in range, with one in Siberia and three in North America. The biggest of them is the muskellunge, or muskie, which may reach more than 30kg (66lb) and 1.5m (5ft) in length, while the Northern pike may exceed 20kg (44lb) and 1m (3.3ft).

The North American pickerels are now regarded by most experts as two species – the Chain pickerel, and two subsubspecies of *E. americanus* known as the Redfin pickerel and the Grass pickerel. All are small fishes, the Redfin and Grass pickerels rarely growing to more than 30cm (1ft) long. The Chain pickerel is somewhat larger and in areas where it cohabits with the others may hybridize and produce fishes that are often claimed to be Redfin or Chain pickerels of record size. It is not always easy to distinguish the two or three species, and even more difficult to establish the true nature of the hybrids.

All pike species are similar in appearance, being slender, elongate fish somewhat laterally compressed with a long, flattened, almost alligator-like snout. The mouth itself is also long and has large pointed teeth. Perhaps the most distinctive feature of pike is the clustering of their dorsal and anal fins. This concentration of finnage at the rear enables them to accelerate rapidly and has endowed them, and also other fish with similar fin arrangements, with the name of "lurking" or "ambushing predators." They skulk among vegetation around the margins of lakes and rivers and surge out to catch passing prey.

Pike are mainly freshwater fish, but a few venture into mildly saline waters in Canadian lakes and the Baltic Sea. Spawning takes place among vegetation in still or gently flowing marginal shallows during the early spring. The female pairs with a male and the two spend several hours together releasing and fertilizing small batches of quite large eggs (2.3–3.0mm, about 0.1in, in diameter). A large female may lay several hundred thousand eggs. Factors known to influence the success of pike reproduction include the degree of inundation by high water levels of terrestrial vegetation, which acts as excellent spawning habitat, and the warmth of the late summer. Young pike are also subject to considerable cannibalism from both their peers and their elders. From the moment they hatch, young pike are predators, initially eating insects and small crustaceans but very soon becoming fisheaters like the adults. Large pike may also occasionally take small mammals and birds.

Pike are highly prized by anglers, especially in Europe. In North America, where salmon species are more diverse, abundant, and freely available, the popularity of pike is not as great, though many fishermen have the aspiration of catching a large muskellunge.

▶ **Right** *The Redfin pickerel (Esox americanus americanus) is widespread throughout North America and inhabits swamps, lakes, and backwaters. Its snout is shorter than that of many other Esox species.*

## Mudminnows
FAMILY UMBRIDAE

The mudminnows are closely related to pike. They were once included in the families Daliidae and Novumbridae, but are now united in one family. Their present disjunct distribution is a relict one, and fossils found in Europe and North America show that their former distribution was much like that of the extant pike. Today they occur in eastern Europe, in the Danube and Dniester river systems (European mudminnow, *Umbra krameri*); in eastern North America (Southern mudminnow, *Umbra pygmaea*, which has been introduced to Europe); in the Chehalis River, Washington State, USA (*Novumbra hubbsi*); in the Great Lakes and Mississippi drainage (*Umbra limi*); and Alaska and Eastern Siberia (Alaska blackfish, *Dallia pectoralis*).

Mudminnows are small fishes, rarely exceeding 15cm (6in) in length. The caudal fin is rounded and the dorsal and anal fins are set far back, as in the pike. Their mottled dark brown or olivaceous coloring is cryptic. All are carnivorous and feed on small invertebrates and larval fishes, which they seize by making rapid lunges. They are sluggish, retiring fishes, hiding among vegetation waiting for the prey to come within striking distance.

Mudminnows are capable of living in high densities in poorly oxygenated swampy areas as they can utilize atmospheric oxygen. They are tolerant of drought, which they escape by burrowing into soft mud and ooze, and also tolerate cold, especially the Alaska blackfish, much as one might expect from where it lives. In many books there are accounts of the Alaska blackfish being able to withstand freezing. This frequently repeated untruth seems to originate from a book by L.M. Turner in 1886. In his *Contributions to the Natural History of Alaska*, he wrote "The vitality of this fish is astonishing. They will remain in . . . grass buckets for weeks, and when brought in the house and thawed out they will be as lively as ever. The pieces which are thrown to the ravenous dogs are eagerly swallowed; the animal heat of the dog's stomach thaws the fish out, whereupon its movements cause the dog to vomit it up alive. This I have *seen* . . ." Sadly for sensation, properly controlled experiments have shown that, although the Alaska blackfish is capable of surviving at very low temperatures, it cannot withstand freezing or being icebound.

⬥ **Above** *Along with many other members of the order Salmoniformes, the European Brown trout (Salmo trutta trutta) is greatly sought after as a food fish.*

### FACTFILE

**PIKES, SMELTS, SALMONS...**

Superorder: Protacanthopterygii

Orders: Esociformes, Osmeriformes, Salmoniformes

Over 300 species in 89 genera and 16 families.

**Distribution** Worldwide in seas and freshwater.

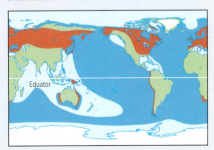

See Salmon, Pike, and Related Families ▷

## Argentines
### FAMILY ARGENTINIDAE

The argentines take their common name from their silvery sheen, and comprise the two genera *Argentina* and *Glossanodon*. They are exclusively marine species. They are also called herring smelts and reveal their osmeroid relationships by having an adipose fin and by superficially resembling the anadromous freshwater osmerid smelts. They are mostly small, usually less than 30cm (12in). They are elongate, slender, silvery fish, darker on the back, usually lacking distinctive markings or coloration. They have scales and a well-developed, rather flaglike dorsal fin high on the back, usually in front of the ventral fins, which are in the abdominal region. The head is longish with a pointed snout, the mouth small and terminal. The eyes are very large, a common feature of fish living at some depth in the sea. Though not well known, argentines are widespread in most oceans of the world; they are found down to about 1,000m (3,300ft), mostly a few hundred meters down, where they probably live in aggregations, if not in coordinated schools. From their teeth and stomach contents we know that they are carnivores, living on small crustaceans, worms and other prey. Their small size and the depths at which they occur mean that they are not of prime importance to commercial fisheries, but they are taken for processing. They also act as a forage fish for larger and more significant food fishes of deep waters.

Although the adults are deepwater fish, the eggs and young are found in the surface waters of the ocean, usually over the continental shelf. Their eggs are 3–3.5mm (0.1in) in diameter. They are slow-growing fish and are long lived, one estimate being that they may live for 20 years or more.

## Microstomatids
### FAMILY MICROSTOMATIDAE

Despite its wide distribution, the family Microstomatidae has been only poorly studied. The Slender argentine is a greatly elongated, mesopelagic species that probably feeds on zooplankton and is generally solitary. It spawns throughout the year in the Mediterranean Sea. The Stout argentine is also greatly elongated and found in continental slope regions, with planktonic eggs and larvae. *Xenophthalmichthys danae* is bizarre, with tubular eyes that look forward like a pair of car headlights.

## Deepsea Smelts
### FAMILY BATHYLAGIDAE

The family Bathylagidae consists of small, dark, large-eyed fishes found worldwide with many species showing daily vertical migrations to depths of about 3,500m (11,500ft). Their diets

◗ **Right** *A river predator par excellence, the Northern pike (Esox lucius) has a streamlined body and an array of sharp teeth with which to devour its prey. It is the most widespread freshwater species in the world.*

are usually dominated by plankton, although euphausiids (luminescent shrimplike crustaceans) are taken by some species. Both eggs and larvae are typically planktonic.

### Barreleyes

FAMILY OPISTHOPROCTIDAE

The family Opisthoproctidae contains six genera and ten species in tropical and temperate seas down to about 1,000m (3,300ft). All species have tubular eyes. In the deep-bodied species of the genera *Opisthoproctus*, *Macropinna* and *Winteria* the eyes point directly upwards. In contrast, in the fragile, slender-bodied forms of the genera *Dolichopteryx* and *Bathylynchnops* the eyes point forwards. The remaining species *Rhynchnohyalus natalensis*, which is known from only three examples, is apparently intermediate.

The Mirrorbelly (*Opisthoproctus grimaldii*) grows to about 10cm (4in) long and lives in the North Atlantic. Its body is silvery, with dark spots on the back. The sides of the body are covered with very deep scales. A swimbladder is present. The skull is so transparent that in live or freshly dead specimens the brain can be seen clearly behind the eyes. The spherical lenses in the tubular eyes are pale green. The ventral edge of the body is flattened and expanded into a shallow trough known as the sole. The base of the sole is silvery but covered with large thin scales and a dark pigment. The sole is believed to act as a reflector for the light produced by bacteria in a gland near the anus. The light from the gland passes through a lens and is then reflected downwards by a light-guide chamber just above the flattened part.

The Barrel-eye (*Opisthoproctus soleatus*), a more widespread species, has a pigmentation pattern on its sole different from that of its only congener *O. grimaldii*, so it is thought that the sole enables species recognition in the areas where the two species live together. The upward pointing, tubular eyes, which afford excellent binocular vision, would easily be able to perceive the light directed downwards. The main food of the North Atlantic species (*O. grimaldii*) seems to be small, jellyfish-like organisms.

The Brownsnout spookfish (*Dolichopteryx longipes*) is slender and very fragile. It is also very rare. The fins are elongated like a filament and there is no swimbladder. The muscles are poorly developed; indeed, it has lost so much of its ventral musculature that the gut is enclosed only by transparent skin. It is, then, probably a very poor swimmer, and the tubular eyes may be advantageous in avoiding predators. Unlike *Opisthoproctus*, there is a light-producing organ associated with the eye. The species has been caught, infrequently, in all tropical and subtropical oceans between 350 and 2,700m (1,150–8,860ft) deep.

### Slickheads, Leptochilichthyids

FAMILIES ALEPOCEPHALIDAE, LEPTOCHILICHTHYIDAE

The family Alepocephalidae comprises the two subfamilies Bathylaconinae and Alepocephalinae, which together contain at least 63 species in approximately 24 genera. *Bathyprion danae* is a pikelike fish living at depths of some 2,500m (8,200ft) in the South Indian Ocean and the North and Southeast Atlantic. It probably hovers waiting for very small fishes or crustaceans to

◑ **Above** Rhynchohyalus natalensis, *a barreleye, emits bacterial bioluminescence The uncanny appearance of the barreleyes explains their other name – spookfishes.*

◑ **Right** The capelin (Mallotus villosus), *a species of smelt, congregates in large shoals, which move inshore to spawn in the spring. In the process, many become stranded, as on this beach in Newfoundland, Canada.*

come close when, so its fin positions would suggest, it surges forward to grab the prey.

The family Leptochilichthyidae is represented only by the genus *Leptochilichthys* which contains just three rare species. Their biology is unknown.

### Tubeshoulders

FAMILY PLATYTROCTIDAE (SEARSIIDAE)

The common name of slickheads originates from the fact that the head is covered with a smooth skin, whereas the body has large scales. Most species are dark brown, violet, or black in color. Light organs are rare among slickheads, but one genus, *Xenodermichthys*, is distinguished by the presence of tiny, raised light organs on the underside of the head and body.

The members of the family Platytroctidae, which was until recently known as the Searsiidae, are deepsea fishes with large, extremely light-sensitive eyes. The lateral-line canals on the head are greatly enlarged and expanded. They are found in all except polar waters and the family is characterized by a unique light organ on the shoulder above the pectoral fin. Light-producing cells are contained in a dark sac which opens to the outside by a backwards-pointing pore. When the fish is alarmed, a bright cloud is squirted out which lasts a few seconds and enables it to escape into the darkness.

A living example of the genus *Searsia* "was seen to discharge a bright luminous cloud into the water on being handled. The light appeared as multitudinous bright points, blue-green in color." There are also series of stripelike or rounded luminous organs underneath the body.

## Smelts
### FAMILY OSMERIDAE

The osmerids or smelts may well have acquired their alternative common name from the fact that the European smelt and several other members of the family have a strong smell like that of a cucumber due to the presence of the compound trans-2-cis-6-nonadienal. Mostly small, silvery fish, smelts live in coastal and brackish cool waters in the northern hemisphere and undertake an anadromous migration to spawn in rivers. Numerous landlocked populations are also known. Smelts are carnivores, feeding on small invertebrates seized with their sharp conical teeth.

Their importance to subsistence fisheries in the far north is significant. They can be numerous and have a high fat content. When not eaten by the original inhabitants of the British Columbian coast, they were dried, and because of their fat content could be set alight and used as a natural candle. Hence *Thaleichthys pacificus* now has the common name of Candle fish.

The ayu (sometimes considered as being within its own monotypic family, Plecoglossidae) is a particularly remarkable member of this family and lives in Japan and adjacent parts of Asia, where it is of great economic importance. Its body is olive brown with a pale yellow blotch on the side. The dorsal fin is expanded and, like the other fins, has a reddish tint. When these colors, especially the reds, are enhanced in the breeding season, the Japanese name for the fish changes from *ayu* to *sabi*, which means rusty. Both sexes become covered in warty nuptial tubercules at the onset of breeding. The upper jaw of the male shortens and the female's anal fin expands. These changes start during the summer and the fish breed in the fall.

The fish mature in the upper reaches of rivers and move downstream towards the sea to breed. Spawning is carried out at night after a 10cm (4in) pit has been excavated. Each female produces

some 20,000 adhesive eggs which hatch in about three weeks, depending on temperature. The larvae stay in the river until they are about 2.5cm (1 in) long when they move into the sea.

This seaward migration of the larvae is part of an interesting survival strategy. If the young stayed in the river, having spawned in the fall, they would have to endure the cold and potentially compete with larger young of the species that spawned in spring (when most fishes spawn). However, during winter the temperature of the sea is more stable than that of the river and at sea food is more abundant. On the other hand, the young ayu have to have developed a physiological (osmotic) mechanism to enable their small bodies to cope with the shock of transferring from fresh to salt water. During winter they feed on zooplankton and small crustaceans and, by spring, when they return to fresh water, they have grown to about 8cm (3in) long. Then they migrate upstream in huge shoals, when thousands are caught and taken to capture ponds to facilitate a rapid growth rate and to provide an easily accessible source of food. The fish that escape continue up to the fast-flowing upper reaches, where each individual establishes a territory for itself among rocks and stones. Here they feed on diatoms and algae until summer or fall when they move downstream to

spawn. The ayu is an annual fish as almost all adults die after spawning. The very small percentage that survive spawning spend the winter at sea and repeat the cycle.

Concomitant with the change of diet from young to adult and the move from salt to fresh water, the teeth change drastically. While at sea the ayu's diet is carnivorous and it uses its conical teeth to catch small crustaceans and other invertebrates. Adults, by contrast, feed on algae and have a whole series of groups of teeth forming comblike structures. Even more unusual is the fact that the teeth lie outside the mouth.

The comb-teeth develop under the skin of the jaw and erupt, shedding the conical teeth, when the fish enter fresh water. Each comb-tooth consists of 20–30 individual teeth, each one shaped like a crescent on a stick: narrow in the plane of the fish but very broad transversely. The gutter of the crescent faces inwards and, because of the different lengths of the arms of the crescent on each tooth, forms a sinuous gutter across the width of the comb-teeth. The combs of the upper and lower jaws juxtapose outside the mouth when it is closed. At the front of each lower jaw is a bony, pointed process that fits into a corresponding recess in the upper jaw. On the midline of the floor of the mouth is a flange of tissue, which is

low at the front but higher at the back where it branches into two. Each branch bends back on itself to run forwards, parallel to the sides of the jaw and decreasing in height towards the front. Muscles link this device with a median bone in the branchial series.

It is known that adult ayus eat algae within closely guarded territories, but exactly how they do so has not yet been explained. Grazing marks have frequently been seen on stones covered by algae in ayus' territories and it is usually stated that these are formed by the comblike teeth. However, as these teeth are outside the jaw, any algae so scraped off would be liable to be washed away by the current and lost.

It is suggested here that the ayu is a filter-feeder in a manner analogous to that of the baleen whales. The ayu's snout is fleshy and slightly overhangs the front of the upper jaw. Behind the snout, at the front of the upper jaw, is a row of about eight small conical teeth. Hanging down from the palate is a complex series of curtainlike structures which have a relationship to the various flanges on the floor of the mouth. It is possible that if the ayu were to face into the current and scrape the algae off the rocks with the conical teeth, the algae so scraped would wash into the mouth. The mouth could then be tightly closed

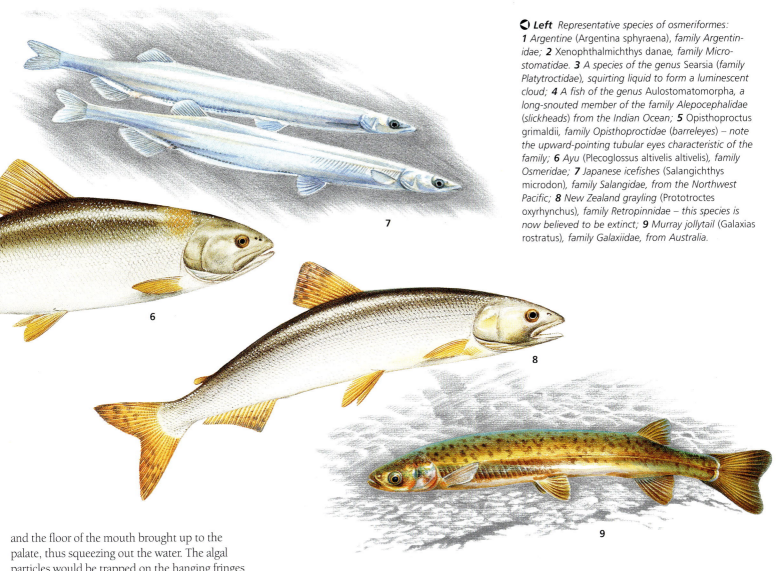

◁ **Left** *Representative species of osmeriformes:*
**1** *Argentine* (Argentina sphyraena), *family Argentinidae;* **2** *Xenophthalmichthys danae, family Microstomatidae.* **3** *A species of the genus* Searsia (*family Platytroctidae*)*, squirting liquid to form a luminescent cloud;* **4** *A fish of the genus* Aulostomatomorpha, *a long-snouted member of the family Alepocephalidae (slickheads) from the Indian Ocean;* **5** *Opisthoproctus grimaldii, family Opisthoproctidae (barreleyes) – note the upward-pointing tubular eyes characteristic of the family;* **6** *Ayu* (Plecoglossus altivelis altivelis)*, family Osmeridae;* **7** *Japanese icefishes* (Salangichthys microdon)*, family Salangidae, from the Northwest Pacific;* **8** *New Zealand grayling* (Prototroctes oxyrhynchus)*, family Retropinnidae – this species is now believed to be extinct;* **9** *Murray jollytail* (Galaxias rostratus)*, family Galaxiidae, from Australia.*

and the floor of the mouth brought up to the palate, thus squeezing out the water. The algal particles would be trapped on the hanging fringes and could be swallowed. How they are swallowed is unknown. If the comb-teeth are a part of the filtration system they can only act as a long-stop, but if so, how the entrapped particles are removed is a mystery. Clearly, much work remains to be done on this enigmatic but commercially important species.

## Icefishes
### FAMILY SALANGIDAE
Noodle fishes of the family Salangidae are very small, slender transparent fishes from the western Pacific. Although marine, they move into estuaries to spawn. Their head is tiny and pointed and the deepest part of the body is just in front of the dorsal fin. The only coloration on the 10cm (4in) long Japanese icefish (*Salangichthys microdon*) is two rows of small black spots on the belly. Although small, they are sometimes so abundant that they can easily be caught for food. To the Japanese they are a delicacy called *shirauwo*.

The shape and transparency of the adult is very similar to that of the larvae of some other fish species. Indeed, if it were not for the fact that sexually mature examples are known, adult specimens

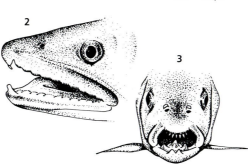

◐ **Above** *The ayu has remarkable dentition:*
**1** *juxtaposing comb teeth on the outside of the jaw;*
**2** *a fleshy snout with a few canine teeth behind it,*
*and* **3** *elaborate skin folds within the mouth.*

of this family would have been thought to be larvae of some unknown species. In lower vertebrates, it is possible for a species to evolve by a process called neoteny or paedomorphosis in which the body development is curtailed whilst sexual development continues as normal. With time, the ability to attain the adult form is lost and a new species is formed. Both the Salangidae and the closely related Sundasalangidae are considered to have evolved in this way and so are said to be neotenic.

## Sundaland Noodlefishes
### FAMILY SUNDASALANGIDAE
The first two of the very small freshwater species that form the family Sundasalangidae from Thailand and Borneo were described as recently as 1981, with another five species discovered in the late 1990s. The body is scaleless and transparent, there is no adipose fin, and several bones in the skull are lacking. Superficially, they resemble the noodle fish but have particular features of the paired fin girdles and gill arches which make them unique. They are among the smallest of all fish species, one of them becoming mature at 1.5cm (0.5in) long.

## New Zealand Smelts

FAMILY RETROPINNIDAE

The family Retropinnidae comprises the two subfamilies Prototroctinae and Retropinninae, commonly known as the southern graylings and southern smelts, respectively, which together contain 5 species in 3 genera.

The scaled, cylindrical southern graylings of the Prototroctinae are represented by just two species: the New Zealand southern grayling (*Prototroctes oxyrhynchus*) and the Australian southern grayling (*P. maraena*). The New Zealand species was first described and named in 1870 when it was abundant and regarded as a good source of food, but the last known specimens were caught by accident in a Maori fish trap in 1923 and it is now presumed extinct. There are only a few records describing live *P. oxyrhynchus*, although like its Australian congener it is known that it had only one ovary or testis. Early reports of its body color are inconsistent. One suggests that it was slaty on the back, merging to silvery on the sides and belly with patches of azure. The fins were orange, slaty dark at the tips and the cheeks had a golden tinge. It apparently migrated regularly from the sea to fresh water, where it spawned. Although they once existed in their millions, today there are less than 40 bodies preserved in the great national museums of the world and a stuffed specimen in the Rotoiti Lodge of the New Zealand Deer Stalkers' Association, Nelson.

*P. maraena* appears to be following the same path towards extinction as its New Zealand cousin and is now severely endangered. Why these two remarkable fish species should have declined so dramatically is unknown for sure, although the extinction of *P. oxyrhynchus* has been attributed to a combination of habitat degradation resulting from deforestation plus the impacts of introduced salmonids. However, neither explanation is regarded as conclusive.

The Retropinninae or southern smelts are slender, small-mouthed fishes from southeastern Australia, Tasmania and New Zealand. Some populations are migratory, while others are landlocked. Because they are very variable in form their taxonomy is far from clear. However, there appears to be two Australian species, including the Tasmanian smelt and two New Zealand species, including the Cucumberfish.

## Galaxiids

FAMILY GALAXIIDAE

The family Galaxiidae comprises the three subfamilies Lovettiinae, Aplochitoninae and Galaxiinae, which together contain about 40 species in 8 genera. The galaxliids are distinctive small fishes found in all the major southern land masses (Australia, New Zealand, South America and South Africa) and also on some of the more remote southern islands such as New Caledonia, Auckland and Campbell and the Falklands. The first galaxiid was collected by naturalists with Captain Cook in New Zealand during 1777. The generic name *Galaxias* was given to the fish because it was a dark, black-olive in coloration and covered with a profusion of small gold spots resembling a galaxy of stars. As a result of these markings, an absence of scales and the presence of smooth leathery skins, galaxiids are fish of distinctive appearance. Unlike some northern relatives, they have no adipose fin but their single dorsal fin is placed over the anal fin well back towards the tail. Most are small, 10–25cm (4–10in) in length, but one species reaches 58cm (23in), while there are several tiny species, 3–5cm (1–2in) long. Most are tubular, cigar-shaped fish with blunt heads, thick fleshy fins and a truncated tail. A few are stocky, thick-bodied fish and most of these are secretive species that skulk among boulders, logs or debris in streams or lakes. Many are solitary, but a few show shoaling behavior. All but about six species have a freshwater distribution, and a few are marine migratory fish in which the larval and juvenile phases are spent at sea.

Migratory species spawn mostly in fresh water and rarely in estuaries. After their eggs hatch, the resulting larvae, about 1cm (0.4in) long, are swept to sea. Their ability to cope with a sudden transition from fresh to sea water shows remarkable flexibility. They spend 5–6 months at sea before migrating back into fresh waters in spring as elongate transparent juveniles. It will be months before these fish reach maturity, at about a year in some species, two to three years in others.

What is known about the spawning of these fish is equally remarkable. The Inanga (*Galaxias maculatus*) is known to spawn in synchrony with the lunar or tidal cycle, spawning over vegetated estuary margins during high spring tides. When these high tides retreat, the eggs are stranded in the vegetation and protected from dehydration only by humid air. Development takes place out of water, the eggs not being reimmersed until the next set of spring tides two weeks later. Then the eggs hatch, releasing the larvae, which are swept quickly out to sea. The Banded kokopu (*G. fasciatus*), from small heavily forested streams, spawns during floods and deposits its eggs in leaf litter along stream margins. When the floods subside, the eggs are left stranded among rotting leaves, where they develop. Hatching cannot occur until there is another flood and then the larvae are swept downstream and out to sea. It is clear that both these modes of spawning involve substantial risks. The breeding habits described above are exceptional and as far as is known most galaxiid species lay their eggs in clusters between rocks and boulders. A few very small species pair up for spawning and lay their eggs on the leaves of aquatic plants.

Although the regions where these fish occur tend to have moist climates, some species have become adapted to surviving droughts and therefore aestivate. Some live in pools that lie on the floor of wet podocarp (southern hemisphere conifer) forests in water usually only a few centimeters deep which covers leaf litter shed from the towering forests above. In the late summer and fall these pools frequently dry up and the fish disappear into natural hollows around the buttresses of trees. They survive for several weeks in these damp pockets until rainfall restores water to the forest floor. The fish wait for the return of water before spawning. As the pools are increasingly replenished, larvae are enabled to disperse around the forest floor and invade available habitats.

That such small fish should have attained importance for commercial fisheries may seem remarkable. However, when European settlers

◔ **Left** Brown galaxias (Galaxias fuscus) *at Woods Point in Victoria, Australia. This species lives in clear, mountain streams above the snowline that have gravelly or rocky substrates.*

arrived in New Zealand in the mid 19th century they found that vast populations of the sea-living juveniles of several *Galaxias* species migrated into rivers during spring. The Maoris of New Zealand exploited huge quantities of them and not surprisingly the Europeans followed their example, calling the tiny fish whitebait on account of their similarity to unrelated fish they knew at home in England. Quantities caught today do not compare with those of the early years, but a good fishery persists in some rivers. Colossal numbers of fish are caught, with each individual weighing only about 0.5g and so requiring about 1,800 fishes to make up a kilogram. The catches of individual fishermen vary from just a few to many kilograms, with exceptional catches reaching several hundred kilograms in a day. These fish make a delicious gourmet seafood and command a correspondingly high price in the shops.

*Aplochiton zebra* is a fairly widespread fish, occurring in rivers of Patagonia and the Falkland Islands where it is called trout. This handsome fish has dark vertical stripes over the back and sides of its scaleless body. Its persistence in the Falkland Islands has unfortunately been placed in jeopardy by the introduction of the Brown trout from Europe, a sad predicament for a species first collected by Charles Darwin when he visited the Falklands. Recent collections suggest that this species may enter coastal waters; otherwise very little is known of its biology.

Historically the very broad distribution of the galaxiid fishes has attracted intense interest. Long ago zoologists asked how a group of freshwater fishes could be so widely distributed around

**⬤ Above** *The Australian smelt* (Retropinna semoni) *lives most commonly in fresh water, but can also tolerate brackish environments. This species is widely distributed throughout southeastern Australia.*

southern lands. Not only is the family as a whole widely dispersed, but the Inanga is found in Australia, Tasmania, Lord Howe Island, New Zealand, Chatham Islands, Chile, Argentina and the Falkland Islands. With such a broad range, this species is one of the naturally most widely distributed freshwater fishes known. Noting the remarkable range of this species, zoologists of the late 19th century suggested that there must have been former land connections between the areas where the fish are present, and so proposed a vicariance biogeography. Some thought that Antarctica or the ancient continent of Gondwana might have been involved. Another explanation is that these fishes dispersed by migrating through the sea (a dispersal biogeography).

This debate has continued into modern times and it is now generally accepted that arguments in favor of a Gondwana-based vicariance biogeography or a dispersal biogeography are not necessarily mutually exclusive. However, a recent extensive consideration of the distribution patterns of galaxiids and other fishes in the southern hemisphere concluded that evidence from areas including genetics, morphology, recent dispersal events, and parasitology all supports, or is consistent with, a dispersal biogeography. The galaxiids are indeed sufficiently ancient to have formerly inhabited Gondwana, but no compelling evidence indicates that their present distribution reflects a former broad Gondwana-based range.

## A PIKE IN THE SOUTHERN HEMISPHERE?

If the galaxiids are the salmonoids of the southern hemisphere, and salmonoids are related to pike, is there a southern hemisphere pike? The answer is probably yes.

Described as recently as 1961, the Salamanderfish (*Lepidogalaxias salamandroides*) is a small fish about 4 cm (1.5in) long, and is the sole member of its family (Lepidogalaxiidae). It is found in numerous localities in western Australia. Originally thought to be a galaxiid, unlike those fishes it has scales, dorsal and anal fins set much further forward, while the anal fin of the mature male is highly modified with

gnarled and hooked rays and peculiar dermal flaps in order to function as an intromittent organ during internal fertilization. The Salamanderfish feeds mainly on aquatic insect larvae and small crustaceans.

Little is known of the biology of this unique species, but it is apparently capable of surviving drought by burrowing in mud or under damp leaves. Its distribution appears to be confined to small, temporary acidic pools and ditches, principally in the sand-plain area between the Blackwood and Kent rivers in Western Australia.

## Salmon, Trout, and Allies

FAMILY SALMONIDAE

The family Salmonidae comprises the three sub-families Coregoninae, Thymallinae and Salmoninae, which together contain about 66 species in 11 genera. Included in this grouping are the salmon, trout, charrs and whitefishes which consitute some of the most famous and important fishes of the northern hemisphere. Unsurprisingly, their great commercial importance as food and sport fishes has ensured that they have been particularly well studied by science.

Members of the subfamily Coregoninae are commonly known as the whitefishes, although this common name may also be applied specifically to at least two species within the subfamily and is also used for a group of completely unrelated species of marine fish. The whitefishes are relatively plain, silvery fish found predominantly in the cold deep lakes of Asia, Europe and North America. There are three genera, although species are highly variable morphologically and genetically leading to continuing debate over classification at this level even when modern molecular techniques are used. A few species are anadromous, but most have exclusively freshwater distributions. Many species such as the vendace and the European whitefish are important for both commercial and recreational fisheries.

The subfamily Thymallinae contains the single genus *Thymallus*, whose name is derived from the supposedly thymelike smell of their flesh. These fishes inhabit cool, swift-flowing rivers, but will sometimes enter brackish water. The grayling is widespread in Asia and Europe, while the slightly more colorful Arctic grayling occurs at higher latitudes in North America.

The subfamily Salmoninae is one of the most important groups of fish in the world, with the Atlantic salmon being its best known species. Many people pay high prices for its flesh and even

**Above** Male and female River or Brown trout (Salmo trutta fario) *attend their nest – a shallow scrape in the substrate – in a fast-flowing, clear stream.*

**Below** A twelve-day-old Brown trout. Larval fish of the family Salmonidae such as this, which have hatched but not yet absorbed their yolk-sacs, are known as alevin. Seen suspended below its body, the yolk-sac forms the alevin's vital first source of energy.

higher prices for the pleasure of trying to catch it by angling in often breathtakingly beautiful surroundings. This species is also much sought after by commercial fishermen, although such activities are now strictly controlled throughout the distribution range of this magnificent fish. Although salmon is now a luxury item, in the 19th century apprentices in London protested about being fed salmon six days a week.

The significance of the only salmon species native to the Atlantic is emphasized by the range of different names applied to each stage of its life history. On hatching, the individual is called an alevin and quickly grows to become a fry. Later, when it is a few centimeters long and has developed dark blotches or parr marks on the body, it becomes a parr. When it later migrates to the sea, the parr marks become covered by a silvery pigment and the fish becomes a smolt. The fish may then remain at sea for one winter and return to fresh water to spawn as a grilse or one-sea-winter fish, or it may stay at sea for one or more additional winters and return to spawn as a larger spring-run or multi-sea-winter fish. After spawning it becomes a kelt, at which stage most fish die although some survive to go back to sea and return again on future spawning migrations.

After adult salmon have spawned in their home streams, the eggs remain in the gravel for a considerable time. Hatching time can be predicted from a knowledge of the local water temperature conditions and is usually between April and May in northern Europe.

The young are about 2cm (0.8in) long on hatching and for the first six weeks or so live in the gravel, feeding on their yolk sacs. With the exhaustion of the yolk supply, they emerge from the gravel and start feeding as fry on insect larvae and other invertebrates. As they grow, they develop into parr and their markings give them camouflage for hunting actively. The length of time spent in fresh water before becoming a smolt varies from five years in the north of the range to one year in the south.

Not all members of the year class migrate to the sea. A few males stay in fresh water to become precociously mature and have been seen shedding sperm in the company of mating adults. The migrating young spend some time in estuaries, acclimatizing themselves for coping with salt water. In the sea they grow rapidly and can reach 14kg (30lb) in 3 years. They feed on fish and spend up to four years in the sea building up strength for the rigors of the spawning migration. When returning to the natal stream for spawning they can travel 115km (70mi) a day.

**◑ Above** *Representative species of salmoniformes:*
*1 Atlantic salmon* (Salmo salar)*; 2 Rainbow trout*
(Oncorhynchus mykiss)*; 3 Grayling* (Thymallus thymallus)*; 4 Sockeye salmon* (Oncorhynchus nerka), *family*
Ophidiidae*; 5 Charr (genus* Salvelinus)*; 6 Sea, Brook*
*or Brown trout* (Salmo trutta trutta)*; 7 Shortjaw cisco*
(Coregonus zenithicus).

⚫ **Above** *Large-scale salmon farming in sea pens, pioneered in Norway in the 1960s, has grown into a lucrative business in many countries. However, disease is a danger with such high concentrations of fishes.*

◗ **Right** *A spawning pair of Sockeye salmon (Oncorhynchus nerka) – on the right, the male with its distinctive hump and hooked jaw. This species is fished extensively on the Pacific coast of North America.*

Some populations of landlocked salmon exist in lakes in the far north of America and Europe. They never grow as large as the others, but still run up streams to spawn. It is thought that their access to the sea was blocked after the last ice age.

There are probably seven species of Pacific salmon, whose generic name *Oncorhynchus* means "hooked snout." Their life history is generally very similar to that of the Atlantic salmon, although two North American species – the Sockeye salmon and the Rainbow trout – and the somewhat doubtful species amago from Lake Biwa in Japan have landlocked forms. In the Atlantic Ocean, the Atlantic salmon grows to about 32kg (70lb) in weight, but in the Pacific Ocean the Chinook salmon has been recorded at 57kg (126lb).

The Eurasian genus *Hucho* includes the Huchen, a slender species from the Danube, and other species in Central Asia. Attempts were made to translocate the huchen to the River Thames in England in the 19th century. Despite rumors of it surviving into the early 20th century, there is no reliable evidence that the introduction succeeded. Such an introduction would not even be attempted by today's more environmentally aware fisheries managers.

The charrs of the genus *Salvelinus* come from the cold deep lakes and rivers of Europe and North America. Only in the very north of the Atlantic are they migratory. The sole European species, the Arctic charr, is very variable in appearance and until relatively recently a different species was named from almost each lake. In the

breeding season the males sport a spectacular deep red on their underside, from which the name charr is derived from the Gaelic *tarr* meaning belly. If anything their flesh exceeds that of the salmon in quality and those lucky enough to have the chance to sample it should have charr steaks, lightly boiled with bay leaves, cold on toast. Despite its common name of Brook trout, the eastern American species *Salvelinus fontinalis* is in fact a charr. In its native haunts, the migratory form can grow to nearly 90cm (3ft) long but the European introductions rarely reach half that length. In Europe, the Brook or Brown trout hybridizes with both the native River or 'other' Brown trout and the introduced Rainbow trout. The offspring of both mismatches are a striped fish called the Tiger or Zebra trout and are sterile.

The Brook trout of Europe has generated much confusion regarding its nomenclature. Being a very variable species in both form and behavior, it has been given a variety of common names, such as Brown trout, Sea trout, Lake trout, and Salmon trout. Brown trout living in lakes may become very large cannibals and are often called Lake trout or ferox. Brown trout that migrate to the sea to feed become very silvery and are called Sea trout or Salmon trout (not a hybrid between a salmon and a Brown trout, though these do occur). As a result of the richer feeding opportunities in the sea, migratory Brown trout reach nearly twice the size of their nonmigratory siblings.

A similar situation occurs on the western coast of North America with the Rainbow trout. This commonly introduced denizen of fish farms in Europe has an extensive natural range from southern California to Alaska. In the northern part of its range it is migratory, and much larger and more intensively colored than in the south. The Canadians call the migratory form the Steelhead trout, whereas the nonmigratory form is referred to as the Rainbow trout. Some years ago a fishery in the United Kingdom bought from North America a large number of Rainbow trout to enhance the trout fishing in their waters. Unfortunately they were provided with the migratory form and very little of their investment ever returned.

Salmon and trout have been introduced into many countries as game and food fishes. The Brown trout is now found in the North American west, almost all southern hemisphere countries, and even in some tropical ones where there are cool streams at high altitudes in which they can thrive. In many cases, the present distribution of the subspecies corresponds to the former extent of the British Empire, where the fish was introduced by keen sport fishermen in colonial service.

To complete this important family, two more poorly known species of uncertain affinities must be mentioned. In the lakes of the Ohrid region on the borders of Albania, the former Yugoslav Republic of Macedonia, and Greece live fish placed in the genus *Salmothymus,* which may be southern landlocked salmon. Finally, the genus *Brachymystax* comes from rivers of Mongolia, China and Korea. No satisfactory conclusions have been reached on its taxonomic relationships, because very few specimens have ever been available for study.                                    IW/RMcD/KEB

# Salmon, Pike, and Related Families

## ORDER ESOCIFORMES

### Pikes
**Family Esocidae**

Freshwater; Northern Hemisphere. Length maximum about 1.5m (5ft). 5 species in 1 genus: **Northern pike** (*Esox lucius*), **Amur pike** (*E. reicherti*), **muskellunge** or **muskie** (*E. masquinongy*), **Chain pickerel** (*E. niger*), *E. americanus* with subspecies **Redfin pickerel** and **Grass pickerel**.

### Mudminnows
**Family Umbridae**

Freshwater; parts of Northern Hemisphere. Length maximum about 15cm (6in). 5 species in 3 genera: **European mudminnow** (*Umbra krameri*), *U. limi, U. pygmaea*, **Alaska blackfish** (*Dallia pectoralis*), *Novumbra hubbsi*. Conservation status: The European mudminnow is classed as Vulnerable.

## ORDER OSMERIFORMES

### SUBORDER ARGENTINOIDEI
SUPERFAMILY ARGENTINOIDEA

### Argentines or Herring smelts
**Family Argentinidae**

Marine; Atlantic, Indian and Pacific oceans. Length maximum about 60cm (24in). 19 species in 2 genera, including: **Alice argentine** (*Argentina aliceae*), **Greater argentine** (*A. silus*), and **Pygmy argentine** (*Glossanodon pygmaeus*).

### Microstomatids
**Family Microstomatidae**

Marine; tropical to temperate seas, Atlantic, Indian and Pacific oceans. Length maximum about 21cm (8in). 17 species in 3 genera, including: **Slender argentine** (*Microstoma microstoma*), **Stout argentine** (*Nansenia crassa*), *Nansenia oblita,* and *Xenophthalmichthys danae*.

### Deepsea smelts
**Family Bathylagidae**

Marine; Atlantic, Indian and Pacific oceans. Length maximum about 25cm (10in). 15 species in 1 genus including: **Longsnout blacksmelt** (*Dolicholagus longirostris*), **Goiter blacksmelt** (*Bathylagus euryops*), and **Eared blacksmelt** (*Lipolagus ochotensis*).

### Barreleyes or spookfishes
**Family Opisthoproctidae**

Marine; tropical to temperate, Atlantic, Indian and Pacific oceans. Length maximum about 25cm (10in). 10 species in 6 genera, including: *Opisthoproctus grimaldii, O. soleatus, Dolichopteryx longipes, Rhynchohyalus natalensis.*

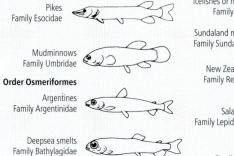

Order Esociformes
Pikes
Family Esocidae

Mudminnows
Family Umbridae

Order Osmeriformes
Argentines
Family Argentinidae

Deepsea smelts
Family Bathylagidae

Slickheads
Family Alepocephalidae

Smelts
Family Osmeridae

Icefishes or noodlefishes
Family Salangidae

Sundaland noodlefishes
Family Sundasalangidae

New Zealand smelts
Family Retropinnidae

Salamanderfish
Family Lepidogalaxiidae

Galaxiids
Family Galaxiidae

Order Salmoniformes
Salmon, trout etc
Family Salmonidae

### SUPERFAMILY ALEPOCEPHALOIDEA

### Slickheads
**Family Alepocephalidae**

Deep sea; all oceans. Length maximum about 76cm (30in). At least 63 species in about 24 genera, including: **Small-scaled brown slickhead** (*Alepocephalus australis*), **Fangtooth smooth-head** (*Bathyprion danae*), the **Black warrior** (*Bathylaco nigricans*), and the **Blackhead salmon** (*Narcetes stomias*).

### Leptochilichthyids
**Family Leptochilichthyidae**

Deep sea; eastern Atlantic, western Indian, and eastern and western Pacific oceans. Length maximum about 30cm (12in). 3 species in 1 genus, including: *Leptochilichthys microlepis.*

### Tubeshoulders
**Family Platytroctidae (Searsiidae)**

Marine; all oceans (absent from Mediterranean). Length maximum about 38cm (15in). 37 species in 13 genera, including: *Barbantus curvifrons, Mentodus crassus.*

### SUBORDER OSMEROIDEI
SUPERFAMILY OSMEROIDEA

### Smelts
**Family Osmeridae**

Marine, anadromous and coastal freshwater; Northern Hemisphere in Arctic, Atlantic and Pacific oceans. Length maximum about 45cm (18in). 13 species in 7 genera, including: **European smelt** (*Osmerus eperlanus*), **Pond smelt** (*Hypomesus olidus*), **Capelin** (*Mallotus villosus*), **Candle fish** (*Thaleichthys pacificus*), **ayu** (*Plecoglossus altivelis*). Conservation status: The **Delta smelt** (*Hypomesus transpacificus*) is Endangered.

### Icefishes or noodlefishes
**Family Salangidae**

Anadromous and freshwater; Sakhalin, Japan, Korea, China to northern Vietnam. Length maximum about 18cm (7in). 11 species in 4 genera, including: **noodlefish** (*Salanx cuvieri*), **Japanese icefish** (*Salangichthys microdon*). Conservation status: *Neosalanx regani* is classed as Vulnerable.

### Sundaland noodlefishes
**Family Sundasalangidae**

Freshwater; Borneo and southern Thailand. Length maximum about 3cm (1in). 7 species in 1 genus, including: *Sundasalanx microps, S. mekongensis.*

### SUPERFAMILY GALAXIOIDEA

### New Zealand smelts
**Family Retropinnidae**

Freshwater and brackish water (some partially marine); New Zealand, Chatham Islands, southeastern Australia and Tasmania. Length maximum about 15cm (6in). 6 species in 3 genera: **cucumberfish** (*Retropinna retropinna*), **Tasmanian smelt** (*R. tasmanica*), **Australian smelt** (*R. semoni*), **New Zealand southern grayling** (*Prototroctes oxyrhynchus*), **Australian southern grayling** (*P. maraena*), **Stokell's smelt** (*Stokellia anisodon*). Conservation status: The New Zealand southern grayling is now classed as Extinct, while the Australian southern grayling is Vulnerable.

### Salamanderfish
*Lepidogalaxias salamandroides*
**Family Lepidogalaxiidae**

Sole member of family. Freshwater; southwestern Australia. Length maximum about 4cm (1.5in). Conservation status: Lower Risk/Near Threatened.

### Galaxiids
**Family Galaxiidae**

Freshwater and diadromous; Australia, New Zealand, New Caledonia, southernmost Africa and southern South America. Length maximum about 58cm (23in). About 40 species in 8 genera, including: **Flathead galaxiid** (*Galaxius rostratus*), **Golden galaxiid** (*G. auratus*), *G. maculatus, G. fasciatus, Aplochiton zebra*. Conservation status: 4 species are Critically Endangered, including the **Swan galaxias** (*Galaxias fontanus*) and **Barred galaxias** (*G. fuscus*); 9 species are Vulnerable, including the **Giant kokopu** (*Galaxias argenteus*) and **Canterbury mudfish** (*Neochanna burrowsius*).

## ORDER SALMONIFORMES

### Salmon, trout, charrs, whitefishes, and allies
**Family Salmonidae**

Freshwater and anadromous; Northern Hemisphere. Length maximum about 1.5m (5ft). About 66 species in 11 genera, including: **Bear Lake whitefish** (*Prosopium abyssicola*), **vendace** (*Coregonus albula*), **European whitefish** (*C. lavaretus*), **grayling** (*Thymallus thymallus*), **Arctic grayling** (*T. arcticus*), **Arctic charr** (*Salvelinus alpinus*), **Brook trout** (*S. fontinalis*), **Atlantic salmon** (*Salmo salar*), **Brown trout** (*S. trutta*), **Chinook salmon** (*Oncorhynchus tshawytscha*), **Humpback** or **Pink salmon** (*O. gorbuscha*), **Sockeye** or **Red salmon** (*O. nerka*), **amago** (*O. rhodiurus*), **Rainbow trout** (*O. mykiss*), **huchen** (*Hucho hucho*). Conservation status: 19 species are endangered, 4 of which are Critically Endangered, including the **Apache trout** (*Oncorhynchus apache*) of the Colorado river system in the United States, and the **Ala Balik** (*Salmo platycephalus*) of Turkey and Central Asia. 5 species are classed as Endangered, including the huchen and 10 species are classed as Vulnerable, including the **bloater** (*Coregonus hoyi*) and the Shortjaw cisco (*C. zenithucus*).

▶ *Right* The Northern pike (*Esox lucius*) is an aggressive, solitary species that lurks in wait for its prey, often poised with its body in an "S" shape, ready to strike. This opportunistic hunter utilizes all kinds of cover for its ambushes; here, a pike emerges from the cockpit of a sunken aircraft. Its marbled green and brown coloration give it excellent camouflage in a range of environments.

# RETURN TO BASE

The life cycle of the Sockeye salmon

THE LIFE HISTORY OF THE SOCKEYE SALMON of the Pacific Northwest exemplifies that of other anadromous species – that is, those that live most of their lives at sea, but return to freshwater streams in order to spawn and eventually die. In the case of the sockeye, which travels further than any other salmon, this remarkable migration may see the fish travel up to 1,600km (1,000 miles).

From spring until late summer, sockeyes run in large schools upstream in an effort to return to the streams in which they were hatched. As they journey up the rivers of Alaska (the Kasilof, Kenai, and Russian) and the Canadian province of British Columbia (the Fraser, Skeena, Nass, and Nootka), they are faced with numerous obstacles and hazards such as rapids and falls. The key to their remarkable "homing" ability is memory and a sense of smell. It has been demonstrated that adult salmon remember and later trace the smell of their birth stream resulting from its combination of chemicals in the water contributed by the surrounding rocks, soils, vegetation, and other factors. Under natural conditions, occasional errors of navigation are made by the fish, which has the advantage of allowing the species to extend its range if more suitable habitat becomes available.

The males usually arrive back first but the females normally select the spawning site, where they are aggressively courted by the males. During maturation, hormonal changes dramatically alter the color of sockeyes – their heads turn green and their backs to a deep red – and the male's jaws elongate to form a hook called the kype. (All seven Pacific salmon species belong to the genus *Oncorhynchus*, meaning "hooked jaw," and the sockeye develops this feature most pronouncedly.)

At the spawning site, a nest or redd is excavated

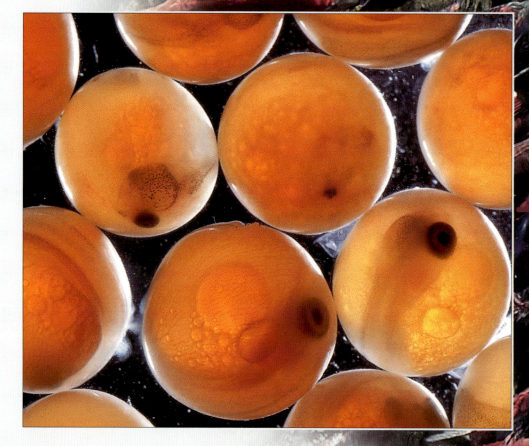

◐ **Above** Laid in the fall, the eggs incubate over winter – protected beneath the gravel, and often several feet of snow and ice. Around one month after laying, eyes begin to appear in the eggs. The fish are most vulnerable in the egg-to-fry stage.

◐ **Below left** Many salmon die on their upstream run, killed by exhaustion, predators, or pollution. Where hydroelectric dams bar their way, "fish ladders" have been built to help them reach hatcheries.

in suitable substrate by vigorous movements of the female's tail until it is up to 3m (10ft) long and 30cm (12in) deep. Depending on the size of the adult fish, female sockeyes can lay between 2,500 and 7,500 eggs. The pair lie alongside one another for spawning and accompany the act with much trembling and jaw opening. The male ejects a milky fluid (milt) containing his sperm onto the eggs to fertilize them. The female then covers the fertilized eggs with gravel for protection until they hatch. Each act of spawning lasts for about five minutes and the whole process may continue for a fortnight. In between, the adults rest in deep holes in the river bed. After each spawning session, the redd is filled in and another excavated. Exhausted by their arduous upstream journey and the rigors of digging and guarding the redds, the adults tend to die about a week after spawning is complete.

After hatching and developing into fry over a period of around a year in the freshwater streams of their birth, or in nearby lakes, the young salmon head downstream to the sea. They are known at this developmental stage as smolts or fingerlings. Once they have entered the Pacific, they range far out into mid-ocean, south of the Aleutian Islands. Here, they will spend 2–4 years maturing and developing their characteristic orange-red flesh that makes them so highly prized by Northwest coast fishermen. Then, in the summer of their fourth year, they head inland to the mouths of the great rivers to begin the cycle anew.

Sockeyes are the most important commercially of all Pacific species. They are caught in purse-seine and gill nets by First Nation and other fishermen. The high fat content (stored for the long migration) makes their flesh particularly rich and flavorful.

**⬥ Above** With their distinctive green heads and red bodies, adult Sockeye salmon in prime spawning condition mass in the Adams River in British Columbia on their annual migration run. Runs in odd-numbered years are generally larger than those in even-numbered years.

**◖ Left** In the late winter, the eggs hatch into alevins, tiny fishes with large attached yolk sacs, from which they gain their nutrition. The orange yolk sacs contain a balanced diet of protein, carbohydrates, vitamins and minerals.

# Bristlemouths and Allies

**b**RISTLELIKE TEETH, LUMINOUS ORGANS, *eyes on stalks – these are some of the characteristics of the order Stomiiformes, a worldwide group of deepsea fishes contained in four families and several subfamilies. The classification of the order is very uncertain and the subject of active research, hence some of the families and subfamilies included here may well change over time.*

Practically all stomiiform species have luminous organs and many also have a luminous chin barbel, thought to act as a lure. They are flesheating fishes with a large, widegaping, toothed mouth. Most are scaleless, black or dark brown in color, but one family in particular, the bristlemouths (Gonostomatidae) are mostly silvery, midwater fishes. Typically an adipose fin is present, but this and the pectoral and dorsal fins have been lost in some lineages.

## Bristlemouths
### FAMILY GONOSTOMATIDAE

The Gonostomatidae are known as bristlemouths because of their fine, bristlelike teeth. The genus *Cyclothone*, with about 12 species, occurs in all oceans. It is probably – along with *Vinciguerria* – the most common genus in the world regarding numbers of individuals: trawls can haul up tens of thousands of these small fish at a time. They feed on small crustaceans and other invertebrates and, in turn, are a most important source of food for larger fishes, including some of their relatives.

The maximum size of a stomiiform species depends upon the richness of the environment. In areas of abundance, such as the Bay of Bengal and the Arabian Sea, a species may reach 6cm (2.5in)

long, but in a polluted area, like the depths of the Mediterranean, or in an area poor in food, they are much smaller. The Mediterranean species *Cyclothone pygmaea* grows to only 2.5cm (1in).

Some species occur worldwide, whereas others have a very limited distribution. As well as a two-dimensional distribution that can be shown on a map, there is also a three-dimensional distribution as species are separated vertically. Generally, silvery or transparent species live nearer the surface than their dark-colored relations. It is also generally true that the species living deeper have weaker and fewer light organs than those living above them. The swimbladder is poorly developed in bristlemouths, which may explain why they do not undertake the extensive daily vertical migrations common in many deepsea fishes.

*Cyclothone* species show differences between the sexes, not with different light-organ patterns, as in the lanternfishes, but in the nature of the nasal complex. In males, as they mature, the olfactory organs grow out through the nostrils; this does not occur in females. In some species, like the Veiled anglemouth, the hydrodynamic disadvantage of the protruding nasal plates (lamellae) is thought to be compensated for by the development of an elongate snout or rostrum.

## Barbeled Dragonfishes
### FAMILY STOMIIDAE

There are currently six subfamilies in the family Stomiidae; however, this may be revised in the light of new research and information.

One of these subfamilies, the scaled dragonfishes (subfamily Stomiinae) includes the single genus, *Stomias*, with about 11 species. Elongated predators, lacking an adipose fin, the scaly dragonfishes are found in the Indo-Pacific and Atlantic Oceans. They have large, easily shed, hexagonal scales that produce a pleasing honeycomb pattern on their dark bodies. *Stomias* species lack a swimbladder, so they can easily undertake extensive daily vertical migrations. There are usually two rows of small light organs along the ventral margin of the body. At their longest, the scaled dragonfishes rarely exceed 30cm (12in).

Members of the snaggletooths (subfamily Astronesthinae) have a dorsal fin that begins slightly behind the midpoint of the body but well ahead of the anal fin; all genera have an adipose fin except for *Rhadinesthes*. They are midwater predators with fairly compressed, elongate bodies that are usually black.

The black dragonfishes (subfamily Idiacanthinae) are elongated, scaleless fishes also lacking a

**FACTFILE**

## BRISTLEMOUTHS AND ALLIES

Class: Actinopterygii

Order: Stomiiformes

About 320 species in over 50 genera and about 4 families.

**Distribution** All oceans within the temperate zones but not uniformly distributed within these limits.
**Size** Length maximum adult 35cm (14in): most are much smaller.

Equator

See families table ▷

◁ **Left** Juveniles and adults of the Atlantic fangjaw (Gonostoma atlanticum) *stay mainly at a depth of 300–600m (980–1,970ft) during the day but at night they go up to between 50–200m (160–660ft). This species is oviparous with planktonic eggs and larvae.*

**⬤ Above** Echiostoma barbatum *belongs to the stomiid family and the subfamily Melanostominae, commonly referred to as the scaleless black dragonfishes. Note the large photophore behind its eye and the tiny photophores all over its body and fins.*

swimbladder. Worldwide in distribution, the number of species is uncertain; there may be fewer than six, or just one variable species.

The North Atlantic species known as the Ribbon sawtail fish is remarkable for extreme differences between the sexes and its most peculiar larvae. The sex of the larvae cannot be determined until they are about 4cm (1.5in) long. They are, however, so peculiar that they were assigned to a separate genus (*Stylophthalmus*) until it was realized that they were the young of *Idiacanthus*. They are stalkeyed – the eyes are at the end of cartilaginous rods which extend up to one-third of the body length. The body is transparent, the intestine extends beyond the tail and the pelvic fins are not developed. However, the pectoral fins (lost in the adult) are well developed. The larva also lacks the luminous organs of the adults.

During metamorphosis (the change from larval to adult form), the eye stalks gradually shorten until the eyes rest in an orthodox (normal) position in the orbit of the skull. The pectoral fins are lost and only the female develops pelvic fins. She also grows a luminous chin barbel, develops rows of small luminous organs on the body and strong jaws with thin, hooked teeth. The male never has a barbel nor teeth, but develops a large luminous organ just below the eye. The female is black, while the male is brown. The male does not grow after metamorphosis and therefore remains less than 5cm (2in) long, whereas the female feeds actively on prey of suitable size and can grow to over 30cm (12in) long.

The general biology of *Idiacanthus* is poorly known. The smallest larvae are caught at the greatest depths and metamorphosing larvae at about 300m (980ft), so they probably spawn at considerable depths. As the catches of larvae are sporadic, it has been thought that they may shoal or otherwise agglomerate. The adults undergo a daily vertical migration from 1,800m (6,000ft) deep during the day to reach the surface at night.

The viperfishes (subfamily Chauliodontinae) contains about six species in the one genus, *Chauliodus*. These are midwater fishes distributed worldwide in oceans between 60° N and 40°S.

Sloane's viperfish has been recorded in all oceans, but distinct and discrete populations have been recognized by some authors. "In all oceans" does not necessarily mean that the species is equally and universally distributed within the stated range. Oceans consist of distinct water masses varying in temperature, salinity, current, food supplies, and the way that fish are distributed within these water masses is exemplified by the distribution of *Chauliodus* species.

Two small species of *Chauliodus*, the Dana viperfish and *C. minimus* (no common name), live respectively in the central water masses of the North and South Atlantic. The larger Sloane's viperfish, lives in the richer waters that flow around the poorer central water masses. It can reportedly grow to over 30cm (12in) long, more than twice the length of the central-water species. Even the oxygen content of water can limit a distribution: *Chauliodus pammelas*, for example, lives only in the deep waters off Arabia and the Maldives, both of which have a low oxygen content. To cope with these conditions, it has gill filaments much longer than those of its relatives.

*Chauliodus* species are highly specialized predators. The second ray of their dorsal fin is elongated, highly mobile, and has a luminous lure at the end. Their teeth vary in shape, but this variation is remarkably consistent throughout each species. The front teeth on the upper jaw have four sharp ridges near the tip and are used for stabbing. The longest teeth (which imply a remarkable gape) are the front two on the lower jaw. Normally, when the mouth is closed, they lie outside the upper jaw, but when they impale the prey, their natural curvature tends to push the prey into the roof of the mouth. At the base of both the second and third upper jaw teeth there is a small tooth sticking out sideways which is thought to protect the large luminous organ below the eye.

These specialized, predatory modifications do not end with the teeth. The heart, ventral aorta (main blood vessel) and gill filaments are all much further forwards than is usual; in fact, they lie between the sides of the lower jaw, the gill filaments extending almost to the front of it. Bearing in mind the fragility and importance of the gill filaments, how does large prey pass through the mouth without damaging them? The answer lies in the backbone. In almost all fish this consists of a series of firmly articulated bones which allow normal flexibility. In these viperfishes, however, the front vertebrae generally do not develop and the spinal column remains a flexible rod of cartilage (softer than bone). Although this is normal in embryonic and juvenile states (where it is known as the notochord), bony vertebrae generally replace it in adults.

Its retention in *Chauliodus* enables the head to enjoy a remarkable freedom of movement. Firstly, as the back muscles pull the head upwards, the hinge between the upper and lower jaws is pushed forwards. At the same time, the mouth is opened and the shoulder girdle, to which the heart is attached, is pulled backwards and downwards. Special muscles then pull the gill arches and their filaments downwards, that is, away from the path of the prey. Finally, movable teeth in the throat clutch the prey and slowly transfer it to the elastic stomach. With the prey stowed away, these organs return to normal.

Viperfishes have been seen alive from a deepsea submersible. They hang still in the water, head lower than tail, with the long dorsal fin ray curved forwards to lie just in front of the mouth. The body is covered with a thick, watery sheath enclosed by a thin epidermis or "skin." This gelatinous layer is thickest dorsally and ventrally and thinnest laterally. It contains nerves, blood vessels and many small luminous organs.

In addition to the lure, *Chauliodus* species have various kinds of luminescent organs (photophores). Along the ventral part of the fish are complex organs with two kinds of secretory cells, a pigment layer and a reflector. This type of organ is specialized below the eye, protected by teeth and transparent bones, with pigment layers and reflectors so arranged that the light shines into the eye. It is believed that this makes the eye more sensitive to light. Small light organs above and in front of the eye are thought to illuminate possible prey, suggesting that sight is an important factor in feeding.

Scattered throughout the gelatinous sheath, as well as inside the mouth, are small, simple photophores which, in life, emit a bluish light. These are spherical and their bioluminous product is secreted into the hollow center of the organ. They are controlled by nerves, unlike the ventral luminous organs, and their function is unknown, but some interesting observations have been made.

When a viperfish is relaxed, its ventral organs produce a bluish light. When touched, though, pulses of light illuminate the whole body. In addition to this, it has been demonstrated in an experiment that the intensity of the ventral photophores can be adjusted to match the amount of light received by the fish from above. In the clearest parts of the oceans, all traces of sunlight have been absorbed at about 900m (3,000ft). Interestingly, fishes below that depth lack ventral photophores. *Chauliodus*, however, lives higher and is therefore affected by low light levels. The photophore near the eye varies its intensity with that of the ventral photophores and presumably, by balancing internal and external light levels, viperfishes can produce the correct level of light from their ventral photophores to match the background illumination, thus making themselves less liable to predation from below.

Species of *Malacosteus*, a blackskinned genus of the subfamily Malacosteinae, are known as loosejaws. They have no floor to the mouth and the stark jaws with their long teeth are reminiscent of the cruel efficiency of gin traps (used – illegally – on land to snare mammals). Some species in this family are unusual in that they have a cheek light organ producing a red light (most photophores produce a blue-green light).

The species of the subfamily Melanostominae are called scaleless black dragonfishes, live in all oceans and are predators. Some species are elongated, while others are squatter, but all have dorsal and anal fins set far back and large, fanglike teeth and rows of small, ventral, luminous organs. Almost all species have chin barbels which can vary from the very small, through multibranched versions, to ones six times the length of the body.

## Deepsea Hatchetfishes and Allies

### FAMILY STERNOPTYCHIDAE

In the family Sternoptychidae species are laterally compressed – flattened from side to side – and deepchested and are therefore known as deepsea hatchetfishes. Some have tubular eyes and, in many, the mouth is vertical. Species in the genus *Argyropelecus* have upwardly directed tubular eyes with a yellow, spherical lens. They feed on very small crustaceans. Some species undergo a small daily vertical migration. The genus *Polyipnus* has over 30 species, mostly in the western Pacific – perhaps the best known are Nutting's hatchetfish

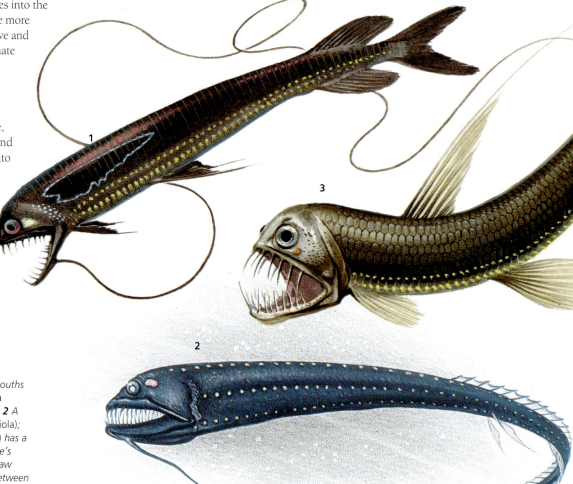

C *Right* Representative species of bristlemouths and allies: **1** Grammatostomias flagellibarba belongs to the scaleless black dragonfishes; **2** A female Ribbon sawtail fish (Idiacanthus fasciola); **3** The Pacific viperfish (Chauliodus macouni) has a row of photophores along its belly; **4** Sloane's viperfish (C. sloani); **5a** The Stoplight loosejaw (Malacosteus niger) has a depth range of between 0–2,500m (0–8,200ft); **5b** Here the Stoplight loosejaw displays its remarkably distensible jaw; **6** Pacific hatchetfish (Argyropelecus affinis).

and the Three-spined hatchetfish. All species stay close to land at depths of between 45–450m (150–1,500ft). Like all members of this family, these hatchetfishes have large, elaborate, downwardly pointing light organs.

The photophores of four species in the genus *Sternoptyx*, which includes the Highlight hatchetfish, have been studied intensively. They have two elliptical patches on the roof of the mouth which lack pigment, reflectors, or colored filters. They luminesce independently of the ventral organs and can glow for about half an hour before gently fading. Apart from, presumably, attracting prey, there is a sort of light guide that lets some of this light to be led close to the eye, where it may be used to balance the light production from the ventral organs so that it matches the background daylight.

The deepsea hatchetfishes are exceedingly beautiful silvery fishes, though what advantage their hatchet shape gives them is unknown. The Pearlsides, a small, spratlike fish often found at night at the surface of the North Atlantic, is thought to be a primitive relative of the deepsea hatchetfishes. It resembles them in many internal details but has a more normal fish shape and is placed in a separate subfamily, the Maurolicinae, along with 13 or so other species belonging to seven genera. The three genera mentioned above have their own subfamly, the Sternoptychinae.

## Lightfishes

Lightfishes are found in the Atlantic, Indian and Pacific oceans, mainly at depths of 200–400m (660–1,300ft) during the day and 100m (330ft) at night. Their diet consists mainly of copepods and they usually feed intensively during the afternoon to early evening. Lightfishes have a similar body shape to the Gonostomatidae and have well developed gillrakers. The lower jaw barbel is absent throughout the family while the adipose fin is present in all genera except *Yarrella*.   KEB/JD

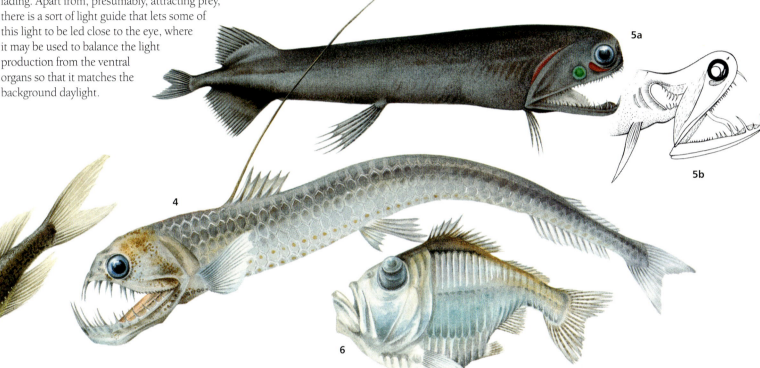

# Bristlemouths and Allies

### Bristlemouths
#### Family Gonostomatidae

26 species in 7 genera. Genera and species include: *Cyclothone pygmaea*, Veiled anglemouth (*C. microdon*), *Diplophos orientalis*, *Manducus greyae*, *Vinciguerria*.

### Barbeled Dragonfishes
#### Family Stomiidae

228 species in 27 genera and 6 subfamilies.
**Snaggletooths** Subfamily Astronesthinae. 30 species in 5 genera. Species include: Snaggletooth (*Astronesthes gemmifer*), Panama snaggletooth (*Borostomias panamensis*), *Heterophotus ophistoma*, *Neonesthes capensis*, *Rhadinesthes decimus*.
**Scaled dragonfishes** Subfamily Stomiinae. Single genus *Stomias* containing about 11 species. Species include: Alcock's boafish (*S. nebulosus*), Blackbelly dragonfish (*S. atriventer*).

**Black dragonfishes** Subfamily Idiacanthinae. Fewer than 6 species in one genus or just one variable species. Species include: Ribbon sawtail fish (*Idiacanthus fasciola*), Pacific blackdragon (*I. antrostomus*).
**Viperfish** Subfamily Chauliodontinae. About 6 species in one genus (*Chauliodus*). Species include: Sloane's viperfish (*C. sloani*), Dana viperfish (*C. danae*), *C. minimus*, *C. pammelas*.
**Loosejaws** Subfamily Malacosteinae. 15 species in 3 genera. Species include: *Aristostomias lunifer*, Shiny loosejaw (*A. scintillans*), *Malacosteus indicus*, Stoplight loosejaw (*M. niger*), *Photostomias guernei*, *P. mirabilis*.
**Scaleless black dragonfishes** Subfamily Melanostominae. About 160 species in 16 genera. Species include: Highfin dragonfish (*Bathophilus flemingi*), *Flagellostomias boureei*, *Grammatostomias flagellibarba*, *Melanostomias melanops*, *Odontostomias micropogon*, Longfin dragonfish (*Tactostoma macropus*).

### Deepsea Hatchetfishes and Allies
#### Family Sternoptychidae

49 species in 10 genera and 2 subfamilies.
**Subfamily Sternoptychinae** c.35 species in 3 genera. Species include: Lovely hatchetfish (*Argyropelecus aculeatus*), Nutting's hatchetfish (*Polypipnus nuttingi*), Three-spined hatchetfish (*P. tridentifer*), Highlight hatchetfish (*Sternoptyx pseudobscura*).
**Subfamily Maurolicinae** c. 14 species in 7 genera. Species include: Pearlsides (*Maurolicus muelleri*), *Sonoda megalophthalma*, *Thorophos nexilis*, Constellation fish (*Valenciennellus tripunctulatus*).

### Lightfishes
#### Family Photichthyidae

About 18 species in 7 genera. Species include: Slim lightfish (*Ichthyococcus elongatus*), Stareye lightfish (*Pollichthys mauli*), *Yarrella blackfordi*.

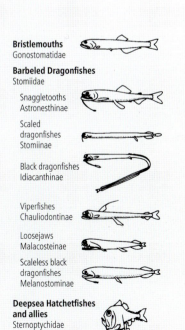

**Bristlemouths**
Gonostomatidae

**Barbeled Dragonfishes**
Stomiidae

Snaggletooths
Astronesthinae

Scaled dragonfishes
Stomiinae

Black dragonfishes
Idiacanthinae

Viperfishes
Chauliodontinae

Loosejaws
Malacosteinae

Scaleless black dragonfishes
Melanostominae

**Deepsea Hatchetfishes and allies**
Sternoptychidae

# LIGHT FROM LIVING FISH

## How fish produce and use illumination

As terrestrial creatures who, in our waking hours, are accustomed to light, we have little appreciation of lifestyles that must cope with continual darkness. Yet that is precisely what life would be like in the depths of the world's oceans were it not for bioluminescence, the production of light by living organisms. Not to be confused with phosphorescence or fluorescence – that is, light produced by non-living things through "excitement" or "stimulation" of crystals – bioluminescence occurs in living organisms and is the result of the chemical reaction of a substance, usually a compound known as luciferin, and an enzyme, referred to as a luciferase. Bioluminescence occurs on land, the best examples probably being fireflies that glow in the evening sky, or fungi that glow on the forest floor. It does not, however, occur in freshwater fishes. Its greatest display, though – both in variety and intensity – occurs in the sea.

Of the more than 20,000 living species of fishes, perhaps 1,000–1,500 bioluminesce. None of the lampreys and hagfishes or lungfishes are known to, but six genera of midwater and benthic (bottom-living) sharks and species representing nearly 190 genera of marine bony fishes are luminescent. This is best seen in the lanternfishes (Myctophidae), the bristlemouths (Gonostomatidae), several of the subfamilies of barbeled dragonfishes (Stomiidae) – for example Melanostominae or scaleless black dragonfishes; Malacosteinae or loosejaws; Chauliodontinae or viperfishes – the slickheads (Alepocephalidae), tubeshoulders (Platytroctidae) and the anglerfishes (various families). Several shallow-water and bottom-living fish families also contain luminescent species, and these are better understood behaviorally and physiologically in that they are easier to capture and study. Among these families are the ponyfishes, slimys or slipmouths (Leiognathidae), flashlight

**Above** *This leftvent species* (genus Linophryne) *of the anglerfish family Linophrynidae is displaying its glowing lure. Species of the family have a barbel hanging from their throat that also generates light.*

**Below** *A complex luminous organ (photophore) from a deepsea hatchetfish* (genus Argyropelecus). *A common pattern is shown here. The light-producing organs are partly screened by pigment cells and backed by a reflective layer which directs the light to the lens, in some cases through filters that change the color of the light emission.*

fishes (Anomalopidae), pinecone fishes (Monocentridae), *Porichthys* species of toadfishes (Batrachoididae), and several of the cardinal fishes (Apogonidae).

The origin of the light and its associated chemistry may be conveniently divided into two categories. The first are those with self-luminous photophores – specialized structures usually arranged in rows and consisting of highly complex lenses, reflectors and pigmented screens. The skin photophores produce light via the photogenic (light-generating) cells and reflect it through the lens and cornealike epidermis (transparent surface tissue). The more than 840 photophores in the belly of the Plainfin midshipman (*Porichthys notatus*) produce a gentle, even glow whose intensity can be slowly modulated (modified) to match the downwelling moonlight upon the sandy bottom.

The second category involves luminous bacterial symbionts – bacteria that live in harmony with their host fish. These are maintained in complex organs and are nurtured by the host fish in exchange for a more brilliant level of light. This extrinsic (externally-generated) form of illumination does not permit the fish to control the intensity or duration of the bacterial light which is produced. In response to this the hosts have evolved fascinating mechanisms, like lids, that allow them to turn off their light when it

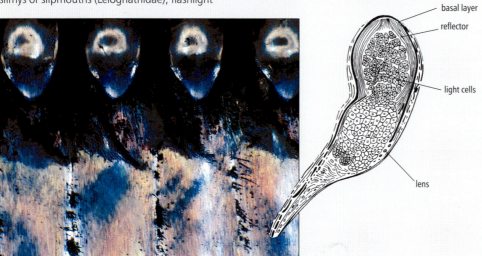

basal layer
reflector
light cells
lens

**Above** *The snaggletooth* Astronesthes niger *develops pale luminous patches with growth on its shoulder and lower sides. This particular species was photographed under ultraviolet light to indicate the fluorescence of photophores on its body and barbel.*

**Right** *The Flashlight fish has a large light organ below the eye which flashes on and off. The light is produced by bacteria housed in cells well provided with blood vessels. The role of the organ is uncertain, but in parts of the eastern Indian Ocean it is used by native fishermen as a bait.*

would be a hindrance or when it is not needed.

What, then, is the function of bioluminescence in fishes? In the case of most deepsea fishes, it is one of camouflage through counter-illumination. Even at 1,000m (3,300ft) in clear tropical waters, downwelling light would silhouette a lanternfish against the light, thus, making it visible to an upward-searching predator, were it not for the weak glow of the rows of photophores on its underside, which cancel out the shadowy form of its silhouette and make it "disappear." Other photophores on its body can be used as well to advertise its species and its sex. The large suborbital light organs (organs located under the eyes) of *Aristos-fomias, Pachystomias* and *Malacosteus* emit red

light, which, when coupled with its red-sensitive retina, might act like a "snooperscope" to hunt prey that can only see blue-green shades. Other uses in the deep sea include luring, as has been achieved by many scaleless black dragonfishes with elongate luminous chin barbels, or angler-fishes with luminous escae (bait) at the end of their modified first dorsal spine (ilicium). Conceal-ment is also a function whereby slickheads and certain grenadiers or rattails (Macrouridae) pre-sumably behave like squids and octopuses, leaving a predator snapping at a luminous ink cloud.

The behavior and bioluminescent function of shallow-water fishes is becoming better under-stood as a result of nocturnal observers with scuba

gear and the improvement in aquarium collecting and husbandry. The pinecone fishes (*Monocentris japonicus* and *Cleidopus gloriamaris*) live in shallow water and apparently lure nocturnal crustacean prey to their jaws with the light organs located in their mouth and on their jaws. Bioluminescence is, however, best perfected in the anomalopid flash-light fishes. These small, black, reef-associated fishes possess an immense light organ directly under each eye, capable of emitting enough light to be seen from 30m (100ft) away. In evening twi-light they migrate up from deep water to feed along the reef edge and return before daylight to the recesses of the deep reef. They use the light for many purposes, including finding food, attracting food, communication and avoiding predators. Flashlight fishes continually blink, either by raising a black eyelidlike structure over the light organ, or by rotating the entire organ into a dark pocket. The living light produced by the Flashlight fish (*Photoblepharon palpebratus*) is the most intense yet discovered.

This brief summary of fish bioluminescence reflects the meager knowledge we have of life in the nocturnal sea. As our ability to descend into the deep ocean at night improves, many more forms of extraordinary behavior associated with bioluminescence are coming to light and our body of knowledge is rapidly expanding. JEM/JD

# Lizardfishes and Lanternfishes

FACTFILE

## LIZARDFISHES AND LANTERNFISHES

Orders: Aulopiformes, Myctophiformes

About 475 species in about 75 genera and 17 families.

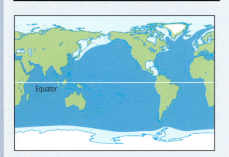

**LIZARDFISHES AND ALLIES** Order Aulopiformes About 225 species in c. 40 genera and 15 families. Shallow to deep water of all oceans. **Length:** maximum up to 2m (6.5ft). Families include: **flagfins** (Aulopodidae); **lizardfishes** (Synodontidae); **greeneyes** (Chlorophthalmidae); **tripod fishes** and **grideyes** (Ipnopidae); **barracudinas** (Paralepididae) and **daggertooths** (Anotopteridae), including the **Daggertooth** (*Anotopterus pharao*); **lancetfishes** (family Alepisauridae), including **Longnose lancetfish** (*Alepisaurus ferox*); **sabertooths** (family Evermannellidae); **pearleyes** (family Scopelarchidae); **telescope fishes** (family Giganturidae).

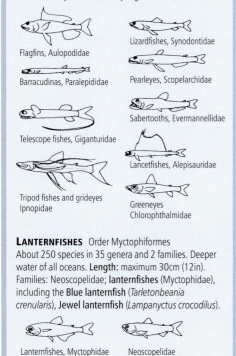

Flagfins, Aulopodidae

Lizardfishes, Synodontidae

Barracudinas, Paralepididae

Pearleyes, Scopelarchidae

Telescope fishes, Giganturidae

Sabertooths, Evermannellidae

Lancetfishes, Alepisauridae

Tripod fishes and grideyes Ipnopidae

Greeneyes Chlorophthalmidae

**LANTERNFISHES** Order Myctophiformes About 250 species in 35 genera and 2 families. Deeper water of all oceans. **Length:** maximum 30cm (12in). Families: Neoscopelidae; **lanternfishes** (Myctophidae), including the **Blue lanternfish** (*Tarletonbeania crenularis*), **Jewel lanternfish** (*Lampanyctus crocodilus*).

Lanternfishes, Myctophidae

Neoscopelidae

○ **Right** One characteristic of the genus *Synodus*, to which this Twospot lizardfish (S. binotatus) belongs, is the single band of palatine teeth which occur on each side of the mouth.

**V**ARIOUS EXTRAORDINARY FISHES BELONG *to the two orders of lizardfishes and lanternfishes: tripod fishes, which perch on the bottom in very deep water on their stiffened pelvic fins and lower tail lobe; grideyes of the genus* Ipnops, *which have greatly flattened eyes covering the top of the skull; that famous delicacy the Bombay duck; the large predatory lancetfish; the bizarre, highly modified telescope fish; the lanternfishes, speckled with luminous organs; and others.*

The 17 or so families in these orders were formerly considered by some authorities to be more realistically included in one order. The arrangement here follows the latest classifications in which just two families, Myctophidae and Neoscopelidae, comprise the Myctophiformes; all the others are Aulopiformes. The myctophiforms are now hypothesized to be more closely related to more advanced teleosts than to aulopiforms.

## Lizardfishes and Allies

### ORDER AULOPIFORMES

The anatomically diverse fishes included in the order Aulopiformes are united as a group by a peculiar arrangement of some of the small bones in the skeleton of the gills. Although the precise function of the gill modification is unknown, it is significant because it has not been observed in any non-aulopiform fishes. Within the order

numerous arrangements of genera and families have been proposed over the past several decades, but the two most recent comprehensive studies of the group divide aulopiforms into four subgroups.

Only one of those groups, the synodontoids, includes members that primarily inhabit warm shallow waters. Flagfin fishes of the family Aulopodidae, the namesake for the order, are among the most primitive aulopiforms. They live in the Atlantic, parts of the Pacific, and around southern coasts. They are scaled, bottom-living fishes with slender bodies and large heads. The second ray of the dorsal fin is characteristically elongate. An adipose fin is present. The teeth are small and lie in closely packed rows. Small, bottom-living invertebrates are the main food.

Flagfins are surprisingly colorful for fishes that may live as far down as 915m (3,000ft); browns, reds, and pinks are well represented among the dozen or so species. *Aulopus purpurissatus* is a highly colored, edible species from Australia. The edges of the scales are crimson against a purple or scarlet background. The fins are yellow with rows of red spots. Its common name of "Sergeant Baker" apocryphally alludes to the name of the soldier who first caught this fish in New South Wales. There is no evidence for this, but many red-colored fishes have a military common name in allusion to the red coats of British troops.

Most other members of this shallow or moderately shallow warm-water fish group belong to the

**⬥ Above** *Generally bottom-dwelling predators, this pair of Lighthouse lizardfish (Synodus jac-ulum) from Wakatobi, Indonesia will hardly leave the substrate except when in flight. This species can be identified by the big black blotch on the caudal peduncle.*

**◗ Right** *By far the most common reef-dwelling lizardfish, the Variegated lizardfish (Synodus variegatus) is often found hiding in the sands of deep lagoons to depths of over 40m (131ft). It preys on small fishes by seizing them from passing schools.*

lizardfish family Synodontidae. Lizardfishes are bottom dwellers, spending time propped up on their pelvic (ventral) fins waiting for their prey to swim by. They get their common name not just from the very lizardlike shape of the head but also from their rapid feeding movements. The most famous family member is the Bombay duck, popular in Indian restaurants as the crispy, salty delicacy eaten before the meal. This dish is the sundried, salted fillet of a large-mouthed, large-toothed fish from the Ganges estuary. Its slender, cylindrical body with a soft dorsal fin and an adipose fin is typical of many lizardfishes. Almost all are predatory, using their curved needlelike teeth to seize fish and invertebrates.

The next subgroup, the chlorophthalmoids, is made up of a diversity of fishes including the moderately shallow greeneyes and the very deep ipnopids. Greeneyes, or chlorophthlamids, are the orthodox members of the group. They are laterally compressed, silvery fishes with large eyes. They grow up to 30cm (12in) long, have dorsal and ventral fins well forward and an adipose fin directly above the anal fin. The common name for the family comes from the green light reflected by the tapetum lucidum (a reflective layer in the retina of the eye) in some species. Yellow eye lenses are common; the yellow coloring is believed to act as a selective filter enabling the fish to "see through" the downwardly directed luminous camouflage emanating from the ventral light organs of the small crustaceans that form its prey.

Greeneyes are widespread and fairly abundant in the North Atlantic, where they shoal at depths of 200–750m (660–2,460ft). In all species the lateral line system is well developed and greatly expanded into special organs on the snout, head, and gill covers. These organs enable the fish to detect the approach of small prey.

The dim light from the perianal organ (an organ around the anus) is produced by bacteria. The presence of this light is believed to enable a fish to maintain contact with its fellows and perhaps to facilitate mating among those in breeding condition. Ten species previously thought to belong to the greeneye family, including the Cucumber fish (*Paraulopus nigripinnis*), lack a perianal organ.

● **Right** *Representative species of lizard-fishes and lanternfishes:* **1** *The Indo-Pacific Gracile or Graceful lizardfish (*Saurida gracilis*) is common in shallow lagoons and reef flats;* **2** *Antarctic jonasfish (*Notolepis coatsi*);* **3** *The Longnose lancetfish (*Alepisaurus ferox*) is oviparous, with planktonic larvae;* **4** *The Metallic lanternfish (*Myctophum affine*) feeds on plankton.*

These ten species are now classified in the genus *Paraulopus* in a new aulopiform family, Paraulopidae, and are believed to be more closely related to the lizardfishes than to the greeneyes. Comprehensive studies of anatomical details often result in major changes in fish classifications.

Tripod fishes of the chlorophthalmoid family Ipnopidae occur as deep as 6,000m (19,700ft). They have been photographed on the deep sea floor resting on their stiffened pelvic fins and the lower lobe of the tail, facing into the current with their batlike pectoral fins raised over the head in the manner of forward-pointing elk horns. The 18 or so species of tripod fish are found worldwide in deep water. However, they are only found in a particular type of oceanic water mass called central oceanic water. Each species of tripod fish lives only in a particular area, defined by subtle parameters of temperature and salinity. *Bathypterois atricolor* may occur in waters as shallow as 300m (1,000ft), whereas *B. longicauda* lives as deep as 6,000m (19,700ft); *B. filiferus* lives only off South Africa, whereas *B. longipes* is circumglobal. All, however, can only live where the seafloor is composed of ooze or very fine sand which permits a firm "foothold" for their fins. One puzzle is that there are large areas of deep sea, for example the North Pacific, with ideal conditions (as far as can be seen) in which they do not live. For deep-sea fish they are common. Off the Bahamas intensive surveys have shown there can be almost 90 fish per sq km (233 per sq mile). The batlike pectoral fins have an elaborate nerve supply, so are sensory, but for what use is not known. The eyes are extremely small. The fish feed on small crustaceans that we can only presume are detected by the fins as they drift past in the current. As with deep-sea organisms in general, there is much that remains unknown, including their life history.

Tripod fishes are grouped with several other genera, including *Ipnops*, in the family Ipnopidae. *Ipnops* comprises 3 species, one of which is called the grideye, that look somewhat like flattened tripod fish without the tripod. They appear to be eyeless. They have achieved fame because of the enigma of the two large, flat, pale yellow plates on the top of the head. For about half a century it was thought that they were luminous organs that directed light upwards. The advent of deep-sea photography revealed that these plates are highly reflective. The flash from a deep-sea camera that photographed one was clearly reflected from the plates. Deep-sea collecting has made more specimens available to scientists, and the puzzle of the plates has been solved: they are a mixture of modified eyes and skull bones. Each plate, which covers half of the head width, is a transparent skull bone. The reflective layer below this is a highly modified eye retina. Ordinary eye structures, like the lens, have been lost; only the light-sensitive retina remains, spread out over the top of the head and protected by the skull. This is remarkable, but it is difficult to understand what it means to the fish. It can detect light coming down from above, yet cannot focus on an object. Moreover, *Ipnops* eats marine worms, which live below it.

The alepisauroid group of aulopiforms represents another diverse assemblage of fishes, all of which inhabit deep oceanic waters. The barracudinas of the family Paralepididae derive their common name from their superficial resemblance to the predatory barracudas of coral reefs, to which they are not related. Barracudinas are slender fishes with large jaws, many small, sharp, pointed teeth on the upper jaw and a mixture of larger stabbing teeth on the lower. A small adipose fin is present and the single, soft-rayed dorsal fin is in the rear half of the body. Scales, when present, are fragile and easily shed. This is thought to be an adaptation for swallowing large prey by permitting easier body expansion. In many species there is a fleshy keel between the anus and the anal fin.

The family is widespread but the range of individual species is more limited. *Notolepis coatsi*, a species growing to more than 10cm (4in) long, is confined to Antarctic waters. The Ribbon barracudina (*Arctozenus risso*) inhabits the eastern North Pacific.

The barracudinas are unusual among aulopiforms in that they have light organs. In the genus *Lestidium* these consist of ducts that extend from the head to the ventral fins. The bacteria therein produce a bright, pale-yellow light. The function of the luminosity is unknown. It is probably not for camouflage because the species with luminous organs have an iridescent skin as well as being translucent. Perhaps the organs function as lighthouses, enabling individuals of the same species to recognize one another.

The eyes of barracudinas are designed in such a way that their best field of binocular vision is directly downward. However, barracudinas seen from submersibles oriented themselves head-up, or nearly so, in the water so that they were looking along a horizontal plane (straight ahead). It is also conjectured that the head-up posture presents a smaller silhouette for predators beneath to spot.

The Daggertooth may grow to 1.5m (4.9ft) and lives in cool polar waters. It was formerly considered part of the barracudina family, but most experts now place it and two congeners in their own family, the Anotopteridae. The Daggertooth can take prey of up to half of its own length; a 75cm (30in) long intact specimen taken from a whale's stomach in the Antarctic was found to contain two barracudinas, 27 and 18cm (11 and 7in) long, both engorged with krill.

Lancetfishes are large, predatory, midwater alepisauroids. None have luminous organs but all have large stabbing teeth and distensible stomachs. Species in the genus *Alepisaurus* can reach 2.2m (7.2ft) in length, but their bodies are so slender that a fish of this size will only weigh 1.8–2.3kg (4–5lb). They are similar in shape to the Daggertooth but have a long, very high dorsal fin that can be folded down into a deep groove along the back and become invisible. The function of this large dorsal fin is unknown but it has

**Above** The Spinycheek lanternfish (Benthosema fibulatum) *grows to a maximum length of 10cm (4in) and at night occurs in the upper 200m of the ocean. The light organs (photophores) are visible here as the small shiny dots.*

been suggested that it might be used like the similarly large dorsal fin of the sail fishes in helping to "round up" shoals of small fishes. The Longnose lancetfish feeds on deep-sea hatchet fish, barracudinas, squids, octopuses and almost anything else available. Most of the fish eaten do not undertake daytime migrations. The very abundant lanternfishes, which do undertake daily migrations, are rarely eaten by lancetfish. Lancetfishes are, however, eagerly eaten by tunas and other surface predators when the opportunity arises.

Other alepisauroids include the closely related mesopelagic sabertooths of the family Evermannellidae and pearleyes of the family Scopelarchidae, some of which may enter more shallow areas at night. As the name suggests, sabertooths have long fanglike teeth typical of many mesopelagic fishes. Pearleyes obtained their name from a white spot, or pearl organ, on the eye. This organ is believed to help the fish detect light from a wide peripheral area. Pearleyes have slightly telescopic eyes that are pointed up and forward.

The last subgroup of aulopiforms contains the bizarre telescope fishes of the family Giganturidae. They are cylindrical, silvery fishes with forward-pointing tubular eyes set back on the snout. Scales and luminous organs are absent. The pectoral fin is set high up on the body; the caudal fin has an elongated lower lobe; adipose and pelvic fins are missing. Also missing are a large number of bones. Indeed, the adult fish has been subjected to a loss of many features typically present in its relatives. Many of the remaining bones are still cartilaginous. The teeth are large, sharp and

depressible, thus easing the passage of large prey. The inside of the mouth and stomach are lined with dense, black pigment which, it has been suggested, blacks out the luminous organs of its last meal. The abdominal region is elastic, meaning that telescope fish are capable of swallowing food much larger than themselves. The pectoral fins are inserted above the level of the gills and are thought to help ventilate them during the slow passage of a large fish down the throat. Certainly, some such device would have to be present, as the normal water currents cannot flow through the blocked mouth to the gills.

Telescope fishes have historically been classified in their own order. The gill skeleton of adults is so highly modified that some of the structures involved in the gill modifications of other aulopiforms are absent. However, in very young telescope fishes, when the gill skeleton is still cartilaginous, the aulopiform arrangement of the gill structures is evident. It is ironic that the young stages provide the best evidence that telescope fishes are aulopiforms: they are so different from adults that until recently they were thought to represent a separate family. Telescope fishes are widespread in tropical and semitropical oceans at depths down to about 3,350m (11,000ft). All are small fishes, rarely exceeding 15cm (6in).

## Lanternfishes and Allies
### ORDER MYCTOPHIFORMES

The 300 or so species in the order Myctophiformes are commonly known as lanternfishes because of the impression created by their extensive speckling of luminous organs. More precise common names for species within this order include Jewel lanternfish and Blue lanternfish, conveying the conspicuous and ornamental nature of the photophores. These carnivorous fishes live in the middle depths of all oceans and rarely exceed 30cm (12in) long. The overall body shape is very similar in all species, but the pattern of light organs differs from species to species and is the basis for species definition. As well as the small photophores there are larger organs – upper and lower glands – mostly near the tail, which indicate the sex of the fish. Usually the female lacks the upper glands and the lower ones are less conspicuous or even absent. The fish react strongly to light signals: one aquarium fish appeared to be most interested in the researcher's luminous wristwatch. Brighter light sources have little effect.

Lanternfishes live 300–700m (1,000–2,300ft) down. There are both silvery-bodied and dark-bodied forms. Many display an upward migration at night, occasionally to as little as 50m (165ft). Those with functional swimbladders have less fat than those without. Fat, being lighter than water, helps the latter maintain neutral buoyancy. Contrary to this, the Blue lanternfish may have no gas in its swimbladder, almost no body fat, and is negatively buoyant – denser than water! KEB/CCB

# Characins, Catfishes, Carps, and Allies

CARPS, CATFISHES, CHARACINS, SUCKERS, *loaches, and their allies are the dominant freshwater fishes in Eurasia and North America and arguably so in Africa and South America. (Only the catfishes are native to Australia.) The approximately 6,500 species are predominantly freshwater fish. Just two families of catfishes and one species of cyprinid are found at sea, although several genera may spend time in brackish water.*

The major groups are well defined (although their relationships remain the subject of much controversy). However, one species – *Ellopostoma megalomycter* from Borneo – is a puzzle, since it does not quite fit in anywhere, although some authorities believe that it belongs within the river loach family (Balitoridae).

## Diverse and Numerous
### CLASSIFICATION AND MORPHOLOGY

The superorder ostariophysi as a whole is divided into two series, the otophysi and the anotophysi, the former containing two hundred times more species than the latter. The otophysi have two main unifying characters. First, the presence of an "alarm substance" or pheromone secreted from glands in the skin when a fish is threatened and which causes a fright reaction in other otophysans. Perhaps understandably, the alarm substance is not present in families of heavily armored catfishes, but less comprehensible is its absence in certain species of the cave-dwelling characins and cyprinids.

The second diagnostic character is the Weberian apparatus. This is an elaborate modification of the first few vertebrae (individual back bones) into a series of levers, known as ossicles, that transmit compression waves of high-frequency sound received by the swimbladder to the inner ear. Consequently, otophysans have acute hearing. No one is certain how this complex "hearing aid" developed, but a clue may come from the anotophysi, which possess "head ribs" that may represent a prototypic form of such a mechanism.

The anotophysi are a diverse and somewhat incongruent group. The milkfish (*Chanos chanos*, sole member of the family Chanidae) is a food fish from the region of Southeast Asia. It looks rather like a large herring with small, silvery scales but lacking ventral scutes ("plates"). Milkfish are intensively cultured in fish ponds in many areas and can grow to well over 1m (3.3ft) in length. They can also tolerate a wide range of salinity.

The Beaked sandfish (*Gonorhynchus gonorhynchus*) is the only member of its family (Gonorhynchidae). A shallow-water species from the temperate and tropical Indo-Pacific, it has an elongate body, long snout, and a ventral mouth. There is no swimbladder. What could be fossil relatives of this species have been found in Alberta, Canada.

Unlike *Gonorhynchus*, the Hingemouth or Snake mudhead (*Phractolaemus ansorgii*) from West African freshwaters has a dorsal mouth that extends like a short periscope. Its swimbladder is divided into small units and can be used for breathing atmospheric air. Growing to little more than 15cm (6in) long, it is confined to the Niger and parts of the Zaïre basin.

The remaining anotophysan family, made up of the knerias and their closest relatives (Kneriidae), consists of small freshwater fishes that feed on algae in tropical and nilotic African freshwaters. They exhibit marked sexual dimorphism whereby the male has a peculiar rosette, of unknown function, on its operculum or gill cover. The genera *Cromeria* and *Grasseichthys* are neotenic, that is, they become sexually mature while still having a larval body form. These two genera are considered by some authorities to be kneriids; others place them in a separate family. Both of these small, transparent fishes from West African rivers – unlike their fellow family members – lack scales and a lateral line.

The characins, catfishes, carps and New World knifefishes are a highly successful group and display a remarkable mixture of evolutionary conservatism and extreme radicalism which, when coupled with the plasticity or variability at the species level, makes their taxonomy very difficult. For such common fish, they are an enigmatic group.                                                    KEB/JD

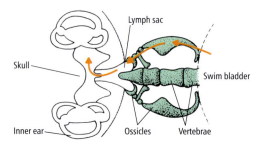

◑ **Above** *Weberian apparatus seen from above, a characteristic feature of many fishes belonging to the series Otophysi. It transmits vibrations from the swimbladder to the inner ear, giving the fish greatly enhanced hearing.*

◐ **Right** *With their short, triangular teeth equipped with razorlike edges for stripping flesh, piranhas (here, a Black-eared Piranha,* Serrasalmus notatus) *are supremely well adapted for feeding on other fishes and carrion. Observations in captivity suggest that the alleged "feeding frenzy" does not occur unless about 20 fish are gathered together.*

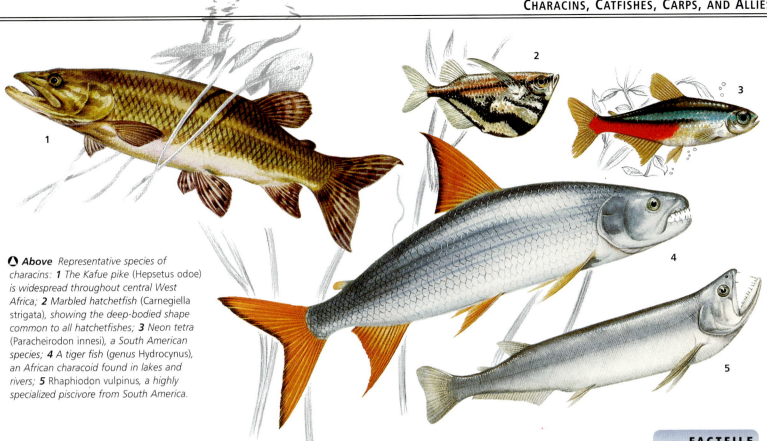

**Above** *Representative species of characins:* **1** *The Kafue pike* (Hepsetus odoe) *is widespread throughout central West Africa;* **2** *Marbled hatchetfish* (Carnegiella strigata), *showing the deep-bodied shape common to all hatchetfishes;* **3** *Neon tetra* (Paracheirodon innesi), *a South American species;* **4** *A tiger fish* (*genus* Hydrocynus), *an African characoid found in lakes and rivers;* **5** Rhaphiodon vulpinus, *a highly specialized piscivore from South America.*

## Characins and Relatives

### ORDER CHARACIFORMES

There are over 1,340 living species of characi-forms, about 210 of which are found in Africa and the remainder in Central and South America. This discontinuous distribution implies that some 100 million years ago, characiforms were widespread in the area of the landmass known as Gondwana-land, which later split to form Africa and South America, Antarctica and Australia.

Superficially, the characiforms resemble members of the carp family (cyprinids) but they usually have a fleshy adipose ("second" dorsal) fin between the caudal and true dorsal fins and have teeth on the jaws but not in the pharynx or throat. In addition to their complete functional set of teeth, characiforms also have a replacement set behind those in current use. In some species all the "old" teeth on one side of the upper and lower jaws fall out and the replacements take their place. Once these are firmly in position, the teeth on the other side of the jaws are replaced. In predatory characiforms all the old teeth drop out and are rapidly replaced in one go. As soon as the replacement teeth are functional, a new set of teeth begins to grow in the tooth-replacement trenches.

There are three families (with several subfamilies) of characiforms in Africa. They are both carnivorous and omnivorous, but are less varied than the Neotropical species. The most primitive African characoid is the Kafue or African pike (*Hepsetus odoe*), the sole member of the family Hepsetidae. It is a fish eater of the lurking-predator type, with a large mouth equipped with strong, conical teeth that prevent the prey's escape. Unusually for characiforms, it lays and guards its several thousand eggs in a floating foam nest (considered a great gastronomic delicacy). On hatching, the larvae hang from the water surface by special adhesive organs on their heads.

The fin eaters or ichthyborids are elongate members of the citharinids (family Citharinidae) that subsist by biting mouthfuls of scales and nipping notches out of other fishes' fins. Their close relatives are two groups of relatively harmless fishes: the grass eaters or distichontids, with which they share the subfamily Distichodontinae, and the moon fishes or citharinids (subfamily Citharininae). Their distinctive feature is scales with a serrated edge (ctenoid scales), unlike all other characins, which have smooth (cycloid) scales.

The final African characiform family is the Alestidae – the African tetras – containing some 18 genera and 100 species. The genus *Alestes* is one of the best-known groups of characoids, thanks to their popularity with aquarists. They are fairly colorful fishes, often with a single lateral stripe and red, orange, or yellow fins. The body can be short and deep or elongate (fusiform). All show sexual dimorphism in anal fin shape; in females the margin is completely straight, while in males it is convex. These fish also exhibit a curious sexual dimorphism in the caudal vertebrae. Yet how they recognize it, and what benefit it confers on them, is unknown. The African tetras have very strong, multicusped teeth, ideal for crushing and grinding their food of insects, fish and insect larvae, plankton and assorted vegetation.

The tigerfishes or water dogs, a genus containing several highly predatory species, have gained notoriety in their native lands. Their generic common name derives from their long, conical teeth, which overlap the outside of the jaws when the mouth is shut, and from their black body stripes (though these are horizontal rather than vertical). The Goliath tigerfish (*Hydrocynus goliath*) from the Congo region grows to over 1.5m (5ft) and weighs more than 45kg (100lb) and is so predatory that there are even unsubstantiated reports of them attacking people. Tigerfishes and water dogs are excellent sport fish. Oddly, tigerfish lose all their old teeth at once. As a result, toothless individuals have occasionally been caught, but it only takes a matter of days for the replacement teeth to emerge and become functional.

### FACTFILE

## CHARACINS, CATFISHES & ALLIES

Superorder: Ostariophysi

Orders: Characiformes, Siluriformes, Cypriniformes, Gymnotiformes, Gonorhynchiformes

About 6,500 species in at least 960 genera and around 60 families.

**Distribution** Worldwide, largely freshwater.

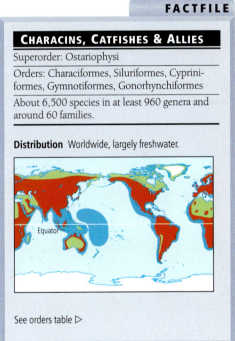

Equator

See orders table ▷

# Characins, Catfishes, Carps, New World Knifefishes, and Milkfishes

SERIES: OTOPHYSI

## Characins and relatives
### Order Characiformes

Freshwaters of Africa, S and C America, and southern N America. Length maximum 1.5m (5ft). Over 1,340 species in over 250 genera and probably 15 families. Families, genera, and species include: Characidae, including Cardinal tetra (*Paracheirodon axelrodi*); African tetras (family Alestiidae), including tiger fishes (genus *Hydrocynus*); freshwater hatchet fishes (family Gasteropelecidae); croaking tetras or glandulocaudines (subfamily Glandulocaudinae); Lebiasinidae, including Splashing tetra (*Copella arnoldi*); Serrasalminae, including piranhas (e.g. genera *Pygocentrus* and *Serrasalmus*), silver dollars (e.g. genera *Metynnis*, *Myleus*), wimple piranhas (genus *Catoprion*). The Naked characin (*Gymnocharacinus bergi*) of Argentina is classed as Endangered.

Note: Characiform classification underwent a major revision in the late 1990s and early 2000. As a result, families and subfamilies changed; the new systematics are reflected in the following pages. A large group of species – including many of the small, colorful, best-known tetras – were also earmarked for further study and placed in a group designated as *incertae sedis*, i.e. of uncertain identity.

## Catfishes
### Order: Siluriformes

Most habitable freshwaters; members of two families (Ariidae, Plotosidae) can inhabit tropical and subtropical seas. Length maximum 3m (10ft). Over 2,400 species in over c. 410 genera and 34 families..Families, genera, and species include: loach catfishes or amphiliids (family Amphiliidae); callichthyid armored catfishes (family Callichthyidae); walking catfishes (family Clariidae), including the Walking catfish (*Clarias batrachus*); crucifix fish (family Ariidae); North American freshwater catfishes (family Ictaluridae), including Blue and Channel catfishes and bullheads (genera *Ictalurus* and *Ameiurus*), flatheads (genus *Pylodictis*) and madtoms (genus *Noturus*); suckermouth armored catfishes or loricariids (family Loricariidae); parasitic catfishes (family Trichomycteridae), including candirús (genera *Vandellia*, *Branchioica*); long-whiskered, antenna catfishes or pimelodids (family Pimelodidae); schilbeids (family Schilbeidae); sheatfishes (family Siluridae), including European wels (*Silurus glanis*); Asian hillstream catfishes or sisorids (family Sisoridae). Thirty-seven species of catfishes are currently classed as threatened to some degree, including the

Critically Endangered Smoky madtom (*Noturus baileyi*), Barnard's rock catfish (*Australoglanis barnardii*), and Cave catfish (*Clarias cavernicola*).

## Carps and Allies, or Cyprinoids
### Order: Cypriniformes

N America, Europe, Africa, Asia almost exclusively in freshwater. Length maximum 3m (10ft). About 2,660 species in around 279 genera and 5 families. Families, genera, and species include: cyprinids (family Cyprinidae), including bighead and silver carps (genus *Hypophthalmichthys*), bream (genus *Abramis*), Common carp (*Cyprinus carpio carpio*), Grass carp (*Ctenopharyngodon idella*), mahseers (genus *Tor*), Roach (*Rutilus rutilus*), snow trouts (genus *Schizothorax*), squawfish (genus *Ptychocheilus*), Tench (*Tinca tinca*), Yellow cheek (*Elopichthys bambusa*); algae eaters or gyrinocheilids (family Gyrinocheilidae); river loaches (family Balitoridae or Homalopteridae); "true" loaches (family Cobitidae), including weather fish (*Misgurnus fossilis* and *M. anguillicaudatus*); suckers or catostomids (family Catostomidae). One hundred and ninety-one species of cyprinids are currently classed as threatened in some measure.

## New World Knifefishes
### Order Gymnotiformes

C and S America, exclusively in freshwater. Length maximum 2.3m (7.5ft). About 62 species in 23 genera and 6 families. Families, genera, and species include: Ghost knifefishes (family Apteronotidae); Electric knifefish or Electric eel (*Electrophorus electricus*); naked-back knifefishes (family Gymnotidae).

SERIES: ANOTOPHYSI

## Milkfish and Allies
### Order: Gonorhynchiformes

Indo-Pacific Ocean; freshwaters in tropical Africa. Length maximum 2m (6.5ft). About 35 species in 7 genera and 4 families. Genera and species include the Milkfish (*Chanos chanos*), Beaked sandfish (*Gonorhynchus gonorhynchus*), and Hingemouth or Snake mudhead (*Phractolaemus ansorgii*).

**Below** The term "tetra" covers a multitude of small characins from South America and Africa. Rummy-nosed tetras (Hemigrammus rhodostomus) inhabit the Orinoco and Amazon river basins in Brazil and Venezuela.

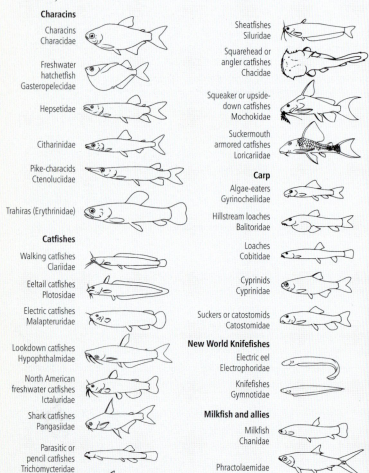

Characins
- Characins — Characidae
- Freshwater hatchetfish — Gasteropelecidae
- Hepsetidae
- Citharinidae
- Pike-characids — Ctenoluciidae
- Trahiras (Erythrinidae)

Catfishes
- Walking catfishes — Clariidae
- Eeltail catfishes — Plotosidae
- Electric catfishes — Malapteruridae
- Lookdown catfishes — Hypophthalmidae
- North American freshwater catfishes — Ictaluridae
- Shark catfishes — Pangasiidae
- Parasitic or pencil catfishes — Trichomycteridae
- Crucifix fishes — Ariidae

Sheatfishes — Siluridae
Squarehead or angler catfishes — Chacidae
Squeaker or upside-down catfishes — Mochokidae
Suckermouth armored catfishes — Loricariidae

Carp
- Algae-eaters — Gyrinocheilidae
- Hillstream loaches — Balitoridae
- Loaches — Cobitidae
- Cyprinids — Cyprinidae
- Suckers or catostomids — Catostomidae

New World Knifefishes
- Electric eel — Electrophoridae
- Knifefishes — Gymnotidae

Milkfish and allies
- Milkfish — Chanidae
- Phractolaemidae

The diversity in Neotropical characins ranges from voracious predators, through tiny vegetarians, to blind subterranean species. The piranhas are the most fabled of all predatory fishes. They are stocky and tough, having a deep head and short powerful jaws with triangular, interlocking, razor-sharp teeth. They are shoaling animals, and feed communally on smaller fish or, allegedly, on larger injured or supposedly healthy prey.

Each piranha makes a clean bite of about 16 cubic cm (1cu in) of flesh. Shoal size then dictates the speed with which the victim is despatched. In some areas, the feeding frenzy is triggered by blood in the water and it takes only a few minutes for a victim to be reduced to little more than a skeleton. People wading or bathing in rivers have also been attacked, but these are rare occurrences. One legend relates how a man and horse fell into the water and were later found with all the flesh picked off, yet the man's clothes were found to be undamaged. Ironically, in reality it is humans who customarily prey on piranhas – large numbers are fished and eaten (usually fried) by river people (caboclos) all along the Amazon and other South American rivers.

Piranhas rarely exceed 60cm (2ft) and are excellent sport fish. Anglers use a stout wire trace to catch them or, quite simply, a hand line with a baited hook. Such is the appetite of hungry

piranhas that an excellent catch can be made in a remarkably short time.

The piranhas' close relatives include vegetarian or omnivorous genera known to aquarists as silver dollars and pacus. Although they are similar in appearance, their nature is quite unlike that of the piranhas. Pacus(Colossoma macropomum) in particular, have strong jaws and grinding teeth with which they can crack hard seeds and fruits. The silver dollars (Metynnis and allies) are more straightforward plant eaters.

The wimple-piranhas (Catoprion spp.) eat the scales of other fish. Their lower jaw is longer than the upper and their teeth are everted, that is, they point outward, which enables them to scrape the scales of their prey in a single upward swipe. In the presence of wary potential prey, they live on insects and other small invertebrates.

The genera of South American "salmons" have many features that suggest they are a primitive group. Catabasis is known only from a single preserved specimen. These fish are presumed to be extant but none have been seen since this specimen was caught in 1900. The trout predator tetras (Salminus spp.) are known as dourados in Brazil and are, apparently, the most primitive characiforms known. Despite its importance as a genus of food and sport fish, the classification of the four species of Salminus is uncertain.

The cachorros (Acestrorhynchus spp.) are the Neotropical genus equivalent of the African genus Hepsetus. They are streamlined pike-like predators with formidable teeth. They often hunt in open water and are capable of producing short, high-speed bursts; they can also leap out of the water.

The family of freshwater hatchetfish (Gasteropelecidae) is completely different. It consists of deep-bodied fish, with long pectoral fins; they rarely exceed 10cm (4in) and are capable of powered flight. The deep chest houses powerful muscles which are necessary for turning the pectoral fins into wings. Prior to flight, hatchetfish may "taxi" for distances of up to 12m (40ft), for most of which the tail and chest trail in the water. The flight phase is marked by a buzzing caused by the very rapid flapping of the fins. The flight distance rarely exceeds 1.5m (5ft) – but can be as long as 39m (100ft) in optimal conditions – and they have been seen at a height of 90cm (3ft) above the water, although a height of up to 10cm (4in) is most common. The energy cost of flight to the fish is unknown, but it is thought that flight is used when they are frightened by predators. Normally, hatchetfish are found near the water surface feeding on insects. Species of elongate hatchetfishes (Triportheus spp.) also have their chest developed into a sort of keel and have large wing-like pectoral fins, similar to those of the other hatchetfish. These fish are able to use the breast muscles and pectoral fins to jump about 1m (3.3ft) above the water surface to escape predators, but this cannot be regarded as true flight.

Most characins are generalized egg scatterers but in some, there is specialized breeding behavior. The male croaking tetras or glandulocaudines, for example, have scales modified into special glands, known as "caudal glands," at the base of the caudal fin or tail. These glands secrete a pheromone – a chemical that the opposite sex are supposed to find irresistible. If the pheromone alone is insufficient to attract a mate, some males are also equipped with a worm-like lure – particularly well developed in the Swordtail characin (Stevardia riisei) to signal to the female of his choice. It is unknown whether this is intended to be a prey mimic or whether it is a visual cue to induce the female to approach, align herself at the right angle beside the male, and allow him to insert sperm into her genital (sexual) opening. These are the only characoids believed to employ internal egg fertilization.

The Splashing tetra (Copella arnoldi), a member of the family Lebiasinidae, lays its eggs on overhanging leaves or rocks, thus avoiding the high predation that eggs experience in water. The male courts a gravid female until the point of egg-laying is reached. Leading her to the overhang of his choice about 3cm (1in) above the water, he makes trial jumps up to this spawning site. The female then follows, sticks briefly to its surface, using water surface tension, and lays a few eggs. The male then leaps and fertilizes them. Alternatively, both fish may jump together. This process continues until about 200 eggs are laid and fertilized. After spawning, the female goes on her way, but the male remains nearby to splash water over the eggs until they hatch. This takes about three days and once the fry fall into the water, the male's "nursemaid" activities are over.

One Panamanian characin, the Sábalo pipón (Brycon petrosus) also lays its eggs out of the water. This species indulges in terrestrial group spawning, with about 50 adults moving by lateral undulations or tail flips onto the banks and laying eggs on the damp ground. Males are distinguished by a convex anal fin and short, bony spicules (tiny needle-like structures) on the fin rays. There is no parental care and the eggs take about 2 days to hatch.

Most of the South American tetras, fishes beloved of aquarists, have received their common name from a contraction of their former scientific group (subfamily) name, Tetragonopterinae (most are now regarded as incertae sedis). Many of these highly successful fishes are brilliantly colored, which, apart from rendering them commercially important in the ornamental aquatic world, holds the members of shoals together in the wild. Tetras are omnivorous to the extent that they will eat anything they can fit into their mouths, although most are predatory, feeding, largely, on small insects and aquatic invertebrates. Within this group is the Mexican Blind Cave Characin (Astyanax jordani).                          BB/JD

# Catfishes

## ORDER SILURIFORMES

There are about 2,400 species of catfishes, assigned to some 34 families. Most are tropical freshwater fishes, but some inhabit temperate regions (Ictaluridae, Siluridae, Diplomystidae and Bagridae) and two families (Plotosidae and Ariidae) are marine.

Catfishes are named for their long barbels, which give them a bewhiskered appearance reminiscent of cats (though barbels are not present in all species and are not diagnostic for the group). Characters defining catfishes include the fusion of the first 4–8 vertebrae, often with modification of the chain of bones or ossicles connecting the swimbladder to the inner ear; lack of parietal bones, i.e. a paired bone on the roof of the skull; a unique arrangement of blood vessels in the head; an absence of typical body scales and strong dorsal and pectoral fin spines.

Although catfishes lack typical scales, the bodies of many are not entirely naked. The thorny, talking catfishes (doradids), the Asian hillstream catfishes (sisorids), and the loach catfishes (amphiliids) all have bony scutes or plates around the sensory pores of the lateral line and sometimes along the back. The loricariid and callichthyid armored catfishes may be completely encased in these scutes. Strong serrated pectoral and dorsal fin spines are widespread in catfishes. Locking mechanisms keep these spines erect and these, coupled with the bony armor, must deter potential predators. Catfish swimbladders may be partially or completely enclosed in a bony capsule. Why this should be is not clear, since the most obvious association of a reduction of the swimbladder and benthic (bottom-hugging) habits, does not hold. For example, reduced and encapsulated swimbladders occur in fast-swimming species of lookdown catfishes (Hypophthalmidae) and bottlenose or barbelless catfishes (Ageneiosidae), while the benthic electric catfishes (Malapteruridae) have the largest swimbladders of all!

There are more catfish species in South America than in the rest of their area of distribution. Both the world's smallest and largest catfishes occur here. The Spiny dwarf catfish (*Scoloplax dicra*, of the family Scoloplacidae) of Bolivia is a minute, partially armoured fish whose total adult length is less than 13mm (0.5in),whereas the Jáu (*Paulicea* sp.) of the family Pimelodidae from Amazonia, can grow to more than 3m (about 10ft). The European wels (*Silurus glanis*) of the family Siluridae can attain a similar size. Of the 16 families in South America, most live in the Amazon Basin, but four are endemic to the Andes.

The suckermouth armored catfishes (Loricariidae) are the largest of all catfish families, with over 600 species. As their name suggests, their mouths are suckerlike with thin, often comblike teeth adapted to scraping algal mats. Most species are active at night and hide during the day in crevices and logs. The males of some species bear long spines on their opercular apparatus (the bones forming the gill cover) and use them in cheek-to-cheek territoriality fights with other males. Twig catfish (*Farlowella* sp.) are especially slim loricariids, long and thin and resembling dead twigs, hence their name.

Closely related to the loricariids are the climbing catfishes (family Astroblepidae). The family's 40 species inhabit Andean torrents. These specialized fishes are able to climb smooth, almost vertical rock faces by utilizing the muscles of the ventral surface and using their pelvic fins to form a sucker.

The callichthyid armored catfishes (Callichthyidae) have mail-like plates thought to be able to resist desiccation when ponds dry up. Several genera (i.e. *Callichthys*, *Lethoplosternum*, *Megalechis* and *Hoplosternum*) can withstand marked temperature changes and propel themselves over dry land with their pectoral spines. They also build floating bubble nests. The genus *Corydoras* – with nearly 200 species – is well-known to aquarists,

who have recorded the breeding habits and development of many species. Unusually, it has been shown that the females of some species of *Corydoras* actually drink sperm when mating and channel these rapidly (and without any deterioration) through their gut, releasing them through their anus, onto a pouch created by their pelvic fins and in which they hold several eggs. Once these sticky eggs have been fertilized, the female places them on a suitable surface and abandons them.

The doradids vary greatly in size, from *Physopyxis lyra* (5cm, 2in) to the Soldier or Snail-eating cat (*Megalodoras irwini*) (1m, 3.3ft). Most species are bottom dwellers and, surprisingly, play an important part in seed dispersal by their fruit-eating habits (the seeds are not digested and pass through the fish unharmed).

The long-whiskered or antenna catfishes (Pimelodidae), with 300 species, is a family of great morphological diversity and includes some of the largest known catfishes, e.g. the Red-tailed cat (*Phractocephalus hemioliopterus*). Most species are omnivorous, but the larger ones are fish eaters or carnivores. One species is recorded as having eaten monkeys that fell in the river. Pimelodids are commercially important in parts of the Amazon Basin.

The parasitic catfishes (Trichomycteridae) contain some 155 species. Some are parasites, inhabiting and laying their eggs in the gill cavities of the larger pimelodid catfishes. The candirú is perhaps the most notorious representative of the family. Mammals (including humans) have had their urethra penetrated by this slender fish when urinating while immersed in a stream. The candirú probably mistakes the flow of urine for water being expelled from the gill chamber of a large catfish. It therefore swims "upstream" and enters the urethra, where it lodges itself with its powerful gill

▶ **Below** *Representative species of catfishes: 1 Armored catfish (Callichthys callichthys), with its distinctive scale pattern; 2 Among sea cats such as the Hardhead catfish (Arius felis), eggs are mouthbrooded by the male; 3 Walking catfish (Clarias batrachus), which can cross land between bodies of water; 4 The candirú (Vandellia cirrhosa) is a parasite that sucks blood from larger fishes' gills; 5 Channel catfish (Ictalurus punctatus), a valued sport fish in the USA; 6 The Frogmouth catfish (Chaca chaca) is a nocturnal predator from southern Asia; 7 Giant catfish (Pangasianodon gigas), an Endangered species from the Mekong River, Vietnam; 8 The Upside-down catfish (Synodontis nigriventis) swims inverted to graze the underside of leaves for live food and algae; 9 The European wels (Siluris glanis) is a large catfish that can, exceptionally, grow to 5m (16.4ft).*

cover spines. Normally, it would rasp a wound in a host's gills and feed on the blood. However, when mistakenly lodged inside the urethra, it cannot swim back out – as it would from the gill chamber of a fish – and therefore causes great pain to the victim. Usually, such trapped candirús can only be removed by surgery.

As well as several eyeless species, there are also two peculiar nonparasitic genera in the Trichomycteridae. They have large fat-filled organs above the pectoral fins. One of them, *Sarcoglanis*, known only from a single specimen 4cm (1.5in) long, was collected in 1925 by Dr. Carl Ternetz in the San Gabriel Rapids on the Rio Negro. Forty years later, Dr. George Myers, in the same locality, caught another similar fish, but belonging to a new genus. Nothing is known about these puzzling forms.

The whale catfishes (Cetopsidae), with 12 species, is also a poorly known group. Some species are particularly voracious and prey on other catfishes by biting out circular pieces of flesh with their sawlike teeth. The Blue whale catfish (*Cetopsis coecutiens*) is, perhaps, the best-known species in this family.

The family of driftwood catfishes (Auchenipteridae) contains about 60 species, characterized by conspicuous spots and stripes. They range from Panama to La Plata and are nocturnal, detrital feeders, inhabiting hollow logs by day where they line up in ranks. Exceptionally for catfishes, driftwood cats employ internal egg fertilization, with the eggs being later released by the female over the bottom or among plants, where they remain, unprotected, until they hatch about one week after release.

The lookdown or loweye catfishes (Hypophthalmidae) are most unusual. Unlike most other catfishes, they feed on plankton which they sieve from the water through fine gill rakers. Long barbels help to funnel the plankton into the mouth. As they are surface feeders, *Hypophthalmus* species have a high fat content and paper-thin bones that increase buoyancy.

Of the eight families of catfishes in Africa, only three are endemic, four are shared with Asia and one, the sea catfishes (Ariidae), also occurs in the coastal waters of Asia, Australia, and North and South America. Although there is less diversity in form among African catfishes than among South American ones, there are many unusual forms, some displaying remarkable parallels with those of South America. The richest diversity of species in Africa occurs in the principal equatorial river basin, the Zaïre, Africa's equivalent of the Amazon. A major difference between the continents, however, is the series of rift valley great lakes in Africa, some of which harbor endemic groups of catfishes.

The most widespread of these are the bagrids (family Bagridae), with over 200 species. Some species of *Bagrus*, a Nilotic catfish genus, weigh over 5kg (11lb). Small bagrids, Zaïrean endemics, live in torrents, while a "flock" of several *Chrysichthys* species, among them the giant of them all, *C. grandis*, which can weigh as much as 190kg (420lb), inhabits Lake Tanganyika. This generalized family also has members in Asia.

The walking catfishes (Clariidae) contain about 30 species and 10 genera. These are long-bodied with long dorsal and anal fins and broad, flat heads. Some species have an organ at the top of the gill chamber that enables them to breathe atmospheric air and so survive when water is deoxygenated. Clariids, like the South American callichthyids, can travel overland from one water body to another, hence their common name. The largest clariid is the Vundu (*Heterobranchus longifilis*), exceeding 50kg (110lb). Other genera are small, anguilliform (eel-like) fishes with burrowing habits; *Uegitglanis zammaranoi* from Somalia is, however, subterranean and eyeless; the Cave clarias (*Clarias cavernicola*) from Namibia is also eyeless. This family also occurs in Asia, but is represented by fewer species there.

The endemic family Malapteruridae, with its two species, is the only family of electric catfishes. All catfishes appear capable of detecting electrical activity, but only *Malapterurus* is actively electrogenic. The dense, fatty electric organ covers the flanks of the fish and gives it a cylindrical, sausage-shaped appearance. These catfishes are capable of generating strong electric impulses (up to 450 volts) which are used for both defense and stunning prey. Some *Malapterurus* specimens exceed 1m (3.3ft) in length and weigh up to 20kg (44lb).

The squeakers or upside-down catfishes (family Mochokidae) are exclusively African. Over 100 of its 170 or so species belong to the genus *Synodontis*, a few species of which can swim upside-down and utilize food on the surface, as well as feeding normally on the bottom. This habit, along with

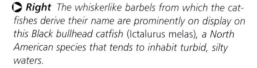

● **Above** *The young of the Saltwater or Coral catfish (Plotosus lineatus)* form rolling "feeding-balls" that resemble giant sea urchins. Plotosids are notorious for the dangerous wounds they can inflict with their pectoral spines, which have venomous glands at the base.

● **Right** *The whiskerlike barbels from which the catfishes derive their name are prominently on display on this Black bullhead catfish (Ictalurus melas), a North American species that tends to inhabit turbid, silty waters.*

● **Below** *The striking transparency of the Glass catfish (Kryptopterus bicirrhis; Siluridae) is a camouflage adaptation, though its physiology is unknown.*

Species of the endemic Asian hillstream catfishes (Sisoridae) with 100 species, and the torrent catfishes (Amblycipitidae) with about 10 species, are small mountain-stream dwellers, clinging to the substrate by the partial vacuum caused by corrugations of their undersides. The two species of the small family of frogmouth catfishes (Chacidae) from Borneo are well-camouflaged, flattened fishes with cavernous mouths and large heads. They resemble some angler fishes and feed in a similar way, apparently being able to lure prey to within reach of their gape.

The shark catfishes (Pangasiidae), numbering about 21 species, is possibly the most economically important of the Southeast Asian catfish families. In Thailand, *Pangasius* species have been pond-reared on fruit and vegetables for over a century and are sold in vast numbers. One of the world's largest freshwater fishes, the Giant catfish (*Pangasianodon gigas*) occurs in the Mekong river, growing to 3m (10ft). Despite the anecdotal evidence of travelers' tales, it too is totally vegetarian.

The tandan catfish family (Plotosidae) contains about 32 species, some of which live in the Indo-Pacific Ocean. However, two genera, *Tandanus* and *Neosilurus* (the eel-tailed catfishes), live in the freshwaters of Australia and New Guinea. Specimens of *Tandanus* can weigh up to 7kg (15lb). These fishes build circular nests, about 2m (6.5ft) in diameter, from pebbles, gravel, and sticks. The several thousand eggs are guarded by the male until they hatch after seven days.

Closely related to the walking catfishes (Clariidae) is the family Heteropneustidae, known as the stinging or airsac catfishes, species of which have long air sacs that extend backwards from each gill cavity. These catfishes can deliver a very potent sting, with enough venom to kill a human.

The sea cats (Ariidae) have a circumtropical, largely marine distribution. Males of this family are mouthbrooders; up to 50 large, fertilized eggs are carried for as long as two months, during which time the male does not feed.

Apart from a few ariid species reaching coastal regions, only one family, the North American freshwater catfishes (Ictaluridae), with its 7 genera comprising some 45 species, is present in North America. The flatheads (*Pylodictis* species) are the largest, growing to some 40kg (88lb). The blue and channel catfishes (*Ictalurus* spp.) form the basis of a large catfishery in the Great Lakes and the Mississippi valley. The madtoms (*Noturus* species) – named for the venomous glands at the base of the pectoral fins – comprise some 25 species. There are also three cave-dwelling, eyeless ictalurids, which appear to have evolved independently. The Mexican blindcat (*Prietella phreatophila*) is known only from a well in Coahuila, Mexico; the Widemouth blindcat (*Satan eurystomus*) and the Toothless blindcat (*Trogloglanis pattersoni*) have only appeared in 300m (1,000ft) deep artesian wells near San Antonio in Texas. It is thought they live in deep water-bearing strata.          GJH/JD

the ability of at least some species to produce sounds, explains the family's common names.

The endemic loach catfish family (Amphiliidae) contains about 47 small species. Some (e.g. the hillstream whiptails, *Phractura* and *Andersonia*) display remarkable parallelism with the South American twig catfishes in their elongate, plated bodies. Amphiliids inhabit the faster, cooler upper reaches of rivers, clinging to the cobbled substrate.

The schilbeid catfishes (Schilbeidae), a family shared with Asia, has about 20 species in Africa. They have a short dorsal fin and compressed, deep bodies. They are fast-swimming shoalers which, in their large numbers, are both important predators on other fishes and, in their turn, form a large food source for fish-eating perches. Schilbeids are ubiquitous fishes that can change their diets easily and have quickly adapted to artificial situations, such as dammed lakes and reservoirs.

After carps and their allies, catfishes are the dominant element of Asia's fish fauna. Compared with African catfishes, Asian catfishes are not well-known, scattered as they are throughout the Indonesian islands and isolated rivers and lakes of China and high Asia. Twelve families occur in and around the continent, seven of which are endemic.

The Bagridae are widely distributed with the species-rich genus *Mystus* (about 40 species) being typical. Most Mystus species are small - around 8-35cm (3.2-14in) in length; some, however, like the Asian Red-tailed Bagrid (*M. nemurus*), can grow much larger, around 60cm (24in) in this case. The accurately-named lancers (*Bagrichthys* spp.) from Borneo and Sumatra are unusual in that the dorsal fin spine of the adults is nearly the length of the fish's body.

The sheathfishes (Siluridae) are a significant family with species in Eurasia, Japan, and offshore islands. The family contains the 2m (6.5ft) long voracious predator, the Helicopter catfish (*Wallago attu*) and the largest of all, the European wels (*Silurus glanis*). The *Wallago* follows shoals of carps in their upstream migrations and can leap clear of the water during a feeding frenzy.

# Carps and Allies

### ORDER CYPRINIFORMES

The cyprinoids form a major lineage of largely freshwater, egg-laying fishes. All lack jaw teeth but most have a pair of enlarged bones in the pharynx or throat, the teeth of which work against the partner bone and a pad on the base of the skull. A less conspicuous unifying feature is a small bone (the kinethmoid) which enables the upper jaw to be protruded, i.e. extended. Most also have scaleless heads. Cyprinoids are indigenous to Eurasia, Africa and North America. Unlike the other major otophysan lineages, they are not native to South America and Australia.

Of the five families, with over 2,660 species and around 280 genera, by far the largest is the family Cyprinidae, with over 2,000. The Cyprinidae – the chubs, minnows, mahseers, carps, barbs, etc.– reflect the distribution of the cyprinoids and are well known to both freshwater anglers and aquarists. Even in areas where they never lived naturally, many are familiar to fishermen and pondkeepers as well as to gourmets.

The Common carp (*Cyprinus carpio carpio*) epitomizes the family. Probably native to Central Europe and Asia, it has been introduced to all continents capable of supporting fish life. The carp is extremely tolerant of a wide range of conditions, so much so, that, in Central Africa, where it was introduced to provide food for expatriates, it has colonized areas so successfully that it is now the commonest cyprinid. In the United Kingdom, to which it was probably introduced in Roman times, it is loved by anglers, for whom catching an 18kg (40lb) specimen is a lifetime's goal. In South Africa, where the carp was introduced in the early 20th century, a 38kg (83lb) specimen was caught.

The Japanese in particular have cultivated carp as objects of beauty; several hundred years of intensive breeding has released the potential colors and many "brocaded" carps (known as Koi)

⊘ *Below* Representative species of cyprinoids, knifefishes, and milkfishes: **1** *Mahseer* (Tor tor), *a native of the Indian subcontinent;* **2** *Shiner* (Notropis lutrensis); **3** *Rosy barbs* (Barbus conchonius) *show marked sexual dimorphism, the male being the more colorful;* **4** *The Common carp* (Cyprinus carpio) *is a popular game and food fish in central Europe;* **5** *Two examples of Gastromyzon, a hillstream cyprinoid that has paired fins forming suction disks, allowing it to cling to rocks;* **6** *Gudgeon* (Gobio gobio); **7** *Luciobrama, a pikelike cyprinoid predator;* **8** *Sucking loach or Chinese algae eater* (Gyrinocheilus aymonieri); **9** *The Flying fox* (Epalzeorhynchous kallopterus) *is a favored aquarium species;* **10** *The Razorback sucker* (Xyrauchen texanus) *has a very limited distribution in the western USA, and is classed as Endangered;* **11** *Ghost knifefish* (Apteronotus albifrons); **12** *Electric knifefish* (Electrophorus electricus); **13** *Milkfish* (Chanos chanos).

are sold for high prices to beautify ponds and aquaria. These colored fishes have become so popular that large breeding and export centers now exist, not just in Japan, but in China, Singapore, Malaysia, Sri Lanka, the US, Israel, and several European countries. In its native Eurasia, the Carp is bred for food, but even there, modifications have been made. Careful selection first produced carp with few scales (Mirror carp), then with none (Leather carp). Further selective breeding has resulted in strains lacking the hairlike, intermuscular bones that create problems for diners.

The majority of cyprinids are smallish fishes, measuring only some 10–15cm (4–6in) long when adult. There are, however, some notable exceptions. The Golden Mahseer (*Tor putitora*) of Himalayan and Indian rivers can grow to 2.7m (9ft) long and can weigh 54kg (120lb). In North America, the Colorado Squawfish

(*Ptychocheilus lucius*) of the Colorado and Sacramento rivers, which was an important food source to the native Americans of those areas (hence the common name), used to grow to over 1.8m (6ft) long. Now, this species is practically extinct in the Colorado (because of damming) and much smaller and rarer in the Sacramento (because of overfishing). Of similar length is the Yellow cheek (*Elopichthys bambusa*) from the Amur River in northern China. Both species are unusual among cyprinids (which are toothless) in that they are specialised fish eaters. Other, but smaller, examples of fish eaters are the Rhinofish (*Barbus mariae*), from a few rivers in East Africa; *Luciobrama macrocephalus* from southern China, a fish with

a disproportionately elongate head; and the Dab Bao or Pla Pak Pra (*Macrochirichthys macrochirus*) from the Mekong River. The last of these is a strongly compressed fish with a large, angled mouth and a hook and notch on the lower jaw. It can also raise its head to increase the gape when lunging at its prey.

Most cyprinids, including the mahseers, will eat almost anything: detritus, algae, mollusks, insects, crustacea, even cheese sandwiches! The bighead and silver carps (*Hypophthalmichthys* spp.) of China are specialized plankton feeders with gill rakers modified into an elaborate filtering organ. One species, the Grass carp (*H. molitrix*), eats plants and has been introduced to many countries to clear weeds from canals, rivers, and lakes.

The shape and distribution of the pharyngeal or "throat" teeth often indicate the diet. Mollusk eaters have crushing, molarlike teeth, which are closely packed; fish eaters have thin, hooked teeth; vegetarians have thin, knifelike teeth for shredding; omnivores come somewhere in between. Yet even within one species, the teeth may vary. In Africa, for example, fish of the species *Barbus altianalis* living in a lake with no snails have "middle-of-the-road" type teeth, while those in a snail-rich lake a few kilometres away, have thicker, lower, more rounded teeth. The young, however, all start off with the same type of teeth.

The widespread and species-rich genus *Barbus* (used here to include, in addition to *Barbus* itself,

genera referred in some works as *Puntius, Capoeta,* and *Barbodes*) derives its name from the (usually) four barbels around the mouth; these are provided with taste buds with which the fish can taste the substrate before eating. A particular specialization of some African species is the varied shape and thickness of the mouth and lips according to diet. A broad-mouthed form with a wide, sharp-edged lower jaw will feed on epilithic algae, i.e. algae that grow as an encrusting layer on rocks. A narrow-mouthed form with thick, rubbery lips feeds by sucking up stones and their associated fauna. The fact that these two extremes are found in one and the same species explains why the fish that is now regarded as *B. intermedius* formerly had over 50 scientific names!

Most cyprinids do not exhibit sexual dimorphism, but some of the small *Barbus* species do. In Central Zaïre, among submerged tree roots, live small "butterfly barbs," 4cm (1.5in) long. including *Barbus hulstaerti* and *B. papilio*. In these strikingly marked species, the males and females have conspicuously different color patterns.

Although, generally, the cyprinids are not as brilliantly colored as the characins, some of the Southeast Asian *Rasbora* species come close. The small Malaysian species, Brittan's rasbora (*Rasbora brittani*) and Axelrod's rasbora (*R. axelrodi*) are the cyprinid equivalents of the popular Glow-light and Neon tetras (order Characiformes).

Totally without color, however, are the subterranean cyprinids. Cave-dwelling members of the genera *Barbus, Garra* and *Caecocypris* have lost all pigment – and their eyes – as a result of living in lightless habitats underground.

The epigean (i.e. above-ground) *Garra* species

are found in Africa, India and Southeast Asia. They are bottom-dwelling fishes with a sucking and sensory disk on the underside of the head. The related "shark" genera (*Labeo* and *Epalzeorhynchos*), with a similar distribution, have an elaborate suctorial mouth and graze on algae. One African species of *Labeo* has specialized in grazing on the flanks of submerged hippopotamuses.

In the cold, mountain streams of India and Tibet live the poorly known snow trout (*Schizothorax* spp.), cyprinids that imitate the life-style of trout and salmon. They are elongate fish, up to 30cm (1ft) long with very small scales (or none at all) except for a row of tile-like scales along the base of the anal fin. Nepalese fishermen capture snow trout by fashioning a worm-shaped wire surrounded by a loop which is tightened when the fish strikes at the "worm."

While it is true that cyprinids are essentially freshwater fishes, some can nevertheless tolerate considerable degrees of salinity. In Japan, species of redfin (*Tribolodon*) have been found up to 5km (3 miles) out to sea. In Europe, the freshwater Roach (*Rutilus rutilus*) and Bream (*Abramis brama*) also live in the Baltic Sea at about 50 percent salinity. These are, however, among the few exceptions.

As if cyprinids were not already a compendium of eccentric habits, at least two species are known to get drunk! In Southeast Asia, both the cigar "sharks" (*Leptobarbus* spp) and the Silver-and-red barb (*Hampala macrolepidota*) gorge themselves on the fermented fruit of the chaulmoogra tree when it falls into the water. They even congregate before "opening time." When intoxicated, these fishes float helpless in the water, but are relatively safe as their flesh is made unpalatable by the alcohol. Counterbalancing such antisocial cyprinid behavior, the Eurasian tench (*Tinca tinca*) has gained a folk reputation as a doctor fish. It is reported that injured fish seek out tench and rub their wounds

in its slime. While it is undeniable that the tench has a copious coating of slime, its healing properties have never been scientifically attested.

The suckers (Catostomidae) have many species in North America and a handful in north Asia. For a long time, they were thought to be the most primitive cyprinoids, due to the shape of their pharyngeal (throat) bones and teeth. Suckers have also developed highly complex sacs from the upper gill-arch bones and it now seems likely, taking into account their distribution, that they are a highly specialized group of cyprinoids. They are generally innocuous, unspectacular fish, apart from two genera, each containing a single species: the Chinese sailfin sucker (*Myxocyprinus asiaticus*) and the Razorback sucker (*Xyrauchen texanus*) from the Colorado River. Both are deep-bodied, with a triangular profile. The function of this peculiar shape is to force them close to the bottom of the river during flash floods (both species live in rivers susceptible to flash floods). These two suckers are therefore a good example of parallel evolution.

The "true" loaches are a family (Cobitidae) of (frequently) eel-like fishes with minute, embedded scales and a plethora of barbels around the mouth. Bony processes enclose most, or all, of the swimbladder, making its normal volume changes rather awkward. All the cyprinoids have a tube connecting the swimbladder to the pharynx, allowing the fish to swallow or expel air, but, with their constricted swimbladder, loaches use this

◁ **Left** The beautifully banded Clown or Tiger loach (*Botia macracanthus*) *is native to freshwater habitats on the Indonesian islands of Borneo and Sumatra. It feeds on crustaceans, worms, and plant matter.*

⬤ **Above** *Familiar and widespread in Europe, where it is fished recreationally, the Roach (Rutilus rutilus) is a highly adaptable fish that can tolerate poor-quality water. So successful is the Roach that it can overrun an area where it has been introduced.*

more often than many. One species, known as the Weather fish or Weather loach (*Misgurnus fossilis*), from eastern Europe, has been kept for centuries by peasants as a living barometer. Its agitation and continued "burping" as it expels air with the changes in atmospheric pressure that accompany the approach of thunderstorms, made it one of the earliest weather forecasters.

Not all of this family are eel-like in appearance, however. One group, the Botinae, have shorter bodies, often compressed, and a pointed snout. There are only three genera in this group, the best known being *Botia* – which includes some popular aquarium fishes, most notably the striking Clown loach (*B. macracanthus*). This species also exhibits a most unusual behavior, resting on its side and giving the impression that it is dead.

Most loaches have small dorsal and anal fins symmetrically placed near the rear of the body. The poorly known, but appropriately-named, long-finned loaches, *Vaillantella* spp., however, have a dorsal fin the length of the body. Loaches (in the broadest sense of the word) can be divided into two subgroups: those that have an erectile spine below the eye, and those that do not. Many are secretive fish, liking to hide under stones during the day. It was an overdue discovery when the first cave-living species was found in Iran in 1976. Since then, two more have been found in southwestern China. Loaches live in Eurasia, not in Africa (apart from an arguably introduced species in European North Africa).

Despite their common name, the gyrinocheilids or algae eaters (Gyrinocheilidae) feed largely on detritus. There are only four species, all from Southeast Asia. They have a ventral, protrusile mouth, like the hose of a vacuum cleaner. With this, they suck in the fine substrate (and scrape off encrusting algae) and filter out the edible material.

*Gyrinocheilus* species lack a pharyngeal tooth apparatus; whether this is lost or has never been developed is unknown. These fishes – often misleadingly called "sucking loaches" – are unique among cyprinoids in that the gill cover is sealed to the body for most of its length, leaving just top and bottom openings. The top opening is covered by a valve and takes in water to oxygenate the gills and expels it through the bottom opening. Thus, breathing, in sharp contrast to other fishes, is through the gill cover, rather than the mouth.

The river loaches, balitorids, or homalopterids (Balitoridae), consist of two subgroups: the flat loaches (Balitorinae), which live mostly in fast-flowing waters, even torrents, in Southeast Asia, and the nemacheilines (Nemacheilinae) which are almost exclusively Eurasian in distribution. Greatly flattened, the Balitorinae have both pectoral and pelvic fins fused into suckers. The mouth is ventral and, while the fish graze on the rich algal growth in such fertile waters the snout is protected by a remarkable development of bones that in other cyprinoids lie below the eye. In the hillstream species, these bones are curved forward in front of the snout, strengthened, and act like the bumpers of a dodgem car.

The nemacheilines are Eurasian eel-like fishes which are very similar in overall shape to the Weather loach and its closest relatives. One species, the enigmatic *Nemacheilus abyssinicus* is African. A Mr Degen was collecting for the British Museum in Ethiopia in 1900. His collection from the mouth of a stream feeding Lake Tsana purportedly contained the specimen described under that name some years later. No more specimens have ever been found; but then, no one has revisited the site and used his collecting techniques. Or perhaps one jar could have been misplaced on a museum shelf?

Equally enigmatic are the description and illustration of *Ellopostoma* from Borneo. The original specimens were lost by 1868 and no more were found for many years. It is now reported from Malaysia and Thailand, however, but is still poorly understood.

## New World Knifefishes
### ORDER GYMNOTIFORMES
The New World knifefishes consist of six families of the order Gymnotiformes. All are eel-like to varying degrees and all lack the pelvic girdle and fins, as well as the dorsal fin. The anal fin, in striking contrast, is extremely long-based, possessing 140 or more rays, and forms the main means of propulsion, both forward and backward. The tail (caudal) fin is either lacking or highly reduced.

New World or South American knifefishes possess electric organs which, in most species, consist of specially modified muscle cells. However, in the ghost knifefishes (family Apteronotidae) modified nerve cells perform this function. In most cases, the electric field is weak and is mainly used to help the fish navigate at night (most species are nocturnal), locate food, and communicate with each other. However, in the Electric knifefish (*Electrophorus electricus*), better known as the Electric eel, powerful impulses capable of (reportedly) stunning a horse can be generated. This species, which can grow to 2.3m (7.5ft), uses electricity to stun its prey and in self-defense, making it both a lethal hunter and a formidable adversary.

## Milkfish and Allies
### ORDER GONORHYNCHIFORMES
One of the most widespread and commercially significant species of the gonorhynchiformes is the Milkfish (*Chanos chanos*). This silvery, streamlined fish, about the size of a Gray mullet, congregates in large shoals in warm waters around island reefs and along continental shelves, and has long been fished and cultivated for food, especially in the Philippines, Taiwan, and Indonesia.

Another marine species, the elongate Beaked sandfish, or Beaked salmon (*Gonorhynchus gonorhynchus*) is found along the shorelines of the southern Pacific, Indian Ocean, and southeastern Atlantic off Namibia and South Africa. It is fished commercially throughout its range.

The freshwater Hingemouth (*Phractolaemus ansorgii*) takes its name from its ability to extend its mouth into a small trunk. Its swimbladder functions as a lung, enabling this species to survive in unoxygenated waters     KEB/GJH/JD

# FISHES UNDERGROUND

## The locations, forms, and lives of cave fishes

THERE ARE AROUND FORTY SPECIES OF FISHES, belonging to some 13 different families, that spend their lives in lightless, underground waters. In some cases, it is uncertain whether an underground (hypogean) population represents a separate species or merely a highly modified population of a surface-living (epigean) species.

Cave fishes are colorless. However, they appear to be pink-colored. This is caused by the blood that runs along tiny vessels (capillaries) that lie close to the skin surface. In a number of cases, the vessels – particularly those that run parallel to the ribs – are extremely distinct and can be seen easily with the naked eye.

Cave fishes also frequently have reduced scales, the degree of reduction ranging from species to species. In fact, at least one species, the Indian Blind Catfish (*Horaglanis krishnai*) is scaleless. Not all cave fishes live in caves, though. Some, for example, live in water-bearing strata or rock layers (known as aquifers) where the rock is honeycombed with water-filled channels.

Subterranean fishes occur in tropical and warm temperate countries that have not been affected by recent glaciation. In Australia, two species, a sleeper goby or eleotrid and a swamp eel or synbranchid, live in the Yardee Creek wells on the North West Cape. Madagascar has two sleeper gobies, while Africa has a barb in the Democratic Republic of Congo (DRC), a swamp eel in Mauritania, and a clariid or walking catfish in Namibia; three species: a catfish and two carps or cyprinids, live in Somalia.

Oman has two species of the cyprinid genus *Garra*. Iran has a subterranean barb and another *Garra*-type cyprinid; Iraq, yet another garrine, as well as the Iraq blind barb (*Typhlogarra widdowsoni*) and – sharing the same sinkhole at the Sheik Hadid Shrine – the much rarer *Caecocypris basimi*. Wells in Kerala, southern India, hold the Indian blind catfish (*Horaglanis krishnai*) a small species from the catfish family Clariidae. Three species (two loaches and yet another garrine) have recently been found in China. Cuba has two freshwater ophidioids – relatives of the marine cusk eels; Mexico has one and also has characoids and a swamp eel. The subterranean fauna of Brazil consists of catfishes and characoids. The USA has a rich cave fauna in many sites, from the Ozark and Cumberland plateaux to Texas, comprising catfish and amblyopsids. There may also be cave fish in New Guinea and Thailand, but Europe has no cave fish.

Some of the cave species known today belong to families or subfamilies that are, basically, marine. Yet the vast majority of cave fishes are found in freshwater habitats. Prime examples of

this are the ophidoids of Cuba, Mexico and the Bahamas, which are found in freshwater limestone wells or pools. *Lucifuga spelaeotus* from Mermaid's Pool in the Bahamas is such a fish; so is its closest relative, *L. dentatus*, from Cuban caves. Yet the family to which they belong (Bythitidae – a member of the order Ophidiiformes, hence the term 'ophidioids'), contains about 90 species, all but a few of which are marine.

Quite how these fishes ended up living in freshwater is open to speculation. In the geological past, fishes living in subterranean saltwater-bearing strata could have been trapped in such underground waters as land masses moved apart through Continental Drift. They would then slowly adapt themselves to brackish or freshwater over a long period of time. Such explanations have been put forward to explain the presence of *Stygichthys* and *Lucifuga* in Cuba. Debate and doubts also surround the possibilities of how these fish came to live where they do. There is some evidence, in at least one instance – that of the Swampfish (*Chologaster cornuta*), a close relative of the American amblyopsids, or cavefishes – of preadaptation. *Chologaster*, for instance, has small eyes and actively shuns light. It is therefore possible that, in desert areas such fish may well have, where possible, followed the falling water-table underground.

The evolution of cave fish was a much-loved subject of Charles Darwin but his views of isolation and natural selection were supplanted by the more recent theory of adaptive shift, which states that cave dwellers can adapt to the dark while still interbreeding with their surface kin – as demonstrated by the blind and eyed types of Mexican tetras, which meet when rivers flow into and out of caves and can be crossbred in the laboratory. However, new research suggests that Darwin's isolation theory may be right after all. Now DNA profiling of the Characiform genus *Astyanax* has clearly distinguished the cave fish from the surface-dwellers, even when living close together. This means that the cave fish cannot have descended from the eyed fish nearby but must have evolved inside the caves a long time ago.

So far as we know, cave fishes live longer than their surface-dwelling relatives. This may be a response to their irregular and sparse food supply, which comes into the cave during floods as detritus, or is provided by other cave animals, all of which are ultimately supported by "the outside."

Reproduction in cave fishes has never been observed in the wild, except in the Cuban ophidioids, which give birth to fully formed young. Other cavefish groups are probably egglayers. In captivity, the only species that is bred in aquaria

◐ **Above** *Mexican blind cave tetras (*Astyanax jordani*) are endemic to Mexico. Once they have spawned, these fishes hide their eggs in the crevices of the rocky caves that they inhabit in the central San Luis Potosí region.*

(b__t by aquarists or by commercial breeders) is the Mexican blind cave tetra or characin (*Astyanax jordani*) which, until recently, was believed to be no more than a cave form of the widespread Mexican tetra (*Astyanax mexicanus*). The reproductive strategies of the surface-living and subterranean species are similar, so much so that in at least one case (*Cueva chica*), they interbreed, producing a whole range of forms, from fully-eyed, fully-

colored specimens, to pink-bodied, completely blind ones.

It is important to be able to breed cave fishes because, first, wild populations have very restricted ranges and are low in numbers and, second, we cannot answer questions about them or improve their chances of survival until we have done so. In some cases, cave fishes have been brought into breeding condition, but some final, essential

ingredient has been missing and the fishes have failed to spawn, or have died. We thus need to identify what these naturally-occurring stimuli or triggers are. Perhaps the torrential flooding of the caves in DRC where the Blind cave barb (*Coecobarbus geertsi*) lives is vital in this case – perhaps not – but, at the moment, not enough is known about the secret lives of these fishes, most of which are facing threats to their survival in the wild.    KEB/JD

# Codfishes, Anglerfishes, and Allies

THE SUPERORDER PARACANTHOPTERYGII IS probably best known for its great commercial importance, the codfishes and their allies being responsible for a huge proportion of the annual marine harvest. The superorder contains a remarkable variety of forms, from species with a typical piscine body plan, like the Trout-perch, Codfish, Hake, and Haddock, to those with peculiar shapes and colors, fishes flattened like a pancake from top to bottom, highly camouflaged fishes, fishes that live inside various invertebrates, and others with bioluminescent lures and reproducing by sexual parasitism.

The superorder, which, following current systematics, comprises five orders, was originally created in 1966 (and somewhat redefined in 1969 and again in 1989), as a taxonomic repository for a number of groups excluded from the major grouping of spiny-finned fishes (Acanthopterygii) – namely, all those forms that were of a similar evolutionary grade but that lacked the characteristics of the spiny-finned fishes. Although the erection of the superorder enabled the acanthopterygians to be somewhat more succinctly defined, the validity of the Paracanthopterygii is still rather tenuous. Over the years, the group has been plagued with problems and confusion, the major difficulty being the lack of unique characters shared by all members of the group. Despite several attempts by some of the best contemporary ichthyologists, there is still no rigorous definition of the group; in other words, there is no satisfactory basis to believe that it constitutes a natural group.

Nearly all members of this superorder are marine, most inhabiting rather shallow water but some living at great depths within the mesopelagic, bathypelagic, and abyssal zones of the major oceans of the world. There are a few (only about 20) exceptional individual species of some otherwise marine families that live in freshwater, along

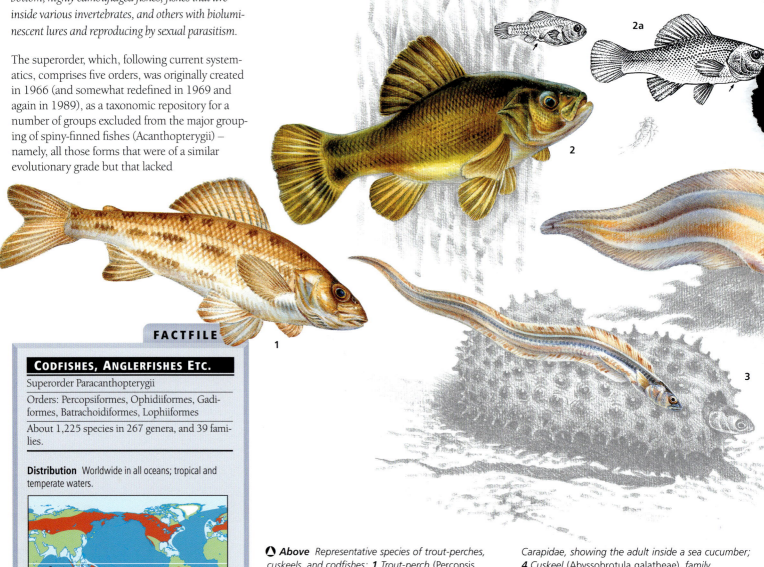

● **Above** *Representative species of trout-perches, cuskeels, and codfishes:* **1** *Trout-perch (Percopsis omiscomaycus), family Percopsidae;* **2** *Pirate perch (Aphredoderus sayanus), sole member of the family Aphredoderidae. One extraordinary feature of this species* **2a** *is the movement of the relative position of its anus while the fish is growing – when still a fry, the anus is sited far back on the body, while it has migrated further forward by the time the fish reaches adulthood;* **3** *Pearlfish (Echiodon drummondi), family* Carapidae, *showing the adult inside a sea cucumber;* **4** *Cuskeel (Abyssobrotula galatheae), family Ophidiidae;* **5** *Threadtailed grenadier (Coryphaenoides filicauda) family Macrouridae;* **6** *Luminous hake (Steindachneria argentea), family Steindachneriidae;* **7** *Poutassou or Blue whiting (Micromesistius poutassou), family Gadidae;* **8** *Atlantic cod (Gadus morhua), family Gadidae;* **9** *Tadpole cod (Salilota australis), family Moridae.*

## FACTFILE

### CODFISHES, ANGLERFISHES ETC.

Superorder Paracanthopterygii

Orders: Percopsiformes, Ophidiiformes, Gadiformes, Batrachoidiformes, Lophiiformes

About 1,225 species in 267 genera, and 39 families.

**Distribution** Worldwide in all oceans; tropical and temperate waters.

Equator

See The 5 Orders of Codfishes, Anglerfishes, & Allies. ▷

with the nine species belonging to the order of trout-perches and their allies that occur exclusively in freshwater habitats in North America.

## Trout-perches and Allies

ORDER PERCOPSIFORMES

The trout-perches and their allies are small fishes, attaining a maximum length of just 20cm (8in). They are thought to be intermediate in structure between soft-rayed, primitive fishes, such as salmon, trout, and herrings, and spiny-rayed, derived forms like rockfishes and basses. They appear to represent remnants of a once larger, more widely distributed assemblage. Fossils clearly belonging to this group (the marine genus *Sphenocephalus*) are rather well known from the Upper Cretaceous period (95–65 million years ago) of Europe. There are, in addition, several fossil genera of freshwater forms from the Eocene (about 55–34 m.y.a.) of North America.

The two species of Trout-perches, family Percopsidae, derive their common name from the presence of a "trout-like" adipose fin combined with their vaguely "perch-like" first dorsal fin, which is spiny in the front, but made up of soft rays behind. The Sand roller (*Percopsis transmon-tana*) is restricted to slow-flowing, weedy parts of the Columbia River drainage in Washington, Oregon, and Idaho. It has scales with a comblike free margin (ctenoid scales) and a cryptic, greenish coloration with dark spots. Reaching a maximum length of about 10cm (4in), it is only half the size of its more widely distributed congener the Trout-perch (*Percopsis omiscomaycus*), which ranges from the west coast of Canada to the Great Lakes and the Mississippi–Missouri river system. Although two rows of spots are present, the body is translucent and the lining of the abdominal cavity can be seen through the sides. Both species feed on bottom-living invertebrates and are themselves eaten by a number of predatory fishes.

The Pirate perch (*Aphredoderus sayanus*), from still and slow-flowing waters of the eastern USA, is the only member of the family Aphredoderidae. A sluggish, dark-hued fish, it grows to a maximum length of 13cm (6in) and lacks the adipose fin of the trout-perches. It feeds on invertebrates and small fishes. Its most unusual feature is the strange development of the vent: in juveniles, the anus is located in the normal position, just ahead of the anal fin, but it moves forward as the fish grows so that in adults it lies beneath the throat.

The family Amblyopsidae contains five genera, three of which live only in caves in the limestone regions of Kentucky and adjacent states. The Swampfish (*Chologaster cornuta*) is an eyed, pigmented species found in sluggish and still waters from West Virginia to Georgia. Despite having functional eyes, it shuns light and hides under stones and logs during the day. The Spring cavefish (*Forbesichthys agassizii*) lives in subterranean waters of Kentucky and Tennessee. It lacks the dark stripe of its only congener but still has functional eyes. In both species, but especially the latter, there are series of raised sense organs on the skin.

The other four species of the family are blind. The Southern cavefish (*Typhlichthys subterraneus*) lacks not only eyes, but pigment and pelvic fins as well. Rows of papillae, sensitive to vibrations, are present on the body and on the tail fin. It is thought to have achieved its wide distribution, from Oklahoma to Tennessee and northern Alabama, by traveling through underground waterways. The Northern cavefish (*Amblyopsis spelaea*) is white, has minute eyes covered by skin, and tiny pelvic fins. Like its relatives, it has vertical rows of sensory papillae on the body. Its reproductive strategy is unusual: the female lays a few relatively large eggs that, once fertilized, are carried in the gill chamber of the mother for up to ten weeks until they hatch. The remaining genus of the family Amblyopsidae, *Speoplatyrhinus*, containing only the Alabama cavefish (*Speoplatyrhinus poulsoni*) is exceedingly rare, being classed by the IUCN as Critically Endangered.

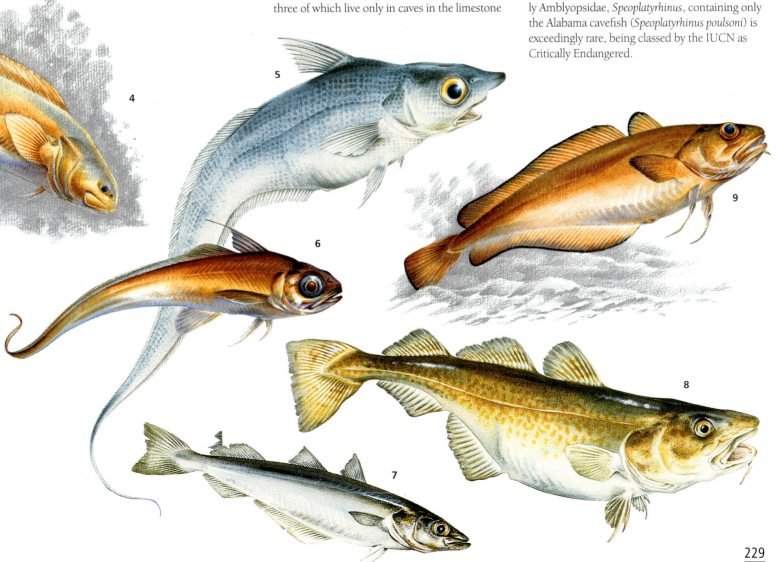

## Cuskeels and Allies

ORDER OPHIDIIFORMES

The cuskeels and their allies constitute five families of rather similar looking forms, all having a rather small head and a long tapering body, with long-based dorsal and anal fins that extend far backwards and are usually attached to the tail. The pelvic fins, if present at all, are located far forward on the body, under the gill covers or even beneath the throat or on the chin.

The carapids or pearlfishes (family Carapidae) occur most commonly in warm tropical seas. All are elongate, slender fishes with long pointed tails. They have a complicated life-history in which they pass through two dissimilar larval stages known as the *vexillifer* and *tenuis* stages. For a long time these two larval forms were thought to belong to two separate, relatively unrelated groups.

All carapids are secretive and live inside the bodies of various marine invertebrates, for example, sea cucumbers, clams, tunicates, sea urchins, or any other animal with a suitable body cavity. Some small species living inside oysters have been found entombed within the shell wall, hence the name "pearl fish." A common Mediterranean species, the Common pearlfish (*Carapus acus*), attains a length of about 20cm (8in). It lives within the body cavity of large sea cucumbers (typically the holothurian species *Holothuria tubulosa* and *Stichopus regalis*) which, like many of its relatives,

it enters tail-first by way of the anus. Rather surprisingly, it has been known to feed on the internal organs of its host. The larvae are free-living and this semiparasitic habit is taken up only by the adult. Carapids usually eat bottom invertebrates or small fishes.

The family Ophidiidae contains little-known but interesting fishes commonly referred to as cuskeels or brotulas. All are elongate fishes with long-based dorsal and anal fins that are often fused with the tail fin. Brotulas are typically deeper-bodied and broader-headed than cuskeels, and have thread-like pelvic fins situated below the rear of the head. The similar-looking pelvic fins of cuskeels are situated beneath the throat. In some species the male has a penis-like intromittent organ that passes packets of sperm to the genital duct of the female. Some species are egg-layers, while in others the eggs hatch inside the mother and emerge as fully formed individuals.

Most of the cuskeels are small, secretive, burrowing fishes from warm seas. The Spotted cuskeel (*Chilara taylori*) from the eastern Pacific burrows tail-first into the sand or rocky crevices. When it emerges from its burrow, it aligns itself vertically, with only the last part of its body in the substrate. The Kingklip (*Genypterus capensis*) is found only off the coast of South Africa from Walvis Bay to Algoa Bay, where it inhabits a wide range of depths from 50 to about 450m

(164–1.476ft). Growing to a maximum length of 1.5m (5ft), it is a giant among the cuskeels. Its flesh is excellent and the liver apparently has a quality much sought after by gourmets. It is not commercially important, however, as catches are irregular and sparse.

The brotulas are found worldwide, mostly in deep waters. The few species that live in shallow waters are shy and secretive, hiding away among rocks or in corals. This tendency to avoid well-lighted habitats may have led to the evolution of cave-dwelling forms in the Yucatán Peninsula of Mexico and in Cuba. The caves are all close to the sea and the water is brackish but variable in salinity. The Mexican blind cavefish (*Ogilbia pearsei*), found only in Balaam Canche Cave, in Yucatán, Mexico, is extremely rare, known from only a very few specimens. Its eyes are minute and covered by skin. Species of the genus *Lucifuga* have the best claim to being freshwater members of the family. Their coloration is remarkably variable, ranging from off-white to deep violet or dark brown. They give birth to fully formed young. The Nassau cavefish (*Lucifuga spelaeotes*) is known only from a single isolated population in the Bahamas. It was discovered in 1967 in Mermaid's Pool, a small freshwater sink in the limestone region near Nassau. Described as new to science in 1970, its future is now seriously threatened by commercial development.

**Left** *Atlantic cod has long been an extremely important commercial fish. Yet at the beginning of the 21st century, overfishing and climate change have seen stocks shrink dramatically, especially in the North Sea.*

## Codfishes and Allies
ORDER GADIFORMES

The Gadiformes, containing the codfishes and their allies, is the largest of the five paracanthopterygian orders, with almost 500 species. It includes numerous commercially important species (together comprising over one-quarter of the world's marine catch), such as the Atlantic and Pacific codfishes, the Hakes, Haddock, Pollock, as well as many smaller and deep-water species of great biological interest but of little or no applied importance.

The group is widely distributed around the world in deep and shallow seas, from the tropics to the far northern and southern polar regions. They are mostly elongate fishes, with the pelvic fins situated far forward on the body, often in front of the pectoral fins. The dorsal and anal fins, sometimes contiguous with the tail fin, are long-based, the dorsal often divided into two or three separate units, the anal often divided into two units. No true spines are present in any of the fins.

Many of the commercially important species form shoals and the number of individuals they contained was enormous, until severe overfishing took its toll. For many years, an estimated 400 million Atlantic cod (*Gadus morhua*) were caught each year in the North Atlantic. At any one time the number of individuals of that species was enormous. A single female Atlantic cod typically produces over six million eggs; thus, if left alone, some fisheries biologists predict that stocks could regain their former abundance in a relatively short period of time.

Some of the 12 currently recognized families in this order are of little relative importance and only brief reference will be made to them.

The Macrouridae, containing the grenadiers or rattails, is a large, widely distrbuted family of deep-water fishes with long, tapering bodies. The mouth is on the underside of a large head, nearly always equipped with an unusually long, pointed snout. In many species the males have drumming muscles attached to the swimbladder that they use to produce surprisingly loud sounds, apparently to attract members of the opposite sex for reproductive purposes. Many have a bioluminescent organ of unknown function, lying lengthwise beneath the skin of the abdomen, with an opening to the outside just in front of the anus.

The Moridae is a worldwide family of deep-sea cods, found in all oceans almost from pole to pole. There are nearly 100 species grouped into 18 genera, nearly half of all species confined to genera *Physiculus* and *Laemonema*. The configuration of dorsal and anal fins is variable, with one to two, but rarely three dorsal fins, and one or two

anal fins. Species in this family rarely exceed a length of 90cm (3ft).

The Blue hake (*Antimora rostrata*), a morid cod despite the common name, has been found in the North Pacific, North and South Atlantic, and Indian Oceans at depths from about 500 to 1,300m (1,650–3,900ft). The first ray of the short-based first-dorsal fin is very long. The body color is dark violet to blackish brown. The Red codling (*Pseudophycis bachus*), again a morid, is common off South Australia, Tasmania, and New Zealand where it is used as a food fish. It occurs in much shallower waters than many of its relatives, from as little as 50m (165ft) but it is most often trawled at depths of 200 to 300m (660–980ft). The first specimen was captured during Captain James Cook's second voyage (1772–75) and described by the famous team of Marcus Elieser Bloch and Johann Gottlob Schneider in 1801. The Japanese codling (*Physiculus japonicus*) has a light organ, as do many other members of this family. The organ is bulbous and has a canal that opens into the rectum near the anus. There is a reflector above the gland and the light shines out through a scaleless area of skin in front of the anus.

The so-called codlets of the family Bregmacerotidae, about 12 species all contained within a single genus (*Bregmaceros*), inhabit the surface waters of tropical and subtropical oceans; all are marine but a few venture into estuaries. Their anal and second dorsal fins are mirror images of each other; both have long bases and are higher at the front and back than in the middle. The first dorsal fin is nothing more than a long single ray, emerging from the dorsal surface of the head just behind the level of the eyes. All are small fishes, attaining a maximum length of only about 12cm (4.7in). The McClelland's codlet (*Bregmaceros mcclellandii*) is as widespread geographically as the rest of the

family but has a considerably greater depth range, from the surface to 4,000m (13,000ft). Members of this family are difficult to characterize and identify, and almost nothing is known of their biology.

The fishes of the Hake family Merlucciidae have elongate bodies, a short first dorsal fin and a much longer second dorsal fin. Both the second dorsal and the anal fins are separate from the tail. In the Pacific hake (*Merluccius productus*) the anal and second dorsal fins possess a deep notch that nearly, but not quite, divides these fins in half. The European hake (*Merluccius merluccius*), the range of which extends into the Mediterranean, can grow to a maximum length of 140 cm (4.6 feet) and weigh more than 15kg (33lb). It has been an important food fish for the population of Western Europe throughout historic times. It is a nocturnal feeder, its large mouth eager for squids and small fishes, even for its own species. They are caught in mid-water, but by day they live close to the bottom. They begin spawning in December, or even as late as April, in water deeper than 180m (600ft), but as the season moves along they migrate and continue to spawn in shallower water. The eggs float at the surface and the future hake stocks are very dependent on the weather. If the wind blows the eggs away from the rich inshore feeding grounds very few young survive, thereby causing the failure of the fishery a few years later.

The Deep-water Cape hake (*Merluccius paradoxus*) is found around South Africa, especially off the west coast where the water is richest. It is very similar to the European hake in appearance but is considerably smaller in size, with females (82cm,

**Below** *The Poor cod (Trisopterus minutus), a small gadoid, occurs in abundance in the Eastern Atlantic and the Mediterranean. It is eaten locally, and also used in the production of fishmeal.*

# The 5 Orders of Codfishes, Anglerfishes, and Allies

## Trout-perches and Allies
### Order: Percopsiformes

North America, from SE United States to Alaska and Quebec. All confined to freshwater. Length 5cm (2in) to a maximum of 20cm (8in). 9 species in 6 genera and 3 families including: Percopsidae, with two species, the **Trout-perch** (*Percopsis omiscomaycus*) and the **Sand roller** (*P. transmontana*); Aphredoderidae, containing a single species, the **Pirate perch** (*Aphredoderus sayanus*); and the **cavefishes** (family Amblyopsidae) 6 species in 5 genera, including the **Spring cavefish** (*Forbesichthys agassizii*) and **Southern cavefish** (*Typhlichthys subterraneus*). The **Alabama cavefish** (*Speleoplatyrhinus poulsoni*) is Critically Endangered, while three other species are classed as Vulnerable.

## Cuskeels and Allies
### Order: Ophidiiformes

Widely distributed in the Atlantic, Pacific, and Indian oceans. Nearly all marine, but some confined to fresh or weak brackish water. Length 5 cm (2in) to a maximum of 2m (6.5ft). About 355 species in 92 genera and 5 families. Families include: **carapids** or **pearlfishes** (family Carapidae) with c.32 species in 7 genera; **cuskeels** (family Ophidiidae) with c.209 species in 46 genera; **viviparous brotulas** (family Bythitidae) with at least 90 species in 31 genera; **aphyonids** (family Aphyonidae) 21 species in 6 genera; **false brotulas** (family Parabrotuli-

dae) 3 species in 2 genera. Seven species are classed as Vulnerable, including the **New Providence cuskeel** (*Lucifuga spelaeotes*).

## Codfishes and Allies
### Order: Gadiformes

Worldwide in all oceans. Almost exclusively marine; one species confined to freshwater, a second with some populations that are confined to freshwater. Length 10 cm (4in) to a maximum of 2m (6.5ft). About 482 species in 85 genera and 12 families including: Ranicipitidae, containing a single species, the **Tadpole cod** (*Raniceps raninus*); Euclichthyidae, containing a single species, the **Eucla cod** (*Euclichthys polynemus*); **grenadiers** or **rattails** (family Macrouridae) 285 species in 38 genera; Steindachneriidae, containing a single species, the **Luminous hake** (*Steindachneria argentea*); **morid cods** or **moras** (family Moridae) c.98 species in 18 genera; **pelagic cods** (family Melanonidae) containing a single genus, *Melanonus*, and 2 species; **Southern hakes** (family Macruronidae) 8 species in 2 genera; **codlets** (family Bregmacerotidae) containing a single genus, *Bregmaceros*, with c.12 species; **Eel cods** (family Muraenolepididae) containing a single genus, *Muraenolepis*, with 4 species; **phycid hakes** (family Phycidae) 27 species in 5 genera; **merluccid hakes** (family Merlucciidae) containing a single genus, *Merluccius*, with 13 species, including the **Atlantic hake** (*M. merluccius*) and **North Pacific hake** (*M. productus*); **codfishes** (family Gadidae) 30 species in 15 genera, including the **Atlantic cod** (*Gadus morhua*), **Burbot** (*Lota lota*), **European ling** (*Molva molva*), **Haddock** (*Melanogrammus aeglefinus*), **Pacific cod** (*Gadus macrocephalus*), **Pollock** (*Pollachius virens*), and **Alaska pollock** (*Theragra chalcogramma*). The **Skulpin** (*Physiculus helenaensis*) is Critically Endangered, while the Atlantic cod and the Haddock are Vulnerable.

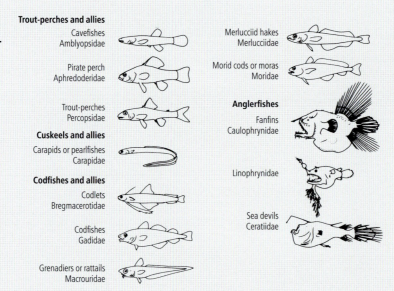

Trout-perches and allies
Cavefishes
Amblyopsidae

Pirate perch
Aphredoderidae

Trout-perches
Percopsidae

Cuskeels and allies
Carapids or pearlfishes
Carapidae

Codfishes and allies
Codlets
Bregmacerotidae

Codfishes
Gadidae

Grenadiers or rattails
Macrouridae

Merlucciid hakes
Merlucciidae

Morid cods or moras
Moridae

Anglerfishes
Fanfins
Caulophrynidae

Linophrynidae

Sea devils
Ceratiidae

## Toadfishes
### Order: Batrachoidiformes

Widely distributed in the Atlantic, Pacific, and Indian oceans. Primarily marine, rarely entering brackish water; a few species confined to freshwater. Length 7.5cm (3in) to a maximum of 57cm (22in). 69 species in 19 genera and 1 family, Batrachoididae including: the **Atlantic midshipman** (*Porichthys plectrodon*), **Oyster toadfish** (*Opsanus tau*), **Splendid toadfish** (*Sanopus splendidus*), and **Venomous** or **Cano toadfish** (*Thalassophryne maculosa*). Five species of toadfish are classed as Vulnerable, including *S. splendidus*.

## Anglerfishes
### Order: Lophiiformes

Worldwide in all oceans. Marine, with rare incursions into brackish or freshwater. Length 6cm (2.5in) to a maximum of 1.5m (5ft). At least 310 species in 65 genera and 18 families including: **goosefishes** or **monkfishes** (family Lophiidae) 25 species in 4 genera, including the **Common goosefish** (*Lophius piscatorius*); **frogfishes** (family Antennariidae) 42 species in 12 genera, including the **Striated frogfish** (*Antennarius striatus*) and the **Sargassum frogfish** (*Histrio histrio*); Tetrabrachiidae, containing a single species, the **Four-armed frogfish** (*Tetrabrachium ocellatum*); Lophichthyidae, containing a single species, **Boschma's frogfish** (*Lophichthys boschmai*); **handfishes** or **warty anglers** (family Brachionichthyidae), containing a single genus, *Brachionichthys*, with 4 species; **gapers**, **coffinfishes**, or **sea toads** (family Chaunacidae) 2 genera and up to 14 species, including the **Redeye gaper** (*Chaunax stigmaeus*) and **Rosy gaper** (*Bathychaunax roseus*); **batfishes** (family Ogcocephalidae) 9 genera and 62 species, including the **Atlantic batfish** (*Dibranchus atlanticus*) and the **Shortnose batfish** (*Ogcocephalus nasutus*); and the 11 families of the deep-sea Ceratioidei, 157 valid species in 35 genera, including the footballfishes (family Himantolophidae) – a single genus, *Himantolophus*, with 18 species, including *Himantolophus groenlandicus*); the Oneirodidae – 62 species in 16 genera, including the Short-rod anglerfish (*Microlophichthys microlophus*) and the Bulbous dreamer (*Oneirodes eschrichtii*); seadevils (family Ceratiidae) – 4 species in 2 genera, including Krøyer's deepsea angler (*Ceratias holboelli*) and the Triplewart seadevil (*Cryptopsaras couesii*), Gigantactinidae (21 species in 2 genera, including *Gigantactis vanhoeffeni*), and Linophrynidae (25 species in 5 genera, including *Borophryne apogon*, *Haplophryne mollis*, and *Linophryne lucifer*). The **Spotted handfish** (*Brachionichthys hirsutus*) of Australia is Critically Endangered.

◖ **Left** The Striped anglerfish (*Antennarius striatus*) *uses a lure comprising a stalk, or illicium, and a bait, or esca. The esca's design, which varies between species, mimics the food of the prey fish, such as a worm. When not in use, the lure is held back against the head.*

2.7ft) and males (53cm, 1.7ft) reaching quite different maximum lengths. This species lives close to the bottom just over the continental slope at depths of 200–850m (655–2,790ft). In contrast to the European hake, spawning probably occurs from September to November. It is fished mainly by bottom trawl but also by longline. When fresh the flesh is delicious and well textured, but loses its flavor and texture with keeping.

Hakes also occur off New Zealand (the Southern hake, *Merluccius australis*), and off the Pacific and Atlantic coasts of South America (the South Pacific or Chilean hake, *Merluccius gayi*; and the Argentine hake, *Merluccius hubbsi*, respectively). Like the other members of this family, these species are all commercially important and when not used as prime food for humans are used as pet food, fishmeal, and fertilizer.

The Gadidae is by far the most commercially important family of the Paracanthopterygii. Most of the approximately 30 species are found on the continental shelves of the northern hemisphere, but members of one genus of Rocklings (*Gaidropsarus*) also occurs off New Zealand, Kerguelen, and South Africa. They have two or three dorsal fins and one or two anal fins, but none of the fins has spines. Many species have a chin barbel and some have additional barbels on the snout.

Practically all species are marine, but an interesting exception is the Burbot (*Lota lota*), an eel-like fish with a mottled brown body. The first dorsal fin is short and just barely makes contact with the long, second dorsal fin. It is widespread throughout sluggish or still waters of cold northern parts of Eurasia and North America. During the last century it was common in rivers on the east coast of England, from Yorkshire south to

○ **Above** *The burbot* (Lota lota) *is the only wholly freshwater species of the order Gadiformes. Characterized by the single barbel on its chin, it lives in wide, slow flowing rivers or in deep lakes, and hunts in the dusk or at night.*

East Anglia, but it is now probably extinct there. Certainly no reliable reports of its presence have appeared in recent years. A major factor contributing to its demise has been the dredging of drains and canals. This has not only removed the weeds that gave the young protection but also increased the speed of currents, to which sluggish species like the Burbot cannot adapt.

The Burbot is a winter and early spring spawner, from November to May, considering its whole area of distribution, but mainly from January to March in Canada. Large females are well known for producing exceedingly large numbers of eggs. Fecundity estimates in Canada range from 45,600 eggs in a 34-cm (13-in) female to 1,362,077 eggs in a 64-cm (25-in) individual. Burbot are largely nocturnal and feed on invertebrates and bottom-living fishes. Although their flesh is nutritious and tasty, and the liver contains a lot of vitamin A, it is not widely accepted as food for human consumption. However, it is fished commercially in Finland, Sweden, and the European part of Russia, and is of minor commercial importance in Alaska and Canada.

The Lings (genus *Molva*), of which there are only two species, look rather like large marine Burbot. The Blue ling (*Molva dypterygia*) is found in the Barents Sea and west to Greenland (including Iceland) and Newfoundland; around the British Isles and south to Morocco and into the Mediterranean Sea. Its sister-species, called simply the

Ling (*Molva molva*), has almost an identical distribution but a much smaller range in Greenland waters and only rarely seen in the northwestern Mediterranean. The Ling is most common at depths of about 300m (1,000ft). A large female can live for 15 years and can weigh as much as 22kg (50lb). It is a commercially important fish, but its main claim to fame is its extraordinary reproductive capabilities. A female Ling 1.5 m (5 feet) long and weighing 24kg (54lb) was found to have 28,361,000 eggs in her ovaries, the largest number of eggs ever recorded for a vertebrate.

The Atlantic cod (*Gadus morhua*) and the Haddock (*Melanogrammus aeglefinus*) are highly prized food-fish from the North Atlantic. During the 19th century, when fishing grounds in the far North Atlantic were first exploited, Atlantic cod measuring 2 m (6.6 feet) in length and weighing up to 90kg (200lb) were recorded. These days, because of intensive fishing, an 18kg (40lb) individual is regarded as a giant and most of those caught commercially average less than about 4.5kg (10lb). Throughout its range the Atlantic cod exists in fairly discrete populations (usually referred to as races), but the migration of individuals from one population to another has precluded the accordance of subspecific status to these groups.

The Atlantic cod spawns in late winter and early spring in depths of less than 180m (600ft). The eggs are pelagic and scattered widely by the currents. The young hatch at the surface and feed on small planktonic organisms, but when they are about two months old, and about 2.5cm (1in) long, they descend to live close to the bottom.

Adult Atlantic cod feed on large invertebrates, but fish form a larger part of the diet as they grow. During the day, individuals form dense shoals off the bottom, but at night they separate and become more or less solitary. The northern populations migrate south to spawn. The lifestyle of the Haddock (*Melanogrammus aeglefinus*) is similar to that of the Atlantic Cod, but they are a much smaller fish hardly reaching 3.5kg (8lb) in weight.

There are many smaller and commercially relatively unimportant gadid genera in both the North Atlantic and North Pacific oceans. Common in the Atlantic are the Poor cod (*Trisopterus minutus*), locally abundant and said to be good eating, but not extensively fished; the Pouting (*Trisopterus luscus*), of which more than 22,000 metric tons have been harvested in good years; the Blue whiting (*Micromesistius poutassou*), with a 708,000 metric-ton annual harvest; the Pollack (*Pollachius pollachius*), not of great commercial importance, but often marketed fresh and frozen; and the Saithe (*Pollachius virens*), a commerically important species, similar to the Atlantic cod and Haddock. In the Pacific, the Pacific cod (*Gadus macrocephalus*) and the Alaska pollock (*Theragra chalcogramma*) are the most abundant and important members of the codfish family. The Pacific cod is now the dominant trawl-caught bottom fish

in British Columbia. In Canada and the western North Pacific, the major types of gear used are trawls, but also longlines, troll, and handlines. Although this species appears to consist of a number of distinct populations, with different behavior patterns, it is overall a biological species quite distinct from the Atlantic cod. The Walleye pollock presently constitutes the largest demersal fish resource in the world. Composed of 12 major stocks distributed in different areas of the North Pacific, the catch in recent years has exceeded 6,700,000 metric tons.

## Toadfishes

### ORDER BATRACHOIDIFORMES

The toadfishes are a group of sluggish, bottom-living fishes, mostly confined to shallow warm seas. The body is short and stout, the head wide, and the eyes lie on top of the head. A large mouth is well equipped with teeth, reflecting a very predatory lifestyle. Many species are cryptically colored and match their background. Some species, such as the Oyster toadfish (*Opsanus tau*) of the eastern American seaboard, exhibit parental care. The large eggs are laid in a protected spot and guarded by the male until they hatch. The Venomous toadfish (*Thalassophryne maculosa*) occurs only along the Caribbean coast of South America at depths of 30 to 60cm (1–2ft). As its common name implies, it can cause serious damage to unwary bathers or fishers. It is said to have the most highly developed stinging apparatus among fishes. Spines in the dorsal fin and on the gill covers are hollow and linked to venom sacs. The fish lies buried in the sand, usually with only its eyes protruding. When trodden on, the spines act like hypodermic needles and inject poison into the offending foot.

The Plainfin midshipmen (*Porichthys notatus*) from the Pacific, and the Atlantic midshipmen (*Porichthys plectrodon*) from the Atlantic, burrow during the day. Each species has a pattern of light organs along its sides that are used in courtship. A wide range of sounds, from whistles to grunts and growls, are produced by swimbladder drumming muscles during courtship.

Some of the species of the genus *Halophryne*, from the Indo-Pacific, can live in fresh water and are sometimes sold in aquarium shops. Poisonous spines on the gill covers, however, should make the aquarist think twice before buying these cryptic predatory fishes.

## Anglerfishes

### ORDER LOPHIIFORMES

The anglerfishes can be conveniently divided into three groups: the first containing the goosefishes or monkfishes; the second, the frogfishes, hand-fishes, gapers, and batfishes; and the third, the deep-sea Ceratioid anglerfishes. Nearly all of the approximately 310 species are characterized by having the first dorsal-fin spine placed on the tip of the snout and modified as a fishing apparatus.

The first two groups contain mostly bottom-dwelling forms while the last is made up of mostly pelagic species living at mesopelagic, bathypelagic, and abyssal depths. Except for rare incursions into mouths of rivers by a few members of the group, all are confined to marine habitats.

The goosefishes or monkfishes (family Lophiidae), about 25 species, are large, depressed, bottom-living fishes. Their heads and mouths are enormous. The Common goosefish (*Lophius piscatorius*) is widely distributed along the European coast from the Barents Sea south to North Africa, to the Mediterranean and Black Sea, and extends from the surface down to 1,000 m (3,280 feet). It can reach a length of 1. m (5ft) and is a voracious predator. Normally this anglerfish feeds from the bottom – hiding among rocks and vegetation and partially buried in sand or mud, its body outline broken up by a series of irregular fleshy skin flaps, it wriggles its brightly colored bait and thereby attracts prey to its gaping mouth. Often, however, this species, along with other members of the family, comes up to the surface to snatch resting geese, ducks, cormorant, gulls, and other seabirds (hence the name "goosefish"). More than one report has described an angler found dead having choked on a seabird a bit too large to swallow. Their voracity is further evinced by reports of lophiids caught in trawls with a belly full of fish, having been unable to resist gorging themselves on their fellow captives. The Goosefish is relatively uncritical about its diet and consumes any food item that comes close.

This and other members of the family, including members of the closely related genera *Lophiodes*, *Lophiomus*, and *Sladenia*, typically move

*Above* The coloring of the Warty frogfish (Antennarius maculatus) *varies enormously according to habitat. It lives on rocky reefs in the Indo-Pacific region and hunts using a large, fish-shaped lure.*

*Left* A diver swimming near a frogfish in the Pacific Ocean. In the open, their distinctive shape makes them easy to spot; however, against reefs, their cryptic coloration is a highly effective camouflage.*

*Below* An aggressive Lophius piscatorius, a member of the goosefish family. This fish is widely sold under the name of Monkfish – perhaps unsurprisingly, minus the head (which accounts for half the body length)!*

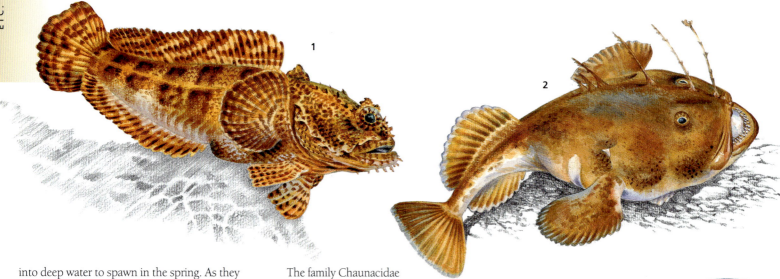

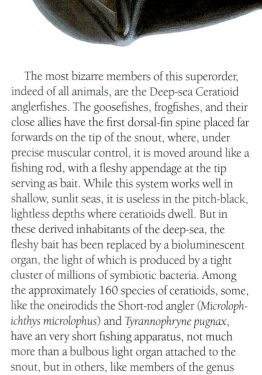

into deep water to spawn in the spring. As they are spawned the eggs emerge from the female embedded within a remarkable ribbon-like mucous sheath or veil up to 9m (30ft) long and 60cm (2ft) wide. The buoyant veil brings the eggs to the surface where they hatch, providing the young developing larvae with a rich food resource of plankton. As they mature, the larvae eventually settle back down to the bottom.

Although often described as "flabby and revolting," the appearance of the Goosefish belies the nature of its flesh, which is delicately flavored and popular in Europe, where it is sold as Monkfish. The flesh of the tail is white and somewhat reminiscent of scampi in texture. Unfortunately, however, *Lophius* and its close allies have been overfished over much of their ranges and are seriously threatened with depletion.

The frogfishes, family Antennariidae, rarely grow longer than about 30cm (12in). They are either flattened from side to side or more nearly globular. Highly cryptic forms, nearly all live camouflaged on the bottom among sea grasses, rocks, and coral. One species, however, the Sargassum frogfish (*Histrio histrio*) lives in warm waters around the world, clinging to floating clumps of Sargassum weed. Like those of other members of the family, its pectoral and pelvic fins are muscular and elongate, resembling arms and legs, allowing it to "crawl" around among drifting vegetation. The lure of the Sargassum frogfish is not well developed, little more than a tiny slender filament, but in bottom-living, closely related forms, such as *Antennarius* spp., the fishing apparatus is strikingly sophisticated in design. In many species the device is long, half the length of the body or more, and equipped with a fleshy terminal bait, often brightly colored. The baits of some species appear to mimic small aquatic creatures, like worms, shrimps, and other crustaceans. The Warty frogfish (*Antennarius maculatus*) of the western tropical Pacific, has a bait resembling a tiny fish. Not only is the mimicry remarkably fishlike, but the angler also moves the bait through the water in such a way that it looks just like a swimming fish.

The family Chaunacidae is represented by two genera, *Chaunax* and *Bathychaunax*, but the number of species is unknown. While much of the scientific literature indicates a single widely distributed species, some ichthyologists estimate as many as 14 species. Living on the bottom at depths of 90 to more than 2,000m (300–6,600ft), the group contains, large-mouthed, loose-skinned, globose forms that attain a maximum length of about 35cm (13.8in). All are pink to deep-reddish-orange.

The batfishes (family Ogcocephalidae) are highly depressed and flattened fishes found around the world in most tropical and subtropical seas. Viewed from above, they are either triangular or round in shape, bearing a narrow elongate tail behind. The mouth is terminal, the eyes are large and placed dorsally, and the arm-like pectoral fins are directed backward. The pelvic fins lie far forward beneath the throat and, like many other benthic anglerfishes, are used in tandem with the muscular pectoral fins for "walking" along the sea floor. The reduced gill openings are located near the hind end of the body, just before the pectoral fins. Most species are inhabitants of deep water (down to about 2,500m; 8,200ft) and all spend the day on the bottom luring prey. The majority of batfishes are rather dull in coloration, a light gray to brown, but the Polka-dot batfish (*Ogcocephalus radiatus*) of the Bahamas and Gulf of Mexico is covered with yellow or reddish orange patches, the tip of the tail is black, and the belly is a bright coppery red. The Circular batfish (*Halieutaea fitzsimonsi*), a South African species, has been recorded in freshwater up the Tugela River in Natal, rather far from the coast. Batfishes in general, and the Shortnose batfish (*Ogcocephalus nasutus*) in particular, perhaps the most common species of the family in the western North Atlantic, are known to eat a wide variety of snails, in addition to some polychaete worms and crustaceans. One wonders how snails could possibly be attracted to wriggling baits such as those displayed by these anglers.

The most bizarre members of this superorder, indeed of all animals, are the Deep-sea Ceratioid anglerfishes. The goosefishes, frogfishes, and their close allies have the first dorsal-fin spine placed far forwards on the tip of the snout, where, under precise muscular control, it is moved around like a fishing rod, with a fleshy appendage at the tip serving as bait. While this system works well in shallow, sunlit seas, it is useless in the pitch-black, lightless depths where ceratioids dwell. But in these derived inhabitants of the deep-sea, the fleshy bait has been replaced by a bioluminescent organ, the light of which is produced by a tight cluster of millions of symbiotic bacteria. Among the approximately 160 species of ceratioids, some, like the oneirodids the Short-rod angler (*Microlophichthys microlophus*) and *Tyrannophryne pugnax*, have an very short fishing apparatus, not much more than a bulbous light organ attached to the snout, but in others, like members of the genus *Gigantactis*, the equipment can be over five times the length of the fish. In members of the genus *Lasiognathus*, the bioluminescent bait is even accompanied by a series of sharp bony hooks.

In *Thaumatichthys*, a rare ceratioid known from

around 30 adult specimens, the fishing apparatus penetrates through the roof of the mouth so that the bait hangs just behind large fang-like teeth. But perhaps least explicable is *Neoceratias spinifer* in which the fishing equipment has been lost altogether – no one knows how this fish catches food.

Deep-sea ceratioid anglerfishes also differ from their shallow-water relatives in having an extreme sexual dimorphism and a unique mode of reproduction in which the males are dwarfed and attach themselves (either temporarily or permanently) to the bodies of relatively huge females. In some species attachment is followed by tissue fusion and, eventually, by a connection of the circulatory systems so that the male becomes permanently dependent on the female for blood-transported nutrients, while the host female becomes a kind of self-fertilizing hermaphrodite.

Although the ceratioids are found worldwide, from high Arctic latitudes to the Southern Ocean, they are patchily distributed, preferring the more highly productive waters. Generally they are found at greater depths in the tropics than at the poles, but all these generalizations can be affected by local factors. Some are relatively shallow-living, for example, *Oneirodes carlsbergi*, which is most commonly found between about 300 and 400m, but most live far below this depth, averaging between 1,000 (3,300ft) and 2,500m (8,200ft), some extending down to at least 3,700m (12,140ft). Most live pelagically far off the bottom, but there is ample evidence that some, for example the Two-rod anglerfish (*Diceratias bispinosus*) and *Bufoceratias wedli*, are closely associated with the bottom; the extremely flattened members of the genus *Thaumatichthys* must certainly lead fully benthic lifestyles. In a most surprising discovery, a species of *Gigantactis* was filmed from a submersible swimming upside-down along the bottom and dragging its bait along the substrate, apparently trolling for benthic-living organisms.    KEB/TP

⊙ **Above** *Representative species of anglerfishes and toadfishes: **1** Oyster toadfish (Opsanus tau), family Batrachoididae. This species, which has venomous dorsal spines, is found along the Atlantic seaboard of the USA south of Massachusetts and in the West Indies; **2** Goosefish (Lophius americanus), family Lophiidae. The enormous, upward-facing jaw of this species is equipped with slender, curved teeth; **3** Longlure frogfish (Antennarius multiocellatus), family Antennariidae; **4** Halieutichthys aculeatus, a species of batfish, family Ogcocephalidae; **5** Anglerfish (genus Melanocetus) family Melanocetidae; **6** Anglerfish (genus Linophryne), family Linophrynidae – the large hyoid barbel indicates that this is a female; **7** Anglerfish (genus Gigantactis), family Gigantactinidae, with a long, whiplike lure on the end of its snout.*

# SEXUAL PARASITES

Reproductive modes among deep-sea ceratioid anglerfishes

AMONG THE MOST BIZARRE AND INTRIGUING of all animals, deep-sea ceratioid anglerfishes, which constitute by far the most speciose group of vertebrates below oceanic depths of about 300m (900ft), differ remarkably from all other living organisms in a variety of ways. Most strikingly, they display an extreme sexual dimorphism and a unique mode of reproduction, in which the males are dwarfed and attach themselves either temporarily or permanently to the bodies of relatively gigantic females. The males of some families are adults at a surprisingly small size. For example, those of some members of the family Linophrynidae are mature at body lengths of only 8–10mm (0.3–0.4in), making them strong contenders for the title of "world's smallest vertebrate." On the other hand, the females of some species grow quite large: females of *Thaumatichthys* and *Gigantactis* are represented by specimens of 30–40cm (12–16in); the record body length for females of the genus *Himantolophus* is 46.5cm (18in); and females of *Ceratias*, by far the largest known of all the ceratioids, grow to at least 77cm (30in).

As well as being smaller than females by an order of magnitude, the males lack a luring apparatus, and those of most species are equipped with large well-developed eyes and relatively huge nostrils. It is hypothesized that the males find females in the dark abyssal depths by using a combination of vision, hence the big eyes, and by homing in on a female-emitted, species-specific smell. As the males mature from larvae to adults the normal jaw teeth are lost, but they are replaced by a set of pincer-like denticles at the anterior tips of the jaws for grasping and holding fast to a prospective mate. Once found, the males bite the female – attachment is usually on her belly, but it could be almost anywhere: on her side, on top of her head, her face, her lip, on one of her fins, even on the bioluminescent bait at the tip of her fishing apparatus. In most ceratioids, the males attach only for a short time, until spawning takes place, and then they let go to begin the search again for another female. But, in a few groups (only eight genera in four of the eleven recognized ceratioid families: Caulophrynidae, Ceratiidae, Neoceratiidae, and Linophrynidae), attachment is followed by fusion of the skin of male and female and, eventually, by a connection of the circulatory systems so that the male becomes permanently dependent on the female for blood-transported nutrients, while the host female becomes a kind of self-fertilizing hermaphrodite. This so-called "sexual parasitism," an approach to reproduction that is unique in all the world to these few groups of deep-sea anglerfishes, usually results in a female with a single attached mate, but some females acquire two or three, and in very rare cases, even seven or eight!

The earliest recorded capture of a deep-sea anglerfish took place in 1833, when a large female was washed ashore on the southwest coast of Greenland, poorly preserved and partially eaten by birds. It was officially described in 1837 as *Himantolophus groenlandicus* by the Danish zoologist Johannes Reinhardt (1776–1845). Although hundreds more specimens were found in subsequent decades, they were not studied closely, and so it escaped biologists' notice that they were all female. The question of where the males were would only be raised, and solved, in the next century.

In 1922, the Icelandic fisheries biologist Bjarni Saemundsson (1867–1940), examining a specimen collected by the recent "round-the-world" deep-sea expeditions of the Danish research vessel *Dana*, was startled to find two little fishes hanging by their snouts to the belly of a large female deep-sea anglerfish identified as *Ceratias holboelli*. Not recognizing them as dwarfed males, he described them as the young of the same species. This view was corrected just three years later, when the British researcher Charles Tate Regan (1878–1943) dissected a small fish attached to another female *C. holboelli* and concluded that it was a parasitic male. Regan wrote that the male fish is "merely an appendage of the female, and entirely dependent on her for nutrition, … so perfect and complete is the union of husband and wife that one may almost be sure that their genital glands ripen simultaneously, and it is not too fanciful to think that the female may possibly be able to control the seminal discharge of the male and ensure that it takes place at the right time for fertilization of her eggs."

Sexual parasitism in ceratioid anglerfishes is now common scientific knowledge, yet there is still much about this remarkable reproductive mode that we do not understand. For example, the physiological mechanisms that allow for sexual parasitism, which have intriguing and potentially significant biomedical relevance, have never been studied. Two especially important questions come to mind: With circulatory systems fused and female fluids diluting those of males, how do males manage the endocrine control that is required for sperm production? How are normal immuno-responses suppressed to enable tissue fusion between males and females? These and many other related questions remain for some future researcher to resolve. KEB/TP

◁ **Left** Unmetamorphosed angler fishes are encased in a protective gelatinous skin. This is a female, as shown by the beginning of the illicium (fishing lure) above the eye.

▷ **Right** At her command, two parasitic males are fused to the body of a female anglerfish (Haplophryne mollis).

# Silversides, Killifishes, and Ricefishes

**f**ISHES THAT FLY, FISHES THAT GIVE BIRTH TO *live young, fishes used to control mosquitoes, and fishes that spawn to the cycles of the moon: these are some of the unusual lifestyles found in the series Atherinomorpha. Some of its members are extremely well known, thanks to their wide use in experimental studies of embryo development and their adaptability to aquarium conditions.*

The series comprises some 1,290 species of minute to medium-sized fishes distributed worldwide in temperate and tropical regions, and inhabiting fresh, brackish, and sea water. The following account recognizes three orders: the silversides, killifishes, and ricefishes and their allies.

## Silversides
### ORDER ATHERINIFORMES

Silversides are characterized by having a silvery lateral band at midbody, hence their common name, but this character is found in many other groups of fishes. Most silversides are narrow-bodied and elongate, though some are relatively deep-bodied, such as species of the rainbowfish genus *Glossolepis* of New Guinea, which are used as food fish. Larval atheriniforms are characterized by a single row of melanophores on the dorsal margin.

Many atherinomorphs have a prolonged development time with fertilized eggs taking one week or more to hatch, as opposed to the more usual time in teleosts of from one to two days. The grunions, in particular the Californis grunion

(*Leuresthes tenuis*), a species of silverside found on the West Coast of North America from southern California to Baja California, Mexico is well-known because of its spawning behavior, which is correlated with the lunar cycle. Grunion spawn during spring tide; the fertilized eggs are stranded during low tide, and hatching is stimulated by the waters of the returning high tide two weeks later.

Silversides, such as species of the North American genus *Menidia* found in coastal and gulf drainages, are used as bait fish. Another common name for silversides is smelts, though they are not related to the true smelts of the salmoniform family Osmeridae.

## Killifishes
### ORDER CYPRINODONTIFORMES

The killifishes are probably best known to the general public in the form of the livebearing fishes in the family Poeciliidae, which are extremely popular in the aquarium hobby. Included among them are the guppy – undoubtedly one of the most commonly kept fishes – and the mosquitofish, which consumes mosquito larvae and pupae and is used throughout the world as a natural mosquito-control agent. Poeciliids are also of great interest to biologists, because there exist populations

🔊 **Below** *The Celebes rainbowfish (Marosatherina ladigesi) is a small silverside from freshwater habitats around the Indonesian island of Sulawesi. Its limited distribution and collection for the aquarium trade have led to it being classified as Vulnerable by the IUCN.*

**FACTFILE**

## SILVERSIDES, KILLIFISHES, ETC.

Series: Atherinomorpha

Superorder: Acanthopterygii

About 1,290 species in about 170 genera, 20 families, and 3 orders.

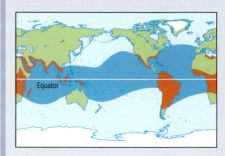

**SILVERSIDES** Order Atheriniformes
290 species in 49 genera and 6 families. Worldwide, fresh and sea waters. **Length** maximum 60cm (24in). Families: Atherinidae; Atherinopsidae, including the grunions (genus *Leuresthes*); Atherionidae; Melanotaeniidae; Notocheiridae; Phallostethidae. **Conservation status:** Six species Critically Endangered, including the Lake Wanam rainbowfish (*Glossolepis wanamensis*) and Glass blue-eye (*Kiunga ballochi*) of Papua New Guinea.

Phallostethidae

Rainbowfishes
Melanotaeniidae

Silversides, Atherinidae

**KILLIFISHES** Order Cyprinodontiformes
800 species in 84 genera and 9 families. Pantropical and north temperate regions in fresh and brackish waters. **Length** maximum 30cm (12in). Families: Anablepidae, including foureyes (genus *Anableps*); Aplocheilidae; Cyprinodontidae; Fundulidae; Goodeidae; Poeciliidae, including guppy (*Poecilia reticulata*), mosquito fish (*Gambusia affinis*); Profundulidae; Rivulidae; Valenciidae. **Conservation status:** Eighteen species are Critically Endangered, including the Monterrey platy (*Xiphophorus couchianus*) of Mexico and the Leon Springs pupfish (*Cyprinodon bovinus*) of Texas, USA.

Four-eyed fishes
Anablepidae

Killifishes
Cyprinodontidae

Goodeids, Goodeidae

Poeciliidae

**RICEFISHES AND ALLIES** Order Beloniformes
200 species in about 37 genera and 5 families. Worldwide, fresh and marine waters. **Length** maximum 1m (3.3ft). Families: flying fishes (family Exocoetidae), halfbeaks (family Hemiramphidae), needlefishes (family Belonidae), ricefishes (family Adrianichthyidae), sauries (family Scombersocidae). **Conservation status:** Two species are Critically Endangered, the Duck-billed buntingi (*Adrianichthys kruyti*) and Popta's buntingi (*Xenopoecilus poptae*), both of Indonesia. Two further species are classed as Endangered, and 8 as Vulnerable.

Ricefishes
Adrianichthyidae

Flying fishes, Exocoetidae

Needlefishes, Belonidae

Sauries, Scomberesocidae

**Above** *The best-known example of a fish that synchronizes its spawning behavior with lunar cycles is the California grunion (Leuresthes tenuis) of the North American Pacific coast. This is a marine species that moves inshore and spawns in the sand of beaches at night, following the highest of the spring tides after both the new and full moons. As the waves roll in, the fish come ashore and deposit and fertilize their eggs in the wet sand near the top of the high-tide mark. The eggs are normally hidden about 8cm (3in) below the surface. The eggs develop in the sand, awaiting the next set of spring tides, some 12–14 days later. Then the eggs hatch and the young are washed into the sea.*

**Left** *Found throughout Central Africa, the Lyretail panchax (Aphyosemion australe) is an oviparous, non-annual killifish species that hangs its eggs on vegetation. Male killifish, such as that shown here, have more flamboyant finnage and coloration than females.*

of some species that are composed entirely, or almost entirely, of females (see Life Without Males).

Other killifishes or killies in the Old and New World tropical families Aplocheilidae and Rivulidae, respectively, are also popular aquarium fishes, as well as pest-control agents. Their popularity as aquarium fishes is no doubt due in part to their bright and beautiful coloration, as well as to their hardy nature, which is so renowned that hobbyists often exchange fishes around the world by mailing them, wrapped only in a plastic bag with a little water and air and shipped in an insulated container. Included in these two tropical families are the annual killifishes, which are so named because adults rarely live longer than one rainy season, at the end of which time they spawn, leaving fertilized eggs in the drying muddy substrate. The eggs spend the dry season buried in the mud, lying quiescent until the rains return the following season. When the rains begin again the eggs are stimulated and hatch, and the cycle is repeated.

North American killifishes are less brightly colored, as are most temperate fishes, but no less well-known, at least to biologists. The Mummichog (*Fundulus heteroclitus*) a species found in brackish water, from Canada to the southern USA, is widely used in experimental embryological studies. Its biology is probably better known than that of any other species of bony fish.

## LIFE WITHOUT MALES

The Amazon molly (*Poecilia 'formosa'*) does not live in the Amazon Basin, but in more northerly, marine waters off Texas and Mexico. The common name of this species denotes the mythical race of woman warriors, and alludes to the fact that, like them, it lives in a society almost entirely devoid of males. In particular, *P. formosa* reproduces by gynogenesis, a form of unisexuality. Sperm is supplied by the males of two closely related species (*P. latipinna* and *P. mexicana*), but its sole function is to trigger cell division in the eggs (a process known as embryogenesis). Because none of the the males' sperm enters the egg and fertilizes it, the paternal genome makes no contribution to the genetic makeup of the next generation, which is, like the one before it, exclusively female. Moreover, as with all unisexual species, Amazon mollies are genetically identical, being descended from a single, founding female.

Some of the most spectacular cyprinodontiforms are those of the genus *Anableps*, found from southern Mexico to northern South America. These are the largest members of the order, some growing to sover 30cm (12in). They are most well-known for the characteristic from which their common name of foureyes (Spanish *cuatro ojos*) is derived; each eye is divided horizontally into two sections: there are separate upper and lower corneas and retinas. *Anableps* species are usually found just below the surface of the water, and seen from above only by the tops of their eyes, which protrude above the surface. The upper eyes are used for vision above the water, whereas the lower eyes are used for vision below.

Killifishes of the families Poeciliidae (subfamilies: Poeciliinae and Goodeinae) and Anablepidae have species that are viviparous (i.e. there is internal fertilization of females by males, and females give birth to live young). Males of these viviparous species have anal fins modified for sperm transfer – in the Poeciliinae and Anablepidae the first few anal rays are usually more elongate and elaborate than those in the rest of the fin and are modified into a gonopodium. In the Goodeinae, males have an anal fin or "notch" known as the spermatopodium. At one time it was thought that all viviparous killifishes formed a natural group – that is, that they were more closely related to each other than any was to a group of oviparous or egg-laying killifishes. Yet this is not the case, with egg-laying killifishes often judged to be more closely related to a particular viviparous group. This insight into killifish relationships has brought a more general awareness that viviparity, though characterized by many complex anatomical and behavioral modifications, is a way of life that has arisen several times within the evolution of killifishes.

## Ricefishes and Allies
### ORDER BELONIFORMES

The order Beloniformes comprises two groups, the ricefishes (Adrianichthyoidei) and the half-beaks, flying fishes, needlefishes, and sauries (Belonoidei or Exocoetoidei).

All ricefishes are contained in a single family. They are so called because they were discovered in Oriental rice paddies. The scientific name of the common ricefish genus *Oryzias* is in fact derived directly from the generic name of rice plants, *Oryza*. Ricefishes are common in fresh and brackish waters from the Indian subcontinent throughout coastal Southeast Asia into China, Japan and along the Indo-Australian archipelago as far as Sulawesi. The Medaka (*Oryzias latipes*) is a well-known model organism in experimental biology.

Halfbeaks are freshwater and marine fishes characterized by an elongate lower jaw and a short upper jaw, hence "half a beak." Most halfbeaks are oviparous, but some, such as the Indo-Australian Wrestling halfbeak (*Dermogenys pusilla*) have internal fertilization and are viviparous.

Species in the family of flying fishes do not exhibit true flight, as the name implies. They have expanded pectoral (and sometimes pelvic) fin rays that allow them to glide for several seconds after they propel themselves above the water surface.

In the needlefish family, species have an elongate upper as well as lower jaw; they are more or less fully beaked. The common name is a reference to the extremely sharp, needlelike teeth in the jaws. Most of the cosmopolitan temperate and tropical needlefishes are marine, whereas some, such as *Potamorhaphis guianensis* of the Amazon, live in fresh water. Needlefishes are characterized by having greenish-colored bones, and also often muscle tissue. This does not, however, prevent them from being used as a food fish.

Sauries are commercially among the most important beloniform fishes. the Pacific saury (*Cololabis saira*), found in both the eastern and western Pacific, is an important species in fisheries in Japan. The scientific name *Scomberesox*, the type genus of the family, is a composite of *Scomber*, a name for mackerels, and *Esox*, the name for pikes and pickerels. Apparently, sauries seemed to early researchers to have features of those two distantly related groups – five to seven finlets behind the dorsal and anal fins being reminiscent of the mackerels, while the moderate-sized jaws with strong teeth resembled those of pikes and pickerels.                      LP

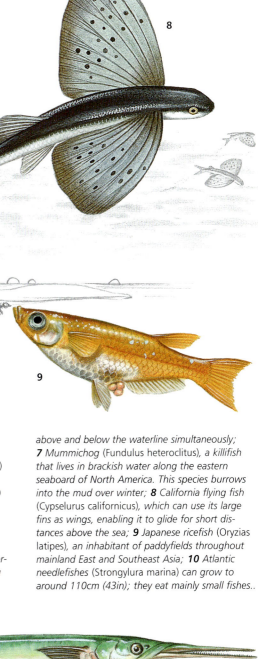

◁ **Left** *Representative species of silversides, killifishes, and ricefishes:* **1** *Goldie River rainbowfish (Melanotaenia goldiei);* **2** *Sandsmelt (Atherina sp.) – this large group of fishes is important commercially;* **3** *The Green swordtail (Xiphophorus helleri) of Central America. Swordtails occur in numerous color forms, reflecting their wide range of habitat and genetic variability;* **4a** *and* **4b** *Female and male guppy (Poecilia reticulata);* **5** *Sailfin molly (Poecilia latipinna). The sail-like dorsal fin characterizes the male;* **6** *Foureyes (Anableps sp.), showing the distinctive divided eye that enables it to see above and below the waterline simultaneously;* **7** *Mummichog (Fundulus heteroclitus), a killifish that lives in brackish water along the eastern seaboard of North America. This species burrows into the mud over winter;* **8** *California flying fish (Cypselurus californicus), which can use its large fins as wings, enabling it to glide for short distances above the sea;* **9** *Japanese ricefish (Oryzias latipes), an inhabitant of paddyfields throughout mainland East and Southeast Asia;* **10** *Atlantic needlefishes (Strongylura marina) can grow to around 110cm (43in); they eat mainly small fishes..*

# Perchlike Fishes

**n**O OTHER ORDER OF FISHES APPROACHES *that of the perchlike fishes in the number of species and the variety of form, structure, and ecology. Indeed, the Perciformes constitute the largest of all vertebrate orders, containing about 150 families with more than 9,300 species. This figure represents almost 40 percent of all fishes.*

Classification of the perchlike fishes continues to be the subject of much debate. Whether they form a natural assemblage is debatable; at present the perciforms are ill-defined and lack a single specialized character (or combination of characters) derived from a common ancestor to define the group (i.e. they are not monophyletic).

The earliest fossil record dates to the Upper Cretaceous (96–65 million years ago). In common with other orders in the larger assemblage known as the spiny-finned fishes, the perciforms have spines in both the anterior part of the dorsal fin (or separately, in front of the soft-rayed dorsal fin) and that of the anal fin. Spines are also present in the pelvic fins.

The large majority of perchlike fishes are marine shore fishes. Only around one-fifth of species – including notably the perches themselves (family Percidae) and most cichlids (family Cichlidae) – inhabit freshwater environments.

## Widespread and Diverse
### PERCIFORM FAMILIES

The most "typical" members of the perciforms, in terms of their morphology, are the species in the **perch family**. The perch body is typically deep and slender; the two dorsal fins are separate; the pelvics are near the "throat" and the operculum ends in a sharp, spinelike point. They are adapted to northern hemisphere temperatures; warm winters retard the maturing of sperm and eggs.

The European perch is a sedentary species that

**◁ Left** *Combtooth blennies are among the smallest perchlike fishes, and some have evolved sophisticated survival strategies. As well as living in crevices, the Red Sea mimic blenny (Ecsenius gravieri) has the same coloration as the venomous Blackline fangblenny (Meiacanthus nigrolineatus), thus avoiding being preyed upon. This phenomenon is known as Batesian mimicry.*

prefers lakes, canals and slow-flowing rivers. The ruffe or pope of Europe and southern England is a bottom-feeding species, frequenting canals, lakes, and the lower reaches of rivers. Confusingly, it has contiguous dorsal fins.

The zander or pikeperch is a native of eastern Europe, but has been widely introduced to other parts of Europe as a sport fish. This predatory species, which takes roach, perch, and sticklebacks, is prized by anglers and valued as a food fish. The North American zander (or walleye) occurs naturally in wide, shallow rivers and lakes.

The North American darters are the most speciose group of percids, with about 145 species. The common name is derived from their habit of darting between stones, as they are bottom-dwelling fishes that lack swimbladders. While many species of darter are brightly colored, often in red and green, the Eastern sand-darter is an inconspicuous translucent species, which buries itself in sandy stream beds with only the eyes and snout protruding.

Like that of all other teleosts, the percid skeleton is basically bone, with some cartilage, though the skeletons of the perciform families of **louvars**

**◁ Left** *Cruising the clear waters of a coral reef, a beautifully marked Coral hind (Cephalopholis miniata) opens its mouth wide to feed. This predatory species will occasioanally take crustaceans, but mainly eats the small Sea goldie (Pseudanthias squamipinnis), a co-member of its own family (Serranidae).*

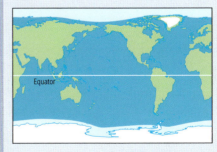

**PERCHLIKE FISHES**

Series: Percomorpha

Superorder: Acanthopterygii.

Order: Perciformes

More than 9,300 species in about 1,500 genera and about 150 families.

**DISTRIBUTION** Worldwide in both marine and fresh waters.

Equator

**SIZE** Length 1cm (0.4in)–5m (16ft); weight up to 900kg (2,000lb)

See Key Families of Perchlike Fishes ▷

(Luvaridae) and **ragfishes** (Icosteidae) are largely cartilaginous. The louvar, the only species in its family, may be related to the mackerels and tunas. It lives in tropical seas, grows to about 1.8m (6ft) and has a tapering, pinkish colored body. Its pectoral fins are sickle shaped; the pelvics are minute; its dorsal and anal fins are long, low and set far back on the body. The louvar feeds on jellyfish; its intestine is very long, with numerous internal projections that increase the absorbent surface area of the gut. The significance of the cartilaginous skeleton remains a mystery.

The ragfish is also the only species in its family. The name comes from its almost boneless appearance, which makes it look like a bundle of rags that has been dropped on the floor. The ragfish grows to some 2.1m (7ft). It is chocolate brown in color, the body shape is elliptical and it lacks scales, spines and pelvic fins. The distribution is the northeastern and mid-Pacific, from Japan to Alaska and southern California, where specimens are occasionally captured in trawls at 18–366m (60–1,200ft). It eats fishes and squid, and is itself fed on by sperm whales.

The large spotted **groupers** in the family Serranidae are voracious predators. Sometimes they are found with black, irregular lumps, either lying

⚫ **Above** *The boldly striated Oriental sweetlips* (Plectorhinchus orientalis) *gathers in small groups in the shelter of seaward coral reefs, hovering motionless in midwater. At the head of this shoal is another perchlike species, the Bluestripe snapper* (Lutjanus kasmira).

in the body cavity or bound by tissue to the viscera: these are mummified sharp-tailed eels. Each eel is swallowed by the grouper and in its death throes punctures the gut; it gets squeezed into the body cavity, where it becomes mummified.

The Queensland grouper, a native of Australian seas, may weigh up to half a tonne and is another sea bass with a hearty appetite! This fish has been known to stalk pearl and shell divers, much as a cat stalks a mouse, a habit that has led to unfounded stories of divers being swallowed by groupers.

The Serranidae family also contains much smaller and highly colorful species, like the colorful anthias, or fairy basslets (genus *Pseudanthias*) that abounds on Indo-Pacific reefs. The huge, swarming schools containing hundreds or even thousands of bright red fishes attracts any sport diver, and has led to these fishes probably being among the most photographed in the world. Apart from that, they, and many related species, are also popular with aquarium hobbyists.

Species in the families of **grunts** (Haemulidae) and **drums or croakers** (Sciaenidae) are pretty, tropical marine fishes that have earned their name from the noise they produce. In the grunts, the sound is produced by grinding together well-developed pharyngeal teeth. The drums' noise is caused by muscles vibrating the swimbladder, not

always attached directly thereto but running from either side of the abdomen to a central tendon situated above the swim bladder. Rapid twitches of the muscles vibrate the swimbladder walls which have a complex structure and act as a resonator to amplify the drumming sound. A swimbladder is absent in the drum genus *Menticirrhus* so this fish produces only a weak noise by grinding its teeth. Both families contain several commercially important food fishes, and are fished for in many parts of the world.

The **barracudas** (family Sphyraenidae) are another group of perciforms reported to attack divers. They are tropical marine fish which in some areas, especially the West Indies, are more feared than sharks. The body is elongate and powerful; the jaws are armed with sharp, dagger-like teeth. Barracudas eat other fish and seemingly herd shoals, making the food easier to catch. Large individuals tend to be solitary, but younger barracudas aggregate in shoals. The barracuda makes very good eating but is notorious for being sporadically poisonous due to the accumulation

of toxin (ciguatera) acquired from the herbivorous fish on which it feeds, who for their part have accumulated the toxins from consumption of seasonal algae (dinoflagellates).

The **mackerels, tunas, and bonitos** or scombrids (family Scombridae) are also delicious perciforms. The scombrids are mainly schooling fishes of the open seas, cruising at speeds of up to 48km/h (30mph). Their bodies are highly streamlined, terminating in a large lunate caudal fin. Some scombrids have slots on the dorsal surface of the body, in which the spiny dorsal fin fits, thus reducing water resistance. Behind the dorsal and anal fins are a series of finlets, the number of which varies according to species. In all species the scales are either very reduced or absent.

The Common mackerel is found on both sides of the North Atlantic. On the European side it ranges from the Mediterranean to Ireland. It is a pelagic fish, which in summer forms enormous shoals at the water's surface near coasts to feed on small crustaceans and other plankton. In winter the shoals disband and move to deeper water,

## HOW TUNA FISH KEEP WARM

Tunas differ from other scombrids and most other teleosts in their ability to retain metabolic heat via a countercurrent heat-exchange system that operates in the muscles and gills. Red muscle occurs in large proportions in tunas. It contains many blood vessels, so the muscle cells are supplied with oxygen- and carbohydrate-enriched blood, enabling them to utilize highly efficient, aerobic metabolism. Aerobic metabolism uses up oxygen and frees energy to drive the muscle and as heat, which is retained in the body by the heat-exchange system. White muscle, found in large proportions in all other fish, has a very poor blood supply and carbohydrate is metabolized anaerobically. which liberates just enough energy to drive the muscle.

Fishes normally lose heat through their gills during respiration, but the tunas' countercurrent heat-exchange system ensures that the metabolic heat is returned to the body. The advantage to the tunas is twofold; the muscles operate at a higher temperature, helping the fish to achieve high speeds and allowing it to range further north.    BB

where the fish approach a state of hibernation.

The skipjack tuna is a cosmopolitan marine species that owes its name to its habit of "skipping" over the surface of the water in pursuit of smaller fish.

The **billfishes** (families Xiphiidae and Istiophoridae), which includes the swordfish, the sailfishes, the spearfishes and the marlins, are all fast-swimming fishes closely related to the scombrids (see Mystery of the Swordfish). They include some of the world's most popular marine sport fishes. Several billfish species are known to be migratory, possibly to follow food. Billfishes are fisheaters; they erect the dorsal fin to prevent prey escaping. They can also use the bill as a club to maim their victims as they rush through a school of fishes.

Sailfishes undergo a remarkable change during their larval development. Larvae of about 9mm (0.3in) have both jaws equally produced, armed with conical teeth; the edge of the head above the eye has a series of short bristles; there are two long pointed spines at the back of the head; the dorsal fin is a long, low fringe and the pelvic fins are represented by short buds. At 6cm (2.4in) they begin to resemble the adult: the upper jaw elongates, the teeth disappear, the dorsal fin differentiates into two fins, the spines at the back of the head

◖ *Left* A school of Sawtooth barracudas (Sphyraena putnamae). *The two parallel rows of sharp teeth in the barracuda's upper and lower jaws are used to slash and tear pieces off their prey; barracudas do not have a wide enough gape to swallow large fish whole.*

◗ *Below* The spinecheek anemonefish (Premnas biaculeatus) *lives in lagoons and around reefs and is commonly associated with the sea anemone species* Entacmaea quadricolor. *Members of this family (Pomacentridae) are mainly from the Indo-Pacific region.*

become reduced and the bristles disappear. Young swordfish also undergo a similar series of changes

Several of the most spectacular and colorful fishes of tropical seas are perciforms. **Butterflyfishes** (family Chaetodontidae) are distributed worldwide in warm waters around coral reefs. Currently, some 115 species are known. Most are very brightly colored, but often with intricate patterns camouflaging the eye, making it difficult for a potential predator to distinguish the head from the tail. Many species have a dark vertical bar that runs through the eye, further disguising it, and to add to the confusion many species also have an eye spot near the caudal fin. Butterflyfishes delude would-be predators by swimming slowly backward. Once the predator lunges at the eye spot, the butterflyfish darts forward, leaving its attacker confused. The Indo-Pacific butterflyfish, also known as the forcepsfish or longnose butterflyfish, is so called because its snout is very long and used like a pair of forceps to reach deep into reef crevices.

The majority of butterflyfishes are obligate coral feeders that are totally dependent on healthy reefs. In many areas where coral death has occurred through direct human impact or by temperature-induced coral bleaching, the number of butterflyfishes has fallen dramatically.

The great beauty of butterflyfishes makes them attractive also to aquarium hobbyists, but – with relatively few exceptions – they are very difficult to keep in captivity, and are best left to highly experienced and skilled aquarium keepers.

Closely related to, and in the past commonly lumped with, the butterflyfishes family are **angelfishes**. Presently placed in their own family, Pomacanthidae, the angelfishes are distinguished from butterflyfishes by their larger, rather rectangular bodies and heavy spines at the base of the gill cover. There are more than 80 species in the family, ranging from tiny dwarf angelfishes, only 8–15cm (3–6in) long, to spectacular giants like the Queen angelfish of the Caribbean, reaching nearly 0.5m (1.6ft). Many are sought-after aquarium fishes, that also do quite well under human care, since most are much less specialist in their feeding requirements than are the butterflyfishes. Several species are quite satisfactory food and occur in most tropical fish markets, but they are rarely of much economic importance.

The twenty-eight species of **clownfishes** (anemonefishes) and **damselfishes** belonging to the Pomacentridae are small, brightly colored fishes of warm shallow seas. Clownfishes live in association with large sea anemones. The relationship is intimate: the fish remains inside the anemone when it withdraws its tentacles. The clownfishes benefit by being protected from predators, so they never stray far from their anemones, but the latter can happily exist without the clownfishes. The anemones' sting-cells are lethal to nonsymbiont fishes, but the clownfishes' mucus coat is considerably thicker than in related species and it

appears to lack the chemical components that triggers the sting-cells. The beautiful color patterns of clownfishes and their fascinating behavior make them some of the most sought-after aquarium fishes. They reproduce easily in captivity and commercial farming of the most popular species is now well established.

The **surgeonfishes** (family Acanthuridae) are another family of colorful reef-dwelling fishes of which there are about 72 species. The name alludes to a razor-sharp, lancetlike spine on either side of the caudal peduncle. In most species the spines lie in a groove and are erected when the fish is disturbed or excited. The spines are a formidable weapon, inflicting slash wounds on the victim,

as the surgeonfish lashes its tail from side to side. Surgeonfishes normally travel solitary or in small groups using their small incisorlike teeth to scrape plants and animals from reefs and rocks. Under special circumstances, however, some species like the spectacular powder-blue surgeonfish gathers in large foraging schools, where the individual is better protected from predators. A few species of surgeonfishes feed on plankton rather than algae. In parts of the Indo-Pacific, surgeonfishes are considered tasty food fish, but the offending caudal peduncle is cut off prior to sale. Several of the smaller and more colorful species are traded for the aquarium hobby.

Members of the family of **stargazers** (Urano-

scopidae) are widely distributed in warm seas and earn their name from their eyes which are set on top of the head so that they appear to be staring at the sky. Stargazers have electric organs situated just behind the eyes, which deliver a shock of up to 50 volts, enough to stun small fish – which are then eaten. The European stargazer is common in the Mediterranean and Black Sea; it grows up to 35cm (14in) and has flaps of tissue in the mouth that resemble worms, tempting potential prey to approach. Predators are deterred from eating the stargazer by grooved spines situated above each pectoral fin. At the base of the spine is a poison gland; as the spine inflicts a wound, poison is trickled into it via the groove. Stargazers are usually

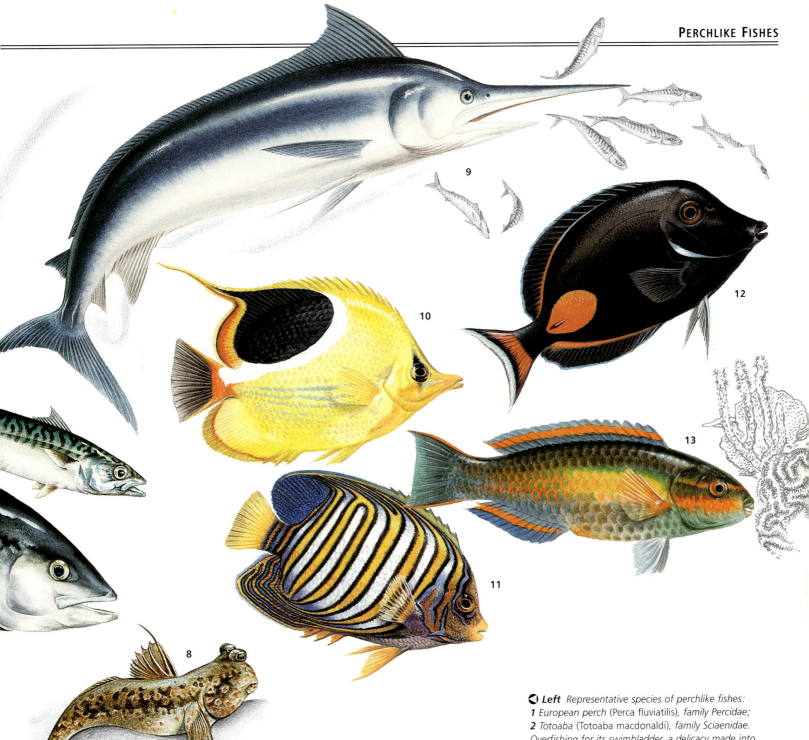

found buried in the sand, with only the eyes and snout tip protruding.

A few perciforms sometimes form unusual relationships with other vertebrates and invertebrates and even with floating objects! The **remoras or sharksuckers** (family Echeneidae) are slim fishes usually associated with sharks, large fishes and occasionally turtles. Their dorsal fin is modified into a sucking disk, the rim of which is raised, and the platelike fin rays can be adjusted to create a strong vacuum between the disk and a remora's chosen partner. It is unknown what benefit such an association is to either the remoras or the animals to which they attach. It has been suggested that remoras are simply "hitching a ride," a

phenomenon known as phoresia, or that they associate with sharks to feed on the scraps they can snatch from the shark's meal. Remoras have been observed entering the mouths of manta rays, large sharks and billfishes, and it has been speculated that they may fulfill a role similar to that of cleaner fish. However, there is no documented evidence of remoras undertaking cleaning duties.

Despite their usual attachment to sharks, remoras are competent swimmers and often leave the "host" to forage. When free-swimming in a group, remoras arrange themselves with the largest on top, smallest at the bottom, reminiscent of a stack of plates. The group swim in a circular fashion; it seems remoras do not like to swim unaccompanied. Ancient legend recounts that remoras can impede the progress of sailing vessels, even stop them. The remora is also reported

◖ **Left** *Representative species of perchlike fishes:* **1** *European perch (Perca fluviatilis), family Percidae;* **2** *Totoaba (Totoaba macdonaldi), family Sciaenidae. Overfishing for its swimbladder, a delicacy made into soup in Southeast Asia, has caused this Mexican species to become Critically Endangered;* **3** *Yellow labidochromis (Labidochromis caeruleus), a mouth-brooding cichlid from Lake Malawi in East Africa; family Cichlidae;* **4** *Crevalle jack (Caranx hippos), an Eastern Atlantic species, family Carangidae;* **5** *Yellowfin tuna (Thunnus albacares), an important commercial food fish, family Scombridae;* **6** *Atlantic mackerel (Scomber scombrus), family Scombridae;* **7** *Dwarf pygmy goby (Pandaka pygmaea), family Gobiidae. At just 1.5cm in length, this species from the Philippines is the smallest freshwater fish in the world;* **8** *Mudskipper (Periophthalmus sp.), an inhabitant of mangrove swamps, family Gobiidae;* **9** *Atlantic blue marlin (Makaira nigricans), family Istiophoridae;* **10** *Saddle butterflyfish (Chaetodon ephippium); family Chaetodontidae.* **11** *Regal angelfish (Pygoplites diacanthus), a popular fish in the aquarium trade, family Pomacanthidae.* **12** *Achilles tang (Acanthurus achilles); family Acanthuridae.* **13** *Princess parrotfish (Scarus taeniopterus); family Scaridae.*

to have magic powers and a potion including one was supposed to delay legal proceedings, arrest aging in women and slow down the course of love!

**Pilotfishes** in the family Carangidae also associate with sharks and rays. It was thought that the pilotfishes guided the sharks to their prey and in return received protection from their enemies by their proximity to such a formidable companion. Sharks and rays are in fact seeking food, and although the pilotfish gain from the hunting efforts of sharks they never lead the foray.

The young of another carangid, the common Horse mackerel, shelter in the bell of the sombrero jellyfish (genus *Cotylorhiza*). Why these small fishes do not get stung is unexplained but possibly the absence of glutathione (an amino acid that stimulates release of sting cells) in their mucus coats protects them.

Members of two other families also associate with jellyfish. Young butterfishes (Stromateidae) are laterally compressed fish which lack pelvic fins and shelter under the protection of the Portuguese man-of-war (genus *Physalia*). The closely related **driftfishes** (Nomeidae) are known as "man-o'-war" fishes and are distinguished from the preceding family by the presence of pelvic fins. Again, it is unknown how these fish gain immunity from the stinging cells of this jellyfish.

Among the **gobies** (family Gobiidae), fishes in the genus *Evermannichthys* habitually live inside sponges. The bodies of these little fishes are slender and nearly cylindrical, allowing them easy access to the larger orifices on the sponge's surface. Scales are either absent or poorly developed, but along the lower posterior line of the sides are two series of large, well-separated scales whose edges are produced into long spines. A further series of four spined scales is situated in the middle line, behind the anal fin. It is thought that these structures are used by the fish for climbing up the inner surfaces of the sponge cavities.

Many Indo-Pacific genera of gobies, for example *Amblyeleotris* and *Cryptocentrus*, are commensal with digging snapping shrimps (genus *Alpheus*). The goby is usually found at the burrow entrance while the snapping shrimp busily excavates it. When danger threatens, the goby dives into the burrow; this also alerts the shrimp which follows the fish inside. The snapping shrimp will not emerge until the goby is once again on sentry duty at the burrow entrance.

The mudskippers, of the genus *Periophthalmus* (family Gobiidae), are found in tropical Africa, Asia, Australia, and Oceania, and spend a great part of their time walking or "skipping" about mangrove roots at low tide. During these periods the branchial chamber is filled with water and oxygen exchange continues over the gills. When the oxygen in this water is exhausted the mudskippers replace it with oxygenated water from a nearby puddle. The mudskippers can also respire through the skin (cutaneously) and have a highly vascular mouth and pharynx through which gaseous exchange can take place; they are therefore often seen sitting with their mouths gaping.

A number of species of **wrasse** (genus *Labroides*; family Labridae) have an unusual "cleaning" relationship with other fishes: they remove ectoparasites and clean wounds or debris. There are some 500 species in the wrasse family, usually nonschooling, brilliantly colored and found on reefs in all tropical and temperate marine waters. The wrasses have well-developed "incisor" teeth that protrude like a pair of forceps from a protractile mouth; in some non-cleaning species these are used for removing fins and eyes of other fishes.

The cleaner wrasse are small, brightly-colored reef dwellers that occupy a specific area, the "cleaner station." Their diet is mostly parasitic organisms on the bodies and gills of fishes. The association between cleaner and customer is not permanent. Fishes requiring "cleaning" congregate at the cleaning stations and follow a specific behavior pattern that invites the cleaner to get to work. The customer allows the cleaner to move all over the body, including such sensitive areas as the eyes and mouth, and even to enter the branchial cavity to remove parasites from the gills. The cleaners benefit by immunity from predation during the cleaning and presumably at other times, since many of the customers are predators on fishes the size of these wrasses.

In North-Atlantic waters there are also species of wrasse that indulge in cleaning behavior on other fishes. The control of parasites in salmon farms is increasingly done with the help of specimens of goldsinny and young ballan wrasse, corkwing wrasse and related species, rather than with biocides. Many wrasse species are eaten, but since most are relatively small and bony, they are more likely to end up in a fish soup than to be cooked by themselves. In Asian waters there are some species that are highly rated as food fish. The prize wrasse in this respect is undoubtedly the Napoleonfish or humphead wrasse, which has been severely overfished in many areas because of the tremendous demand for large specimens. It can grow to a stunning 230cm (7.5ft), weighing up to nearly 200kg (440lb), but large specimens are getting increasingly rare.

The **parrotfishes** family (Scaridae) is closely related to the wrasses and many species secrete a mucous nightshirt that surrounds the whole body. This mucous cocoon may take up to half an hour to secrete and as long for the fish to release itself from. Interestingly this cocoon is not secreted every night but only under certain conditions, the causal factors of which are a mystery. It seems that the mucous cocoon may be a protective device, preventing odors from the parrotfishes reaching predatory fish, such as moray eels.

Species in the **leaffish** family (Nandidae) rely on crypsis (pretending to be something else) to

## THE MYSTERY OF THE SWORDFISH

The swordfish is the sole representative of its family (Xiphiidae). It is a solitary fish, and may weigh up to 675kg (1,000lb). The snout is produced into a powerful, flattened sword. Swordfish live in all tropical and subtropical oceans but will enter temperate waters, occasionally straying as far north as Iceland.

The sword has a coat of small denticles similar to those found on sharks. Its function is unknown, but suggestions include a weapon (i.e. the swordfish strikes a shoal of fishes with lateral movements and then devours the mutilated victims) and as extreme streamlining, with the snout acting as a cutwater.

There are numerous accounts of large fish attacking boats, but often there is no attempt to discriminate between swordfish, spearfish, and sailfish, all of which have similar habits. There is no doubt that a swordfish could pierce the bottom of a boat and have the sword snap off in its struggles to withdraw it. In the Natural History Museum, London there is a sample of timber that a swordfish snout has penetrated to a depth of 56cm (22in). It is also reported that the wooden sailing ship HMS *Dreadnought* sprang a leak on a voyage from Ceylon (Sri Lanka) to London. Examination of the hull revealed a 2.5cm (1in) hole punched through the copper sheathing, which was reputed to have been made by a swordfish. Periodically swords are found in whale blubber. Whether these attacks on ships and whales are deliberate is unclear. The most likely explanation is that when a swordfish, which can travel at speeds up to 100km/h (60mph), encounters a boat or whale it finds it impossible to change course in time, and a collision becomes inevitable.                    BB

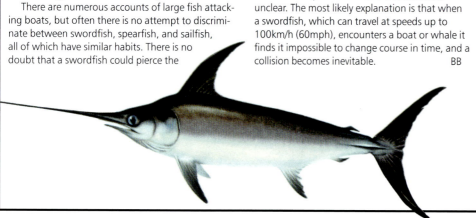

◗ **Right** *Parrotfishes derive their name from the fact that their jaw teeth are fused together and resemble a parrot's beak. Like the birds, they are also characterized by vibrant colors, a feature amply displayed by this Scarus sp. parrotfish sleeping on a reef off Borneo.*

catch their food. They are found in tropical fresh waters in Africa, Southeast Asia and South America. The Southeast Asian leaffishes are very perchlike – none mimics leaves and the body is only slightly compressed. The most common leaffish of this area is *Badis badis* (sometimes placed in a family of its own, Badidae) which has a large number of different color forms and is found in streams of India and Indochina. The most spectacular leaffishes are those found in South America. These are deep-bodied fish with soft dorsal fin rays: they closely resemble floating leaves in both contours and marks – even a "stalk" is present, protruding from the lower jaw. Leaffish usually hide beneath rocks or in crevices, where they look like a dead leaf, then dart out to capture prey. The most famous leaffish, *Monocirrhus polyacanthus*, is found in the Amazon and Rio Negro basins of South America. Its body is leaf-shaped and tapered toward the snout, with an anterior barbel mimicking a leaf stalk. The fish reaches about 10cm (4in) in length and is a mottled brown similar to dead leaves. It drifts with the current; on approaching a potential meal, the leaffish bursts into action and, assisted by its large protrusile mouth, engulfs fishes up to half its size.

The perciform family with the largest numbers of species is that of the **cichlids** (Cichlidae). Even a conservative estimate indicates that there are at least 1,300 species, and some scientists believe the final count may reach around 5,000! To put this in context, only about 3,000 species of freshwater fishes have so far been recorded from the entire continent of South America. Cichlids are widely distributed in freshwaters of Central and South America, Africa, Syria, Iran, Madagascar, southern India, and Sri Lanka. Over half of the presently known cichlid species are found in Africa, especially the Great Lakes (Victoria, Malawi, and Tanganyika), each of which boasts 100 or more endemic species. The high number of endemisms and apparently rapid speciation make the cichlid fauna of these lakes interesting examples in evolutionary theory. Lake Malawi alone may actually hold about 1,000 species, of which the vast majority are endemic, but the taxonomy is controversial and normal definitions of what constitutes a species are often difficult to apply to cichlids. Cichlids are characterized by a single nostril on each side of the head and two lateral lines on each side of the body. The pharyngeal bone is triangular, lying on the floor of the "throat"; its function is to break up food against a hard pad at the base of the skull, and it is of diagnostic importance in the identification of species.

Cichlids have evolved all kinds of dentition that allow them to cope with a varied diet. Vegetarians have bands of small, notched teeth in the jaws, sometimes with an outer chisel-like series for cutting weed or scraping algae off rocks. Fish-eating species have large mouths armed with strong, pointed teeth for securing struggling fish. The

## SHOOTING DOWN INSECTS

Six species of archer fish (*Toxotes* spp.) occur naturally in both fresh and salt water from India and Malaysia to northern Australia. Their remarkable hunting technique involves spitting droplets of water at their prey. The archer fish has a groove in the roof of the mouth. The tongue is thin and free at the front but thick and muscular with a midline fleshy protuberance at the back. Once the tongue and protuberance are pressed against the roof of the mouth, the groove becomes a narrow tube. The thin, free end of the tongue acts as a valve. When the archer fish spots an insect, the tongue is pressed against the roof of the mouth, the gill covers are jerked shut and the tip of the tongue is flicked, shooting out drops of water. Archer fish are able to compensate for refraction of light by placing the body vertically below the prey. A fully grown fish can shoot down an insect from up to 1.5m (5ft), whereas babies can only shoot a few centimeters without loss of accuracy. Experiments with adult archer fish suggest, however, that their aim may be quite haphazard and the "downing" of an insect owes more to sheer firepower than to sharp shooting.                                    BB

◑ **Above** The Wolf-eel (Anarrhichthys ocellatus) *lies in wait in rock crevices or among kelp beds for its prey (smaller fish, crustaceans, mollusks, and sea urchins). All the five species in the family to which it belongs (Anarhichadidae) are equipped with large, conical canine teeth at the front of the jaw and strong molars at the rear, with which they can deliver a powerful bite. Wolffishes inhabit the far northern waters of the Atlantic and Pacific and grow up to 2.5m (80in).*

◐ **Right** *Native to small streams in the Orinoco river basin in South America, the Ram cichlid (Mikrogeophagus ramirezi) is a small, brightly colored fish that is very popular with aquarists. It spawns on the substrate, and the adults guard their eggs and fry.*

◓ **Below** *The Lace or Pearl gourami (Trichogaster leeri; family Osphronemidae) of Southeast Asia is one of the "labyrinth fishes," so named for the accessory breathing organs on either side of their heads that enable them to breathe atmospheric air.*

mollusk-eating varieties have strong, blunt pharyngeal teeth to grind up mollusks, although in some species the lateral jaw teeth are modified, enabling the fish to remove the snail from its shell before swallowing it. Finally, in some species the dentition is greatly reduced and deeply embedded in the gums of a very distensible mouth. These species (paedophores) feed almost entirely on the eggs and young of mouthbrooding cichlids, which they force the parent to "cough up."

Cichlids are very popular aquarium fishes and some species, like the freshwater angelfish and the discus fishes count, like the goldfish, among the truly domesticated fishes, of which a huge number of stunning color breeds have been produced.

The **gouramis** (Osphronemidae), the **climbing gouramis** (Anabantidae), the **kissing gouramis** (Helostomatidae) and the **snakeheads** (Channidae) are four more perciform families renowned for their ability to breathe atmospheric air. The first three families are also called labyrinth fishes for their labyrinthlike accessory breathing organs. These breathing organs are located at the top of each gill chamber; they are hollow and formed from highly vascular skin lining the gill chambers. As the fish grows, the organs become more convoluted, increasing the surface area available for respiration. These fishes rely on atmospheric air for survival and quickly suffocate if denied access to the surface of the water.

One of the most spectacular labyrinth fishes is the Siamese fighting fish. This species is customarily brightly colored in aquaria, but has a rather unexciting, brownish-red coloration in the wild. This is another example of selective breeding being used to produce appealing, domesticated forms of fishes – similar to the enhancement by breeding of certain features in other pet animals, such as dogs and cats.

The **snakehead** family is related to the gouramis but contains long cylindrical fishes with flattened, rather reptilian-looking heads. These fish inhabit rivers, ponds and stagnant marsh pools in Southeast Asia. The various species of snakehead differ in the extent to which each has developed the habit of breathing air. The accessory breathing organs are simpler than those found in anabantoids, consisting of a pair of cavities lined with a vascular thickened and puckered membrane. These lunglike reservoirs are not derived from the branchial chambers but are pouches of the pharynx.

The snakeheads are also able to move overland, but do so by a rowing motion of the pectoral fins. During prolonged periods of drought, snakeheads survive by burying themselves in mud and estivating; in hot, dry weather they become torpid. Since several species are popular food fishes that are often sold in food markets while still alive, there is a constant risk of snakeheads being introduced into areas where they do not occur naturally. Many are large, voracious predators, and where accidental introductions have taken place, the snakeheads have inflicted terrible damage on the local fauna. It is therefore extremely important that those handling live snakeheads are aware of the dangers and avoid spreading them to new areas. At the time of writing, 13 US states have banned ownership of live snakeheads.　　KEB/SF

# Key Families of Perchlike Fishes

The order Perciformes, with over 9,300 species in about 1,500 genera and over 150 families, is the largest of all fish orders – indeed, of all vertebrate orders.

## Sea basses or groupers
### Family Serranidae

Primarily marine worldwide. 449 species in 62 genera including: Black sea bass (*Centropristis striata*); Coney (*Cephalopholis fulva*); Queensland grouper (*Epinephelus lanceolatus*); Black grouper (*Mycteroperca bonaci*); hamlets (genus *Hypoplectrus*); Swallowtail seaperch (*Anthias anthias*); Sixstripe soapfish (*Grammistes sexlineatus*); Kelp bass (*Paralabrax clathratus*); Tattler (*Serranus phoebe*); Atlantic creolefish (*Paranthias furcifer*); Sand perch (*Diplectrum formosum*).

## Perches
### Family Percidae

Freshwater worldwide. 162 species in 10 genera including: European perch (*Perca fluviatilis*); Yellow perch (*Perca flavescens*); ruffe or pope (*Gymnocephalus cernuus*); North American darters (genera *Ammocrypta, Crystallaria, Etheostoma, Percina*) including Eastern sand-darter (*Ammocrypta pellucida*), Crystal sand-darter (*Crystallaria*

*asprella*), and Slackwater darter (*Etheostoma boschungi*); pikeperches or zanders (genus *Sander*), including zander (*S. lucioperca*), North American zander or walleye (*S. vitreus*), sauger (*S. canadensis*).

## Drums or croakers
### Family Sciaenidae

Marine and freshwater worldwide. 270 species in 70 genera including: Freshwater drum (*Aplodinotus grunniens*); Silver croaker (*Bairdiella chrysoura*); White weakfish (*Atractoscion nobilis*); Silver seatrout (*Cynoscion nothus*); White croaker (*Genyonemus lineatus*); Black drum (*Pogonias cromis*); Queenfish (*Seriphus politus*); Polla drum (*Umbrina xanti*).

## Wrasses
### Family Labridae

Marine waters worldwide. 500 species in 60 genera including: goldsinny (*Ctenolabrus rupestris*);Ballan wrasse (*Labrus bergylta*); Corkwing wrasse (*Symphodus melops*); Tautog (*Tautoga onitis*); Napoleonfish or Humpback wrasse (*Cheilinus undulatus*); Spanish hogfish (*Bodianus rufus*); California sheephead (*Semicossyphus pulcher*); Señorita (*Oxyjulis californica*); Slippery dick (*Halichoeres bivittatus*); Bluehead

(*Thalassoma bifasciatum*); African clown wrasse (*Coris formosa*); Birdmouth wrasse (*Gomphosus coereleus*); Harlequin tuskfish (*Choerodon fasciatus*).

## Butterflyfishes
### Family Chaetodontidae

Worldwide, in coral reef environments. 114 species in 10 genera including: Spotfin butterflyfish (*Chaetodon ocellatus*); Forceps fish (*Forcipiger longirostris*); bannerfishes (genus *Heniochus*), including Horned bannerfish (*H. varius*); Blacknosed butterflyfish (*Johnrandallia nigrirostris*); Longnosed butterflyfish (*Prognathodes aculeatus*); Western talma (*Chelmonops curiosus*).

## Angelfishes
### Family Pomacanthidae

Worldwide, in tropical waters. 74 species in 9 genera including: dwarf angelfishes (genus *Centropyge*), including Coral beauty (*C. bispinosus*) and Cherubfish (*C. argi*); Rock beauty (*Holacanthus tricolor*); Queen angelfish (*H. ciliaris*); Regal angelfish (*Pygoplites diacanthus*); Griffis angelfish (*Apolemichthys griffisi*); Blackstriped angelfish (*Genicanthus lamarck*).

## Cichlids
### Family Cichlidae

Worldwide, exclusively freshwater. c.1,300 species in 105 genera including: discus (genus *Symphysodon*); Freshwater angelfish (*Pterophyllum scalare*); Longfin tilapia (*Oreochromis macrochir*); Julidochromis marlieri; Jewel fish (*Hemichromis bimaculatus*); Egyptian mouthbrooder (*Pseudocrenilabrus multicolor*); Malawi eye-biter (*Haplochromis compressiceps*); Keyhole cichlid (*Aequidens maronii*); Ramirez's dwarf cichlid (*Mikrogeophagus ramirezi*); Jack Dempsey (*Cichlasoma octofasciatum*); *Uaru amphicanthoides*; Mango tilapia (*Sarotherodon galilaeus*); Oscar (*Astronotus ocellatus*).

## Combtooth blennies
### Family Blenniidae

Mostly marine, occasionally brackish, rarely freshwater; worldwide distribution. 345 species in 53 genera including: Midas blenny (*Ecsenius midas*); Bicolor blenny (*E. bicolor*); Redlip blenny (*Ophioblennius atlanticus*); Ocellated dragonet (*Synchiropus ocellatus*); Jewel blenny (*Salarias fasciatus*); Striped blenny (*Chasmodes*

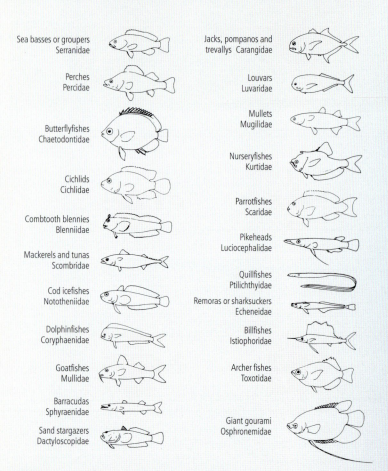

Sea basses or groupers — Serranidae
Perches — Percidae
Butterflyfishes — Chaetodontidae
Cichlids — Cichlidae
Combtooth blennies — Blenniidae
Mackerels and tunas — Scombridae
Cod icefishes — Nototheniidae
Dolphinfishes — Coryphaenidae
Goatfishes — Mullidae
Barracudas — Sphyraenidae
Sand stargazers — Dactyloscopidae
Jacks, pompanos and trevallys — Carangidae
Louvars — Luvaridae
Mullets — Mugilidae
Nurseryfishes — Kurtidae
Parrotfishes — Scaridae
Pikeheads — Luciocephalidae
Quillfishes — Ptilichthyidae
Remoras or sharksuckers — Echeneidae
Billfishes — Istiophoridae
Archer fishes — Toxotidae
Giant gourami — Osphronemidae

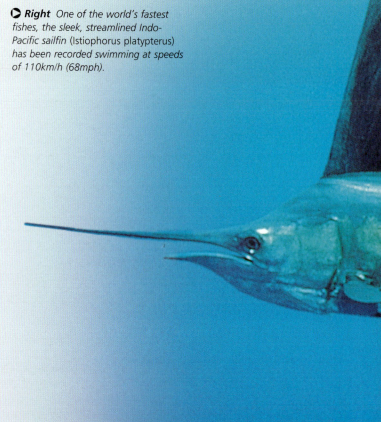

**◗ Right** *One of the world's fastest fishes, the sleek, streamlined Indo-Pacific sailfin (*Istiophorus platypterus*) has been recorded swimming at speeds of 110km/h (68mph).*

*bosquianus*); Barred blenny (*Hypleurochilus bermudensis*); Feather blenny (*Hypsoblennius hentzi*); Molly miller (*Scartella cristata*); Disco blenny (*Meiacanthus smithi*); Forktail blenny (*M. atrodorsalis*); Muzzled blenny (*Omobranchus punctatus*).

## Gobies
### Family Gobiidae

c.1,875 species in 212 genera. Mostly tropical marine and brackish environments. Species and genera include: Bluecheek goby (*Valenciennea strigata*); Giant goby (*Gobius cobitis*); mudskippers (genus *Periophthalmus*), including Barred mudskipper (*P. argentilineatus*); Lemon goby (*Gobiodon citrinus*); Yellow prawn-goby (*Cryptocentrus cinctus*); Catalina or Blue-banded goby (*Lythrypnus dalli*); Golden-banded goby (*Brachygobius doriae*); Blackeye goby (*Rhinogobiops nicholsii*); Clown goby (*Microgobius gulosus*); Bridled goby (*Coryphopterus glaucofraenum*); Frillfin goby (*Bathygobius soporator*); Highfin goby (*Gobionellus oceanicus*); Spotted fringefin goby (*Eviota albolineata*); Transparent goby (*Aphia minuta*); Tusked goby (*Risor ruber*).

## Mackerels, tunas, and bonitos
### Family Scombridae

49 species in 15 genera. Tropical and temperate seas worldwide. Species include: Atlantic mackerel (*Scomber scombrus*); Horse mackerel (*Trachurus trachurus*); Skipjack tuna (*Katsuwonus pelamis*); Little tunny (*Euthynnus alletteratus*); Atlantic bonito (*Sarda sarda*); Albacore (*Thunnus alalunga*); Yellowfin tuna (*T. albacares*); Cero (*Scomberomorus regalis*); Spanish mackerel (*S. maculatus*); Plain bonito (*Orcynopsis unicolor*).

## Other families, genera, and species include:

**glassfishes** (family Chandidae), including the Indian glassperch (*Parambassis ranga*); **dottybacks** and **eelblennies** (family Pseudochromidae), including Orchid dottyback (*Pseudochromis fridmani*), Carpet eel blenny (*Congrogadus subducens*); **prettyfins** or **longfins** (family Plesiopidae), including comet (*Calloplesiops altivelis*); **jawfishes** (family Opistognathidae); **sunfishes** (family Centrarchidae), including bluegill (*Lepomis macrochirus*); **louvar** (*Luvarus*

*imperialis*) sole species of Luvaridae; **ragfish** (*Icosteus aenigmaticus*) sole species of Icosteidae; **cardinal fishes** (family Apogonidae), including Banggai cardinalfish (*Pterapogon kauderni*); **remoras** or **sharksuckers** (family Echeneidae); **dolphinfishes** (family Coryphaenidae, genus *Coryphaena*); **jacks, pompanos** and **trevallys** (family Carangidae), including pilotfish (*Naucrates ductor*); **snappers** (family Lutjanidae); **grunts** (family Haemulidae), including sweetlips (genus *Plectorhinchus*), porkfish (*Anisotremus virginicus*); **threadfins** (family Polynemidae, genera *Polynemus, Eleutheronema*); **goatfishes** (family Mullidae), including Red mullet (*Mullus surmuletus*); **moonfishes** (family Monodactylidae); **archerfishes** (family Toxotidae, genus *Toxotes*); **leaffishes** (family Nandidae); **hawkfishes** (family Cirrhitidae); **damselfishes** (family Pomacentridae), including clownfishes (genera *Amphiprion, Premnas*); **parrotfishes** (family Scaridae); **eelpouts** (family Zoarcidae); **wolffishes** (family Anarhichadidae); **weeverfishes** (family Trachinidae); **stargazers** (family Uranoscopidae), including European stargazer (*Uranoscopus scaber*);

**dragonets** (family Callionymidae); **rabbitfishes** (family Siganidae); **surgeonfishes** (family Acanthuridae), including Powderblue surgeonfish (*Acanthurus leucosternon*); **barracudas** (family Sphyraenidae); **billfishes** (family Istiophoridae), including sailfishes (genus *Istiophorus*); **swordfish** (*Xiphias gladius,* family Xiphiidae); **gouramies** (family Osphronemidae), including Siamese fighting fish (*Betta splendens*); **snakeheads** (family Channidae).

About 269 species of perchlike fishes are threatened, with 5 Extinct in the Wild, including *Haplochromis lividus* and *Platytaeniodus degeni*; 55 species are Critically Endangered, including the Warsaw grouper (*Epinephelus nigritus*), totoaba (*Totoaba macdonaldi*), and Dwarf pygmy goby (*Pandaka pygmaea*); 28 species are Endangered, including the Bluestripe darter (*Percina cymatotaenia*); and 136 species are Vulnerable, including the Mexican darter (*Etheostoma pottsi*), Bigeye tuna (*Thunnus obesus*), and the Humpback wrasse.

# Flatfishes

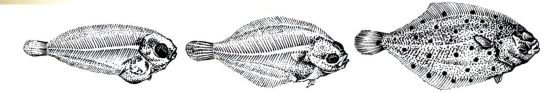

**a** S THE COMMON NAME FOR THE ORDER indicates, flatfishes are noted for their flattened body shape, with eyes present on only one side of the body. Furthermore, the scientific order name Pleuronectiformes derives from the Greek for "side swimmers." Unique among fishes in being asymmetrical, flatfishes are believed to have evolved from a generalized symmetrical percoid (sea bass) body pattern in a fish that habitually rested on its side.

There are about 570 pleuronectid species, divided into 11 families. The members of the most primitive family – the Psettodidae – have rather perch-like pectoral and pelvic fins; only the eyes and long dorsal fin distinguish them from the seaperch, suggesting that flatfish evolved from perchlike ancestors.

All adult flatfish are bottom-living fish but their eggs, which contain oil droplets, float at or near the sea surface. The larvae take a few days to hatch; the fish appear symmetrical, with an eye on each side of the head and a ventrally situated mouth, further suggestive of their perchlike ancestry. When about 1cm (0.5in) long a metamorphosis occurs which has profound effects on the symmetry of the skull and the whole fish. The changes are initiated when one eye migrates

◔ ◑ **Above and right** Flatfishes start life as normal-shaped fish with an eye on each side and a horizontal mouth. As the larva grows, ABOVE, one eye migrates to the other side of the head and the mouth twists until the adult comes to lie permanently on one side. The consequent deformation in the adult can be seen in this image of a Leopard flounder (Bothus pantherinus) RIGHT from Tonga in the Indo-Pacific Ocean.

across the head to lie alongside the other, its passage being assisted by resorption of the cartilaginous bar of skull separating them. The nostril simultaneously migrates to the eyed or colored side. Except in the psettodids, the mouth also twists into the same plane as the eyes. The eye that migrates often characterizes particular families. Members of families such as the Scophthalmidae and the Bothidae are called "lefteye flounders" because their right eye usually migrates, so the uppermost, colored side is the left one. Pleuronectidae are right-eyed flounders because ultimately the right side is uppermost. In the psettodids equal numbers are found lying on either side.

While these radical changes are taking place the little fish sinks to the sea bottom. Flatfish do not have a swimbladder, so they remain lying at or near the bottom, on their blind side. The body shape of adult flatfishes is quite variable – the European turbot and its relatives are nearly as

## FLATFISHES

Series: Percomorpha

Superorder: Acanthopterygii

Order: Pleuronectiformes

About 570 species in about 123 genera and 11 families. Species and families include: **scaldfishes** (family Bothidae), including Peacock flounder or Plate fish (*Bothus lunatus*), European scaldfish (*Arnoglossus laterna*); **turbot** or **lefteye flounders** (family Scophthalmidae), including European turbot (*Psetta maxima*), megrim (*Lepidorhombus whiffiagonis*); **pleuronectids** or **right-eye flounders** (family Pleuronectidae), including plaice (*Pleuronectes platessa*), European flounder (*Platichthys flesus*), Lemon sole (*Microstomus kitt*), halibut (*Hippoglossus hippoglossus*); **psettodids** (family Psettodidae); **soles** (family Soleidae), including European sole (*Solea solea*); **tongue fishes** or **tongue soles** (family Cynoglossidae); **American soles** (family Achiridae), including **Drab** or **Freshwater sole** (*Achirus achirus*).

**DISTRIBUTION** Worldwide in both marine and fresh waters.

**SIZE** Length 4.5cm (1.8in) – 2.5m (8ft); **weight** 2g (0.07oz) –316kg (697lb)

Psettodids Psettodidae

**CONSERVATION STATUS** The halibut is classed as Endangered and the Yellowtail flounder (*Pleuronectes ferrugineus*) is classed as Vulnerable.

---

broad as long, whereas the tongue soles (family Cynoglossidae) are long and narrow. Frequently, flatfish bury themselves, by flicking sand or by wriggling movements of the body, leaving just their eyes and upper operculum (gill cover) exposed. There is a special channel that connects the gill cavities. Water is pumped from the mouth over both sets of gills, but the expired water from the gills on the buried side is diverted through the channel and expired from the exposed side.

Many flatfish are predominantly brown on the colored side, although they often have spots and blotches of orange thus enabling them to blend with the substrate. The pleuronectids, however, are masters of disguise among fish as they can change their color to match the substrate. When

placed on a chequered board some species can reproduce the squares with reasonable accuracy. All flatfish are carnivorous but their methods of catching prey are quite diverse. Scaldfishes, members of the left-eyed family Bothidae, are daytime hunters that feed on other fish. They swim actively after their prey and have very acute vision. Species of soles (family Soleidae) and tongue soles (Cynoglossidae) hunt at night for mollusks and polychaete worms, which they locate by smell. These families of flatfish both have innervated filamentous tubercles instead of scales on the blind side of the head which probably enhance their sense of smell. The pleuronectids are intermediate: some, like the halibut, actively prey on fishes, and others, like plaice, hunt polychaete worms and crustacea, relying on smell and visual acuity to locate their prey.

The majority of flatfishes are marine, but a few species can live in sea or fresh water. The European flounder frequently migrates up rivers to

feed and is found up to 65km (40 miles) inland in the summer, returning to spawn in the sea in the fall. The American flatfish, the Drab sole (*Achirus achirus*) is a freshwater species, often kept by aquarists. It has a large surface area to weight ratio and can suspend itself by surface tension at the water surface. It can also "stick" itself to rocks or the sides of aquaria by creating a vacuum between the underside of its body and the substrate.

There is no obvious difference between the sexes in most species of flatfishes, although among the scaldfishes the male often has some filamentous dorsal and pelvic fin rays or other visible sexual dimorphism.

Many flatfishes, such as Dover sole, flounder, and halibut, are highly esteemed as food fishes, and some have considerable commercial importance. The peculiar structure of flatfish is very convenient for cooks. They cook quickly and evenly. They are easily filleted, and the bones are rarely troublesome.                    BB/KEB/SAF

# Triggerfishes and Allies

**f**ASCINATED BY THEIR BIZARRE FORMS AND *traits, the 1st-century Roman author Pliny the Elder included pufferfishes and oceanic sunfishes in his 37-volume encyclopedia* Naturalis Historiae. *Today, tetraodontiforms make up 5 percent of the world's tropical marine fishes and remain one of the most specialized groups of teleost fishes.*

The Tetraodontiformes are an order of mostly marine fishes that have the teeth fused into a beak. Among their number are poisonous fishes, inflatable fishes, and one of the largest oceanic teleosts. None have scales; instead, they are covered either with spines or with skin so thick that little can penetrate it.

The triggerfishes (Balistidae) are named for the interlocking triggerlike mechanism of their first and second dorsal fin spines; the small second spine must be released before the larger first spine can be depressed. Triggers, with their bony scales, have an easily recognized overall appearance, with their opposite and almost symmetrical dorsal and anal fins actively undulating as the major propulsion mechanism. Many have striking color patterns and inhabit coral reefs. The filefishes (Monacanthidae) are rather similar to triggerfishes, but have very small, rough scales and the dorsal spines are much further forward than in the triggerfishes. Filefishes have extremely small mouths and feed by picking up small invertebrates. Many have an expandable dewlap between the chin and the anal fin.

The boxfishes and cowfishes in the family Ostraciidae have been described as bony cuboid boxes with holes for the mouth, eyes, fins and the vent. Some species also have two small, hornlike processes over the eyes, hence the common name cowfish. The rigid outside skeleton (exoskeleton) is formed by fused bony scutes. Boxfishes are slow-swimming, brightly colored fishes of shallow tropical seas. In case their armor should be thought inadequate against predators, boxfishes can also secrete a virulent toxin if molested. There are about 33 species, some of which can grow up to 60cm (2ft); most are shorter than 30cm (1ft).

The pufferfishes or blowfishes (Tetraodontidae) derive their common names from their ability to inflate the body with water (or air if lifted above water) as a defense tactic. In the inflated state they

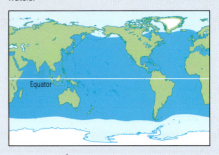

⊙ **Above** *Ocean sunfish (Mola mola) jump from a juvenile length of just 0.6cm (0.25in) up to a length of 3m (9.8ft) when fully developed. California sea lions usually prey upon the juveniles.*

## FACTFILE

### TRIGGERFISHES AND ALLIES

Series: Percomorpha

Superorder: Acanthopterygii

Order: Tetraodontiformes

About 340 species in about 100 genera and 9 families: **spikefishes** (Triacanthodidae); **triple-spines** (Triacanthidae); **triggerfishes** (Balistidae), including Picassofish or humuhumu (*Rhinecanthus aculeatus*); **filefishes** (Monacanthidae); **box-fishes** or **trunkfishes** (Ostraciidae), including cowfishes (genus *Lactoria*); **pufferfishes** or **blow-fishes** (Tetraodontidae), including fugu (genus *Takifugu*) and sharpnose puffers or tobies (genus *Canthigaster*); **porcupinefishes** (Diodontidae); **molas** or **oceanic sunfishes** (Molidae), including Ocean sunfish (*Mola mola*); **Three-toothed puffers** or **pursefishes** (Triodontidae).

**DISTRIBUTION** Worldwide in tropical and temperate waters.

Triggerfishes Balistidae

Porcupinefishes Diodontidae

Three-toothed puffers Triodontidae

Molas or oceanic sunfishes Molidae

**SIZE** Length 2.5cm–3m (1in–9.8ft); **weight** maximum 2,300kg (5,000lb).

**CONSERVATION STATUS** 3 species are classed as Vulnerable, including the Queen triggerfish (*Balistes vetula*).

⊙ **Below** *This night-foraging Black-blotched porcupinefish (Diodon liturosus) is displaying the distinctive defensive form taken by pufferfishes and porcupinefishes. When inflated like this – either with water or air – the lateral spikes of the scutes stick out.*

● **Above** *Among the most highly prized of the aquarium fishes, the lone Clown triggerfish (Balistoides conspicillum) inhabits Indo-Pacific waters. Its bright yellow mouth is thought to deter predators.*

are literal balls that both look inedible and are extremely difficult for a predator to grasp. Untypical of the order, several pufferfishes actually live in freshwater.

The Freshwater pufferfish is a striking black and yellow species widespread throughout the Zaïre system and some other West African rivers. This, and some of the other African freshwater species, are occasionally kept in aquaria, but they are aggressive inhabitants. All pufferfishes are very poisonous but, despite that, some are valued as a delicacy. Particularly in Japan, some species are eaten as *fugu*. The fishes are prepared by specially trained cooks, to avoid any possibility of the toxic parts being eaten or contaminating the flesh. The lethal poison, tetraodotoxin, is found in the fish's gut, in the liver, ovary, and skin. Serious poisoning has resulted from ill-prepared *fugu*.

The oceanic sunfishes (Molidae) are the giants of the order. The Ocean sunfish is the largest species, probably weighing up to 2,300kg (5,000lb). Seen from the side this brownish-blue fish is nearly circular, with the caudal fin reduced to a mere skin-covered fringe, but with the dorsal and anal fins produced into "oars" used for locomotion. It is most often seen lying on its side at the surface, allegedly basking but probably dying. A rare film of a young specimen alive shows that it swims rapidly in an upright position by vigorous sculls of the expanded fins. The fish's diet consists of jellyfish, crustaceans, mollusks, and zooplankton. Below the scaleless skin is a very thick layer of tough gristle. Although not common, the Ocean sunfish lives worldwide in tropical and subtropical waters.                    BB/KEB/SAF

● **Above** *The strange-looking Longhorn cowfish (Lactoria cornuta) has no known sexual dimorphism and feeds on benthic invertebrates by blowing jets of water at the sandy substrate. Adults are solitary, while juveniles are often found in small groups.*

# Seahorses and Allies

**U**NUSUAL AND VERY DISTINCTIVE IN SHAPE, *it is not surprising that many people find it hard to believe that seahorses are actually a type of fish. With their upright posture, horselike head, and strong prehensile tail, they certainly present an unfamiliar picture. However, seahorses are only the better known members of a large diverse group of fishes within the order Syngnathiformes.*

As well as the seahorses, the other members of the order Syngnathiformes – pipefishes, trumpetfishes, cornetfishes, snipefishes, and shrimpfishes – are an almost entirely marine group. Only a few pipefish species live permanently in fresh water. Important unifying characters of these fish are long snouts with a small terminal mouth, the elongation of the first

## FACTFILE

### SEAHORSES AND ALLIES

Series: Percomorpha

Superorder: Acanthopterygii.

Order Syngnathiformes

About 241 species in 60 genera and 6 families: **seahorses** and **pipefishes** (family Syngnathidae), including seahorses (genus *Hippocampus*); **ghost pipefishes** (family Solenostomidae); **trumpetfishes** (family Aulostomidae); **cornetfishes** (family Fistulariidae); **snipefishes** (family Macrorhamphosidae); **shrimpfishes** (family Centriscidae).

**DISTRIBUTION** Worldwide in tropical and temperate seas; some in brackish and fresh water.

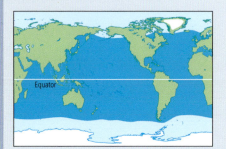

Equator

**SIZE** Length 2cm (0.8in)–1.8m (5.9ft).

Shrimpfishes Centriscidae

**CONSERVATION STATUS** At least 27 species are threatened, including the River pipefish (*Syngnathus watermeyeri*) which is Critically Endangered and the Cape seahorse (*Hippocampus capensis*) which is Endangered; the rest are classed as Vulnerable (20 are seahorses).

Seahorses and pipefishes Syngnathidae

few vertebrae (in the shrimpfish, the first six vertebrae form over three-quarters of the length of the vertebral column) and the peculiar structure of the first dorsal fin which, when present, consists not of fin rays but of prolonged processes associated with the vertebrae.

The shrimpfishes have an extremely compressed body entirely enclosed in thin bony sheets. Only the downturned posterior part of the body is free, allowing tail-fin movement for locomotion. They live in shallow warm seas, sometimes among sea urchin spines where they shelter for protection. The deep-bodied snipefish lives in deeper water and is covered with prickly denticles and a row of scutes on the chest. Apart from the lack of parental care, little is known of their reproductive behavior.

The pipefishes, however, show a remarkable series of reproductive adaptations. The simplest strategy, in the subfamily of nerophiine pipefishes, is for the eggs to be loosely attached to the

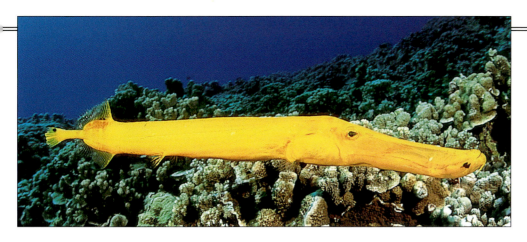

● **Above** *One of three species in the family Aulostomidae, the quirky, slow-moving Chinese trumpetfish (Aulostomus chinensis) uses stealth and camouflage to prey on small fishes and shrimps.*

◐ **Left** *Measuring up to 30cm (12in) long, the Pacific seahorse (Hippocampus ingens) is one of the world's largest seahorse species. Seahorses use their prehensile tails to cling onto plants, corals, or sponges; here, the Pacific seahorse is on a Red gorgonian coral.*

◑ **Below** *In the warm southern oceans lives the Harlequin ghost pipefish (Solenostomus paradoxus). The larger female (pictured) has capelike pelvic fins that form a pouch. Within this, the eggs are attached to short filaments.*

abdomen of the male. A more elaborate condition is present in some syngnathines where the eggs are individually embedded in spongy tissue covering the male's ventral plates. Further protection in other groups is provided by the development of lateral plates partially enclosing the eggs. In all cases it is the male that carries the eggs.

The seahorses – which are merely pipefishes with the head at right angles to the body, a prehensile tail, and a dorsal fin adapted for locomotion – exhibit the ultimate in egg protection. The trend seen in the development of protective plates is continued until a full pouch (or marsupium) is formed, with a single postanal opening. The female has an ovipositor by which the eggs are

placed in the male's pouch until the pouch is full. Apparently this simple act is not always done without mishap, and some eggs may be lost.

Hatching time varies with temperature, the young leaving the pouch between 4 and 6 weeks after the eggs were deposited. In some larger species, the male helps the young to escape by rubbing his abdomen against a rock, in others there are vigorous muscular spasms which may expel the young with considerable velocity. After "birth" the male flushes out his brood sac by expansion and contraction to expel egg remains and general debris to prepare for the next breeding season. This may occur relatively soon, and three broods a year are not unknown.

Over the last several years, increasing focus has been put on the conservation status of seahorses. Destruction of marine seagrass habitats, which are important to most seahorse species, is continuing at an alarming rate worldwide. Added to this is the commercial fishing of seahorses for the Chinese traditional medicine trade, which is thought to exacerbate the problem in some areas. Small-scale fishing also takes place for the curio and aquarium trade. As of May 2004, all seahorse species have had some limited protection through CITES trade regulations, and there are efforts in many countries, including China, to increase farming. Hopefully, habitat destruction will also slow down, helping to protect these marvelous fishes.

Apart from small numbers for the aquarium trade, the other groups of Syngnathiformes have little economic value.                          KEB/SAF

# Other Spiny-finned Fishes

t HE REMAINING ORDERS OF SPINY-FINNED *fishes span a huge variety of forms and ecologies. Groups represented range from the familiar stick-lebacks to the exotic and highly diverse families of the order Scorpaeniformes.*

## Squirrelfishes and Allies

### ORDER BERYCIFORMES

The Beryciformes (with five families) are large-headed marine fishes found in temperate and tropical oceans, many in deep water and cave habitats. Most families have rough scales, a characteristic alluded to in the common name of the Monocentridae – pinecone fishes. This family comprises just four species in two genera (*Mono-centrus* and *Cleidopus*). These rounded little fishes live in small schools in the Indo-Pacific Ocean. The body is covered with irregular bony plates and the soft-rayed dorsal fin is preceded by a few large, alternately angled spines. The pelvic spines

⬤ **Above** *The Pinecone or Pineapple fish (Cleidopus gloriamaris), which inhabits the western Pacific, is covered in a mosaic-like pattern of rough scales. It lives in caves, or around rocky ledges and coral reefs.*

⬤ **Right** *The lugubrious appearance of the bottom-dwelling John Dory (Zeus faber) deters some people from eating it, even though it is an excellent food fish. It can grow to a length of 66cm (26in).*

## Other Spiny-finned Fishes

### Squirrelfishes and Allies
**Order: Beryciformes**

Temperate to tropical oceans. Length maximum 60cm (2ft). About 130 species in 18 genera and 5 families, including: **squirrel-** and **soldierfishes** (Holocentridae); **alfonsinos** (Berycidae); **flashlight fishes** (Anomalopidae); **pinecone fishes** (Monocentridae), including *Monocentrus japonicus.*

### Dories and Allies
**Order: Zeiformes**

Oceans in mid-to deep water. Length maximum about 1m (3.3ft). About 39

species in at least 20 genera and 6 families, including: **dories** (genus *Zeus*; family Zeidae), including John Dory (*Z. faber*); **boarfish** (*Capros aper*).

### Pricklefishes, Whalefishes and Allies
**Order: Stephanoberyciformes**

Oceanic, all oceans except Arctic and Mediterranean. Length maximum 40cm (1.3ft). About 86 species in 28 genera and 9 families, including: **bigscales** and **ridge-heads** (Melamphaidae); **mirapinnids** (Mirapinnidae), including hairyfish (*Mirapinna esau*); **flabby whalefishes** (Cetomimidae)

### Swamp eels and Allies or Synbranchids
**Order: Synbranchiformes**

Mainly freshwater (a few occasionally in brackish waters) of C and S America, Africa, Asia, Indo-Australian archipelago, and NW Australia. Length maximum 1.5m (5ft). About 87 species in 12 genera and 3 families, including: **swamp eels** (Synbranchidae), including Marbled swamp eel (*Synbranchus marmoratus*), Rice eel (*Monopterus albus*); **spiny eels** (Mastacembelidae), including the Lesser spiny eel (*Macrognathus aculeatus*); **chaudhuriids** (Chaudhuriidae), including *Nagaichthys filipes*. The Blind swamp eel (*Ophisternon infernale*) is Endangered.

### Sticklebacks
**Order: Gasterosteiformes**

Worldwide in marine, brackish and fresh water. Length maximum 20cm (8in). About 216 species in 11 genera and 5 families including: **sticklebacks** (Gasterosteidae), including Brook stickleback (*Culea inconstans*), Fifteen-spined stickleback (*Spinachia spinachia*), Four-spined stickleback (*Apeltes quadracus*), Nine-spined stickleback (*Pungitius pungitius*), Three-spined stickleback (*Gasterosteus aculeatus*); **seamoths** (Pegasidae); **Armored stickleback** (*Indostomus paradoxus*; only species in the family Indostomidae);

**tubesnouts** (Aulorhynchidae), including the Tube-snout (*Aulorhynchus flavidus*) and Tubenose (*Aulichthys japonicus*). *Pungitius hellenicus* is Critically Endangered and *Pegasus laternarius* is Vulnerable.

### Mailcheeked fishes
**Order: Scorpaeniformes**

Worldwide in sea and fresh waters (though distribution more disjunct in fresh waters). Length maximum 2m (6.5ft). Nearly 1,300 species in about 266 genera and 25 families, including: **flying gurnards** (Dactylopteridae); **scorpion-fishes** (Scorpaenidae), including lionfish (*Pterois volitans*), Atlantic redfish (*Sebastes marinus*), stonefishes (genus *Synanceia*), including Indo-Pacific stonefish (*S. veru-cosa*); **sea robins** or **gurnards** (Triglidae); **sablefishes** (Anoplopomatidae); **sculpins** (Cottidae), including bullhead (*Cottus gobio*), Shorthorn sculpin (*Myoxocephalus scorpius*); **armored sea robins** and **pogges** (Agonidae); **lumpfishes** (Cyclopteridae); **Australian prowfishes** (Pataecidae). 10 species are threatened – 3 are Critically Endangered, including the Pygmy sculpin (*Cottus paulus*); 2 are Endangered, including the Acadian redfish (*Sebastes fasciatus*); and 5 are Vulnerable, including the St. Helena deepwater scorpionfish (*Pontinus nigropunctatus*). The Utah Lake sculpin (*Cottus echinatus*) is now Extinct.

**Squirrelfishes and allies**
Pinecone fishes
Monocentridae

**Dories and allies**
Dories
Zeidae

**Pricklefishes, Whale-fishes and Allies**
Bigscales and ridgeheads
Melamphaidae

**Swamp eels and Allies**
Mastacembelidae

**Sticklebacks**
Sticklebacks
Gasterosteidae

Seamoths
Pegasidae

Armored stickleback
Indostomidae

**Mailcheeked fishes**
Stonefishes
Synanceiidae

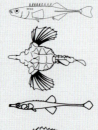

Australian prowfishes
Pataecidae

**FACTFILE**

**OTHER SPINY-FINNED FISHES**

Series: Percomorpha

Superorder: Acanthopterygii.

Orders: Beryciformes, Zeiformes, Stephanoberyciformes, Synbranchiformes, Gasterosteiformes, Scorpaeniformes

At least 1,858 species in about 355 genera, 53 families and 6 orders.

The best known of all members of Beryciformes are the squirrel- and soldierfishes in the family Holocentridae. Most of the 66 known species are twilight- and night-active coral reef inhabitants. During the day they stay in caves and crevices on the reef, where they stand out with their bright red color patterns and are easily spotted by sport divers. They are hardy aquarium fishes, but too voracious to be really popular. Being fairly small and very bony fishes, most species are not in great demand as food, although they are found in fish markets worldwide.

## Dories and Allies
ORDER ZEIFORMES

The order Zeiformes comprises deep-bodied, extremely compressed fishes. The most familiar species is the John Dory, which has pronounced protrusile jaws and feeds on small fishes and crustaceans. The origin of its common name is a subject of much debate. Some argue that it derives from the French *jaune d'orée* (with a yellow edge) in allusion to the yellowish color of the body. In some countries, its common name is the vernacular for "St. Peter's Fish" (*Saint-Pierre* in French, *pez de San Pedro* in Spanish). This name alludes to the single dark blotch on each side, which are romantically thought to represent the thumb and forefinger prints of St. Peter, who allegedly took tribute money from its mouth. The same distinction has, however, been accorded to the haddock in other countries (even though the biblical incident that is the source of the story took place in the Sea of Galilee, which is freshwater!). The John Dory is found in the eastern Atlantic and Mediterranean, and the same or possibly distinct, related species also occur in the Indian Ocean and the Pacific. The fish yields excellent, bone-free fillets of white flesh, and is particularly highly prized in the Mediterranean and Australia.

are massive and erectile. Although pinecone fishes do not grow to more than 23cm (9in) long, they are commercially viable in Japan, where they are eaten. They have two small luminous organs on each side of the lower jaw with colonies of bacteria providing the light. The blue-green light can be "switched" off and on by closing and opening the mouth.

Luminous organs are also present under the eye in the nocturnal flashlight fishes of the family Anomalopidae. Each organ is a peculiar flat white in daylight but at night glows with a blue-green light. The luminous organs blink on and off when functioning and are controlled in some species by rotating the entire gland, and in others by covering it with a eyelid-like membrane. The light is turned on and off in repeated patterns, typically with some 10 seconds light and 5 seconds darkness. The fishes probably have three main advantages from this: first, the light helps the fishes to keep together in the otherwise total darkness;

second, the light probably attracts planktonic crustaceans that the fishes feed on; and finally, the light confuses potential predators so they miss their prey. The flashlight fishes occur on reefs in the Red Sea, Indo-Pacific and the Eastern Pacific Ocean, in schools from 20 to 50 specimens, normally in depths below 30 meters (c. 100ft). Apart from a very limited demand for the aquarium trade, they are of no commercial importance although, if caught, the luminous gland is removed and used as bait in subsistence fisheries.

The family Berycidae contains mid- to deepwater, large-eyed species with compressed bodies, commonly known as alfonsinos. Most species are red or pink, and are therefore sometimes sold under the confusing names of "redfish" or "red bream." The flesh is excellent and fetches a good price at market. The two very similar species, the Splendid alfonsino (*Beryx splendens*) and the Alfonsino (*B. decadactylus*), are found together circumglobally in tropical and subtropical seas.

## Pricklefishes, Whalefishes, and Allies

ORDER STEPHANOBERYCIFORMES

The order Stephanoberyciformes (of which some families are sometimes placed in a separate order, Cetomimiformes) is poorly known, but contains fascinating oceanic deepwater fishes. The bigscale fishes or ridgeheads of the family Melamphaidae, of which there are some 33 species, are especially notable. They are small (maximum 15cm/6in) subcylindrical fishes with large heads, blunt short snouts and long, abruptly narrowed caudal peduncles. The scales are typically very large and clearly distinguishable. Another peculiar member of the order is the hairyfish of the family Mirapinnidae, characterized by a short, hairlike pile that covers the body. It also has two halves of caudal fin overlapping and large, winglike pelvic fins. The species is thought to spend most of its time in very deep water, but is so far known from a single 5.5cm (2.2in) specimen caught at the surface north of the Azores.

## Swamp Eels and Allies

ORDER SYNBRANCHIFORMES

The order Synbranchiformes consist of eel-like freshwater fishes. The swamp eels (family Synbranchidae) occur in South and Central America, West Africa, southern Asia, and Australia. Their common name derives from their shape, and from the fact that they often live in poorly oxygenated waters. Instead of having a gill opening on each side of the head there is a single, common slit on the underside. In some species the gill chamber is divided internally into two chambers by a tissue dividing wall (septum). Often the gill chamber is distensible and, by filling it with water, the fish can "breathe" while traveling overland. Species in stagnant water absorb atmospheric air either through a modified section of the gut, well provided with blood vessels, or via lunglike chambers extending from the branchial cavity. In both cases the air is taken in through the mouth.

At least one swamp eel species, the Marbled swamp eel (*Synbranchus marmoratus*), can burrow in the mud and estivate much like the lungfish, so

avoiding droughts. Pectoral and pelvic fins are absent, and the dorsal and anal fins are reduced to mere ridges of skin without fin rays.

The Rice eel from Asia has colonized irrigation ditches in paddyfields. They grow to 1m (3.3ft) long and are an important source of food, not least because they can stay alive, hence fresh, for

a long time if kept moist. The male makes a bubble nest, where the female lays the eggs. They and the newly hatched young are guarded by the male.

The family Mastacembelidae, or spiny eels, are also greatly valued in some areas as food fishes. More colorful species are kept as aquarium fishes. Spiny eels are found in a wide variety of habitats, ranging from the clear East African inland seas to quite swampy areas. Many are airbreathers and utilize this ability to survive in poorly aerated water or mud. Like many other species, the Lesser spiny eel spends the daytime in a mud burrow, excavated by rocking and wriggling movements that submerge it at a constant rate, leaving only the tips of the nostrils protruding.

⟡ **Right** Representative synbranchid species: **1** The Lesser spiny eel (Macrognathus aculeatus) inhabits large rivers in Southeast Asia; **2** The Rice eel (Monopterus albus) of southern Asia burrows into the mud in dry periods. It is valued as a food fish.

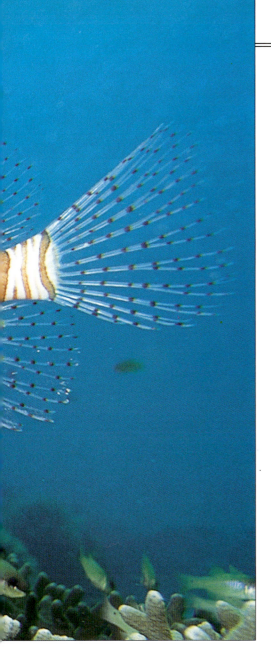

◁ **Left** *The Red lionfish (Pterois volitans), a member of the order Scorpaeniformes, is a formidable predator. Hunting at night, it uses its fanned-out pectoral fins to corner small prey, which it stuns with its venomous dorsal spines before swallowing them whole.*

▶ **Right** *The body of the Short dragonfish (Eurypegasus draconis), a species of sea moth, is protected by bony plates with a reticulated pattern that give the fish excellent camouflage against rocky substrates. It is widespread in oceans from the Red Sea east to the central Pacific.*

## Sticklebacks
### ORDER GASTEROSTEIFORMES

The most commonly known fishes of the order Gasterosteiformes are the sticklebacks. The "humble" stickleback is found in most fresh, brackish and sometimes coastal waters throughout Eurasia and northern America. It is highly variable in form, and some authors consider there to be a large species complex rather than a single species, *Gasterosteus aculeatus*. Although mostly "three-spined," two- and four-spined individuals occur. There are populations in Canada that never have pelvic fins. Freshwater forms usually have fewer bony scutes than brackish or marine forms. Generally, sticklebacks never grow to more than 7.5cm (3in) long but in lakes in the Queen Charlotte Islands, off the coast of British Columbia, there are dark pigmented forms that grow to 20cm (8in) long.

The Fifteen-spined stickleback is a solitary marine species, living in marine water on the European Atlantic coast. The Nine-spined stickleback (which usually has 10 spines) has at most only a few small scutes. It is nearly as widespread as the Three-spined but rarely enters brackish or saline waters. Two genera are confined to northern America: the Brook stickleback (usually with 5 spines), which is fairly widespread and may even be found in coastal waters of reduced salinity in the north; and the Four-spined stickleback, which only occurs in the northeastern part of northern America. Despite the presence of protective spines on the back and in the pelvic fins, sticklebacks form an important part of the food chain and are eaten by larger fish, birds and otters.

The tubesnouts are primitive relations of the stickleback found in the cooler waters either side of the North Pacific. The American species known as the Tube-snout, which resembles the European Fifteen-spined stickleback, lives in huge shoals. No nest is built but the female lays sticky eggs along the stipe of the giant kelp (large seaweed) which is first bent over and then glued down. The male defends the eggs. Its Japanese relative, the Tubenose, is poorly known, but is reputed to lay its eggs inside a seasquirt (*Cynthia*).

Related to sticklebacks, but superficially very different, are the sea moths (Pegasidae). They are small, tropical marine fishes with a body encased in bony scutes and variously developed snouts. There are only five species, in two genera. Because of their curious shape, and the fact that the shape is maintained when the fish is gutted and dried, they are often sold as curios in the Far East. Apart from the fact that they are bottom-living egglayers and eat small invertebrates like worms and crustaceans, little is known about their biology.

In Burma, Cambodia, western Malaysia, and Thailand, a peculiar species known as the Armored stickleback is found. It lives in freshwater swamps with soft bottoms and dense vegetation. The systematic position of this species has been much discussed. Superficially the species resembles the

## THE RED BREAST OF THE THREE-SPINED STICKLEBACK

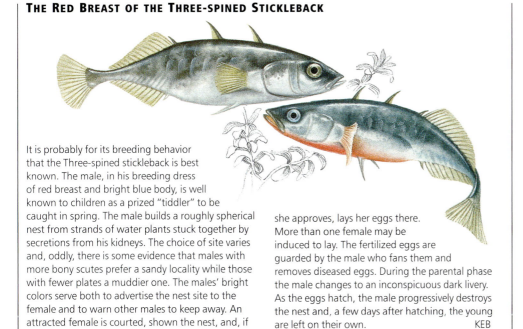

It is probably for its breeding behavior that the Three-spined stickleback is best known. The male, in his breeding dress of red breast and bright blue body, is well known to children as a prized "tiddler" to be caught in spring. The male builds a roughly spherical nest from strands of water plants stuck together by secretions from his kidneys. The choice of site varies and, oddly, there is some evidence that males with more bony scutes prefer a sandy locality while those with fewer plates a muddier one. The males' bright colors serve both to advertise the nest site to the female and to warn other males to keep away. An attracted female is courted, shown the nest, and, if she approves, lays her eggs there. More than one female may be induced to lay. The fertilized eggs are guarded by the male who fans them and removes diseased eggs. During the parental phase the male changes to an inconspicuous dark livery. As the eggs hatch, the male progressively destroys the nest and, a few days after hatching, the young are left on their own.                                            KEB

above-mentioned tubesnouts, but various morphological evidence suggests that it could have its closest relatives among the Syngnathiformes. Currently, it is generally thought to be most closely related to the sea moths.

## Mailcheeked Fishes

### ORDER SCORPAENIFORMES

Mailcheeked fishes or Scorpaeniformes are an order of predominantly shallow-water marine fish, but the order also contains some notable deepwater species, like the Atlantic redfish that is found off the North-Atlantic coasts at 100–1,000m (330–3,300ft) depth. Like the redfish, many other Scorpaeniformes species are also predominantly reddish in color. Otherwise, they have a general appearance rather similar to that of the Perciformes – spiny first dorsal fin, ctenoid scales, spines on the head and pelvic fins well forward). The order contains about 25 families, including the sea robins or gurnards, the fascinatingly beautiful coral-reef lionfishes, the extremely poisonous stonefishes of Australasia, the sculpins, and the armored sea robins and pogges.

Some sculpins, species of the family Cottidae, are common in fresh water. The large head of *Cottus gobio* has given it the name bullhead in the United Kingdom. The vast majority of the approximately 300 sculpin species known are, however, marine. The greatest diversity occur along the North Pacific coastline, but there are also many species in Atlantic coastal areas. Most occur in shallow areas, but a few are known from waters as deep as 2,000m (6,600ft). Although some species are eaten, mainly in soup, hardly any have much commercial value. In Greenland, large specimens of the Shorthorn sculpin (*Myoxocephalus scorpius*, which grows to 60cm/2ft) are cooked in a similar way to cod, and are eaten with pleasure.

The flying gurnards (family Dactylopteridae) are not gurnards, neither do they fly. The myth that they are capable of flight arises from their greatly expanded, colorful, fanlike pectoral fins. The actual purpose of these fins may well be to frighten away potential predators. The "flying"

gurnards are heavily built, bottom-living fish with a heavy, bony skull. They spend most of their time "walking" along sandy bottoms, using their transformed, fingerlike pelvic fins to probe for crustaceans, mollusks and worms that hide in the substrate, as is known also in the true gurnards or sea robins (family Triglidae).

Most scorpionfishes have venomous fin spines that can inflict nasty wounds on humans, as many fishermen will know from experience. In some species the venom can have lethal effects. This is particularly true for the Indo-Pacific stonefish, which possesses the strongest venom and most sophisticated venom apparatus that is known from any fish. Attached to the 9th through 13th dorsal fin spine are large venom glands, which at the slightest pressure squirt venom through a slit in the fin spine into the victim who carelessly handles or accidentally steps on the well camouflaged, bottom-living fish. Stings cause immediate burning pains, often followed by inflammation of lymph glands, breathing difficulties, vomiting, and muscular spasms. Deaths have occurred, and even in mild cases, the recovery period may last several months. KEB/SAF

⬇ **Below** *The venom in the dorsal fin spines of the Reef stonefish* (Synanceia verrucosa) *is highly toxic and has occasionally caused human fatalities. Even so, the fish still falls prey to the larger sharks and rays.*

# Oarfishes and Allies

**k**NOWN AS "KING OF THE HERRINGS" BY *northern Europeans, the oarfish (Regalecus glesne) and other Lampridiformes have found a place in folklore as harbingers of abundance or paucity of food fish. Previously placed within the series Percomorpha, the Lampriformes are now considered to occupy their own superorder, Lampridiomorpha. Lampridiform fish are scarce, spectacular in color, weirdly shaped, and cause great excitement when washed ashore.*

The oarfish is a silvery, ribbonlike fish, with a red dorsal fin the length of its body. The head profile resembles that of a horse. The anterior rays of the dorsal fin are elongated like a mane and the scarlet pelvic fins are very long with bladelike expansions at the end (hence its common name). The caudal fin is reduced to a few

⬥ **Above 1** *The extraordinary oarfish (Regalecus glesne), the longest of all fishes, is rarely seen;* **2** *The Opah or Spotted moonfish (Lampris guttatus) is sometimes taken as by-catch in long-line fishing for tuna.*

streamers. This spectacular fish, which grows to over 9m (30ft) long, is thought to have been the origin of many sea-serpent stories, since they often mention a red mane.

The oarfish, one of only two species in the family Regalecidae, is found worldwide and probably lives in moderately deep water when healthy (those at the surface are usually moribund). Almost nothing is known of its biology. Examples caught with a full stomach reveal a diet of small crustaceans. Largely on theoretical grounds, it has been convincingly reasoned that the oarfish swims at an angle of 45°, with the long red mane streaming out horizontally. The blades of the pelvic fins bear a large number of chemoreceptor cells. The pelvic fins are now regarded as chemical probes that are held out in front of the animal so that the fish can detect its prey before it reaches it, and organize its respiratory cycle for maximum efficiency in sucking in the small crustaceans. Locomotion is probably by undulations of the dorsal fin, producing an upright attitude and relatively sedate passage through the water.

As regards body shape, there are two distinct groups of Lampridiformes. The Lophotidae, Stylephoridae, Regalecidae, and Trachipteridae have ribbon-shaped bodies; propulsion is effected largely by the dorsal fin and the skin has prickles or tubercles whose function is to lessen water drag. The other group contains the family Veliferidae

and the opahs or moonfishes (Lamprididae). The body is deep and propulsion is by enlarged, winglike pectoral fins powered by powerful red muscles attached to an enlarged shoulder girdle.

The coloration of the opahs is extraordinary. Their back is azure, which merges into silver on the belly. The sides have white spots and the whole is overlaid with a salmon-pink iridescence that fades quickly after death. The fins are bright scarlet. Despite being toothless and of a seemingly cumbersome shape, they feed on midwater fishes and squid, which testifies to the swimming efficiency of the winglike pectoral fins. There is one worldwide species, which reaches 1.5m (5ft) in length and over 90kg (200lb) in weight.

The ribbonlike lophotids are known as crest fishes because the bones of the top of the head project forward over the eyes and in front of the mouth like a dorsal keel. The expansion of the bones is used as a base to attach some of the muscles that work the locomotory dorsal fin. Apart from their surrealistic shape, they also possess an ink sac that lies close to the intestine and discharges via the cloaca. Very few undamaged specimens have been found, but they grow to over 1.2m (4ft) long. Their distribution is uncertain, but they have been found off Japan and South Africa.

The ribbonfishes (family Trachipteridae) have the silvery body and fins of their relatives as a

color pattern. Some add dark spots and bars to this pattern. As with many of the long-bodied lampridiforms, the swimbladder is reduced and the skeleton correspondingly lightened, thus achieving neutral buoyancy. When adult, the caudal fin consists of a few rays of the upper lobe, elongated and turned upwards at right angles to the body. The ribbonfishes' lifestyle is thought to be like that of other members of the order.     KEB/SAF

---

**FACTFILE**

## OARFISHES AND ALLIES

Superorder: Lampridiomorpha

Order: Lampridiformes

About 19 species in 12 genera and 7 families. Families include: **crestfishes** (Lophotidae); **ribbonfishes** (Trachipteridae): **opahs** or **moonfishes** (Lamprididae); **oarfishes** (Regalecidae).

**DISTRIBUTION** Oceans worldwide.

Ribbonfishes Trachipteridae     Opahs or moon-fishes Lampridae

**SIZE** Length 30cm (12in) – 11m (36ft); **weight** up to 270kg (600lb)

267

# Bichirs, Coelacanths, and Lungfishes

**t**HESE THREE VERY DISTINCT GROUPS OF *fishes are grouped together here solely on the grounds that all are anachronistic – in other words, they all appear to belong to past times, rather than the present. The popular contradiction in terms "living fossils" may be an appealing cliché to describe them, but does not really advance our understanding of their relationships.*

Fossil coelacanths first appeared in rocks of the Devonian period (417–354 million years ago) and continued to occur until about 70 million years ago when, along with the dinosaurs, they disappeared from the fossil record. Since the coelacanth was rediscovered in 1938 and again in 1952 around two hundred have been transferred to scientific institutions but, although its anatomy has been detailed, little is known of its biology and its taxonomic relationships are still an unresolved controversy. Indeed, in a symposium volume published by the California Academy of Sciences in 1979 there are several contradictory papers each advocating different groups of fishes as the closest relatives of the coelacanth.

## Bichirs

### POLYPTERIDAE

The bichirs are endemic to the freshwaters of Africa. The family contains just two genera, the true bichirs with, at least, ten species in one genus (*Polypterus*) and the Rope or Reedfish – the sole representative of its genus (*Erpetoichthys*). To which other major group of fishes the bichirs are related is a source of much debate. Almost every group has been suggested at one time or another over the last century.

Bichirs are primitive-looking fishes. They have thick, diamond-shaped scales that articulate by a "peg and socket" joint, gular (throat) plates, and an upper jaw that is fixed to the skull. As a group, they retain a surprising number of primitive features, ranging from the tail skeleton, to the possession of two lungs (see below). Yet their fossil record is scanty, the oldest known remains coming from deposits of the Cretaceous period (142–65 million years ago). All the fossils are in Africa, largely within the present area of distribution.

True bichir species owe their generic name (*Polypterus*, from ancient Greek, means "many-fins") to the row of small finlets on the back, each consisting of a stout spine supporting a series of rays. This arrangement is sometimes referred to as a "flag and pole" system – hence the group's alternative name, flagfishes. The pectoral fin has a

**◐ Above** *True to its common name, the Ornate bichir (Polypterus ornatipinnis) has an intricate marbling on its skin. This species is found throughout the basin of the Congo River in Central Africa, and in Lake Tanganyika.*

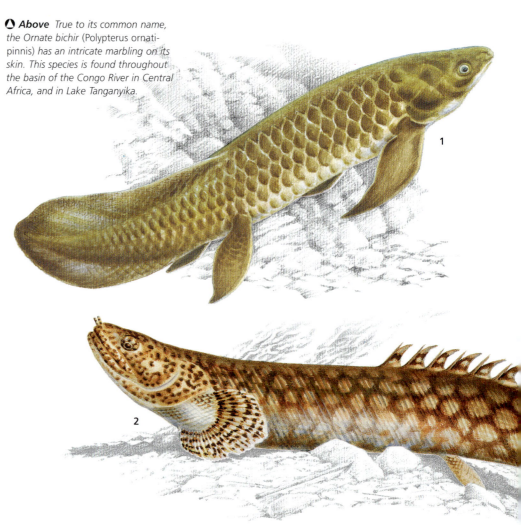

stout, scale-covered base and, although the tail is symmetrical in appearance, its internal structure retains the primitive, upturned, heterocercal condition in which the upper lobe skeleton is longer than the lower one, as in sharks.

Bichirs live in sluggish fresh waters and their swimbladders have a highly vascularized lining that is used as a lung, enabling them to live in poorly oxygenated conditions. Shallow swampy waters, such as those produced when rivers overflow, are preferred for spawning, during which several hundred eggs are laid among vegetation and abandoned. These usually hatch in less than a week, yielding young bichirs with well-formed external gills, another primitive characteristic.

Bichirs are largely nocturnal fishes, not known for an active lifestyle. At night they feed on smaller fishes, amphibians, or large aquatic invertebrates. Within Africa, they are confined to the tropical regions in drainages emptying into the Atlantic Ocean or the Mediterranean. Living bichirs generally grow no longer than 75cm (2.5ft), although the Congo bichir (Polypterus endlicheri congicus) can attain a maximum length close to 1m (3.2ft). However, to judge from the size of the scales, some fossil species might have been twice as long.

The Reedfish is a slender, eel-like version of the true bichirs. It lacks pelvic fins and the subsidiary rays on the isolated spines. A much smaller species than most bichirs (it can grow only to around 40cm/16in), it is found exclusively in reedy areas in coastal regions of West Africa near the Gulf of Guinea. It appears to eat mostly aquatic invertebrates.

## Coelacanths
### COELACANTHIDAE
Much of the biology of the coelacanth has to be inferred from its anatomy and catching records, since no specimens have been kept alive for long.

Apart from the mysterious first catch (see In Search of Old Fourlegs), all subsequent coelacanths had, until recently, been caught off the islands of Grand Comore and Anjouan at depths of 70–400m (230–1,300ft). Most had been caught during the first few months of the year in the monsoon season. These two islands are composed of highly absorbent volcanic rock and it has been argued, with some possible corroboration from its kidney structure, that the coelacanth lives in areas where fresh rainwater leaks out into the sea. In 2000, the range of this species (Latimeria chalumnae), was dramatically expanded, with the direct observation of some live specimens within the Sodwana Bay Jesser Canyon of the St. Lucia Marine Reserve off the northern Kwazulu-Natal coast of South Africa.

The coelacanth has the build of a lurking predator and fish remains have been found in the stomach. It has very large eggs: 20 about the size of a tennis ball (around 9cm/3.5in across, making them the largest fish eggs known) were found in a 1.6m (5.3ft) long female. The only known embryos, which still had yolk sacs and were therefore probably not close to birth, were more than 32cm (12.5in) long and it has been estimated that the gestation period is well over a year. The females are larger than the males and can live for at least 11 years.

Although L. chalumnae and its recently (1997) discovered relative, L. menadoensis, are superficially similar to the last known fossilized coelacanths, there are some interesting anatomical differences. In the present-day coelacanths, unlike their Cretaceous forebears, the swimbladder is nonfunctional and is filled with fat. The fish, however, retain the peculiar triple tail, the lobed paired fins, a skull with a hinge in it, and the rough cosmoid scales of their fossil ancestors.

It might perhaps be supposed that the discovery

**FACTFILE**

## BICHIRS, COELACANTHS, & LUNGFISHES
Orders: Polypteriformes, Coelacanthiformes, Ceratodontiformes, Lepidosireniformes

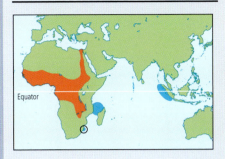

Equator

### ORDER POLYPTERIFORMES

**BICHIRS OR POLYPTERIDS**
Family Polypteridae
10 species in 2 genera. Freshwaters in Africa. **Length** maximum c. 1m (3.3ft), but most smaller. Species and genera include: bichirs (Polypterus spp.) and Reedfish or Ropefish (Erpetoichthys calabaricus).

### ORDER COELACANTHIFORMES

**COELACANTHS**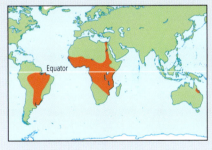
Family Coelacanthidae
2 species in 1 genus: Latimeria chalumnae and L. menadoensis. Oceans off Comoro Islands (between Madagascar and Africa), Eastern Cape and Kwazulu-Natal (South Africa), NW Sulawesi (Indonesia). **Length** maximum 1.8m (5.9ft). **Conservation status:** L. chalumnae is classed as Critically Endangered.

Equator

### SUPERORDER CERATODONTIMORPHA
ORDERS CERATODONTIFORMES, LEPIDOSIRENIFORMES

**LUNGFISHES** Families Ceratodontidae, Lepidosirenidae and Protopteridae
6 species in 3 genera. Freshwaters of Brazil, Paraguay, Africa, and Queensland (Australia). **Length** maximum 2m (6.5ft). Species and genera include: **Australian lungfish** (Neoceratodus forsteri), **South American lungfish** (Lepidosiren paradoxa), and **African lungfish** (Protopterus spp.).

Australian lungfishes
Family Ceratodontidae

South American lungfishes
Family Lepidosirenidae

African lungfishes
Family Protopteridae

**◁ Left** Representative species of lungfishes, bichirs, and coelacanths: **1** Australian lungfish (Neoceratodus forsteri), the most stout-bodied of the lungfishes; **2** Short-finned bichir (Polypterus palmas); **3** Coelacanth (Latimeria chalumnae) – once the sole coelacanth species, a Southeast Asian relative has now been found.

of such "anachronistic" organisms would resolve many disputes about evolution, yet, in truth, these extraordinary fishes only generate more questions: Why, for example, have some anatomical changes occurred but not others? Why, if they have kidney similarities with freshwater fishes, do they live in the sea? How long do the embryos take to develop? How are the eggs fertilized internally? Does cannibalism between embryos exist, as has been suggested? Are populations really as widely scattered as they appear to be? And how can we explain the huge geographical gap that exists between the two species?

## Lungfishes

LEPIDOSIRENIDAE, PROTOPTERIDAE, CERATODONTIDAE

The three genera and six species of lungfishes are now confined to the freshwaters of the Amazon, West and Central Africa and the Mary and Burnett Rivers in the far southeast of Queensland in Australia. Their fossils, by contrast, are found in rocks from Greenland to Antarctica and Australia. As with some other ancient fishes, we know that they represent an important organizational advance somewhere in the evolution from aquatic vertebrates to land-living vertebrates, but exactly how they fit in is still a matter of some uncertainty.

Living lungfishes are grouped into three families: the South American lungfish (*Lepidosiren paradoxa*) has its own family, the Lepidosirenidae, while the African *Protopterus* (4 species) form the Protopteridae. The Australian species, *Neoceratodus forsteri*, is the sole representative of its family, the Ceratodontidae.

*Neoceratodus* retains more of the primitive features of its Devonian ancestors than do its relatives. It has large, overlapping scales and lobed, paired fins fringed with rays that retain the primitive characteristic of being more numerous than their supporting bones. The dorsal, caudal, and anal fins are all joined up. Unlike its relatives, though, the Australian lungfish cannot survive

drought and will die if it is out of water for any length of time. The lungs open by a ventral slit in the gullet or oesophagus; the air tube then runs dorsally (namely, along the back) so that the partially two-lobed lungs lie dorsal in a similar position as the swimbladder in bony fishes, but not like the lungs in other vertebrates, which lie ventral to the gut or alimentary tract. The Australian lungfish, while being able to breathe atmospheric air in adverse conditions, normally uses its gills for respiration.

Lungfishes are carnivores, and when fully grown (about 1.5m, 5ft) will eat large invertebrates, frogs, and small fish. The teeth consist of a pair of sharp plates in each jaw, which work in a shearing action.

Reproduction in the Australian lungfish has been observed in shallow water in August when, after a rudimentary courtship consisting of the male nudging the female, the eggs are scattered

over a small area of dense weed and fertilized. There is no indication of any further parental concern. Although native to two small river systems, the interest in this rare species is such that stocks have been transplanted into other Australian rivers. At least three of the introductions have been successful and the fish have bred.

The biology of the African species is better known. At least two, the African lungfish (*Protopterus annectens*) from west and southern Africa and the Spotted lungfish (*P. dolloi*) from the Zaïre basin, are known to survive drought by a type of summer hibernation (estivation) in cocoons. The widespread East African species, the Ethiopian or Speckle-bellied lungfish (*P. aethiopicus*) is thought to be capable of estivating, but rarely does so in the wild as its waters are less likely to dry up. The same applies to *P. amphibius*.

African lungfish are more elongate than their Australian relatives. Small scales cover the body and the paired fins are long and threadlike. They are aggressive predators and, in the case of the Ethiopian lungfish, can grow to more than 2m (6.5ft) long. The lungs are paired and lie in a ventral position, as in terrestrial vertebrates – and in

⊙ **Below** *Estivation in the African lungfish.* **1** *As the waters evaporate, the fish burrows into the mud;* **2** *It then turns back on itself and* **3** *settles in the base of the burrow with its tail wrapped around itself;* **4** *Finally, it secretes a mucous sheath that stops it drying out.*

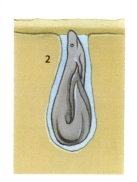

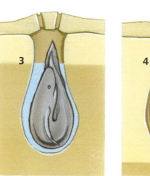

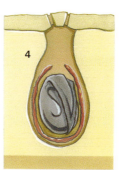

**◑ Above** *Inhabiting swampy floodplains with oxygen-poor waters in the basins of the Amazon and Paraná rivers, the South American lungfish (Lepidosiren paradoxa) satisfies its oxygen requirements by breathing air at the surface.*

sharp contrast to their Australian relative. The use of lungs in breathing requires a four-chambered heart, so, unlike bony fish, the lungfishes' auricle (upper heart chambers) and ventricle (lower heart chambers) are functionally divided by a partition so that blood is circulated to the lungs as a bypass from the normal body and gill circulation – as happens in mammals, humans included.

All the African lungfishes build nests. In the Ethiopian lungfish, it often takes the form of a deep hole dug by the male, which then guards the newly-hatched young for about two months. As well as driving away would-be predators, he also aerates the water in the nest. The nest of the Spotted lungfish is much more elaborate and has an underwater entrance. The terminal brood chamber in which the eggs develop may be in swampy ground and may be open at the top. Aeration vents are also built into it by the male.

The larvae of African (and South American) lungfish have external gills, the degree of development varying with the amount of oxygen in the water. At metamorphosis (i.e. the change from the juvenile to the adult form), the external gills are usually resorbed and the lung and gill respiration takes over. Occasionally, however, vestigial (tiny) external gills remain throughout life.

*Protopterus annectens* lives in swamps and rivulets that are prone to drying out, often for months on end. In order to survive such harsh conditions, the fish burrows into a tube that it excavates in the soft mud as the water level falls. Using its mouth and general body pressure, the lungfish widens out the bottom of the tube until it can turn around. As the water drops below the opening of the tube the fish then closes the mouth of the tube with a plug of porous mud, curls up in the lower chamber and secretes large quantities of a special mucus that hardens to form an encasing cocoon with only an opening for the mouth. The cocoon retains moisture while the porous mud plug allows breathing. During estivation, as in hibernation, the metabolic rate is greatly reduced and the basic energy needed for

survival comes from the breakdown of muscle tissue. In this state, lungfishes have been known to survive four years of drought, although, normally, an incarceration of only a few months would be necessary. Eventually, when the rains return and the river floods again, the waters dissolve the cocoon and the fish emerges.

The South American lungfish (*Lepidosiren paradoxa*) looks similar to the African species, with an eel-like body and feeler-like pectoral fins, but with fleshier-based, wider pelvic fins. It also possesses the general characteristics of a cartilaginous vertebral column and a common opening for the waste products, eggs and sperm.

*Lepidosiren* is able to estivate, but its refuge is much simpler than that of its African relatives and no cocoon is produced. An elaborate nest is made in the breeding season, during which time the pelvic fins of the male bear a large number of blood-rich filaments. The function of these is unknown, but hypotheses have included the release of oxygen into the water of the nest, or alternatively, that the filaments act as supplementary gills to reduce the number of visits to the surface while the fish is guarding its young.      KEB/JD

# IN SEARCH OF 'OLD FOURLEGS'

## The discovery of the Coelacanth

IT IS UNIVERSALLY ACCEPTED IN BIOLOGY THAT the absence of records does not imply certainty of extinction. The coelacanths represent perfect examples of this.

On a hot summer's day in 1938 Captain Goosen's boat, *Nerine*, docked at East London in South Africa. At that time, Marjorie Courtenay-Latimer was the curator at the East London Museum and local skippers were accustomed to her frequent visits to the port to obtain fish specimens for the museum. At 10.30 a.m. on 22 December she was telephoned and told that the *Nerine* had returned with some specimens for her. Among the catch was a large blue fish with flipper-like fins and a triple tail which she had never seen before. After several attempts she found a taxi driver willing to take her and her 1.5m (5ft) long, oily, smelly prize back to the museum. There, after searching through reference books, the nearest she could come to identifying the fish was as "a lung fish gone barmy."

Realizing that her find was important, she tried to contact Dr J. L. B. Smith (whose name will be forever linked with the fish), the ichthyologist at Rhodes University, Grahamstown. It was then mid-

summer in South Africa and temperatures were high. How, therefore, was this important scientific find to be preserved? The local mortuary refused to have the corpse in its cold store, so finally, a local taxidermist, Mr R. Centre, although admitting inexperience in fish-stuffing, agreed to help. He wrapped the body in cloth, soaked it in formalin and placed it in a makeshift ichthyosarcophagus ("fish coffin").

On 26 December there was still no reply from Smith. An examination of the body showed that the formalin had not penetrated and that the internal organs were rotting. Pragmatism dictated that the decaying parts should be thrown away and what could be preserved should be preserved.

On 3 January 1939 a telegram arrived from J.L.B. Smith. It read "most important preserve skeleton and gills = fish described." The ensuing search of local rubbish heaps failed to find the discarded organs. Parallel disasters now revealed themselves. The early photographs taken of the fresh fish had been spoiled, while the museum trustees, not thinking the fish to be important, had ordered the skin to be mounted before, on 16 February, Smith finally arrived. He stared at the

mounted skin and said: "I always knew, somewhere, or somehow, a primitive fish of this nature would appear."

He described the fish as *Latimeria chalumnae*, in recognition of Marjorie Courtenay-Latimer and the Chalumna River, off which the fish had been caught.

Why had this conspicuous, spiny-scaled fish remained unnoticed for so long? Its large eye and lurking predator shape seemed to suggest that it did not normally live off East London. Unless the only living specimen had been caught, there must be more – but where?

The hunt was long and extremely exciting. It took 14 years, involved a great deal of work and almost entailed commandeering the South African Prime Minister's private aircraft. For all the details the reader is referred to J. L. B. Smith's book, *Old Fourlegs: The Story of the Coelacanth* (London: Longman, Green, 1956), as well as Keith Thomson's similarly-titled book, *Living Fossil: The Story of the Coelacanth* (Hutchinson Radius, 1991).

Just before Christmas 1952 (note the date again), Smith received a telegram from Captain Eric Hunt in the Comoro Islands. It read: "repeat cable just received have five foot specimen

◐ *Left and below* The discovery of the coelacanth was one of the most important zoological finds in history. Marjorie Courtenay Latimer meticulously sketched and noted the dimensions of the fish that she found on the East London quayside in 1938. Fourteen years later, in 1952, the long search for the first intact specimen came to an end; J. L. B. Smith (left) and Eric Hunt (right) proudly display their find at Dzaoudzi in the Comoro Islands.

◐ **Above** *"Old Fourlegs" is something of a mis-nomer, since the coelacanth swims conventionally and does not, as Smith speculated, propel itself along the seafloor with its prominent pelvic and anal fins. This specimen was sighted off the Comoros.*

◑ **Right** *Arnaz Erdmann swimming with a* Latimeria menadoensis. *Fishermen in Sulawesi had long referred to their indigenous coelacanth as* Rajah Laut, *or "King of the Sea."*

coelacanth injected formalin here killed 20th advise reply hunt Dzaoudzi."

Although this discovery was very exciting to the scientific community, the inhabitants of the Comoro Islands (where Dzaoudzi is located) were unmoved. They were familiar with this fish, had dubbed it *Gombessa* (meaning 'taboo' in reference to its foul taste) and thought it a worthless catch, although the coarse scales could be used to roughen bicycle tyre inner-tubes when mending punctures!

All subsequent findings of coelacanths were made off Comoro waters, making this the center of coelacanth distribution for many years. Then, in September 1997, Mark and Arnaz Erdmann, biologists honeymooning in Sulawesi, Indonesia (some 10,000 km/6,200 miles away from the Comoros) came across a fish in a local market that dramatically updated the coelacanth story and destroyed the Comoro Islands' exclusive claim as the only place on earth where the coelacanth was found.

The Sulawesi fish was definitely a coelacanth, but of a slightly different type. This was confirmed ten months later when a live specimen was landed. These coelacanths were different in color to the Comoro ones (brown with golden-colored flecks, instead of bluish with pinkish-white flecks). DNA studies corroborated the difference, and the new coelacanth was named *Latimeria menadoensis*.

On 28 October 2000, divers in Jesser Canyon in Sodwana Bay, in a marine reserve off the northern Kwazulu-Natal coast of South Africa, spotted three live coelacanths at a depth of 104m (340ft). One month later, three further specimens were filmed in the same area. These finds suggested that the coelacanth might be more widespread in the western Indian Ocean than was once thought.

Diving at such depths can be extremely dangerous and, in this case, ended in tragedy for one of the divers, who never regained consciousness following a blackout after surfacing.            KEB/JD

# Sharks

THE TALES OF ANCIENT MARINERS AND *modern media hyperbole have given most people the idea that sharks are savage predators, but this is only true of a minority of species. A group of fishes that have survived for around 400 million years, the elasmobranchs – sharks, skates and rays – have five or more gill slits on either side of their heads and a cartilaginous skeleton. These characteristics distinguish them from most other fishes, which have a single gill cover on each side of the head and bony skeletons. Sharks have exceptional sensory organs, and some give birth to live young.*

With few natural predators, many sharks grow slowly, mature late, and have very few young. The recent increase in affluence in Southeast Asia has led to a huge demand for shark fins to supply the shark fin soup market. Sharks are now being fished at a much greater rate than they can reproduce and some species are threatened with extinction if this trend continues.

## Sophisticated Hunters
### TEETH AND SENSORY SYSTEMS

A notable feature of sharks is their teeth. In the large highly predatory sharks these are large and razor sharp, used for shearing and shredding their prey into bite-sized pieces. When biting, the shearing is often aided by body motions such as rotating the body or rapid shaking of the head. Those preying on fishes have long, thin teeth to help them catch and hold on to struggling and slippery fish. Sharks that feed on the bottom

**⬤ Above** *Not all sharks are large. The Australian marbled catshark (Atelomycterus macleayi) only grows to around 60cm (2ft). Catsharks are named for their elliptical, catlike eyes. They are also characterized by two dorsal fins set far back.*

### FACTFILE

### SHARKS

Class: Chondrichthyes

Orders: Chlamydoselachiformes, Hexanchiformes, Heterodontiformes, Orectolobiformes, Scyliorhiniformes, Triakiformes, Odontaspidiformes, Isuriformes, Carcharhiniformes, Squaliformes, Squatiniformes, Pristiophoriformes.

At least 370 species in at least 74 genera, 21 families and 12 orders (other taxonomic accounts, e.g. Nelson 1994 (3rd edn.) list only 8 orders).

**DISTRIBUTION** Worldwide in tropical, temperate and polar oceans at all depths.

Equator

**SIZE** Length 15cm–12m (6 inches–40ft); **weight** 1–12,000kg (1–26,500lb).

See The 12 Orders of Sharks ▷

have flattened teeth for crushing the shells of their mollusk and crustacean prey. At any one time most sharks may have several rows of teeth in their mouths. Only the first row or two are actively used for feeding, the remaining rows are replacement teeth in various stages of formation with the newest teeth being at the rear. As a tooth in the functioning row breaks or is worn down, it falls out and a replacement tooth moves forward in a sort of conveyor-belt system. The largest species, the Basking shark and the Whale shark, have minute teeth that play no role in feeding; rather, they feed in a similar way to the baleen whales, filtering the water for plankton. Basking sharks have modified gill rakers while Whale sharks have spongy tissue supported by the gill arches and can also swallow small shoaling fishes.

Sharks find their prey through a number of sensory systems. Many have better eyesight than

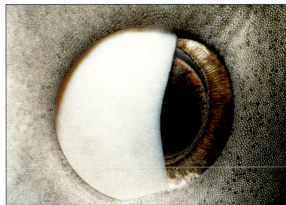

was once believed and unlike most bony fishes, are able to control the size of the pupil. Sharks that hunt in dim light or the dark have a tapetum that reflects the light so that it stimulates the retina a second time; in the dark, light reflected from these eyes makes them shine like those of a cat. Many sharks have a nictitating membrane, which serves as a protective eyelid. When the fish gets close to its prey, it closes this membrane and switches over to other sensors, particularly its 'Ampullae de Lorenzini'. Great white sharks do not have nictitating membranes but roll their eyes backward for protection while striking prey. The Ampullae de Lorenzini are a series of pits around the snout; they are sensitive to other stimuli, but their use as electroreceptors is of prime importance. Using these electroreceptors, sharks are capable of picking up an impulse of just one-millionth of a volt, which is less than the electrical

◖ *Above* Millions of years of evolution have given sharks the beautifully stream-lined shape and powerful musculature that make them such efficient hunters. In addition, the snout is equipped with highly sensitive scent detectors. This Grey reef shark (Carcharhinus amblyrhynchos) exemplifies such adaptations.

◖ *Above right* Triangular, sawlike teeth make the Great white shark (Carcharodon carcharias) a fearsome predator. These serrated teeth are designed to tear chunks of flesh from the flanks of large prey, as the shark shakes its head from side to side.

◖ *Right* A nictitating membrane closing over the eye of a Tiger shark (Galeocerdo cuvier). This requiem shark species eats a wide variety of prey, including other sharks and sea snakes, and the membrane helps protect its eyes during an attack.

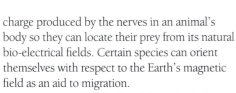

charge produced by the nerves in an animal's body so they can locate their prey from its natural bio-electrical fields. Certain species can orient themselves with respect to the Earth's magnetic field as an aid to migration.

In common with all other fishes, sharks have a lateral-line system – a series of sensors along both sides of the body that pick up pressure waves caused by the movements of another animal or even by the shark itself approaching a stationary object. Some species have sensory barbels around their mouth that taste the seabed for prey. Sharks have a keen sense of smell and can detect one part of blood in a million parts of seawater!

### Frilled Shark
ORDER CHLAMYDOSELACHIFORMES

The most primitive living shark is the Frilled shark (*Chlamydoselachus anguineus*), sole representative of this order. It has broad-based, tricuspid (trident-like) teeth which are otherwise found only in fossil sharks. Its common name is derived from its long, floppy gill flaps, forming a frill around the head. Its primitive and unique characteristics place it in its own family. First discovered off Japan on Sagami Bay in the 1880s, deep trawling has shown that it lives at depths of 300–600m (1,000–2,000ft) over a wide area off the coasts of Australia, Chile, California, Europe, and South Africa (where specimens may possibly be a separate *Chlamydoselachus* species). It grows to 2m (6ft) long and has a thin, eel-like body and feeds on small fishes swallowed whole. The female develops eggs in her body, producing 6–12 young per litter (i.e. the species is viviparous).

### Six- and Seven-gilled Sharks
ORDER HEXANCHIFORMES

The six- and seven-gilled sharks (also known as the cow sharks) are so named because they have developed one or two extra sets of gill slits. They prefer cold water, and in the tropics live in deep water. No nictitating membrane is present in these species. They reach 4.5m (15ft) in length and feed on other fishes. The upper-jaw teeth are long and tapered while the lower-jaw teeth are short and wide with unique, strong, multiple serrations. They too develop eggs internally and produce up to 40 young.

### Catsharks and False Catsharks
ORDER SCYLIORHINIFORMES

The catsharks and false catsharks comprise about 18 genera and 87 species. Mostly living in cold or deep waters, they are found worldwide and many have mottled patterns and do not lose this pigmentation pattern as they mature. Living on or near to the seabed, they feed on mollusks, crustaceans, and bottom-dwelling fishes. Some species have sensory barbels that help them locate their prey.

Most species are small, maturing at about 1–1.5m (3–4.5ft) but some are larger, such as the False catshark, which may reach 3m (9ft). When threatened, the aptly named swell sharks swallow water or air into their stomachs, enlarging their girth to three or four times its normal size.

### Smooth Dogfish Sharks
ORDER TRIAKIFORMES

The smooth dogfish sharks (triakoids) live in the shallows of tropical, subtropical, and temperate seas. They are moderately large sharks, reaching about 2m (6ft) in length. Despite the fact that they are bottom dwellers, feeding on mollusks, crustaceans and fishes, they do not lie or crawl on the sea bed. Most species have modified crushing and grinding teeth.

The Leopard shark from the eastern North Pacific has a beautiful color pattern with dark gray to black spots on a silvery background, which makes it popular for public aquariums.

Virtually all species make long migrations, spending winters in the tropics and migrating to

**Left** *Representative species of sharks:* **1** *Frilled catfish* (Chlamydoselachus angineus; *sole member of the order Chlamydoselachiformes), the most primitive form of shark;* **2** *Necklace carpetshark* (Parascyllium variolatum; *order Orectolobiformes);* **3** *Whale shark* (Rhincodon typus; *order Orectolobiformes)– this Vulnerable species is the world's largest fish;* **4** *Cuban ribbontail catshark* (Eridacnis barbouri; *order Scyliorhiniformes);* **5** *Leopard shark* (Triakis semifasciata; *order Triakiformes), caught both commercially and as a game fish in the Eastern Pacific;* **6** *Goblin shark* (Mitsukurina owstoni; *order Odontaspidiformes) – this species has specialized jaws that can suddenly project far forward to catch prey;* **7** *Great white shark* (Carcharodon carcharias; *order Isuriformes);* **8** *Thintail thresher* (Alopias vulpinus; *order Isuriformes), widespread in tropical and temperate waters;* **9** *Longnosed sawshark* (Pristiophorus cirratus; *order Pristiophoriformes) – this species occurs only off southern Australia;* **10** *Ornate angelshark* (Squatina tergocellata; *order Squatiniformes), from the Eastern Indian Ocean.*

temperate waters in the summer. Evidence suggests that these migrations are regulated by water temperature and this in turn affects where the sharks spawn. Females of these species develop embryos in the uterus and deliver 10–20 young at a time. Although these sharks are considered harmless to humans there is at least one authenticated instance of the Leopard shark attacking a man in northern California.

## Horn or Port Jackson Sharks
### ORDER HETERODONTIFORMES

The horn sharks live in the Indian and Pacific oceans. Sluggish, bottom dwellers up to 1.65m (5.4ft)-long, they lie, sometimes in groups, under kelp beds or on shallow rocky reefs and occasionally sandy patches during the day and disperse to feed at night when their prey are most active. The genus name, *Heterodontus* (Greek for "different teeth") alludes to the fact that they have pointed front teeth and rear teeth fused molar-like into crushing plates – ideal for holding, breaking, and then crushing shelled mollusks and crustaceans. Stockily built, speciies of this order have prominent brow ridges above their eyes, which give them the appearance of having horns – hence the name horn sharks. Oviparous, they lay eggs, which are unique in having a screw-shaped spiral form. The female forces these into crevices between rocks or pieces of coral and each egg case contains one pup (baby shark).

## Orectoloboids
### ORDER ORECTOLOBIFORMES

The orectolobiformes are closely related families of sharks that are tropical to subtropical fishes. They are mostly found in the Indo-Pacific while two species are found in the Atlantic Ocean.

In size the orectolobiformes range from the epaulette sharks – 1m (3ft) long – to the Whale shark, which has been reliably reported as reaching over 12m (40ft) in length and is the world's largest fish. In most species the young are born with spotted or banded patterns, which fade as the animals' mature.

Most species lay eggs (oviparous), but a few develop them internally (viviparous). Usually less than 12 young are produced per litter.

All species except the Whale shark are bottom dwellers, the skeletons of the pectoral fins are modified so that they can actually use the fins for walking on the seabed, even when disturbed many species will crawl away rather than swim.

Most orectolobiformes feed on mollusks and crustaceans and have teeth for crushing and grinding. All have sensory barbels around the mouth. The carpet sharks mainly eat fishes, so they have long, thin teeth. The Whale shark is a filter feeder, having its gill arches specially modified to filter out the planktonic organisms and small animals that it feeds on such as krill, squid, anchovies, sardines and mackerel. Its redundant teeth are

⚫ **Above** *Off the coast of Costa Rica, Central America, a pack of Whitetip reef sharks (Triaenodon obesus) gather to hunt. These small, slim sharks are sluggish during the day, but become active at night. They often occur in lagoons and on coral reefs.*

⚫ **Below** *Distinct features of horn sharks, such as the Port Jackson shark (Heterodontus portusjacksoni) include hornlike ridges above the eyes, pointed front teeth and crushing rear-teeth plates, and a bottom-dwelling habit.*

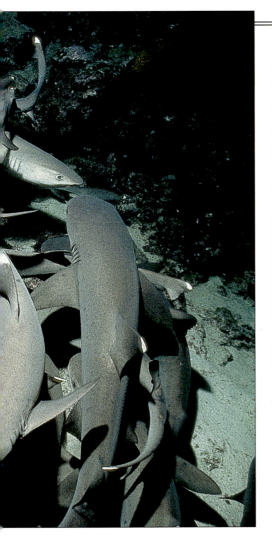

○ **Above** *Lesser spotted dogfish embryos in their egg capsules ('mermaid's purses'). Sharks have three modes of egg development. Most are viviparous, with eggs developing and hatching in the womb. In some viviparous species, the eggs develop in the womb connected to the wall by a yolk 'placenta'. These two types give birth to fully developed young. The third type (represented by the dogfish) is oviparous, with the female attaching fertilized eggs to vegetation.*

○ **Above** *The Spotted wobbegong (Orectobolus maculatus) has a flattened head and distinctive coral-shaped skin flaps around the edge of its snout. It inhabits shallow coastal waters off southern Australia.*

minute. The Whale shark's vast bulk requires constant fuel, so it swims continuously, filtering the ocean for its food. Found worldwide, in all tropical, subtropical and warm temperate seas, when first described by Smith, the generic name used was *Rhineodon* but in a later descriptions he used both *Rhincodon* and *Rhineodon*. *Rhincodon* is now the accepted version; some researchers feel that it should be placed in a separate family.

### Sand Tiger, False Sand Tiger, and Goblin Sharks
ORDER ODONTASPIDIFORMES

The sand tiger, false sand tiger, and goblin sharks are all fairly large, reaching 3–3.5m (10–12ft) in length. The sand tiger sharks (5 species, with a new one possibly found off Columbia's Malpelo Islands) are found worldwide in shallow, temperate and tropical waters. Largely fish-eaters, they have long, thin teeth that protrude from the mouth to give a ferocious, snaggle-toothed appearance. This, combined with their docile nature, has made them favorites in public aquariums. Known as the Tiger Shark in North America, Grey Nurse Shark in Australia and Spotted Raggedtooth Shark in South Africa, this is one species whose scientific name has changed from *Carcharias taurus* to *Eugomphodus taurus* to *Odontaspis taurus* and is now back to *Carcharias taurus*.

Reproduction in this order is viviparous – embryos develop in the uterus – but as with many shark species, there is intrauterine cannibalism. The female begins with 6–8 embryos per uterus but as they grow, the largest in each oviduct devours its siblings, embryos and other unfertilized eggs;

only two young are eventually born.

The False sand tiger shark or Crocodile shark lives in deeper waters off China and East and West Africa. The Goblin shark is perhaps the most bizarre-looking of all living sharks. Projecting from its "forehead" is a flattened, spade-shaped, horn-like growth whose function is unknown, the mouth can extend forward under this horn or retract under the eye. The Japanese fishermen that first caught it called it *Tenguzame*, which means "Goblin shark." Like the Frilled shark, it was originally caught in the 1890s in Japan's Sagami Bay. Since then, it has been caught worldwide at depths of 300m (1,000ft) and more. However, apart from its length, 4.3m (14ft), little is known about this species, although DNA studies suggest that it became specialized early in its evolution. While alive, Goblin sharks are a translucent pinkish-white colour, but become very dark brown shortly after death.

### Requiem Sharks
ORDER CARCHARHINIFORMES

The requiem sharks are probably the largest group of living sharks, with about 100 species in 10 genera. In body shape and behavior they are the "typical" shark people think of. They reach 3.5m (11.5ft) in length and occur in all tropical and temperate seas.

The Bull shark is found in tropical to subtropical coastal waters worldwide and enters fresh water for lengthy periods. It has been reported 3,700km (2,300 miles) up the River Amazon, 2,900km (1,800 miles) up the River Mississippi, more than 1,000km (620 miles) from the ocean in the River Zambezi and in Lake Nicaragua. Originally sharks from these fresh waters were wrongly thought never to enter the ocean and thus to be distinct species and were appropriately named after the waters that they were found in, for

# The 12 Orders of Sharks

## Frilled Shark
### Order: Chlamydoselachiformes

Lives off coasts of California, Chile, Europe, S Africa, Japan, Australia. 1 family – Chlamydoselachidae – containing the sole species *Chlamydoselachus anguineus*. One South African species may be a separate subspecies.

## Six- and Seven-gilled sharks or hexanchoids
### Order: Hexanchiformes

Worldwide in cold marine waters at shallow to moderate depths. 1 family – Hexanchidae – containing 5 species in 3 genera including: Bluntnose sixgill shark (*Hexanchus griseus*), Bigeye sixgill shark (*Hexanchus nakamurai*),Broadnose sevengill shark (*Notorynchus cepedianus*), Sharpnose sevengill shark (*Heptranchias perlo*). The Bluntnose sixgill shark is presently classed as Vulnerable.

## Horn or Port Jackson sharks
### Order: Heterodontiformes

Tropical Western Indian and Eastern and Western Pacific Oceans. 1 family – Heterodontidae – containing 8 species of the genus *Heterodontus,* including: Horn shark (*H. francisci*), Crested bullhead shark (*H. galeatus*), Japanese bullhead shark (*H. japonicus*), Port Jackson shark (*H. portusjacksoni*), Zebra bullhead shark (*H. zebra*).

## Orectoloboids
### Order: Orectolobiformes

Indo-Pacific Ocean; 2 species in Atlantic Ocean. About 31 species in 13 genera and 7 families, including: banded catsharks and epaulette sharks (family Hemiscyllidae), including epaulette sharks (genus *Hemiscyllium*); carpet sharks (family Orectolobidae), including the Spotted wobbegong (*Orectolobus maculatus*); collared carpet sharks (family Parascylliidae), including the Necklace carpetshark (*Parascyllium variolatum*) and the Barbelthroat carpetshark (*Cirrhoscyllium expolitum*); nurse sharks (family Ginglymostomatidae), including the Nurse shark (*Ginglymostoma cirratum*) and the tawny nurse shark (*Nebrius ferrugineus*); Whale shark (*Rhincodon typus*, sole species of the family Rhincodontidae). The Whale shark and the Bluegray carpet shark (*Heteroscyllium colcloughi*) are both classed as Vulnerable.

## Catsharks and False catsharks
### Order: Scyliorhiniformes

Worldwide in cold or deep marine water. About 87 species in at least 15 genera and 3 families including: catsharks (family Scyliorhinidae), including Lesser spotted

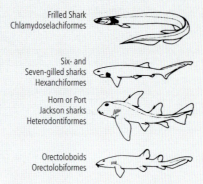

Frilled Shark
Chlamydoselachiformes

Six- and
Seven-gilled sharks
Hexanchiformes

Horn or Port
Jackson sharks
Heterodontiformes

Orectoloboids
Orectolobiformes

Catsharks and
False catsharks
Scyliorhiniformes

Smooth dogfish
sharks
Triakiformes

Sand tiger sharks
and allies
Odontaspidiformes

Thresher, Mackerel and
Megamouth sharks
Isuriformes

Requiem sharks
Carcharhinoidiformes

Spiny dogfish
and Allies
Squaliformes

Angel sharks
Squatiniformes

Sawsharks
Pristiophoriformes

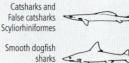

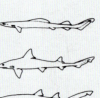

dogfish (*Scyliorhinus canicula*), swell sharks (genus *Cephaloscyllium*); False catshark (*Pseudotriakis microdon*; family Pseudotriakidae), 2 species, one on both sides of the North Atlantic and one in the Western Pacific; finback catsharks (family Proscylliidae), including Cuban ribbontail catshark (*Eridacnis barbouri*), Graceful catshark (*Proscyllium habereri*), and the Slender smooth-hound (*Gollum attenuatus*). Four species are listed as Lower Risk/Near Threatened, including the Pyjama shark (*Poroderma africanum*).

## Smooth dogfish sharks
### Order: Triakiformes

Worldwide in tropical, subtropical and temperate seas. 1 family – Triakidae – containing about 30 species in 9 genera, including: Whiskery shark (*Furgaleus macki*) of the eastern Indian Ocean; Longnose houndshark (*Iago garricki*) of the western Pacific; Leopard shark (*Triakis semifasciata*) of the eastern North Pacific, the Tope (Soupfin) shark (*Galeorhinus galeus*) and the Sailback houndshark (*Gogolia filewoodi*). The Whitefin tope shark (*Hemitriakis leucoperiptera*) is Endangered while 3 species are Vulnerable, including the Tope shark, and 4 species are classed as Lower Risk/Conservation Dependent and 3 as Lower Risk/Near Threatened.

## Goblin sharks and allies
### Order: Odontaspidiformes

Worldwide in tropical and temperate seas. 7 species in 4 genera and 3 families, including: False sand tiger shark or Crocodile shark (*Pseudocarcharias kamoharrai*; sole species of the family Pseudocarchariidae); Goblin shark (*Mitsukurina owstoni*; sole species of the family Scapanorhynchidae); sand tiger sharks (family Odontaspididae), including Sand tiger shark (*Carcharias taurus*) and Bigeye sand tiger (*Odontaspis noronhai*). The Sand tiger shark is Vulnerable and the Crocodile shark is Lower Risk/Near Threatened.

## Thresher sharks and allies
### Order: Isuriformes

Worldwide in tropical and temperate seas. 10 species in 6 genera and 3 families including: mackerel sharks (family Isuridae), including Basking shark (*Cetorhinus maximus*), Great white shark or man-eater or White shark (*Carcharodon carcharias*), Shortfin mako shark (*Isurus oxyrinchus*), Porbeagle shark (*Lamna nasus*), Salmon shark (*Lamna ditropis*); Megamouth shark (*Megachasma pelagios*; Megachasmidae); thresher sharks (family Alopiidae), including Bigeye thresher (*Alopias superciliosus*). Both the Basking shark and the Great white shark are Vulnerable, while the Shortfin mako and the Porbeagle shark are Lower Risk/Near Threatened.

## Requiem sharks
### Order: Carcharhiniformes

Worldwide in tropical and temperate seas. 1 family – Carcharhinidae – containing about 100 species in 10 genera including: Blacktip reef shark (*Carcharhinus melanopterus*), Bull shark (*C. leucas*), Silvertip shark (*C. albimarginatus*), Oceanic whitetip shark (*C. longimanus*), hammerhead sharks (genus *Sphyrna*), Great hammerhead shark (*S. mokarran*), Scalloped hammerhead (*S. lewini*), Tiger shark (*Galeocerdo cuvier*), and Blue shark (*Prionace glauca*). The Ganges shark (*Glyphis gangeticus*) and the Pondicherry shark (*C. hemiodon*), along with several new species that are awaiting description, are Critically Endangered; 2 species are Endangered: the Borneo shark (*Carcharhinus borneensis*) and the Speartooth shark (*Glyphis glyphis*), and 2 are Vulnerable: the Smoothtooth blacktip (*Carcharhinus leiodon*) and the Sharptooth lemon shark (*Negaprion acutidens*).

## Spiny dogfish and allies
### Order: Squaliformes

Worldwide in cold or deep seas. 1 family – Squalidae – containing about 70 species in around 12 genera including: bramble

sharks (genus *Echinorhinus*), Bramble shark (*E. brucus*), Prickly shark (*E. cookei*), cigar or cookiecutter sharks (genera *Isistius, Squaliolus*) including the Cookiecutter shark (*Isistius brasiliensis*), sleeper sharks, including the Pocket shark (*Mollisquama parini*), Common Spiny dogfish (*Squalus acanthias*). The Spiny dogfish is classed as Lower Risk/Near Threatened.

## Angel sharks
### Order: Squatiniformes

Worldwide in tropical and temperate seas. 1 family – Squatinidae – containing about 10 species of the genus *Squatina*, including: Angelshark (*S. squatina*), Hidden angelshark (*S. occulta*)Australian angelshark (*S. australis*), African angelshark (*S. africana*), and the Angular angelshark (*S. guggenheim*). The Hidden angelshark (*S. occulta*) is Endangered and 2 species are Vulnerable – the Angelshark and the Angular angelshark.

## Sawsharks
### Order: Pristiophoriformes

Bahamas, off coast of S Africa, western Pacific Ocean from Japan to Australia. 1 family – Pristiophoridae – containing 5 species in 2 genera: Sixgill sawshark (*Pliotrema warreni*),Longnose sawshark (*Pristiophorus cirratus*), Shortnose sawshark (*P. nudipinnis*), Japanese sawshark (*P. japonicus*), Bahamas sawshark (*P. schroederi*).

Note: Nelson 1994 and the Fishbase database (www.fishbase.org) list only 8 orders of sharks. The Scyliorhiniformes and the Triakiformes are subsumed within the Carcharhiniformes, and the Frilled shark within the Hexanchiformes, while the Odontaspidiformes and Isuriformes merge to form a new order, the Lamniformes.

▷ **Right** *A Scalloped hammerhead shark (Sphyrna lewini) being cleaned by two Angelfishes. Widespread throughout the world's warmer oceans, hammerheads are often caught in commercial fishing, either intentionally (their fins are highly prized) or as bycatch.*

instance *Carcharhinus nicaraguensis*.

All *Carcharhinus* species are widespread, and in summer some migrate long distances into temperate waters. They have a metallic gray or brown dorsal coloration. Some, however, have the edges of their fins tipped with white or black, hence the names, Silvertip, Whitetip and Blacktip sharks.

The largest requiem shark, the Tiger shark, reaches over 6m (20ft) in length and is unquestionably one of the most dangerous of all sharks. As a scavenger it will swallow anything that it can get down its throat – including shoes, cans, birds, and human body parts. Juvenile Tiger sharks have dark bands on a silvery gray background, a coloration from which their name derives, but these bands fade with age.

The hammerhead sharks are so called because of the large lateral expansions of their heads with their eyes set on the ends. Except for their unique heads, which define the genus (or, possibly, two genera), they are typical requiem sharks. It has been mooted that their hammer-shaped heads help streamline their bodies, or give them a better field of vision, but more research suggests that the elongate head contains extra electrodetectors, the Ampullae de Lorenzini. Hammerhead sharks are often seen moving their heads from side to side like a metal detector above sandy bottoms and then burrowing into the sand to grab hidden fishes – mostly stingrays; they also make regular migrations following the earth's magnetic field. The Great hammerhead shark is the largest, growing to more than 5m (15ft) long while the Scalloped hammerhead is the one most seen by divers.

## Spiny Dogfish and Allies
### ORDER SQUALIFORMES

The spiny dogfish sharks are cold-water forms, worldwide in distribution. All develop eggs viviparously, producing about 12 young per litter. In size they range from less than 30cm (1ft) to over 6m (20ft). Many, especially the deepwater species, feed on squid and octopus.

In the North Atlantic, the Common Spiny dogfish – also known as the Pickled Dogfish or Spurdog – is an important food fish. Tens of millions are caught every year and stocks are collapsing. Spiny dogfish rarely exceed 1m (3ft) in length, travel in schools and migrate long distances, moving into Arctic waters each summer. Each dorsal fin is preceded by a spine, which has venom-producing tissue at its base. The venom is painful to humans, but not fatal.

Many deepwater species, especially in the genus *Etmopterus*, have light-producing organs along the sides of their body, possibly attracting their deepwater squid prey as well as providing camouflage through "counter-illumination." Their large eyes are very sensitive at low light levels.

The small but very thin cigar sharks (especially genus *Isistius*) are equipped with greatly elongated teeth in their lower jaw. They swim up to a larger animal (a fish, squid, or even a cetacean), bite it, and then, with a twist of the body, cut out a perfectly circular piece of flesh from their prey. This feeding technique has given rise to their alternative common name – "cookiecutter sharks."

Sleeper sharks, the giants among spiny dogfish sharks, are the only sharks that permanently inhabit Arctic waters, often under the ice. They feed on seals and fishes, and are thought to be the only sharks with flesh that is poisonous to both humans and dogs.

The bramble sharks are unusual in having extremely large, flat dermal denticles ("teeth") widely dispersed over the skin, giving them a "brambly" appearance. There are probably two species, one in the Atlantic (*Echinorhinus brucus*) and one in the Pacific (*Echinorhinus cookei*). Although large, over 2.7m (9ft) long, their skeleton is not calcified so it is extremely soft.

## Thresher, Mackerel and Megamouth Sharks
### ORDER ISURIFORMES

The thresher, mackerel, and megamouth sharks are among the largest sharks in the world and are found in tropical and temperate seas.

The thresher sharks derive their name from the extremely long, thin upper lobe of their caudal fin, which may be as long as the rest of their body. Swimming into a school of small fishes, they are believed to use their tail like a whip, thrashing it among the school, killing or stunning the fishes, which are then eaten. They grow to some 6m (20ft) and give birth to only a few young, but the pups of the largest species are about 1.5m (5ft) long!

An exciting shark discovery was that of the aptly named Megamouth, which was only first captured off Hawaii in November 1976. Over 5m (16ft) long, it has now been found off Japan, Indonesia, the Philippines, the USA, Brazil and Senegal. The Megamouth shark is a filter-feeder

that migrates vertically, spending the day at depth and rising to about 12m (40ft) to feed at night. It has been speculated that the lining of the roof of its mouth may attract prey with bioluminescence. Researchers think that it is distantly related to the Basking shark, but is sufficiently different to be considered separately. The Megamouth is preyed upon by the Cookiecutter shark (*Isistius brasiliensis*); it is also feared that, with the growth in deep-water fishing, this species will increasingly be taken as bycatch.

The family of mackerel sharks contains some of the best known sharks, including the Porbeagle, Mako, Basking, and the unjustifiably notorious Great white sharks. They are large and most live in all tropical and temperate seas. The Basking shark can reach 10m (33ft) but is only found in temperate seas. All have an unusual caudal fin with the lobes being nearly equal in length, caudal keels on either side of the tail, and are relatively fast swimmers; most species are fish-eaters. Some species are known for "breaching" – making spectacular leaps into the air. The reason for this behavior is not known, but it has been suggested that it is an attempt to dislodge skin parasites. The Basking shark is known to have collided with boats during such leaps. Most, if not all, species are homoiothermic – that is, they maintain their body temperature above that of their surroundings.

Reaching over 6m (20ft) in length, the Mako shark is one of the fastest fish in the world, and

has been recorded swimming at speeds over 95km/h (60mph).

The world's most notorious shark by far is the Great white shark – also called the White pointer, Blue pointer, Man-eater, or simply the White shark. It is the species most often cited in references to shark attacks on humans, although many of these should actually be ascribed to the Tiger shark and the Bull shark (see Shark Attacks). Feeding primarily on marine mammals (the only shark to do so), its broad, serrated teeth are

**⬤ Above** *Strips of Whale shark meat drying in the Philippines. For millions of people who depend on subsistence fishing, sharks are a plentiful and cheap source of protein. Exploitation for their meat, fins, and other byproducts has endangered many species.*

**⬤ Below** *The huge-mouthed Basking shark (Cetorhinus maximus) of the mackerel shark order inhabits temperate waters, feeding on plankton near the surface. Its gill rakers are well developed, while its teeth are vestigial. Despite its great size and terrifying appearance, it poses no threat to humans.*

designed for biting large chunks of flesh from whales, seals, and sea lions. Known to reach 6.7m (20ft) in length, its average length is 4.5m (15ft). Reproduction is viviparous and the developing embryos are then nourished by eating unfertilized eggs (oophagy). Like many sharks, the Great White shark is countershaded, only the belly is white, the dorsal surface being blue-gray to gray-brown or bronze.

At around 2.7m (9ft) long, the Porbeagle and the Salmon shark (sometimes known as the Pacific porbeagle) are the smallest members of the mackerel shark family. They live in the Atlantic and Pacific oceans respectively.

The Basking shark is second in size to the Whale shark. Commonly 10m (33ft) long, it is a filter feeder. Its teeth are minute and modified gill rakers are used for sieving the plankton. Its liver yields vast amounts of oil and the fish has been the subject of local fisheries in the North Atlantic. The Basking shark's name comes from its behavior of swimming and resting at the surface.

## Angelsharks
### ORDER SQUATINIFORMES

The angelsharks are extremely distinctive in appearance; being very flat, they are considered to be more closely related to the skates and rays than to the more "typical" sharks. They grow to more than 1.8m (6ft) in length and there are about 12–18 species in the genus *Squatina*, found in all tropical to temperate seas. An anterior lobe of the pectoral fins extends in front of their gill slits. They have long, thin teeth, and lie camouflaged in fairly shallow water, waiting for prey to swim by, before swiftly lunging out and capturing it in their highly protrusible jaws. Though normally lethargic, they can move very rapidly when catching prey. The angelsharks are viviparous, producing about 10 young per litter.

## Sawsharks
### ORDER PRISTIOPHORIFORMES

Having long, flat, blade-like snouts edged with teeth of varying sizes, sawsharks bear a striking resemblance to sawfishes; however, they are true sharks. They are quite rare and grow to a length of about 1.8m (6ft). One species, the Sixgill saw-shark (*Pliotrema warreni*), has an extra set of gills. The genus *Pristiophorus* has seven species, most of which inhabit the western Pacific and Southwestern Indian Ocean, but also including one Atlantic species found in deep water off the Bahamas, Cuba and Florida. They have a pair of long thin barbels under the saw-like rostrum, which help them find their mollusk and crustacean prey on the sea floor. Their teeth are flat and broad for crushing and their "saws" appear to be used only for defense. Sawsharks are viviparous, producing 3–22 young per litter with the saw-teeth folded back at birth, thus preventing injury to the mother.                JJ/GDi

## SHARK ATTACKS

The most famous characteristic of sharks is their alleged propensity to kill and eat humans. But very few shark species have been implicated in unpro-voked attacks. The idea that sharks are waiting for people to enter the water so that they can attack them is false. To put it in perspective, every year more people are killed by bee-stings, 10 times more people are killed by lightning and thousands more people are killed by other people or in automobile accidents, than by sharks. The International Shark Attack File authenticates 70–100 unprovoked shark attacks annually with 5–15 fatalities.

The Great white shark has the worst reputation for attacking humans. Yet Great whites feed mainly on sea mammals. The shark usually surprises its prey with one huge bite, and then retreats to allow its victim to die. For this reason, many humans survive the attack of a Great white shark if they are saved before being consumed. Death, however, may result from massive blood loss or damage to organs.

Attacks by other species of sharks are for feeding. Statistically, the next most dangerous sharks are the Tiger, Bull, and Sand tiger shark. Divers dive unmolested among shoals of 300 Scalloped hammerhead sharks, though there is thought to be a small risk from Great Hammerhead sharks. All predatory sharks feed most actively at dawn and dusk and most sharks will scavenge when the opportunity occurs. Their sensors home in on the smell of dead fishes being carried by spear-fishermen, as well as the vibrations from dying, speared, or hooked fishes and fishes that are already under attack by other predators so many attacks are linked to these events. Similarly the vibrations given by bathers splashing on the surface will attract sharks. To any predatory fish, any other fish on the surface would appear to be

one that is in trouble and therefore easy prey. Divers that are submerged are at much less risk than divers or swimmers on the surface.

Despite their proven sensitivity to blood, sharks are heavily attracted to decaying flesh; divers and fishermen chum for sharks with fish-oil, dead fish-es, frozen fishes or horsemeat. Problems linked to this occur when bathers and surfers are in the water in areas near to where abattoirs discharge their waste or fishermen clean their catch. In recent years, divers have ventured near or into bait-balls – tightly-knit shoals of fishes that are already under attack by sharks or dolphins, so it is not surprising that some of them have been bitten in error. Similarly, changes in current patterns sometimes bring shoals of fishes close inshore – aerial shots taken off Florida showed bathers frolicking among such shoals but oblivious to the sharks that were feeding on them. Another common fallacy is that sharks will not attack in the presence of dolphins.

Every year more and more divers enter the water and many of them go out of their way to get close to sharks. This should increase the chances of a shark attack but it does not happen. In fact, the reverse is true and more and more people realize that if they are sensible about where they go and what they do, the chance of such an attack is rare.

A great deal of research has gone into preventing shark attacks. Various chemicals (including detergents and a skin secretion produced by the Red Sea Moses sole), striped wetsuits, all-enclosing bags, air bubbles, methods of slowing one's heart-beat and electric fields have all been tried. Most measures are useless, while others will deter some species of sharks but actually attract others! Net-ting works well for all sizes of sharks off popular bathing beaches but often kills many of them. Heavy chain-mail suits are useful when hand-feeding sharks up to 2m (6ft) long but the only sure way of avoiding attack by the larger predatory sharks is to be inside a sturdy cage.                JJ/GDi

⬤ **Below** *A Great white shark inspects a caged diver off Australia. Attacks by this species may often be a case of mistaken identity – a swimmer or surfer, seen from below, looks much like a seal.*

# Skates, Rays, and Sawfishes

**t**HE MERE MENTION OF RAYS TO A MARINER *conjures up images of gigantic breaching devil-fishes, venomous stingrays, the electric ray or numbfish, which can stun the unwary. All these reputations reflect truth and are based on anatomical adaptations, but what these relatives of sharks are really doing is responding defensively to our attempts to catch them. Skates and rays are edible and consumed by most fishing cultures.*

Skates and rays are found worldwide; some species commute into brackish water and 18 species of the three genera of subfamily Potamotrygoninae live in freshwater rivers with Atlantic drainage in South America. Some species of sawfish are known to swim up rivers, even as far as Lake Nicaragua.

The order is most closely related to the angel-sharks and sawsharks. All have their pectoral fins extending well in front of the gill arches and fused to the sides of the head, and gill slits underneath the body. Mostly sedentary, feeding on mollusks, crustaceans and small fishes, they have large openings (spiracles) positioned clear of the bottom that take in water clear of sand and silt and then pump it over the gills and out through the ventral gill slits.

## Extraordinary Forms
### SKATE, RAY, AND SAWFISH FAMILIES
Members of the sawfish family are easily recognized by the "saw" that emerges from the front of the body, a similar protuberance to that of sawsharks. It is used both to capture food and as a defensive weapon. Swimming into a school of fishes, sawfishes rapidly slash their saw back and forth, stunning or killing fishes in the school, then consuming any immobile individuals. The saw is also used to dig for prey hidden in the substrate.

The number of teeth on the saw varies with the species. The teeth within the jaw are short and flattened for crushing the shells of crustaceans and mollusks. Including the saw, the Green sawfish can measure over 7m (24ft). The Freshwater sawfish is mostly found in rivers and lakes but occasionally enters the sea. Female sawfishes develop their eggs internally (viviparous). Living in waters that are heavily fished and subject to pollution, most sawfish species, such as the Common sawfish, are in danger of extinction.

◗ **Right** *Golden cownose rays* (Rhinoptera stein-dachneri) *make an eerie sight as they gather en masse off the Galápagos Islands. Shoals may contain hundreds of individuals.*

## FACTFILE

### SKATES AND RAYS

Class: Chondrichthyes

Order: Rajiformes

Over 465 species in 62 genera and 12 families.

**Distribution** Worldwide in tropical, subtropical, and temperate waters.

**Size** Length 30cm–7.3m (1–24ft); width 10cm–6.7m (4 inches–22ft).

See Skate, Ray, and Sawfish families ▷

Species in the guitarfish and shovelnose ray families look like sawfishes without saws, but have larger pectoral fins. They range in length from about 75cm (2.5ft) for the Atlantic guitarfish to about 3m (10ft) in the Whitespotted guitarfish. The Skarkfin or Bowmouth guitarfish has an unusual mouth that undulates, rising and falling like waves. They feed in shallow water on mollusks and crustaceans and have flattened crushing teeth. All species develop their eggs internally.

Members of both *Rhinobatos* and *Rhynchobatus* have a fairly long front extension (rostrum) thus giving the front part of the body, the disk, a heart-shaped appearance. The remaining genera (*Rhina, Platyrhina, Zapteryx* and *Platyrhinoides*) have much shorter rostra and the disk looks round. Many species have enlarged dermal denticles, often called thorns, on their dorsal surface.

All members of the electric ray and Lesser electric ray families produce electricity. Most live in shallow water though some occur at great depths. Slow swimmers, spending most of their time on the seabed, they feed on fishes and invertebrates, which they capture by stunning them with electric shocks. Their electric organs, composed of modified muscle tissue, are between the pectoral fins and the head, one on each side. The electric shock from these organs can reach 220 volts and is also used in defense. In ancient Greece and Rome, the shocks of the species *Torpedo nobiliana* were used

as a treatment for maladies such as headache.

The Lesser electric ray grows to about 30cm (1ft) whereas the Atlantic torpedo ray grows to over 2m (6ft) long. Their disks are round, the tail short and stubby in most species and the eyes usually small. In some species, e.g. the Blind Numbfishes from deep water off New Zealand, the eyes are very poor, the fish use electroreceptors to see. The skin is entirely free of scales in all species and is often beautifully marked. For reproduction, eggs develop internally until hatching.

The largest group of skates and rays is the Rajidae family, with over 250 species. They are found worldwide in cool waters – even in the tropics they are common in deep, cold water, at depths greater than 2,100m (7,000ft). Always closely associated with the seabed where they hide in the sand or mud with only their eyes and spiracles protruding, they feed mostly upon mollusks and crustaceans, although they occasionally catch fishes. The smallest species, the Little skate, which is common off the Atlantic coast of North America, only reaches about 50cm (20in) long. The Big skate from the Pacific coast of North America has been recorded at over 2.5m (8ft).

The enlarged pectoral fins of species in this family and their fairly long snout give the disk a diamond shape. The enlarged pectoral fins of stingrays, eagle rays and manta rays as well as skates are often called wings; and from their grace-

ful up-and-down movements in swimming it is easy to see why. In some skates the pelvic fins have been greatly enlarged and elongated and they can use these to "walk" over the seabed. The tails of skates have weak electric organs; long, thin, and covered with strong, sharp thorns, they are used as a defense weapon. Most species have

---

## Skate, Ray and Sawfish Families

**Eagle rays and Mantas**
**Family Myliobatidae**

Worldwide in tropical and subtropical oceans. About 42 species in 7 genera including: **Spotted eagle ray** (*Aetobatus narinari*), **Bat ray** (*Myliobatis californica*), **Manta ray** (*Manta birostris*).

**Electric rays**
**Family Torpedinidae**

Tropical and subtropical oceans, mainly in shallow water. 14 species in 2 genera including: **Atlantic torpedo ray** (*Torpedo nobiliana*), **Marbled electric ray** (*T. sinuspersici*).

**Lesser electric rays and Allies**
**Family Narcinidae**

Tropical and subtropical oceans, mainly in shallow water. About 24 species in 9 genera including: **Lesser electric ray** (*Narcine brasiliensis*), **Blind numbfish** (*Typhlonarke aysoni*).

**Guitarfishes**
**Family Rhinobatidae**

Tropical and temperate areas of the Atlantic and Indo-Pacific oceans. About 45 species in 7 genera including: **Whitespotted guitarfish** (*Rhynchobatus djiddensis*), **Atlantic guitarfish** (*Rhinobatos lentiginosus*). Con-

servation status: **Brazilian guitarfish** (*Rhinobatos horkeli*) Critically Endangered.

**Sawfishes**
**Family Pristidae**

Tropical/subtropical oceans in coastal, estuarine and freshwater. c. 6 species and 2 genera, including: **Common sawfish** (*Pristis pristis*), **Freshwater sawfish** (*P. microdon*), **Green sawfish** (*P. zjisron*), **Narrow sawfish** (*Anoxypristis cuspidata*). Conservation status: 2 species Critically Endangered – **Largetooth sawfish** (*P. perotteti*) and Common sawfish.

**Skates**
**Family Rajidae**

Worldwide, mostly in deep-sea waters but a few species are found in shallow, inshore waters. Over 250 species in at least 18 genera including: **Big skate** (*Raja binoculata*), **Little skate** (*R. erinacea*). Conservation status: 2 species are Endangered, including the **Blue** or **Common skate** (*Dipturus batis*), 1 is Vulnerable and 3 are Lower Risk/Near Threatened.

**Stingrays**
**Family Dasyatidae**

Tropical and subtropical oceans. About 70 species in c. 9 genera. 3 genera in S Ameri-

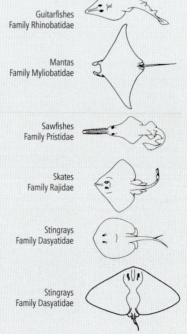

Guitarfishes
Family Rhinobatidae

Mantas
Family Myliobatidae

Sawfishes
Family Pristidae

Skates
Family Rajidae

Stingrays
Family Dasyatidae

Stingrays
Family Dasyatidae

ca inhabit fresh water. Species include: **Atlantic stingray** (*Dasyatis sabina*), **Southern stingray** (*D. americana*), **Manzana ray** (*Paratrygon aireba*). Conservation status: 5 species Endangered, including the **Pincushion ray** (*Urogymnus ukpam*), and 3 species are Vulnerable.

**Deepwater stingray**
**Family Plesiobatidae**

Mozambique, Hawaii and (perhaps) S China. Sole species *Plesiobatis daviesi*.

**Sixgill stingrays**
**Family Hexatrygonidae**

Off S Africa, W Pacific from Hong Kong to Japan. 6 species in 1 genus, including: **Sixgill stingray** (*Hexatrygon bickelli*).

**Round stingrays**
**Family Urolophidae**

W Atlantic, E Indian and Pacific Oceans. About 40 species in 3 genera, including: **Spotted round ray** (*Urobatis maculatus*).

**Butterfly rays**
**Family Gymnuridae**

Atlantic, Indian and Pacific Oceans; some species enter estuaries. About 14 species in 2 genera, including: **California butterfly ray** (*Gymnura marmorata*).

**Shovelnose and Shark rays**
**Family Rhinidae**

Indo-West Pacific Ocean. About 6 species in 2 genera, including: **White-spotted shovelnose ray** (*Rhynchobatus djiddensis*), **Shark ray** (*Rhina ancylostoma*).

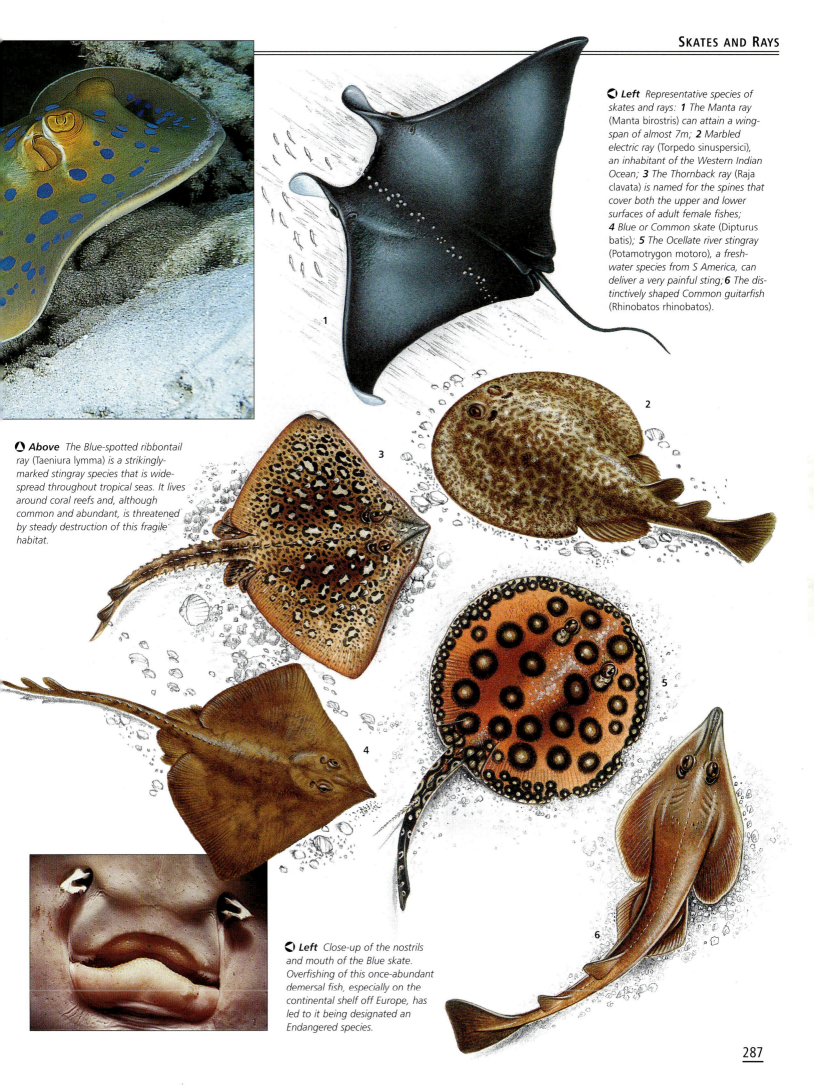

◑ **Left** *Representative species of skates and rays:* **1** *The Manta ray* (Manta birostris) *can attain a wing-span of almost 7m;* **2** *Marbled electric ray* (Torpedo sinuspersici), *an inhabitant of the Western Indian Ocean;* **3** *The Thornback ray* (Raja clavata) *is named for the spines that cover both the upper and lower surfaces of adult female fishes;* **4** *Blue or Common skate* (Dipturus batis); **5** *The Ocellate river stingray* (Potamotrygon motoro), *a freshwater species from S America, can deliver a very painful sting;* **6** *The distinctively shaped Common guitarfish* (Rhinobatos rhinobatos).

◑ **Above** *The Blue-spotted ribbontail ray* (Taeniura lymma) *is a strikingly-marked stingray species that is widespread throughout tropical seas. It lives around coral reefs and, although common and abundant, is threatened by steady destruction of this fragile habitat.*

◑ **Left** *Close-up of the nostrils and mouth of the Blue skate. Overfishing of this once-abundant demersal fish, especially on the continental shelf off Europe, has led to it being designated an Endangered species.*

287

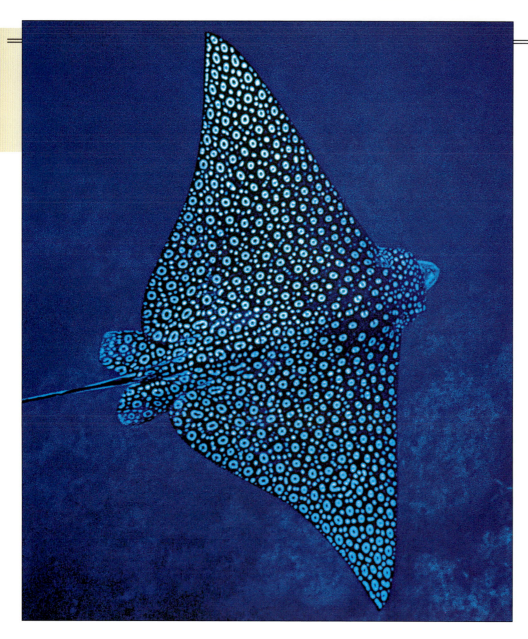

spines or thorn-like structures or "bucklers" on the dorsal surface of the body.

Typical skates (Rajidae) have two dorsal fins on the tail, Arynchobatidae have one and Anacanthobatidae none. Skate egg cases are leathery oblong capsules with stiff pointed horns at the corners, often washed up on beaches they are called "mermaid's purses." Like sharks, skates and rays live longer and produce fewer young than most fishes, so they are particularly vulnerable to overfishing. Heavily fished for their tasty wings, populations are decreasing rapidly in many parts of the world.

Stingrays are named for the one or more spines on the dorsal side of their tail. They are found worldwide in warm tropical and subtropical waters, some migrating into temperate waters in the summer. They spend a lot of time camouflaged on the seabed, often partially covered by sand. They can swim rapidly when disturbed, or in pursuit of fish. They also eat mollusks and crustaceans, and have flat, crushing teeth. The disk can be diamond-shaped or almost round, causing a distinction between the round stingrays and the square stingrays. Two genera are called butterfly rays (*Gymnura* and *Aetoplatea*) with reference to

**○ Above** *Exquisitely patterned and hydrodynamically streamlined, a Spotted eagle ray* (Aetobatus narinari) *glides through the waters of the Caribbean.*

their wide wings and short, stubby tails.

The spines on stingrays' tails have venom sacs and are used for defense, the fish striking out with their tails if stepped on. Each spine has angled barbs, which allow easy penetration, but make it very difficult to remove. Sharks, especially hammerheads, prey on stingrays and are seemingly immune. The venom is painful but rarely fatal to humans, like most fish venoms it is a high molecular weight protein that is easily broken down by heat; the wound should be immersed in water that is as hot as one can stand for 60–90 minutes. When wading in shallow water, one should shuffle rather than lift one's feet .

The Atlantic stingray only measures about 30cm (1ft) across its disk. The largest species is the Indo-Pacific Smooth stingray, which has a total length of over 4.5m (15ft) and a disk width of over 2m (7ft). Several deaths have been attributed to this species in Australia. Even very large specimens will lie in shallow water and impale

swimmers in the chest or abdomen with their large spine, which can be 30cm (1ft) long.

Although most species are marine, some South American genera live only in fresh water (e.g. *Potamotrygon* and *Paratrygon*). Their osmoregulatory physiology has adapted so completely to fresh water that they rapidly die in salt water, their upper limit of salt tolerance being about 50 percent that of seawater. They have an almost perfectly circular disk and are all beautifully marked with spots and bars. Lying in shallow water, covered by mud, they are feared for their poisonous spines. Like all other stingrays, the females develop their eggs internally, with up to twelve young per litter.

The three genera (*Myliobatus*, *Aetobatus* and *Rhinoptera*) of eagle rays – named for their large pectoral wings – are found worldwide in tropical and subtropical seas. Their wingspan can reach 2.4m (8ft). They have no frontal protrusion (rostrum), giving them a pug-nosed appearance. Their whiplike tail may be more than twice the length of their disk, with one or more spines at its base. The wings taper and are pointed at the tips, and both the eyes and spiracles are large. The teeth are fused into large crushing plates. They eat shellfish, which they find by squirting water from the mouth and blowing away the sand. Eagle rays can swim fast enough to breach and glide through the air.

The manta rays are the giants of the skates and rays and have one of the largest brains among fishes. Although stingless, they are closely related to the stingrays. The manta, whose name comes from the Spanish word for blanket or cloak, reaches a wingspan of over 6.7m (22ft) while the smallest juveniles have wingspans of little more than 1m (40 in). The wingspan of mobulas (devil rays) is 1–3m (3–10ft). The mouth of mantas is located at the front of the head and the teeth are only in the lower jaw, while that of mobulas is situated slightly beneath the head and the teeth are in both jaws. Mobulas are primarily pelagic.

Giant filter-feeders, mantas have two extensions of the pectoral fins called cephalic lobes that project forward from the head and are used to funnel plankton and fish-fry into the mouth. These lobes resemble horns – hence the name devilfish, though this also alludes to their habit of rubbing against anchor lines to remove skin parasites, causing the anchors to drag. Usually solitary except when breeding, they can be pelagic but prefer areas near land. When food is plentiful they will stay inshore around a single reef. As with Basking sharks, when plankton rises to the surface in the afternoon, they feed at the surface. Like eagle rays they can swim at great speed and make spectacular breaches, possibly to dislodge parasites. Reproduction is ovoviviparous, the one or two young hatch from eggs inside the mother and are nourished with a milky fluid from projections in the uterus until born alive. Mantas have been fished commercially in the Philippines and the Sea of Cortez and are often caught in drift-nets. JJ/GDi

# Chimaeras

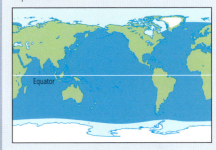

⬆ **Left** *It is easy to see how the Ratfish (Chimaera monstrosa) earned its common name.*

**a** LARGE, BLUNT HEAD, AN ERECTABLE *spine in front of the first dorsal fin, and a gill cover over the four gills that leaves a single opening are some characteristics of the chimaeras. Named for the she-monster of Greek mythology, which had a lion's head, a goat's body and a serpent's tail, these ugly relations of the sharks are also known as ratfish or rabbitfish; one of the generic names* (Hydrolagus) *literally means "water* (hydros) *rabbit* (lagus)".

Chimaeras occur in cold water, often at great depths – some have been recorded as deep as 2,400m (8,000ft). They are poor swimmers. Instead of using powerful side-to-side body movements like most fishes, especially sharks, they swim by flapping their pectoral fins, which makes them bob up and down in a clumsy fashion. Chimaeras usually keep close to the sea floor and have been observed motionless on the bottom, perched on the tips of their fins.

Like all cartilaginous fishes, the males have pelvic claspers to introduce sperm into the female. However, male chimaeras also have a second pair of retractable claspers in front of the pelvic fins that are probably used to hold the female during mating. Mature males also have a clasper on the forehead. Long-nosed and plow-nosed chimaeras have elongated, fleshy and flexible head projections (rostra), which are covered with electrical and chemical receptors.

Chimaeras are durophagous – a term meaning that they habitually feed on items that are hard. Their teeth are fused together to form three crushing plates, one in the lower jaw and two in the upper jaw, which are used to crush the shells of their food, mollusks, crustaceans and a few small fishes. Their large eyes are adaptations to low ambient light.

Young chimaeras are covered by short, stout dermal denticles (minute teeth) which are lost as they mature, except in long-nosed chimaeras which keep some of them for life. All chimaeras lay fairly large eggs, 15–25cm (6–10in) with a hard leathery shell that hatch in 6–8 months.

Most sharks take in water through the mouth to pass over the gills but chimaeras take in water through large nostrils connected to special channels, which direct the water to the gills. Unlike sharks, chimaeras have their gills in a common chamber protected by a flap (operculum).

The flesh of chimaeras is mostly eaten in Australia, New Zealand, and China, though the fillets are best pre-soaked in fresh water to remove the slight taste of ammonia. In the past, chimaera liver was used as a source of machine oil.   JJ/GDi

⬇ **Below** *The Plownose chimaera or Ghost shark* (Callorhincus milii) *occurs in the southwestern Pacific Ocean, off New Zealand and Southern Australia. It uses its distinctive plow to search out its main food item, shellfish.*

## FACTFILE

### CHIMAERAS

Class: Chondrichthyes

Order: Chimaeriformes

31 species in 6 genera and 3 families.

**Distribution** Subarctic, subantarctic, temperate and tropical waters.

**Size** Length 60–90cm (2–3ft) in most species to 1.8–2.2m (6–8ft) in *Chimaera monstrosa* and *Hydrolagus purpurescens*.

**SHORT-NOSED CHIMAERAS**
Family Chimaeridae
21 species in 2 genera, *Chimaera* and *Hydrolagus*. Atlantic, Pacific and Indian oceans.

**LONG-NOSED CHIMAERAS**
Family Rhinochimaeridae
6 species in 3 genera, *Rhinochimaera*, *Harriotta* and *Neoharriotta*. Scattered localities worldwide in temperate and tropical seas.

**PLOW-NOSED CHIMAERAS OR ELEPHANT FISHES**
Family Callorhinchidae
4 species of the genus *Callorhinchus*. Southern Hemisphere.

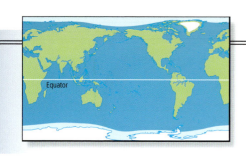

# WHALES & DOLPHINS

**m**AMMALS EVOLVED ON LAND, AND MOST *people still generally think of them as terrestrial animals. Yet over two-thirds of the surface of the planet is covered with water, so it is hardly surprising that in the course of evolutionary time some of them should have taken advantage of the expansive aqueous niche. Whales and dolphins have subsequently adapted to the physical properties of water and evolved in ways that would not have been possible had they remained on land; only supported by water's dense buoyancy could the largest whales have reached their present size.*

Adaptation to the watery environment has given the whales and dolphins a fishlike appearance, and it was not until 1758 that, thanks to the great Swedish biologist Carolus Linnaeus, they were in fact recognized as mammals. It took even longer to reveal the adaptations that have enabled them to spend their entire lives in oceans and seas; animals that encircle the whole world underwater and feed as deep as 1,500m/4,900ft (even 3,000m for sperm whales) have inevitably been difficult for land-dwelling humans to study. Technology – so much the enemy of whales in other ways – is, however, now helping us to understand their requirements and their complexity.

In fact, whales are clearly distinguished from fish by a number of specifically mammalian features. They are warm-blooded, breathe air through lungs, and give birth to living young that are suckled on milk secreted by the mammary glands of the mother. Unlike most land mammals, they do not have a coat of hair for warmth, as this would impede their progress through the water, reducing the advantage gained by the streamlining of the body. Of the three marine mammal orders – besides Cetacea, to which whales and dolphins belong, these comprise Pinnipedia (seals, sea lions, and walruses) and Sirenia (dugongs and manatees) – it is the whales and dolphins that are most specialized for life in the water; pinnipeds must return to land or ice to breed.

One half of the order Cetacea comprises the generally small dolphins and porpoises. They belong to the suborder Odonteceti, or toothed whales, which in total accounts for 72 of the 85 cetacean species. The toothed whales feed mainly on fish and squid, which they pursue and capture with jaws usually containing a large array of teeth. In contrast, most of the great whales belong to the suborder Mysticeti, the baleen whales; these have a system of horny plates – the baleen – in place of teeth, using them to filter or strain planktonic organisms and larger invertebrates, as well as schools of small fish, from the sea.

## Body Shape, Locomotion, and Diving
### ANATOMY AND PHYSIOLOGY

The largest animal ever to have lived on this planet is the Blue whale. It reaches a length of 24–27m (80–90ft) and weighs 130–150 metric tons, equivalent to the weight of 33 elephants – the largest terrestrial mammal. Such an enormous body could only be supported in an aquatic medium, for on land it would require limbs so large that mobility would be greatly restricted. Though populations have been severely reduced by overhunting, the Blue whale still survives today.

Despite their size and weight, whales and dolphins are very mobile, their streamlined bodies

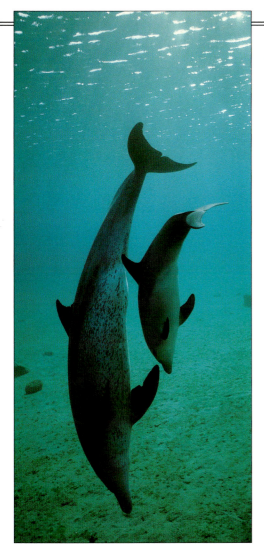

○ **Left** *A mother and calf Bottlenose dolphin diving to feed in the Red Sea. These dolphins are often seen in captivity, as they appear to be an intelligent species that can learn complex tasks quickly. Some people even claim to have seen wild Bottlenoses using their tail to flip fish onto a beach before retrieving them.*

ideally adapted to fast movement through water. The head is elongated in comparison to other mammals, and passes imperceptibly into the trunk, with no obvious neck or shoulders. Rorquals, river dolphins, and the white whales have neck vertebrae that are separate, allowing greater flexibility; the remainder of the species have between two and seven fused together.

Whales' skeletons still bear signs that their ancestors were once land mammals with four legs, but hind legs have now entirely disappeared from the outside of the body. In fact, few body parts protrude to create drag. Instead of ears, cetaceans merely have two tiny openings that lead directly to the organs of hearing. The male's penis is completely hidden within muscular folds, and the teats of the female are housed within slits on either side of the genital area. The only protuberances are a pair of horizontal fins or flippers, a boneless tail fluke, and, in many species, an upright but boneless dorsal fin of tissue that is firm and fibrous.

In most of the toothed whales the jaws are extended as a beaklike snout, behind which the

**ORDER: CETACEA**
14 families; 40 genera; 85 species

**TOOTHED WHALES**
Suborder: Odontoceti

**RIVER DOLPHINS** Families Lipotidae, Iniidae, Platanistidae, and Pontoporiidae
5 species in 4 genera in 4 families
Yangtze river dolphin (*Lipotes vexillifer*), Amazon dolphin (*Inia geoffrensis*), Ganges dolphin (*Platanista gangetica*), Indus dolphin (*P. minor*), and La Plata dolphin (*Pontoporia blainvillei*).

**DOLPHINS** Family Delphinidae
At least 36 species in 17 genera
Includes Pantropical spotted dolphin (*Stenella attenuata*), Common dolphin (*Delphinus delphis*), Killer whale (*Orcinus orca*), Pilot whale (*Globicephala melas*), Risso's dolphin (*Grampus griseus*), White-beaked dolphin (*Lagenorhynchus albirostris*).

**PORPOISES** Family Phocoenidae
6 species in 3 genera
Includes Harbor porpoise (*Phocoena phocoena*) and Finless porpoise (*Neophocaena phocaenoides*)

**BELUGA AND NARWHAL** Family Monodontidae
2 species in 2 genera: beluga (*Delphinapterus leucas*) and narwhal (*Monodon monoceros*).

**SPERM WHALE** Family Physeteridae
1 species *Physeter catodon (macrocephalus)*

**PYGMY SPERM WHALES** Family Kogiidae
2 species in 1 genus: Pygmy sperm whale (*Kogia breviceps*) and Dwarf sperm whale (*K. simus*).

**BEAKED WHALES** Family Ziphiidae
At least 20 species in 6 genera
Includes Northern bottlenose whale (*Hyperoodon ampulatus*), Blainville's beaked whale (*Mesoplodon densirostris*), and Cuvier's beaked whale (*Ziphius cavirostris*).

**BALEEN WHALES**
Suborder: Mysticeti

**GRAY WHALE** Family Eschrichtiidae             p256
1 species *Eschrichtius robustus*

**RORQUALS** Family Balaenopteridae             p262
8 species in 2 genera
Includes Blue whale (*Balaenoptera musculus*), Fin whale (*Balaenoptera physalus*), Minke whale (*Balaenoptera acutorostrata*), Humpback whale (*Megaptera novaeangliae*).

**RIGHT WHALES** Family Balaenidae             p270
3 species in 3 genera
Includes Bowhead whale (*Balaena mysticetus*) and Northern right whale (*Balaena glacialis*).

**PYGMY RIGHT WHALE** Family Neobalaenidae     p270
1 species *Caperea marginata*

*Note* As with several other mammalian orders, the taxonomy of the cetaceans is in considerable flux. For example, the classification established in 1993 accepted 11 genera, 41 families, and 78 species.

○ **Left** *The Pygmy killer whale (Feresa attenuata) is a predatory species, about which little is known. They have occasionally been known to prey upon the off-spring of some species of dolphins, and are found principally in the coastal waters off Japan, Hawaii, and South Africa.*

○ **Above** *The tail flukes, powered by huge back muscles, are the great whales' sole source of propulsion. The Northern right whale, in common with other species, usually only raises its tails flukes clear of the water before making a deep dive. One speculation is that this species may use its tail as a sail in high winds.*

forehead rises in a rounded curve or "melon." Unlike the baleen whales (or any other mammal) they possess a single nostril; the two nasal passages, which are separate at the base of the skull, join close below the surface to form a single opening – the blowhole. In extreme cases, one passage is devoted to sound production, leaving the other as the sole breathing tube. The blowhole typically takes the form of a crescent-shaped slit protected by a fatty and fibrous pad or plug. Efficient adaptation means that the slit is closed by water pressure, but can be opened by muscular action when the whale surfaces to breathe. The skull bones of the nasal region are usually asymmetrical in their size, shape, and position, although porpoises and the La Plata dolphin have symmetrical skulls.

The baleen or whalebone whales differ from toothed whales in a number of ways. They are generally much larger, and the baleen apparatus takes the place of teeth in the mouth. The baleen grows as a series of horny plates from the sides of the upper jaw, occupying the position of the

upper teeth in other animals. Baleen whales feed by straining large quantities of water containing plankton and larger organisms through these plates. The paired nostrils remain separate, so that the blowhole is a double hole forming two parallel slits that are close together when shut. Other features specific to baleen whales are single-headed ribs and a breast bone (sternum) composed of a single bone articulating with the first pair of ribs only. All baleen whales have symmetrical skulls, though the size and shape varies between species.

Like all mammals, cetaceans are warm-blooded, using part of the energy available to them to maintain a stable body-core temperature, in their case of 36–37°C (97–99°F). The sea is a relatively cool environment, with temperatures usually below 25°C (77°F), and cetaceans lack fur coats, instead insulating the vital organs that lie just inside their skin with blubber – a layer of fat up to 50cm (20in) thick in the Bowhead whale. Larger species have a distinct advantage over smaller ones, having less surface area over which to lose

heat in relation to their body mass. This may explain why the smaller dolphins do not occur at very high latitudes. The liver is also an important fat store, and in some species there are significant quantities of fat (up to half the body's total) in the form of oil laid down in the skeletal bones.

Whales and dolphins rely upon controlled bloodflow from the body core to the skin and appendages for heat regulation. Unlike land mammals, whose insulation typically overlies vascular circulation to the skin, the insulating blanket of cetacean blubber is penetrated by massive, contorted spirals of blood vessels called *retia mirabilia* (mainly arteries, but also including some thin-walled veins) that usually form blocks of tissue on the inner dorsal wall of the thoracic cavity and on the extremities or periphery of the body. These vessels function as countercurrent heat exchangers, maintaining a heat differential between oppositely-directed flows and so increasing the amount of heat transferred. Such heat exchangers in the flippers, flukes, and fins serve to conserve body

## DOLPHIN AND WHALE BODY PLANS

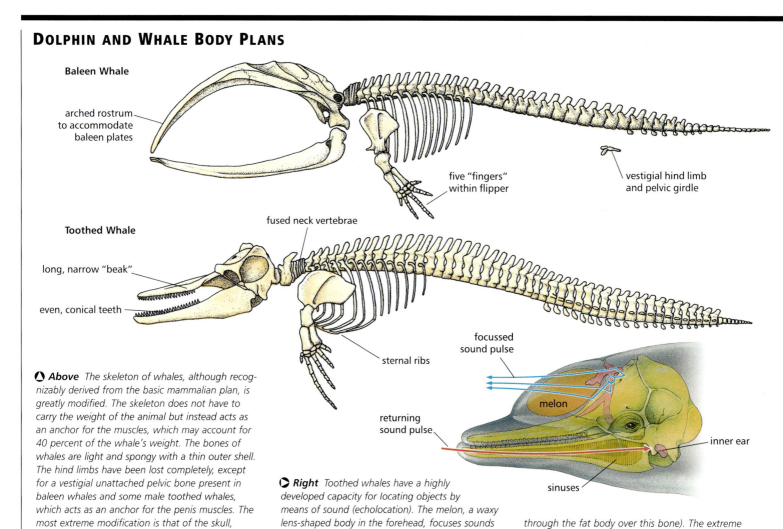

**Baleen Whale**

arched rostrum to accommodate baleen plates

five "fingers" within flipper

vestigial hind limb and pelvic girdle

**Toothed Whale**

fused neck vertebrae

long, narrow "beak"

even, conical teeth

sternal ribs

focussed sound pulse

returning sound pulse

melon

inner ear

sinuses

◑ **Above** The skeleton of whales, although recognizably derived from the basic mammalian plan, is greatly modified. The skeleton does not have to carry the weight of the animal but instead acts as an anchor for the muscles, which may account for 40 percent of the whale's weight. The bones of whales are light and spongy with a thin outer shell. The hind limbs have been lost completely, except for a vestigial unattached pelvic bone present in baleen whales and some male toothed whales, which acts as an anchor for the penis muscles. The most extreme modification is that of the skull, which is greatly extended in both baleen and toothed whales. The loss of teeth in baleen whales and associated changes have produced a skull with a grotesque form, unlike that of any other animal.

◖ **Right** Toothed whales have a highly developed capacity for locating objects by means of sound (echolocation). The melon, a waxy lens-shaped body in the forehead, focuses sounds produced in the nasal passages (more focussing is achieved by reflections off the skull and air sacs). Returning sound waves are channeled to the inner ear through oil-filled sinuses in the lower jaw (and

through the fat body over this bone). The extreme sensitivity of this system is assisted by the isolation of the inner ear from the skull by means of a bubbly foam. Sound is thus very precisely channeled without the interference of extraneous resonances.

temperature, the arteries being closely surrounded by veins. Cold blood from the veins extracts heat from the arterial blood coming from the body core, so that the blood returning to the body is warmed and heat loss is consequently minimized. Countercurrent heat exchangers also exist close to male genitalia, to cool the testes, and in Gray whales' tongues. As well as needing to conserve heat, when large whales (or active small whales) are in warm water, they have a heat dumping problem. In such circumstances, the countercurrent system can be overridden by flushing more blood through the arteries, collapsing surrounding veins, and so diverting blood to a superficial return pathway, where it can be cooled.

◖ **Right** *The Humpback whale occurs in a worldwide distribution. Here, a juvenile Humpback is seen swimming with its mother. Its distinctive flippers, with their white, scalloped leading edges picked out by the refracted underwater light, are already well developed. The flippers can grow up to 5m (17ft) in length.*

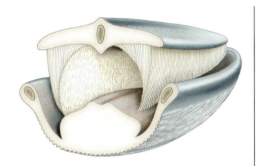

◐ **Above** *Baleen apparatus. Instead of teeth, baleen whales have two rows of fringed plates hanging from the upper roof of the mouth. They evolved from the curved transverse ridges of the palate found in many land mammals. Despite the commercial name applied to them ("whalebone") they are not made of bone, but toughened skin.*

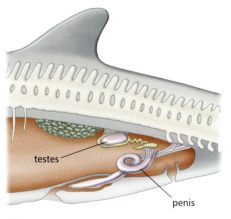

◑ **Above** *The genitals of whales are internal, only a genital slit being visible. In males, the penis lies coiled on the floor of the abdominal cavity, held there by a retractor muscle. The penis is very mobile and is often used as a sensory organ in a variety of social interactions.*

Whales propel themselves mainly by vertical strokes of their powerful tails (unlike fish, which propel themselves by sideways movements). This movement is powered by a great muscle mass that occupies the upper region of the animal. Most cetaceans have a well-defined dorsal fin that is presumed to stabilize the animal, although it also plays a role in temperature regulation.

The skeletal structure of the forelimbs is similar to that of the human arm, but the limbs have been modified to form paddle-like flippers that are used for steering. Whereas the rigid hull of a ship creates turbulence as it passes through the water,

a cetacean minimizes this through flexibility; its blubber is not tightly fixed to the underlying muscular tissues, and there is a very well-developed system of dermal ridges beneath the skin. From the smooth, outer, cellular layer of the epidermis comes a secretion of tiny droplets of a high polymer of ethylene oxide; one speculation is that these droplets assist the shedding of epidermal cells into the water and may help to maintain a laminar flow, reducing turbulence and drag by dissipating the energy of the impeding vortices.

Cetaceans spend almost all their lives underwater, sometimes at great depths. Yet they must surface to breathe air, since, unlike fish, they do not take up oxygen from the water. When they dive, they must hold their breath.

When a man dives for longer than he can hold his breath, he takes with him an aqualung – a cylinder of compressed air. This is necessary because the air pressure within his lungs must equal or slightly exceed the pressure of the water around him; otherwise, he cannot expand his chest to breathe. Under compression, the nitrogen in the air dissolves in the fluids and tissues of his body to their full capacity, and when he ascends the dissolved nitrogen comes out of solution in the form of bubbles of gas. These may appear in any part of the body; in the joints they cause the painful condition called "the bends." In contrast, when a cetacean dives it takes just enough air to fill its relatively small lungs; only a proportion of the air is nitrogen, so that the amount that could dissolve in the body fluids and tissues from one filling of the lungs is rather small. But even this small amount does not enter the blood and tissues, because the cetacean's lungs compress as it dives, driving the air into the windpipe and its branches and into the extensive nasal passages, whose thickened membrane linings prevent gas exchange to the tissues. In cetaceans the chest is comparatively flexible and the diaphragm set very obliquely, so that the pressure of the abdominal viscera pushing against it on one side makes the lungs on the other side collapse.

As a cetacean ascends, its lungs gradually expand again; the blowhole opens wide, and the foul-smelling air accumulated during the dive is expelled explosively. This produces a cloud of spray – the spout – as water from around the blowhole is forced into the air. All whales perform this "blowing," although it is less visible in smaller species. As soon as the animal has exhaled, it takes in fresh air; the air sacs of the lungs return to their expanded condition for maximum gas exchange, and the whale is ready to dive again.

Cetaceans can remain underwater for quite extended periods – up to an hour or more for Northern bottlenose and Sperm whales. A molecular store called myoglobin supplies the muscles with oxygen, allowing them to function without fresh oxygen for longer than in land mammals.

## Sound Production and Echolocation
### UNDERWATER NAVIGATION

There is little light deep underwater, so cetaceans rely mostly on senses other than sight to inform them about their surroundings and to help them locate food. They have a highly developed sense of hearing, and communicate with each other by producing a wide variety of sounds. The toothed whales, which pursue agile fish and squid, locate their prey by using sonar. They emit intense, short pulses of sound mainly in the ultrasonic range (20–220kHz). In dolphins, each click lasts from 10 to 100 milliseconds and may be repeated as many as six hundred times per second. These clicks, along with other sounds, bounce off objects in their path, producing echoes from which the animal is able to build up a complete sound "picture" of its surroundings. Sperm whales produce click pulses that last about 24 milliseconds and consist of a series of up to nine individual clicks that reverberate rapidly. The repetition rate of the pulses is adjusted so that the echo of one click pulse returns from the target before the next pulse is emitted. These click pulses are very intense and can be heard several kilometers away.

It was once thought that echolocatory clicks were produced by the larynx, but now they are known to come from the nasal sac region just inside the blowhole. In the upper nasal sac passages is a structure called the "monkey lips"/dorsal bursa complex. All toothed whales and dolphins except the Sperm whale possess two bilaterally-placed complexes located just below the ventral floor of the vestibular air sac and composed of a pair of fatty-filled anterior and posterior dorsal bursae embedded in a pair of monkey lips (a slitlike opening), a resilient cartilaginous blade, and a stout blowhole ligament, all suspended within a complex array of muscles and air spaces. Although the heads of Sperm whales superficially look different from those of dolphins, it is now believed that they produce sound in much the same way. Air is forced between the monkey lips, causing the complex to vibrate. The periodic opening and closing of the lips breaks up the air flow and determines the repetition rate of the click train. When the lips slap together during click production, vibrations are thought to be produced in the bursae. A high-speed video endoscope has been used recently upon captive dolphins to confirm the role of this complex in sound production. Once sound is generated, it is propagated through the melon (or junk in the case of Sperm whales). The core of the melon consists of low-density lipids, which serve as an acoustic lens to focus directional beams in front of it.

◗ **Below** *The size and pattern of whales' water spouts is extremely diverse. The spout of smaller whales is quite inconspicuous, however, the spout of the Gray whale can reach 3m (10ft). Some species have two blowholes and produce a V-shaped spout.*

The baleen whales have not yet been shown to use echolocation as toothed whales and dolphins do, and may instead rely on sight to locate the swarms of plankton on which they feed. However, they can emit very loud pulses of sound at low frequencies (from 15Hz to 30kHz) and for short durations that, as revealed by SOSUS (SOund SUrveillance System) arrays deployed by the US Navy in deep waters, are audible over tens to hundreds of kilometers across the deep-ocean channels. The low frequencies of Blue and Fin whale tones have very long wavelengths, from 50m at 30Hz to100m at 15Hz. A typical Blue whale call lasts for 20 seconds and in water is approximately 30km in length. If these sounds were used for echolocation, they would not be able to discriminate targets finer than those wavelengths. They may therefore be used primarily to detect largescale oceanic features like continental shelves, or possibly the sharp differences in water density associated with cold-water upwellings.

Baleen whale sounds may also serve a communicatory function, particularly if individual calls vary and are recognizable. In toothed whales and dolphins, which are often social, signature whistles provide opportunities for individual recognition, and these might lead to the evolution of geographic or pod-specific dialects.

## Evolution

### CETACEAN ANCESTRY

The origins of present-day cetaceans are poorly understood, although the introduction of new molecular techniques in the 1990s has led to an extensive re-evaluation of relationships on the basis of a combination of fresh molecular and morphological information. However, whereas morphology indicates that cetaceans are most closely related either to Artiodactyla (even-toed ungulates) or to Perissodactyla (odd-toed ungulates), molecular data suggest cetaceans and hippopotamid artiodactyls may form extant sister taxa, with Ruminantia (antelope, deer, and kin) being the next most closely related.

Mammals recognizable as cetaceans first appear as fossils in rock strata from the early Middle Eocene. The first was *Pakicetus,* of the Protoceridae, an elongated aquatic animal with reduced hind limbs and a long snout. Classified within a separate suborder called Archaeoceti, such mammals flourished during the Eocene epoch, but most were extinct before the end of the Oligocene, and none survived beyond the Miocene. However, even by the late Middle and early Upper Eocene, they had become so specialized that they could not have been the ancestors of modern cetaceans.

Looking further back in time, members of the terrestrial suborder Mesonychia may have given rise to the archaeocetes (and thence to all other cetaceans) at the end of the Cretaceous and then colonized the sea during the Paleocene. These are

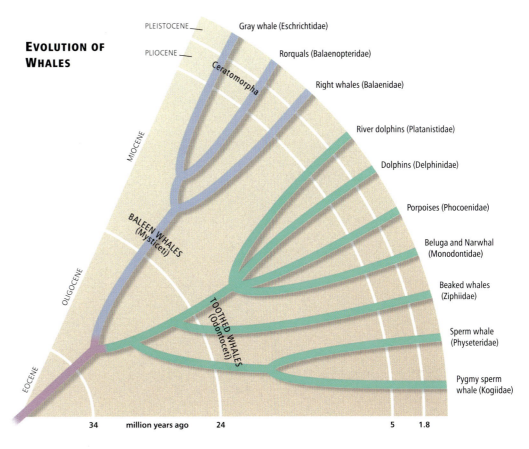

**EVOLUTION OF WHALES**

PLEISTOCENE — Gray whale (Eschrichtidae)

PLIOCENE — Rorquals (Balaenopteridae)

Ceratomorpha

Right whales (Balaenidae)

River dolphins (Platanistidae)

MIOCENE

Dolphins (Delphinidae)

BALEEN WHALES (Mysticeti)

Porpoises (Phocoenidae)

Beluga and Narwhal (Monodontidae)

OLIGOCENE

Beaked whales (Ziphiidae)

TOOTHED WHALES (Odontoceti)

Sperm whale (Physeteridae)

EOCENE

Pygmy sperm whale (Kogiidae)

34    million years ago    24    5    1.8

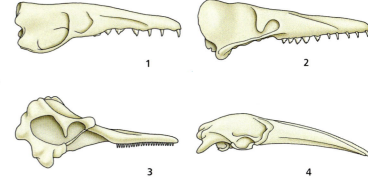

▷ **Right** The modifications to bone structure and teeth that have been involved in the evolution of the whale skull.
**1** Protocetus, a land-based creodont with carnivore-like teeth;
**2** Prosqualodon, an intermediate form; **3** The Bottlenose dolphin, a modern toothed whale, showing the uniform teeth;
**4** a rorqual, showing the most extreme modification of the bone structure, loss of all the teeth, and their replacement by baleen (not shown).

1    2    3    4

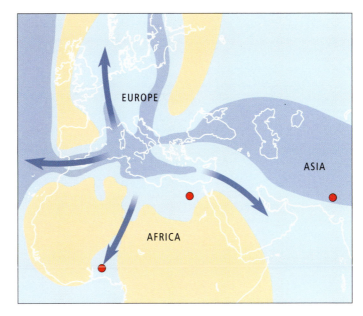

EUROPE

ASIA

AFRICA

◁ **Left** The Tethys Sea was an enormous trough in the earth's crust. It formed a seaway that separated Europe and Africa, continued across the Middle East, and then southeast to Myanmar (Burma). It is the probable center of whale evolution: dispersal routes show how modern distribution came about.

original extent of the Tethys Sea

expansion of the Tethys Sea during the Eocene

source of the remains of the oldest known whales

possible dispersal route

thought to share with the suborder Arctocyonia (the likely ancestors of present-day ungulates and their relatives) ancestry from the Condylarthra (otherwise known as creodonts). The Mesonychidae resemble the archaeocetes in a number of skull and dental characteristics, and although the similarities are not all clear-cut, they appear at present to be the most likely ancestors of the Cetacea.

Most of the early archaeocete remains come from the Mediterranean–Arabian Gulf region, which during the Paleocene formed a narrow arm of the western part of the ancient Tethys Sea. It was probably here that populations of terrestrial creodonts started to colonize marshes and shallow coastal fringes during the late Paleocene, exploiting niches vacated at the end of the Cretaceous by the vanishing plesiosaurs, ichthyosaurs, and other reptiles. As population pressure on resources intensified during the Eocene, we can speculate that selection would have favored adaptations for the capture of fast-moving fish rather than the sluggish fish and freshwater and estuarine mollusks that previously formed their main diet.

This was the age of mammals, with massive adaptive radiation into many species; such rapid evolution may help to explain the sparse fossil record for this period, with forms developing relatively specialized cetacean characters quite quickly. During the Eocene, the warm waters of the western Tethys Sea were dominated by the archaeocetes, but as the climate started to deteriorate and the Tethys Sea enlarged during the Oligocene, they probably declined in density and abundance, and by the Miocene were being entirely replaced by odontocetes and mysticetes. The progressively more aquatic mode of life resulted in a backward and upward shift of the external nostrils, and the development of ways to seal them against water. The long, mobile neck, functional hind limbs, and, eventually, most of the pelvic girdle were all lost, together with any remaining coat, and horizontal tail flukes developed for propulsion. The body became more torpedo-shaped to provide greater streamlining, and a dorsal fin developed for hydrodynamic control and temperature regulation.

Most modifications of the archaeocete skull towards an odontocete (toothed whale) form involved the telescoping of the front of the skull, which probably paralleled the development of acoustic scanning as a means of location, thereby aiding the capture of agile prey. At the same time, various specialized organs developed – notably the melon, spermaceti organ, and nasal diverticula. Their functions are thought to relate to the processing of sounds and, in the case of species like the Sperm whale, possibly also to diving. Later, sexual selection may have favored greater development of some of these in males of species in which competition for mates is important.

The teeth of archaeocetes were differentiated into incisors, canines, and grinding teeth. These teeth either became modified during the Eocene, forming the long rows of sharp, uniform teeth typical of present-day toothed whales, or later, mainly in the Oligocene, gave rise to the baleen plates: the remarkable feeding structures that evolved from the curved transverse ridges of the palate. Most present-day baleen whales still have the

△ **Above** *Small prey for large mammals; individual Antarctic krill grow to a maximum size of just 7.5cm (3in); however, they exist in staggering numbers, totaling some 500–750 million tonnes. Krill is the principal food of the large baleen whales, particularly the Blue whale, but also the Fin, Sei, and Minke whales.*

◁ **Left** *Humpback whales "bubble net" feeding. One or two Humpbacks work together, swimming up beneath a shoal, all the while spiraling and blowing bubbles. The fish will swim in through the barrier of bubbles to join their companions but will not swim out, so the "net" effectively concentrates the shoal.*

▽ **Below** *Feeding strategies vary from species to species of dolphin. Some herd shoals in an apparently cooperative manner, while others feed independently. Here, a Bottlenose dolphin is seen chasing a shoal of baitfish. Bottlenose dolphins have also been seen to temporarily disable fish by knocking them out of the water with their powerful tail.*

developmental precursors of teeth (buds) in the early stages of fetal development, a further indication of their common ancestry with the toothed whales, which is also supported by anatomical and chromosomal evidence.

The earliest true toothed whales were the squalodonts, a group of short-beaked whales with triangular, sharklike teeth. These were possibly most abundant in the late Oligocene to early Miocene, dispersed throughout the Southern Hemisphere, but by the middle Miocene they were being superseded by representatives of families with living relatives. In particular, the *Ziphiidae* (beaked whales) can be traced back to a squalodont ancestor, and so can other groups including the *Physeteridae* (Sperm whales) and, in fresh and brackish waters, the *Platanistidae* (river dolphins), *Delphinidae* (true dolphins), and *Phocoenidae* (porpoises). Sperm whales, which have a much more marked asymmetry of the skull than any other odontocetes and a quite distinct chromosomal structure, almost certainly diverged early in the history of the line, around the mid-Oligocene. However, recent molecular evidence refutes the idea that they may be more closely related to baleen whales than to other toothed whales.

While the toothed whale skull was becoming modified to contain acoustic apparatus, the baleen whale skull became adapted to a different lifestyle. The upper margin of the "forehead" of the skull underwent considerable forward extension, probably mainly to combat the stresses on the skull and jaws imposed by the wide opening and closing of the mouth at irregular intervals as the animals feed.

## A Generalist Diet
### FOOD AND FEEDING

From the predatory Killer whales, which feed on other cetaceans, Sea otters, and pinnipeds, through fish- and cephalopod-pursuing dolphins to Humpback and Blue whales sieving krill, cetacean diets encompass much of what is on offer from the sea. Many small toothed whales appear to have generalist diets, opportunistically taking in a range of shoaling open-sea fishes, but the extent to which diets overlap between species within a region remains poorly known. Among the baleen whales, the thickness and number of baleen plates is related to the size and species of prey taken. Thus the Gray whale, a highly selective seabottom feeder, has a shorter, stiffer baleen and fewer throat grooves (usually 2–3) than the rorquals (with 14–100), and is thereby adapted for "scouring" the sea bottom. In the rorquals, the baleen is longer and wider. In the Blue whale, the plates may reach a width of nearly 0.75m (2.5ft); in the other rorquals they are correspondingly narrower, and this dictates the diet of each. In the Right and Bowhead whales the baleen is extremely long and fine and these whales feed on the smallest planktonic invertebrates of any of the baleen whales.

Whereas baleen whales and some toothed whales, such as the Sperm whale, Northern bottlenose whale and Harbor porpoise, may tend to feed independently, a number of small toothed whales appear to herd shoals cooperatively by a combination of breaching and fast surface-rushing in groups. Communication between individuals presumably is carried out by vocalization (high-pitched squeaks, squeals, or grunts) and perhaps also by particular types of breaching. These latter activities often seem to be quite complex, but until we can routinely follow marked individuals (preferably below water), we cannot be sure of the extent of cooperation between individuals.

## Ecology and Behavior
### LIFESTYLE AND BREEDING

The different evolutionary courses that the baleen and toothed whales have taken have strongly influenced their respective ecologies. Generally speaking, the ocean areas with the highest primary productivity (quantities of phytoplankton), and hence the most fish and squid dependent upon this, are close to the Poles (where 150–250mg of carbon are fixed from light energy per square meter daily in a season), whereas at tropical latitudes productivity is relatively low (though rich upwellings of nutrients do occur patchily – high in coastal waters but at rates of 50–100mg of carbon per square meter per day in open waters where there is no upwelling). Polar regions show great seasonal variations, and during the summer the rapid increase in temperature, sunlight, and daylength, and the relatively stable climatic conditions, allow phytoplankton – and hence zooplankton and higher organisms such as fish and squid – to build up to very high densities.

During the 120-day period of summer feeding, the great baleen whales probably eat about 3–4 percent of their body weight daily. Present-day whale populations in the Southern Ocean (including all species of baleen whales) consume about 40 million metric tons of krill each year. Before these whale populations were exploited by man, the figure may have been as high as 200 million tons. Thus, during part of the year (about four months in the Southern Ocean, but often more than six months in the North Pacific and North Atlantic, where productivity is lower), the great whales migrate to high latitudes to feed, and here they may put on as much as 40 percent of their body weight as blubber. During the rest of the year, feeding rates may be reduced to about a tenth of the summer value, which results in much of the blubber store being used by the time the whales return to the feeding grounds.

Why should the great baleen whales use up the food they have stored in their blubber to migrate to regions nearer the Equator where there is little food? There are several speculative answers, yet no definitive one. Many smaller cetacean species spend all the year at high latitudes and appear to be perfectly capable of rearing their young in this relatively cool environment. Breeding at high latitudes in winter would be constrained by lack of food, but in summer primary productivity is very high and water temperatures are also much more favorable.

One explanation why the larger whales travel to warm waters to breed is that the growth rates required for the young to attain anything like the large size of their parents, together with the energy intake required by mothers to sustain both themselves and their calves, would require a

⬆ **Above** A Killer whale beaches on the coast of Patagonia, Argentina, and snatches a South American sea lion. This species has fewer teeth than most toothed whales, but they are large and strong for seizing large fish, squid, and other marine vertebrates. The Killer whale does not chew its food but swallows it whole or in large chunks, which it tears off.

⬇ **Below** One of the functions of breaching is to communicate with other whales, but it may also serve to panic or stun shoals of fish, making it easier to feed on them. Humpback whales are very adept at breaching and have been observed to leap clear of the water belly-up, reenter headfirst, and circle underwater to return to the starting position.

longer period of high productivity than is available in a polar summer. This proposition is supported by the observation that plankton has a short season of abundance, whereas fish and squid are available year-round, and the great whales that undertake extensive migrations are mostly plankton-feeders (although some migratory Humpback whales depend more on fish). Secondly, the answer may be historical. The earliest fossil remains of baleen whales, from about 30 million years ago, occur in low latitudes of the North Atlantic. With the juxtaposition of continental land masses by tectonic plate movement and changes in sea temperature during the Cenozoic era, they radiated and dispersed toward the poles. As with some long-distance migrant bird species, the present-day movements of the great whales may be partly a vestige of earlier times, in their case of an epoch when high productivity was to be found in more equatorial regions. For this to apply, however, the energetic costs of latitudinal long-distance travel would need to be small, for selection pressures would otherwise have eliminated this behavioral trait. A third explanation is that whales avoid breeding in polar and subpolar seas because they experience high predation pressures there, due to the higher density of Killer whales. A full understanding of whale migration still eludes science. However, it is worth noting that some large baleen whales, such as the Fin whale, do not necessarily show strong latitudinal migrations.

Whereas baleen whales feed chiefly on zooplankton, the toothed whales feed largely on either fish or squid. All three prey groups have comparable energy values, weight for weight, and although this takes no account of differences in protein, fat, or carbohydrate contents, daily feeding rates are comparable across groups. Body size appears to be the factor that determines whether or not toothed whales move out of high latitudes in winter; smaller species have relatively higher feeding rates, irrespective of diet (the smallest species put on 8–10 percent of body weight daily, compared with 3–5 percent for the largest), but total daily intake for a smaller individual is obviously proportionately lower.

The smaller cetaceans may be found at most latitudes. Even though they range over large areas – for example, the home range of the Pantropical spotted dolphin in the North Pacific appears to be 320–480km (200–300mi) in diameter – they do not tend to make strong north–south migrations.

Although the differences in migratory habits cannot be entirely attributed to diet, other cetacean features do appear to be related to what the animals eat. Plankton- and fish-feeding species all have gestation periods of between 10–13 months whatever their size, whereas squid-feeders have periods of the order of 12–16 months. The longer gestation may reflect the relative food values (protein, fat, and carbohydrate amounts,

rather than simply energy values) of the different prey, or it may relate to the relative seasonal availabilities of those prey. Amongst large whales, lactation periods are relatively longer in the squid-feeding Sperm whale than in plankton-feeding baleen whales. Among smaller cetaceans, the pattern is similar, though less clear-cut: squid-feeding species have lactation periods varying from 12–24 months, whereas in fish-feeding species they are generally around 10–12 months.

The social systems of whales may also be influenced by diet. In the plankton-feeders such as the Right and Bowhead whales, males may compete with one another to mate with a single female, but spend most of their time either singly or in pairs; small groups of usually less than 10 individuals occur primarily at feeding concentrations or during long-distance movements. We have little information on the social systems of rorquals, but male Humpback whales seasonally advertise themselves to females, singing long songs and breaching repeatedly; they form "floating leks," in which males consort temporarily with females for mating purposes, rebuffing or displacing other males. On the other hand, at least some of the squid-feeding whale species form stable groups, often matriarchal with young of both sexes, to which adult males attach themselves for short periods for mating purposes; other groups can comprise bachelor males, which may also travel alone. This system is exemplified by the Sperm whale. The pilot whale may be more akin to the Killer whale, with males remaining in their natal group, in contrast to the Sperm whale, in which males disperse. Microsatellite DNA studies of the Long-finned pilot whale indicate that the species travels in matrifocal kin groups, with males mating with two or more females though rarely with members of their own pod. The Killer whale, which has a mixed diet of squid, fish, marine birds, and mammals, also forms very stable, matrilineal social groups, each typically consisting of an older mature female, her male and female offspring, and the offspring of the

○ **Above** *A pair of Bottlenose dolphins mating. The mating season varies according to the geographical location of the dolphins and the waters that they inhabit. The gestation period is usually about one year. The newborn may not be fully weaned until they are 18 months old, but will begin taking some solids from about 6 months.*

second generation's mature females. Mature males remain with the pod into which they were born, and movement or exchange of individuals among pods has not been documented. Genetic studies suggest that male Killer whales do not mate with closely-related pod members but rather with members of other pods in ephemeral encounters. Most fish-feeders, however, have a rather fluid social system, with mixed groups or family units (which may simply be mother–calf pairs) that aggregate on the feeding or mating grounds, and also during long-distance movements. Individuals come and go so that the group is not stable, though it may have a constant core. In several species studied, it seems that there is no stable pair bond (long-term associations being mainly between female kin), and both sexes are promiscuous.

Although almost certainly rare, hybridization between Fin and Blue whales does occur, despite an evolutionary separation of 5 million years or more. Hybridization between more distantly related mammalian species may not be excluded, but it is probable that the Blue and Fin whales are nearly as different in their mitochondrial DNA sequences as hybridizing mammal species can be – as different, in fact, as chimps and humans.

## Location and Life History
### DISTRIBUTION
Cetaceans are not randomly distributed over any region but instead seem to favor certain oceanographic features such as upwellings (where food concentrations tend to occur), or undersea topographic features such as continental shelf slopes (which may serve as cues for navigation). Breeding areas for most cetacean species (particularly

small toothed whales) are very poorly known, but are better known for some of the large whales.

Gray and Right whales seem to require shallow coastal bays in warm waters for calving, whereas balaenopterids such as Blue, Fin, and Sei whales possibly breed in deeper waters further offshore. The former group thus has more localized calving areas than the latter.

During the period of mating, some cetacean species congregate in particular areas. These may be the same warm-water areas as those in which calving occurs during the winter months, or they may be on feeding grounds at high latitudes during the summer, as with many small toothed whales. Mating is usually seasonal, but in a number of gregarious dolphin species sexual activity has been observed during most months.

The lengths of the gestation and lactation periods naturally dictate the frequency with which a female may bear young. Cetaceans give birth to single young. In the smaller fish-feeding species (such as porpoises), a female may reproduce every year; among the large plankton-feeding whales, the period is every alternate year (in some species perhaps only every 3 years); in squid-feeding species, females bear young every 3–7 years; while in the Killer whale, with its mixed diet, females reproduce at intervals of 3–8 years. Furthermore, many species do not reach sexual maturity for a number of years (4–10 years in plankton- and fish-feeders, 8–16 in squid feeders and in the Killer whale). It is thus not surprising that most species are long-lived (12–50 years in the smaller species, but 50–100 years in the large baleen

whales like the Bowhead and the Sperm, as well as the Killer whale).

Natural mortality rates seem to decrease in different whale species as their size increases, with those for juveniles being somewhat higher than the ones for adults. Current estimates are 9–10 percent per annum for Minke whales; 7.5 percent for Sperm whales; and 4 percent for Fin whales. The long maturation in squid-feeders probably results from their need for a long period to learn efficient capture of the relatively difficult and agile squid prey. There is evidence for differences in annual mortality rates between sexes in some

**Above** Whaling was a far more dangerous activity before the advent of explosive harpoons and factory ships. This scene of early whalers being tossed about in their small boat by a harpooned whale is an example of scrimshaw, the art of engraving pictures onto whalebone or whale ivory – in this instance, a Sperm whale's tooth.

**Above left** Dolphins figure widely in classical art and literature – including works by Aristotle, Aesop, and Herodotus – often as rescuers of people in peril at sea. This Greek bowl, made in the 5th century BC, depicts an incident involving Dionysus, the god of wine. Attacked by pirates, the god retaliated by transforming his assailants into the benign form of dolphins.

**Below** Pictorial representations of whales exist as far back as the Stone Age. However, following the introduction of scientific classification by Linnaeus, works such as this 18th century engraving – intended primarily as a typological aid – became widespread.

species, for instance Killer whales (3.9 percent in adult males and 0.5–2.1 percent in adult females) and Sperm whales (6–8 percent in males and 5–7 percent in females).

## Whales and Man

### AN HISTORICAL OVERVIEW

Man has interacted with whales for almost as long as we have archaeological evidence of human activity. Carvings showing whaling activities have been found in Norse settlements from 4,000 years ago, and Alaskan Eskimo middens 3,500 years old contain the remains of whales. It is quite possible, of course, that at this time whales were not so much actively hunted as taken primarily when entering nearshore waters to strand. However, with the likely seasonal abundance of whales in the polar regions as the oceans warmed after the Pleistocene, it would be surprising if these early hunters had not actively exploited them.

At about the same time (3,200 years ago), the Ancient Greeks incorporated dolphins into their culture in a nonconsumptive way, for they appear on frescoes in the Minoan temple of Knossos in Crete, and many Greek myths refer to the animals' altruistic behavior. One describes how the lyric poet and musician Arion was set upon by the crew of the boat in which he traveled from Italy. When they threatened to kill him, he asked the favor of playing one last tune, which was so sweet that it attracted a school of dolphins. Seeing them, Arion leapt overboard and was carried to safety on a dolphin's back. The Greek philosopher Aristotle (384–322BC) was the first to study cetaceans in any detail, and even though some of his information was incorrect and contradictory, many of his detailed descriptions of their anatomy clearly indicate that he had dissected specimens.

The earliest record of regular whaling in Europe comes from the Norsemen of Scandinavia, in around 800–1000AD. Basque seafarers were also among the first to exploit whales; by the 12th century, there are accounts of extensive whaling in the Bay of Biscay. Early fisheries probably concentrated on Right and Bowhead whales, since they are slow-moving and float after death due to their high oil content. A Gray whale population that once existed in the North Atlantic was probably hunted to extinction by the early 18th century.

From the Bay of Biscay, whaling gradually spread northward up the European coast and across to Greenland. By the next century the Dutch and then the British started whaling in Arctic waters. During the 17th century, whaling from eastern North America was also getting under way. All through this period, the whalers used small sailing ships and struck their prey with harpoons hurled from rowing boats. The whales were then towed ashore to land or ice floes, or cut up and processed in the sea alongside the boat. In contrast, whaling in Japan, which developed around 1600, used nets and fleets of small boats.

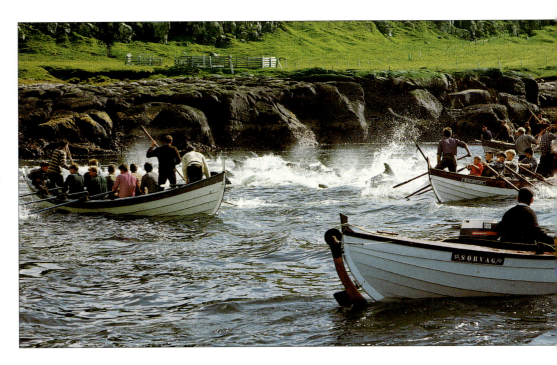

As vessels improved, whalers started to pursue other species, notably the Sperm whale. In the 18th and 19th centuries, the whalers of New England (USA), Britain, and Holland moved first southward in the Atlantic and then west into the Pacific around Cape Horn, and eastwards into the Indian Ocean around the Cape of Good Hope. In the first half of the 19th century, whaling started in South Africa and the Seychelles. By this time, the Arctic whalers had penetrated far into the icy waters of Greenland, the Davis Strait, and Svalbard, where they took Bowhead, Right, and, later, Humpback whales. Whaling for Right whales also started up in the higher latitudes of the Pacific off New Zealand and Australia, and from 1840 onward for Bowheads in the Bering, Chukchi, and Beaufort seas.

Overhunting brought about the collapse of whaling in the North Atlantic by the late 1700s, and in the North Pacific during the mid-1800s. Sperm whaling flourished until about 1850, but then declined rapidly. The situation worsened after 1868, when a Norwegian, Svend Foyn, developed an explosive harpoon gun and steam-driven vessels replaced the sailing ships. Both these innovations had a significant impact on the remaining great whales, allowing ships to pursue even the fast-moving rorquals. By the late 1800s, populations of Bowheads and Right whales had declined markedly. British Arctic whaling ceased in 1912.

By the end of the 19th century, whalers were concentrating on the Pacific and the waters off Newfoundland and the west coast of Africa. Then, in 1905, they discovered the rich Antarctic feeding grounds of Blue, Fin, and Sei whales. In 1925 the first modern factory ship began working in the Antarctic and the industry ceased to be land-based. As a result Antarctic whaling expanded

○ **Above** *Small-scale whaling, like this Pilot whale hunt on the Faeroes, still persists in some places. Both the USA and Russia, for example, are permitted limited catches by indigenous peoples of the Arctic Circle, for whom whaling has long been a traditional way of life.*

rapidly, with 46,000 whales taken in the 1937–38 season, until, yet again, populations declined to commercial extinction. The largest and hence most valuable of the rorquals, the Blue whale, dominated the catches in the 1930s, but had declined to very few by the mid-1950s, and was eventually totally protected in 1965. As these populations declined, attention turned to the next largest rorqual, and so on down.

Sperm whales continued to be taken following the population collapse in the 1850s, though with a world catch of only about 5,000 annually until 1948. Catches then increased quite rapidly, with about 20,000 a year being taken, mainly in the North Pacific and the Southern Hemisphere, until 1985, when the species became protected.

Until the middle of the 20th century, the whaling industry was dominated by Norway and the United Kingdom, with Holland and the United States also taking substantial shares. After World War II, however, these nations abandoned deep-sea whaling, and the industry was largely taken over by Japan and the Soviet Union, although many nations continued coastal whaling. Data from the former Soviet Union that has recently come to light show, for example, that from 1951–71 at least 3,368 Southern right whales were taken, even though the species had officially been under international protection since 1935.

Originally, the most important product of modern deep-sea whaling was oil; that of baleen whales was used in margarines and other foodstuffs, and that of Sperm whales in specialized lubricants. From about 1950, however, chemical products and meal for animal foodstuffs became increasingly important, although meat from baleen whales was also highly valued for human consumption by the Japanese. The Soviet Union, on the other hand, used very little whale meat and instead concentrated upon Sperm whales for their oil. By the late 1970s, whale catches in the Antarctic were yielding 29 percent meat, 20 percent oil, and 7 percent meal and solubles.

Over the last 30 years public attention and sympathy has increasingly turned towards the plight of whales. People watching whales off the eastern United States and in the lagoons of California were impressed by their confiding nature and fascinating behavior. At the same time, most of the great whales were continuing to decline in number as a result of overexploitation. The International Whaling Commission was set up in 1946 to regulate whaling activities, but it remained generally ineffective because the advice of its scientific committee was often overruled in the interests of short-term commercial considerations.

In 1972, the US Marine Mammal Act prohibited the taking and importing of marine mammals and their products except under certain conditions, such as by some native peoples, Inuits, and Aleuts for subsistence purposes or for the making of native handicrafts. In the same year, the United Nations Conference on the Human Environment called for a 10-year moratorium on whaling. The latter was not accepted by the International Whaling Commission, but continued publicity and pressure from environmental bodies and concern expressed by many scientists over the difficulties in estimating population sizes and maximum sustainable yields, finally had an effect. In 1982, a ban on all commercial whaling was agreed upon, and this took effect from 1986. Following the conservationist stance taken by the majority of IWC member nations during the 1980s and 90s, a separate management organization called NAMMCO (North Atlantic Marine Mammal Commission) was formed alongside the IWC, bringing together those countries like Norway, the Faeroes, Iceland, Greenland, and parts of Canada that wished to continue whaling in the North Atlantic. Within the IWC itself, Norway continued taking Minke whales for scientific purposes and, from the late 1990s, restarted an annual commercial take of a few hundred animals. Japan continues to lobby for the resumption of commercial whaling.

With the largely global ban on whaling, a number of large whale species have shown signs of recovery. Humpback whales in the western North Atlantic were estimated to number 10,600 in 1999, with the well-studied summering population in the Gulf of Maine growing at a rate of 6.5 percent per annum. The eastern North Pacific Blue whale population is also showing some encouraging signs of recovery, with 2,000 animals estimated in the 1990s and a trend toward increasing population size over several years. However, the status of some baleen whale populations is causing great concern, due to their overall scarcity and various associated problems, including human-induced mortality. All populations of Northern right whales are seriously endangered; there are little more than 300 left in the northwestern Atlantic, and only a few tens in the eastern North Atlantic. The Bowhead whales of the Okhotsk Sea and various parts of the eastern Arctic, Gray whales in the western North Pacific, and Blue whales in several areas all also remain at perilously low numbers.

Harbor porpoise particularly vulnerable. Sometimes high pollutant burdens have been linked with disease and mass die-offs, as during the early 1990s when more than 1,000 Striped dolphins died of a morbillivirus in the Mediterranean. In that instance the animals were found to have large concentrations of PCBs (polychlorinated biphenyls) in their tissues, which affect the immune system, reducing resistance to disease.

Destruction of suitable habitat by the building of coastal resorts, breakwaters that change local current patterns and encourage silting, and dams that regulate water flow in rivers, all pose additional threats. Species most vulnerable are usually those that are rare and localized in distribution, like the vaquita in the Gulf of California or the baiji (*Lipotes vexillifer*) on the Yangtze River in China.

The greatest threat of all for many species may come from commercial fishing. In some instances, independent observers aboard vessels have been able to estimate incidental takes, and comparisons with population estimates have shown that the mortality from these activities is unsustainable. Every year, the world's fisheries draw up an estimated 27 million metric tons of nontarget marine life that is simply discarded back into the sea, dead or dying. This figure represents a quarter of the global catch, and a wide variety of species are affected. On the continental shelf of Europe and North America, the Harbor porpoise is particularly at risk. Further offshore, the more pelagic dolphins like the Striped, Common, Spinner, and Spotted varieties are sometimes taken in large numbers. Even the great whales fall victim to particular fisheries, adding further pressure upon rare and endangered species.

Direct competition with fisheries for food may represent a further pressure, though this is one that is very difficult to disentangle from other effects upon the marine ecosytem. As particular prey species become scarce through overexploitation, others may take their place and the structure of marine communities alters. Although many cetacean species have catholic diets and appear able to switch prey species, we have little understanding of the longterm consequences for them.

Finally, increasing industrialization has contributed to widespread climate changes. These may have a variety of consequences upon cetacean populations. Sea temperature rises are likely to affect the composition of cetacean species in a particular region. With the melting of portions of the ice cap, the rise in water levels will affect the marine communities of shallow seas. And the greater frequency of storms may result in less stable climate systems elsewhere and the breakdown of plankton frontal systems, on which many cetaceans depend. All these pressures are unlikely to evoke the same passions as direct killing by humans, but nevertheless they will have to be addressed if these magnificent creatures are to continue to grace our seas.                              PGHE

◐ **Above** *Without human intervention there is still significant danger for the world's whale populations. Human concern for these creatures no longer simply extends to attempts to curtail whaling; operations are carried out to help whales that have become stranded, or – as is the case with this Gray whale at Barrow, Alaska – trapped in pack ice.*

◐ **Left** *Iceland, which withdrew from the International Whaling Commission in the 1990s, is one of a handful of countries that still pursues whaling activities in the North Atlantic. At a processing plant in Hvalfjördhur, the carcass of a huge Fin whale is stripped of its flesh in readiness for its eventual resale as meat.*

◐ **Below** *A diver swims alongside a Right whale off the coast of Argentina. Despite the massive size of the Right whale – average length is about 14m (46ft), average weight around 22,000kg (48,400lb) – they exist on a diet of tiny crustaceans, which are mostly only a few millimeters in diameter. They feed by swimming along, mouth open, near the surface.*

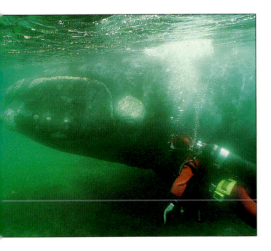

## ◼ Changing Marine Environments
### NEW THREATS

The story of man's often unhappy relationship with whales does not end here. Even if we terminated commercial whaling forever, or acquired sufficient knowledge to manage whale populations in a sustained manner, cetaceans would continue to face a variety of other threats of mankind's making. The marine environment is being modified in many parts of the world as human populations increase and become more industrialized, making greater demands upon the sea either by removing organisms for food or by releasing toxic waste products. Acoustic disturbance comes from seismic testing during oil and gas exploration, from loud military sonar, and from motor-vessel traffic. Although it is difficult to determine the longterm consequences, short-term negative reactions have been observed in several species, and there is some evidence that extended exposure to loud sounds may cause hearing damage. Besides emitting sounds, vessels may also pose a direct threat of physical damage through collisions. The most endangered of all the great whales, the Northern right whale, which numbers just 300 animals, faces the threat of ship strikes off the eastern seaboard of the United States. Another new danger is that of high-speed ferries, which are being introduced into many parts of the world and are already resulting in collisions with slower-moving cetaceans like Sperm and Pilot whales.

Toxic chemical pollution, particularly from heavy metals, oil, and persistent chemicals, may also have serious harmful effects in enclosed bodies of water such as the Baltic, Mediterranean, and North Seas, making coastal species such as the

# Dolphins

**F**ROM THE DOLPHINS THAT RESCUED THE
lyric poet Arion from pirates in Greek mythology
to the eponymous Killer whale hero of the 1993
Hollywood movie Free Willy, dolphins have always
had a special appeal for humankind. It has been
argued that their intelligence and developed social
organization are equaled only by the primates –
perhaps even only by humans – while their general
friendliness and apparent lack of aggression have
been compared favorably with our own.

This anthropocentric view has in recent years
required modification, as it has become apparent,
for example, that aggression is a not uncommon
element of dolphin behavior. Even so, the more
we find out about dolphins' learning abilities,
social skills, and life below the waves, the more we
marvel at the great variety of behaviors and social
structures they exhibit as different populations or
species adapt to local conditions.

## Agile and Intelligent
### FORM AND FUNCTION

The family Delphinidae is a relatively modern
group, having evolved during the late Miocene,
about 10 million years ago. They are the most
abundant and varied of all cetaceans.

Most dolphins are small to medium-sized animals, with well-developed beaks and a central,
sickle-shaped dorsal fin that curves backwards.

They have a single, crescent-shaped blowhole on
top of the head, with the concave side facing forwards, and have functional well-separated teeth in
both jaws (anything from 10 to 224, though most
have 100–200). The majority of delphinids have a
forehead melon, although this is indistinct in
some species, for example the tucuxi, and entirely
absent in *Cephalorhynchus* species; the melon is
pronounced and rounded to form an indistinct
beak in Risso's dolphin and the two species of
pilot whales, and tapered to form a blunt snout in
Killer and False killer whales. Killer whales also
have rounded, paddle-shaped flippers, whereas
the pilot whales and False killer have narrow, elongated flippers.

The wide variation in color patterns between
species can be categorized in a number of ways.
One classification recognizes three types: uniform
(plain or evenly marked), patched (with clearly
demarcated pigmented areas), and disruptive col-

◁ **Left** *Bottlenose dolphins mainly inhabit tropical
and subtropical waters. This individual clearly displays
the short beak that is characteristic of the species.
Bottlenoses also commonly have the white patch seen
here on the tip of the lower jaw.*

oration (black and white). Color differentiation
helps individuals to recognize one another, and
colors may also help conceal hunters from their
prey. Dolphins feeding at depths where the light is
dim are often uniform, while surface feeders tend
to be countershaded (dark above, light below) so
that they blend into the background when lit from
above. The color patterns of some species may
also act as anti-predator camouflage: saddle patterns afford protection through their counterlight-
ing effect, while spotted patterns blend in with
sun-dappled water. Criss-cross patterns have both
countershading and disruptive elements.

Dolphins, like other toothed whales, rely greatly on sound for communication. Their sounds
range from a narrow band and modulated whistles
to trains of clicks of 0.2 kHz into the ultrasonic
range around 80–220 kHz; these appear to be
used for tracing prey by echolocation, and possibly also for stunning it. Although different whistles have been categorized and associated with
particular behaviors, there is no evidence of a
language with syntax.

Dolphins can perform quite complex tasks
and are fine mimics capable of memorizing long
routines, particularly where learning by ear is

involved. In some tests they rank with elephants. Bottlenose dolphins can generalize rules and develop abstract concepts. Dolphins have large brains relative to body size – adult Bottlenose dolphins weighing 130–200kg (290–440lb) may have a brain of about 1,600g (3.5lb) weight; in comparison, the brains of humans weighing 36–95kg (80–210lb) range from 1,100–1,540g (2.4–3.4lb). They also have a high degree of folding of the cerebral cortex, comparable with that found in primates. These features are considered to be indications of high intelligence.

Brain tissue is metabolically expensive to produce, and is therefore unlikely to evolve unless there is a strong benefit. Several different functions have been ascribed to the large brains exhibited by some cetaceans. (Not all species have large brains, however; mysticetes have relatively small brains). One suggestion is that processing acoustic information requires greater "storage" space than visual information; another explanation is that cetaceans may simply need larger brains to do the same tasks that land mammals

◐ **Left** *Bottlenose dolphins leaping. Dolphins may use this behavior to herd fish and for sexual display, but also sometimes leap just for the fun of it. Such displays of graceful agility have helped secure dolphins a special place in the human imagination.*

◑ **Below** *Juvenile Atlantic spotted dolphins in the Atlantic waters around the Bahamas. The patterns on many dolphins may help to conceal them from their prey or from predators, as light playing near the surface blends with the dolphin's coloration and breaks up its outline.*

achieve with smaller ones. A third hypothesis is that brain power plays an important part in social evolution, and that extended parental care, cooperation with conspecifics in feeding and defence, alliance formation, and individual recognition with individual-specific social bonding may together have favored cerebral development.

Dolphins' oft-cited lack of aggression has been exaggerated. Bottlenose species, and perhaps also spinners, develop dominance hierarchies in captivity, in which aggression is manifested by directing the head at the threatened animal, displaying with an open mouth, or

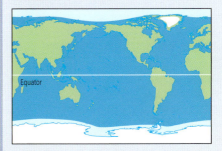

## FACTFILE

### DOLPHINS

Order: Cetacea

Family: Delphinidae

At least 36 species in 17 genera, including common or saddleback dolphins (*Delphinus*, 3 species); spinner, spotted, and striped dolphins (*Stenella*, 5 species); white-sided and white-beaked dolphins (*Lagenorhynchus*, 5/6 species); southern or piebald dolphins (*Cephalorhyncus*, 4 species); hump-backed dolphins (*Sousa*, 3 species); bottlenose dolphins (*Tursiops*, 2 species); right whale dolphins (*Lissodelphis*, 2 species); pilot whales (*Globicephala*, 2 species).

**DISTRIBUTION** All oceans

Equator

**HABITAT** Generally over the continental shelf, but some open sea.

**SIZE** Head–tail length from 1.2m (3.5ft) in Heaviside's dolphin to 7m (23ft) in the Killer whale; weight from 40kg (88lb) to 4.5 tonnes (4.4 tons) in the same two species.

**FORM** Snout beaklike (versus blunt in porpoises) and teeth spade-shaped (versus cone-shaped in porpoises); body form slender and streamlined. Pectoral and dorsal fins sickle-shaped, triangular, or rounded; dorsal fin positioned near middle of back, except in right whale dolphins, which lack a dorsal fin.

**DIET** Primarily fish or squid; Killer whales also eat other marine mammals and birds.

**BREEDING** Gestation 10–16 months (13–16 months in the Killer whale, False killer whale, pilot whales, and Risso's dolphin; the rest 10–12 months).

**LONGEVITY** Up to 50–100 years (Killer whale).

See species table ▷

clapping of the jaw. Fights have also been observed in the wild, in which scratches and scrapes have been inflicted by one individual running its teeth over the back of another; and some species, for example Bottlenose dolphins, are known to attack individuals of other, smaller species (for example, Spotted and Spinner dolphins); they have even been known to kill Harbor porpoises.

## Different Diets, Different Forms
### DIET

Differences in diet between dolphin species are reflected in their body shapes and dentition. For example, those species that feed primarily upon squid generally have the most rounded foreheads, blunt beaks, and (often) reduced dentition.

Killer whales, whose diet also includes marine mammals and birds, have particularly enlarged foreheads. One theory is that this is an adaptation for receiving and focusing sound signals to obtain an accurate picture of the location of agile, fast-moving prey. The other members of the family feed primarily upon fish: all appear to be opportunist feeders, probably catching whatever species they encounter within particular size ranges. Some – for example, bottlenose and hump-backed

dolphins – are primarily inshore feeders, though they also prey on both bottom-dwelling and open-sea fish. Other species, such as members of the genera *Stenella* and *Delphinus*, are more pelagic, feeding further out to sea on shoaling fish – both those found close to the surface such as anchovy, herring, and capelin, and those located at great depths, including lantern fish.

Most dolphins are partial to squid and even shrimps. These overlaps make it difficult to determine the extent of competition among species. One way to avoid having to share food is to avoid other dolphins with similar dietary requirements. In the tropical eastern Pacific, Spotted dolphins feed largely on open-sea fish near the surface, whereas the related Spinner dolphin feeds at deeper levels; and the two may also feed at different times of the day.

Deeper-ocean dolphins tend to travel in herds of up to 1,000 or more, whose members may cooperate in the capture of shoaling fish (see Cooperative Killers). Inshore species usually form smaller herds of 2–12 individuals, possibly because they are feeding on prey at low densities. Offshore, dolphin schools may spread out to form a band that may be anything from 20m (66ft) to several kilometers wide. Small groups of 5–25 tend to coalesce within the larger assemblage. The dolphins often follow underwater escarpments or other landmarks, and they also exploit tidal currents to ensure efficient journeying. When shoaling fish are present in large numbers, the dolphins come together in feeding activity that may sometimes appear frenzied but in fact involves cooperation to herd the shoal into a

tight ball, through which the dolphins weave picking off mouthful after mouthful.

Radio-tracking studies have shown that dolphins may have home ranges varying in size from about 125sq km (48sq mi) in the Bottlenose to 1,500sq km (580sq mi) in the Dusky dolphin. Successive generations of Bottlenose dolphins have been observed occupying the same range for more than 28 years. Individual movements of more than 1,800km (1,140mi) a year have been recorded in Spotted dolphins, and are probably not uncommon for open-sea species.

## Home Is Where the Group Is
### SOCIAL BEHAVIOR

Although most species have an open social structure, with individuals entering and leaving the herd over periods of time, some, such as pilot whales and the Killer whale, seem to have more stable group membership. Genetic data from Long-finned and observational data from Short-finned pilot whales suggest that pods are composed primarily of related females and their offspring, although one or more unrelated adult males may associate with the group when there are opportunities

for mating. Grown-up offspring of both sexes stay with their mothers, although adult sons may move among pods to mate before returning to their natal pods. Herds of bottlenose dolphins seem to comprise family groups of male, female, and calf, or else mother–calf pairs, which may aggregate to form larger herds, some of which may be segregated by sex and age. Among bottlenoses there is evidence of strong male–male bonds. The animals' mating system is as yet imperfectly understood, but generally appears to be promiscuous. The frequent scars observed in some species appear to be most prevalent on males, suggesting male–male competition for mating access to females. Polygyny may also occur, but, whatever the mating system, the male–female and male–calf bonds are relatively weak.

Sexual behavior occurs throughout the year, although there is usually a peak in calving during the summer months, even in lower latitudes. One calf is born, and it remains with the mother for several months; she will continue to feed it with milk for up to 3.5 years. Many species therefore breed at minimum intervals of 2–3 years (rising to 7–8 years in the case of Killer and pilot whales). The age of sexual maturity probably ranges from 5–7 years (in Commerson's, Spinner, and Common dolphins) up to 16 years in the male Killer whale, with most species breeding at about 8–12 years of age.

Many species undertake seasonal migrations in search of food; these are usually offshore–inshore movements, although they can be latitudinal. If discrete calving areas exist, they have rarely been identified, although they may be in deeper offshore waters where there is less turbulence from coastal currents. Adults and young in several species may then move into shallower waters to exploit prey that aggregate around reefs and seamounts.

Dolphins are gregarious, though the large herds of 1,000 or more generally only occur during long-distance movements or among concentrations at major food sources. In most cases, herd membership is fluid; individuals may enter or leave the group over a period of weeks or months, with only a minority remaining within it for a longer time. There is rarely any indication of the stable, well-developed social organization typical of primates, although in a few species such as the Killer whale, kin relations can last a lifetime. It has not been easy to determine the extent to which dolphins cooperate with one another in infant rearing and prey capture, but even if we accept that some of the more gregarious species do so, such behavior is also found among primates, carnivores, and birds.

◑ **Above** *The characteristic poses of 13 dolphin species.* **1** *Bottlenose dolphin* (Tursiops truncatus); **2** *Rough-toothed dolphin* (Steno bredanensis); **3** *Atlantic white-sided dolphin* (Lagenorhynchus acutus); **4** *Atlantic spotted dolphin* (Stenella frontalis); **5** *Common dolphin* (Delphinus delphis); **6** *Northern right whale dolphin* (Lissodelphis borealis); **7** *Dusky dolphin* (Lagenorhynchus obscurus); **8** *Atlantic humpbacked dolphin* (Sousa teuszii); **9** *Melon-headed whale* (Peponocephala electra); **10** *Commerson's dolphin* (Cephalorhynchus commersonii); **11** *False killer whale* (Pseudorca crassidens); **12** *Killer whale* (Orcinus orca); **13** *Risso's dolphin* (Grampus griseus).

▶ **Right** *A heavily scarred male Risso's dolphin. Prominent weals like this are caused by fights over feeding territories or mating, which may sometimes be prolonged and vicious.*

## The Problem with Gill-nets

CONSERVATION AND ENVIRONMENT

Large herds of dolphins sometimes concentrate at feeding areas, and conflict can result if these coincide with human fisheries. Many dolphins are caught and drowned in gill-nets. Inshore species such as Dall's and Harbor porpoises are most at risk, but in the late 1960s and early 1970s the eastern Pacific purse-seine tuna fishery annually caused the death of between 150,000 and 500,000 individuals – mainly Spinner and Atlantic spotted but also Common dolphins. Subsequently, the numbers later fell thanks to the introduction of various methods of making the nets more conspicuous to dolphins, including the application of lines of floats at the water's surface, as well as of panels through which captured dolphins could escape. By the end of the century, the numbers of animals killed accidentally each year had fallen to about 3,000 (all from non-US vessels, since the United States ceased this fishing activity in the region from 1995).

Yet incidental capture in fishing gear continues to be a worldwide problem. Bottom-set gill-nets in the North Sea kill several thousand Harbor porpoises a year, a larger number than the local populations can sustain. Mitigation measures such as "pingers" (acoustic alarms) have been shown to reduce kills substantially in some circumstances, most recently off Denmark and the UK. Such techniques are now being applied more widely, but they will not be effective in every situation.

Less obvious threats to dolphins come from inshore pollution by toxic chemicals and disturbance from boats. A recent study of stranded porpoises in the UK found that those with high pollutant burdens were significantly more likely to be diseased, and the same factors may well be at work in Common and Bottlenose dolphins in the western Mediterranean and off southern California. The rise in recreational traffic in coastal waters poses threats to species like Bottlenose dolphins that share those waters, whilst the introduction of high-speed ferries in many parts of the world has led to collisions with pilot whales.

Dolphin hunting is not widespread. It continues off the coasts of Japan and South America and on a small scale off many tropical islands. Until recently, large numbers of Common dolphins were taken in the Black Sea (Turkish catches were 40,000–70,000 annually until 1983, when the practice was outlawed, although poaching still continues in a minor way). Finally, direct competition for particular fish species may be an important potential threat as man increasingly exploits the marine environment for food.     PGHE

## THE MYSTERY OF MASS STRANDINGS

Dolphins have long been found stranded on dry land; in fact, up to the 1970s, virtually all information about cetaceans came from carcasses found on coasts. Most such animals have died at sea and been washed ashore, but some strand while alive. Such incidents are most conspicuous when groups of animals strand together, a phenomenon that is particularly prevalent among pilot and False killer whales.

In some cases, mass strandings can be directly related to a particular cause. From 1989–92, several hundred Striped dolphins that washed ashore along the Mediterranean coasts of Spain, France, Italy, and Greece were found to have a morbillivirus infection, but also very high levels of PCBs (polychlorinated biphenyls). It has been suggested that the animals, weakened by food shortage, mobilized their blubber reserves, where the pollutants were stored in an inert state, thus lowering their resistance to disease. Mass mortality from disease has been reported along the eastern seaboard of North America in a number of species, particularly Bottlenose dolphins.

The cause of mass strandings of live animals is rarely known. While disease and old age may explain many individual cases, they are obviously unlikely to lead to an entire herd coming ashore, so the explanation may be that most of the stranded animals were simply following a leader – usually an experienced older animal (which among species with matriarchal societies would normally be a female). So far as we know, mass-stranding species tend to form fairly stable herds; they are also pelagic, so they are less likely to be familiar with shallow coastal areas and more likely to become disorientated. Other theories that have been put forward to explain the phenomenon include infection of the inner ear by nematode parasites, disturbing the animals' balance or echolocation abilities; the effects of upsetting sounds, such as underwater explosions or magnetic disturbances; and disorientation after the animals have followed prey into unfamiliar or shallow waters.

▼ **Below** *Stranded Long-finned pilot whales. Pilot whales appear to strand in large numbers more frequently than any other whale; however, this may just be a result of their abundance.*

# SLEEK SPINNERS

## School life of the Spinner dolphin

THE SLENDER DOLPHINS LEAP HIGH OUT OF THE water, twisting and spinning rapidly around their longitudinal axes. The movement instantly identifies these as Spinner dolphins, inhabitants of oceans throughout the tropics and subtropics.

Spinner dolphins of Hawaii rest and socialize during the day within protected bays and along shallow coastlines, in tight groups of usually 10–100 animals. At night, they move into deep water 1km (0.6mi) or more offshore, and dive to 100m (330ft) or more to feed. When this occurs, the group spreads out.

The groups are ephemeral. During the night, many individual dolphins change their companions, so by the time that they head shoreward at dawn, group membership is partially reshuffled. This shifting is not random, however, as small subgroups of 4–8 animals, possibly related, stay together for up to four months and possibly longer, changing group affiliations at will. Ties between some dolphins last throughout their lives.

The dolphins may range up to 100km (60mi) along the coast daily, though subgroups have a preferred "home area." The shallow water is usually calmer than the open ocean, making resting and socializing easier, and deepwater sharks that prey on dolphins are rarer and more easily detected.

It is likely that Spinners recognize their group mates – and possibly more distant individuals – far from their home area. When Spinners meet after a long separation, surface leaping, spinning, and

tailslapping takes place. There is also much vocalizing, which may be part of a greeting ceremony.

Hawaiian Spinner dolphins have the advantage of the shoreline for protection. In deep waters, Spinners mix with Atlantic spotted dolphins, and adopt a mutual defense strategy: Spinner dolphins feed mostly at night, Spotted dolphins feed mostly during the day. Each species helps the other while it is resting by guarding against the danger of surprise attack by large, deepwater sharks.

Deepwater Spinners may cover several thousand kilometers in a few months. It is not known whether their social affinities are as transient as those of their Hawaiian relatives. Perhaps the open-ocean school, which travels together and may number 5,000–10,000 animals, has its coastal equivalent in the population of many of the interchanging groups of the Hawaiian coast.

The open-ocean dolphins also associate with Yellowfin tuna in the tropical Pacific. The tuna may benefit from the excellent echolocation abilities that dolphins use to help find and identify prey. Since the tuna often swim below the dolphins, movements, such as breaking ranks in the face of a shark attack, may be easily detected by the dolphins, so the benefits may be mutual.

In the past four decades, a downside of such associations has emerged for both species. Dolphins surface to breathe, and so are easily spotted by fishermen, who set their nets around dolphin–tuna schools. In the past, many dolphins

used to drown after becoming entangled in the tuna nets. Over the past 20 years, tuna fishermen have adopted special nets and practices to reduce the threat to dolphins. A panel of finer mesh is used in that part of the net furthest from the fishing boats, where the fleeing dolphins used to get snared and drown as the net was being tightened (pursed). The dolphins can thus now escape over the net rim, while the tuna usually dive and are retained in the net. However, things can still go wrong, especially if a net canopies above dolphins attempting to get to the surface to breathe.

Helpfully, one further aspect of dolphin behavior has also been recognized. Dolphins caught in tuna nets often lie placidly as if feigning death (although the rigidity may be due to shock). Such dolphins were previously thought to have drowned, and were hauled up onto the deck of the vessel, where they did indeed die. Now the divers who monitor the nets signal to colleagues in small boats stationed around the net to manually help such unmoving animals over the net rim. Although some animals may be missed, the divers do their best to release dolphins entangled in the mesh – a good example of humans attempting to live in harmony with other animals.      BW/RSW

⬤ *Below  A school of Hawaiian Spinner dolphins. Following legislation in the USA, deaths of these dolphins in fishing bycatch fell from about 180,000 in 1972 to just over 100 in 1993.*

# Dolphin Species

DOLPHIN TAXONOMY IS COMPLICATED BY the fact that several genera, such as *Delphinus, Stenella, Sousa,* and *Sotalia,* include species that are virtually indistinguishable in physical appearance. Controversy remains, but genetic analysis has added weight to the morphological differentiation of at least two species of Common dolphin that live together but have different lengths of beak. Two separate species of spotted dolphin are now recognized – the Pantropical and the Atlantic – while Spinner dolphins have recently been divided into the Long-snouted and the Clymene varieties.

As more studies are conducted on populations inhabiting remote regions of the world, evidence for further species will no doubt come to light, and it is likely that there will be further splits within genera. For example, at present only two species of the genus *Tursiops* are recognized, *T. truncatus* and *T. aduncus*; the latter distinguished both genetically and externally by its spotted undersurface. Within these groupings, however, some inshore and offshore populations show both morphological and genetic differences, and variation between populations in the Indo-Pacific is by no means clear-cut. The nomenclature adopted below follows Rice (1999).

## Commerson's dolphin
*Cephalorhynchus commersonii*
Commerson's or Piebald dolphin

Cool waters of southern S America and Falkland Islands, possibly across Southern Ocean to Kerguelen Island.
HTL 1.3–1.4m; WT c.50kg.
FORM: dark gray on back but with large white-pale gray cape across front half, extending down across belly, leaving only small black area around anus; white area also on throat and chin, so that dark gray frontal region is confined to forehead. Snout and broad band across neck region to flippers. Rounded black flippers and centrally placed low rounded dorsal fin. Short, rounded snout with no melon and very short beak. Small, stout, torpedo-shaped body.

## Black dolphin
*Cephalorhynchus eutropia*
Black, Chilean, or White-bellied dolphin

Coastal waters of Chile.
HTL c.1.6m; WT c.45kg.
FORM: black on back, flanks, and part of belly but with three areas of white, variable in extent, on throat, behind flippers,

and around anal area; thin, pale gray or white margin to lips of both jaws; sometimes pale gray area around blowhole. Low triangular dorsal fin, centrally placed with longer leading edge and blunt apex. Short, rounded snout with no melon and very short beak. Small, stout, torpedo-shaped body, with keels above and below tail stock.

## Heaviside's dolphin
*Cephalorhynchus heavisidii*

Coastal waters; W coast of southern Africa.
HTL 1.2–1.7m; WT c.40kg (max. 74kg).
FORM: black on back and flanks, white belly, extending upwards as three lobes, two on either side of the flipper, and one from anal region up along flanks to tail stock. Small, oval-shaped black flippers, and centrally-placed, low, triangular dorsal fin. Short, rounded snout with no melon and no distinct beak. Small, fairly stout, torpedo-shaped body.

## Hector's dolphin                    En
*Cephalorhynchus hectori*

Coastal waters of New Zealand.
HTL 1.2–1.4m; WT c.40kg.
FORM: pale to dark gray around anus. Rounded black flipper and centrally placed low, rounded dorsal fin. Short, rounded snout with no melon and a short beak. Small, stout, torpedo-shaped body, narrowing at tail stock.
CONSERVATION STATUS: North Island subpopulation Critically Endangered.

## Rough-toothed dolphin
*Steno bredanensis*

Offshore waters of all tropical, subtropical, and warm temperate seas.
Male HTL 2.3–2.4m; WT c.140kg. Female HTL 2.2–2.3m; WT c.120kg.
FORM: dark gray to dark purplish-gray on back and flanks, and white throat and belly; pinkish-white blotches on flanks round to belly; often scarred with white streaks. Centrally-placed, sickle-shaped dorsal fin. Long, slender beak not clearly demarcated from forehead, white/pinkish-white on both sides, including one or both lips and tip of snout. Slim, torpedo-shaped body, keels above and below tail stock.

## Atlantic hump-backed dolphin
*Sousa teuszii*

Coastal waters and river systems of W Africa. Possibly a form of Indo-Pacific hump-backed dolphin which it closely

resembles, differing in having fewer teeth and more vertebrae.
HTL about 2.0m; WT c.100kg. Shape and coloration variable.
FORM: dark gray-white on back and upper flanks, lightening on lower flanks to white belly; young uniformly pale cream. Small but prominent triangular, centrally-placed dorsal fin, sickle-shaped in young, becoming more rounded later. Rounded flippers. Long slender beak with slight melon on forehead. Stout, torpedo-shaped body, with distinct dorsal hump in middle of back (on which is dorsal fin) and similar marked keels above and below tail stock.

## Indo-Pacific hump-backed dolphin
*Sousa chinensis*

Coastal warm waters of E Africa to Indonesia and S China.
HTL 2.0–2.8m; WT c. 85kg. Shape and coloration variable.
FORM: dark gray-white on back and upper flanks, usually lightening on lower flanks to white belly; adults may develop spots or speckles of yellow, pink, gray, or brown; young uniformly pale cream. Small but prominent triangular, centrally-placed dorsal fin, sickle-shaped in young, becoming more rounded later. Rounded flippers. Dorsal fin and flippers may be tipped white. Long slender beak (with white patch on tip in some individuals) with slight melon on forehead. Stout, torpedo-shaped body, with distinct dorsal hump in middle of back (on which is dorsal fin) and similar marked keels above and below tail stock.

## Indian hump-backed dolphin
*Sousa plumbea*

Coastal waters; E Africa to Thailand. Size and form as for *S. chinensis,* but coloration darker. Regarded by some as synonym for *S. chinensis.*

## Tucuxi
*Sotalia fluviatilis*

Orinoco and Amazon river systems and coastal waters of NE South America and E Central America.
HTL 1.4–1.8m; WT 36–45kg.
FORM: coloration variable geographically and with age; medium to dark gray on back and upper flanks with brownish tinge, lighter gray sometimes with patches of yellow-ocher on lower flanks and belly; two pale gray areas sometimes extend diagonally upwards on flanks. Coloration lightens with age, sometimes becoming

cream-white. Small, triangular, centrally-placed dorsal fin. Relatively large spoon-shaped flippers. Pronounced beak (mid- to dark gray above, light gray-white below), and rounded forehead. Small, stout, torpedo-shaped body. Orinoco population (previously recognized as a separate species, *S. guianensis*) generally darker, sometimes with a brownish band extending from anal area diagonally upwards over flanks to leading edge of dorsal fin.

## Bottlenose dolphin
*Tursiops truncatus*

Atlantic and temperate N Pacific. Coastal waters of most tropical, subtropical and temperate regions.
HTL 2.3–3.9m; WT 150–200kg.
FORM: usually dark-gray on back, lighter gray on flanks (variable in extent), grading to white or pink on belly. Some spotting may be present on belly. Centrally placed, tall, slender, sickle-shaped dorsal fin. Robust head with distinct, short beak, often with white patch on tip of lower jaw. Stout, torpedo-shaped body, with moderately keeled tail stock.

## Indian Ocean bottlenose dolphin
*Tursiops aduncus*

Indo-Pacific and Red Sea.
HTL 2.3m; WT 150 kg.
Form as for *T. truncatus*, though sometimes darker in coloration. Regarded by some as synonym for *T. truncatus.*

## Atlantic spotted dolphin
*Stenella frontalis*

Subtropical and warm temperate Atlantic.
HTL 1.9–2.3m; WT c. 100–110kg.
FORM: coloration and markings variable with age and geographically; dark gray to black on back and upper flanks, lighter gray on lower flanks and belly (sometimes pinkish on throat); white spots on upper flanks, dark spots on lower flanks and belly, absent at birth but enlarging with age; spotting also decreases away from coasts of N America; distinct dark gray-black area (or cape) on head to dorsal fin; pronounced pale blaze on flanks, slanting up on to back behind dorsal fin. Slender, sickle-shaped, centrally-placed dorsal fin; pale, medium, or dark gray or pinkish flippers. Long, slender beak, both upper and lower lips white or pinkish, and distinct forehead. Slender to relatively stout (in coastal populations) torpedo-shaped body with marked keel below tail stock (sometimes also one above tail stock).

○ **Above** *A school of Southern right whale dolphins off the coast of Peru. This species' common name comes from the fact that, like the Right whale, it has no dorsal fin.*

## Pantropical spotted dolphin [LR]
*Stenella attenuata*

Tropical Pacific, Atlantic, and Indian Ocean. Size and form as for *S. frontalis*, but with black circles around eyes and a broad black stripe from origin of flipper to corner of mouth (which fades as spotting increases), giving a banded appearance to the light gray sides of the head.
CONSERVATION STATUS: LR Conservation Dependent.

## Spinner dolphin [LR]
*Stenella longirostris*

Probably in all tropical oceans. At least four different races.
HTL 1.7–2.1m; WT c. 75kg.
FORM: dark gray, brown, or black on back; lighter gray, tan, or yellowish-tan flanks, and white belly (purplish or yellow in some populations); distinct black to light gray stripe from flipper to eye. Slender erect to sickle-shaped centrally-placed dorsal fin, often lighter gray near middle of fin; relatively large black to light gray flippers. Medium to long, slender beak and distinct forehead. Slender to quite stout, torpedo-shaped body, which may have marked keels above and below tail stock.
CONSERVATION STATUS: LR Conservation Dependent.

## Clymene dolphin
*Stenella clymene*
Clymene or Short-snouted spinner dolphin

Warm temperate to tropical Atlantic.
HTL 1.8–2.1m; WT c. 75kg.
FORM: dark gray back, lighter gray flanks, and white belly. Slender, sickle-shaped dorsal fin; relatively large dark to light gray flippers. Short beak and distinct but sloping forehead. Slender to moderately stout torpedo-shaped body, which may have marked keels below and occasionally above tail stock.

## Striped dolphin [LR]
*Stenella coeruleoalba*
Striped, Euphrosyne, or Blue-white dolphin

All tropical, subtropical, and warm temperate seas, including Mediterranean.
HTL 2.0–2.4m (male), 1.85–2.25m (female); WT 70–90kg (rarely to 130 kg).
FORM: dark gray to brown or bluish gray on back, lighter gray flanks, and white belly; two distinct black bands on flanks, one from near eye down side of body to anal area (with short secondary stripe originating with this band, turning downwards towards flippers) and the other from eye to flippers; most have additional black or dark gray fingers extending from behind dorsal fin forward and about halfway to eye; black flippers. Slender, sickle-shaped, centrally-placed dorsal fin. Slender, long beak (but shorter than Common dolphin) and distinct forehead. Slender, torpedo-shaped body.
CONSERVATION STATUS: LR Conservation Dependent.

## Common dolphin
*Delphinus delphis*
Common or Saddleback dolphin

All tropical, subtropical, and warm temperate seas, including Mediterranean and Black Seas. Usually offshore waters.
HTL 1.8–2.2m (male), 1.7–2.1m (female); WT 80–110kg (male), 70–100kg (female).
FORM: coloration variable; black or brownish-black on back and upper flanks; chest and belly cream-white to white; hourglass pattern of tan or yellowish tan on flanks becoming paler gray behind dorsal fin where it may reach dorsal surface; black stripe from flipper to middle of lower jaw, and from eye to base of beak; flippers black to light gray or white (Atlantic population). Slender, sickle-shaped to erect dorsal fin, centrally placed. Long, slender beak and distinct forehead; slender, torpedo shaped body.

## Long-beaked common dolphin
*Delphinus capensis*

Eastern N Pacific. Size and form as for *D. delphis*, but with a longer beak and one or two gray lines running longitudinally on lower flanks. Only recently recognized as a separate species from *D. delphis*.

## Arabian common dolphin
*Delphinus tropicalis*

Arabian Sea, Gulf of Aden, and Persian Gulf to the Malabar Coast of India and the South China Sea. Dimensions and form as for *D. capensis*, of which some authorities consider it a separate population.

## Fraser's dolphin
*Lagenodelphis hosei*
Fraser's or Sarawak dolphin

Warm waters of all oceans.
HTL 2.3–2.5m; WT 160–210 kg.
Form: medium-dark gray on back and flanks, white or pinkish-white belly; two parallel stripes on flanks: upper cream-white, beginning above and in front of eye, moving back and narrowing to tail stock; lower more distinct, dark gray-black from eye to anus; sometimes also a black band from mouth to flipper; white throat and chin, but tip of lower jaw usually black. Small, slender, slightly sickle-shaped dorsal fin, pointed at tip, centrally placed. Very short rounded snout with short beak. Fairly robust torpedo-shaped body, with marked keels above and below tail stock.

## Peale's dolphin
*Lagenorhynchus australis*
Peale's or Black-chinned dolphin

Cold waters of Argentina, Chile, and the Falkland Islands.
HTL 2.0–2.2m; WT c. 115kg.
FORM: dark gray-black on back, white belly; light gray area on flanks from behind eye to anus, and, above this, a narrow white band behind the dorsal fin extending backwards, enlarging to tail stock; thin black line running from leading edge of black flipper to eye. Centrally-placed, sickle-shaped fin. Rounded snout with short black beak and torpedo-shaped body.

## White-beaked dolphin
*Lagenorhynchus albirostris*

Temperate and subpolar waters of N Atlantic, mainly on continental shelf. HTL 2.5–2.8m (male), 2.4–2.7m (female); WT 300–350kg (male), 250–300kg (female).
FORM: dark gray or black over most of back, but pale gray-white area over dorsal surface behind fin (less distinct in young individuals); commonly dark gray-white blaze from near dorsal surface, behind eye, across flanks and downward to anal area; white belly. Centrally-placed, tall (particularly in adult males), sickle-shaped dorsal fin. Rounded snout and short beak, often light gray or white. Very stout torpedo-shaped body, with very thick tail stock.

## Atlantic white-sided dolphin
*Lagenorhynchus acutus*

Temperate and subpolar waters of N Atlantic, mainly along shelf edge and beyond.
HTL 2.1–2.6m (male), 2.1–2.4m (female); WT 215–234kg (male), 165–182kg (female).
SKIN: black on back, white belly, gray flanks but with long white oval blaze from below dorsal fin to area above anus; directly above but originating slightly behind the front edge of white blaze is an elongated yellow band extending back to tail stock. Centrally-placed, sickle-shaped dorsal fin, relatively tall, pointed at tip. Rounded snout with short, black beak; stout, torpedo-shaped body with very thick tail stock (particularly in adult males), narrowing close to tail flukes. Recently re-assigned by some authorities to a separate genus, *Leucopleurus*.

## Dusky dolphin
*Lagenorhynchus obscurus*

Circumpolar in temperate waters of S Hemisphere.
HTL 1.8–2.0m; WT c. 115kg.
FORM: dark gray-black on back, white belly; large gray area (varying in intensity) on lower flanks. extending from base of beak or eye backwards and running to anus; light gray or white areas on upper flanks extending backwards from below dorsal fin as two blazes which generally meet above anal region and end at tail stock. Centrally-placed, sickle-shaped dorsal fin, slightly more erect and less curved than rest of genus, commonly pale gray on posterior part of fin. Rounded snout with very short black beak and torpedo-shaped body.

## Pacific white-sided dolphin
*Lagenorhynchus obliquidens*

Temperate waters of N Pacific.
HTL 1.9–2.0m; WT about 150kg; male slightly larger than female.
FORM: dark gray or black on back, white belly, large, pale gray oval area on otherwise black flanks in front of fin above flipper and extending forward to eye, which is encircled with dark gray or black; narrow, pale gray stripe above eye running along length of body and curving down to anal area where it broadens out; pale gray blaze also sometimes present on posterior part of centrally-placed, sickle-shaped dorsal fin. Rounded snout with very short black beak and torpedo-shaped body.

## Hourglass dolphin
*Lagenorhynchus cruciger*

Probably circumpolar in cooler waters of Southern Ocean.
HTL 1.6–1.8m; WT c. 100kg.
FORM: black on back, white belly, two large white areas on black flanks forward of dorsal fin to black beak and backward to tail stock, connected by narrow white band; area of white variable in extent. Centrally-placed, sickle-shaped dorsal fin, usually strongly concave on leading edge. Rounded snout with very short black beak and torpedo-shaped body.

## Northern right whale dolphin
*Lissodelphis borealis*

Offshore waters of temperate N Pacific.
HTL 2.1–3.1m; WT c. 70kg.
SKIN: black on back and flanks, extending down around navel; white belly, in some individuals extending up flanks around flipper so that only the tips are black; otherwise, flippers all black. Juveniles light gray to brown on back and flanks. Dorsal fin absent. Rounded snout with distinct beak and white band across bottom of lower jaw. Small, slender, torpedo-shaped body, with marked keel above tail stock.

## Southern right whale dolphin
*Lissodelphis peronii*

Offshore waters of Southern Ocean, possibly circumpolar.
HTL 1.8–2.3m; WT c. 60kg.
FORM: black on back and flanks, white belly extending upwards to lower flanks behind flippers and forward across forehead in front of eyes so that entire back is white; flippers all white. Dorsal fin absent. Rounded snout with distinct beak. Small, very slender torpedo-shaped body, with underside of tail fluke white.

## Risso's dolphin
*Grampus griseus*
Risso's or Gray dolphin

All tropical and temperate seas.
HTL 3.5–4.0m (male), 3.3–3.5m (female); WT c.40kg (male), c.35kg (female).
FORM: dark to light gray on back and flanks, palest in older individuals, especially leading edge of dorsal fin, so that head may be pure white; many scars on flanks of adults; white belly enlarging to oval patch on chest and chin. Long, pointed black flippers; tall, centrally-placed, sickle-shaped dorsal fin (taller and more erect in adult males). Blunt snout, rounded with slight melon. No beak. Stout, torpedo-shaped body, narrowing behind dorsal fin to quite narrow tail stock.

## Melon-headed whale
*Peponocephala electra*
Melon-headed whale or Many-toothed blackfish

Probably all tropical seas.
HTL 2.3–2.7m (males slightly larger than females); WT c. 160kg.
FORM: black on back and flanks; slightly lighter on belly; areas around anus, genitals, and lips pale gray or white. Pointed flippers. Sickle-shaped, centrally-placed dorsal fin. Rounded head (though snout slightly more pointed than in *Feresa attenuata*) with slightly underslung jaw, and slender body with slim tail stock.

## Killer whale    [LR]
*Orcinus orca*
Killer whale or orca

All oceans.
HTL 6.7–7.0m (male), 5.5–6.5m (female); WT 4,000–4,500kg (male), 2,500–3,000kg (female).
FORM: black on back and sides, white belly extending up the flanks and a white oval patch above and behind the eye; indistinct gray saddle over back behind dorsal fin. Rounded, paddle-shaped flippers and centrally placed dorsal fin, sickle-shaped in female and immatures, but very tall and erect in male. Broad, rounded head and stout, torpedo-shaped body.
CONSERVATION STATUS: LR Conservation Dependent.

## Pygmy killer whale
*Feresa attenuata*

Probably all tropical and subtropical seas.
HTL 2.3–2.7m (male), 2.1–2.7m (female); WT 150–170kg (male and female).
SKIN: dark gray or black on back, often lighter on flanks; small but conspicuous white zone on underside from anus to tail stock and around lips; chin may be entirely white. Flippers slightly rounded at tip. Sickle-shaped, centrally-placed dorsal fin. Rounded head with underslung jaw; slender body.

## False killer whale
*Pseudorca crassidens*

All oceans; mainly tropical and warm temperate.
HTL 5.0–5.5m (male), 4.0–4.5m (female); WT c.2,000kg (male), c.1,200kg (female).
FORM: all black except for a blaze of gray on belly between the flippers, which have a broad hump on the front margin near middle of flipper. Tall, sickle-shaped dorsal fin just behind midpoint of back, sometimes pointed. Slender, tapered head, underslung jaw, and long, slender body.

## Long-finned pilot whale
*Globicephala melas*
Long-finned pilot whale or Pothead whale

*G. m. melas* temperate waters of N Atlantic; *G. m. edwardi* all waters of all seas in S Hemisphere.
HTL 5.5–6.2m (male), 3.8–5.4m (female); WT c.3,000–3,500kg (male), 1,800–2,500kg (female).
FORM: black on back and flanks, with anchor-shaped patch of grayish-white on chin and gray area on belly, both variable in extent and intensity (lighter in younger animals). Some have gray dorsal fin. Long, sickle-shaped flippers, and fairly low dorsal fin slightly forward of midpoint, with long base, sickle-shaped (in adult females and immatures) to flag-shaped (in adult males). Square, bulbous head, particularly in old males, with slightly protruding upper lip and robust body.

## Short-finned pilot whale    [LR]
*Globicephala macrorhynchus*

All tropical and subtropical waters but with possible separate form in N Pacific.
HTL 4.5–5.5m (male), 3.3–3.6m (female); WT c.2,500kg (male), c.1,300kg (female).
FORM: black on back, flanks, and most of belly, with anchor-shaped gray patch on chin and gray area on belly (lighter in younger animals). Long, sickle-shaped flippers, and fairly low dorsal fin, slightly forward of midpoint, with long base, sickle- to flag-shaped. Square, bulbous head especially in old males, with slightly protruding upper lip and robust body.
CONSERVATION STATUS: LR Conservation Dependent.

## Irrawaddy dolphin
*Orcaella brevirostris*

Coastal waters from Bay of Bengal to N coast of Australia.
HTL 2–2.5m; WT c.100kg.
FORM: blue-gray on back and flanks, lighter gray on belly. Stout, torpedo-shaped body and tail stock; robust, rounded head with distinct melon but no beak; small, sickle-shaped dorsal fin with rounded tip, slightly behind centre of back. Sometimes regarded as a member of the Monodontidae family.

# A DOLPHIN'S DAY

## Moods of the Dusky dolphin

THE SLEEK, STREAMLINED DOLPHINS WERE LEAPING around the Zodiac rubber inflatable at Golfo San José, off the coast of southern Argentina. When the divers entered the cool water, a group of 15 dolphins repeatedly cavorted under and above them, approaching the humans to within an arm's length and showing no fear of these strangers from another world.

These were Dusky dolphins, whose playful behavior indicated that they had recently been feeding and socializing, for Dusky dolphins have different moods, and will not interact with humans when they are hungry or tired.

Season and time of day also affect their behavior. These small, round dolphins feed on Southern anchovy during summer afternoons. Nighttime is spent in small schools of 6–15 animals not more than about 1km (0.6 mi) offshore. When danger approaches in the form of large sharks or killer whales, they retreat close inshore to hide in the turbulence of the surfline.

In the morning, the dolphins begin to move into deeper water 2–10km (1–6 mi) out, line abreast, each animal 10m (33ft) or more from the next, so that 15 dolphins may cover a swath of sea 150m (500ft) or more wide. They use echolocation to find food, and, because they are spread out, they can sweep a large area of ocean. When a group locates a school of anchovy, individuals dive down and physically herd it to the surface by swimming around and under the fish in an ever-tightening formation.

The marine birds that gather above the anchovy to feed, and the leaping of the dolphins around the periphery of the school, indicate what is going on to human observers as far as 10km (6 miles) away. Other small groups of dolphins, equally distant, will also see such activity, and move rapidly toward it.

The newly-arrived dolphin groups are immediately incorporated into the activity; the more dolphins present, the more efficiently they are able to corral and herd prey to the surface. Five to ten dolphins cannot effectively herd prey and so give up quickly, but groups of 50 have been seen to feed on average for 27 minutes. By mid-afternoon groups of as many as 300 dolphins (normally scattered in 20 to 30 small groups covering a total area of about 1,300sq km/500 square miles) may come together to feed for 2–3 hours. There is much social interaction in such a large group, and considerable sexual activity, particularly toward the end of feeding. Mixing in large groups allows individuals a wider choice of mates, and thus avoids the problems of inbreeding. Both males and females will mate with more than one partner, but females do seem to be particular about the partners they will allow close.

Play must wait for resting and feeding to end, but it is nonetheless a crucial activity. In order for dolphins to function effectively while avoiding predators, hunting for food, and cooperatively herding prey, they must know each other well and communicate efficiently. Socializing helps to bring

this about. Toward the end of feeding, they swim together in small, ever-changing subgroups, with individuals touching or caressing each other with their flippers, swimming belly to belly, and poking their noses at each others' sides or bellies. At this time, the dolphins will readily approach a boat, ride on its bow wave if it is moving, and swim with divers in the water.

In the evening, the large school splits into many small groups once again, and the animals settle down near shore to rest, the mood changing abruptly to quiescence once again. Although there is some interchange of individuals between small groups from day to day, some of the same dolphins travel together on subsequent days. Indeed, some Dusky dolphins have been observed to stay together for as long as 12 years.

Occasionally in summer, and for much of the winter, anchovy are not present, so Dusky dolphins feed in small groups on squid and bottom-dwelling fish, mainly at night. Such prey does not occur in large shoals, so the feeding dolphins stay in small groups and remain in somber mood. Winter and hunger do not make for a playful dolphin, but in summertime the living is easy and the dolphins are high!

BW

🔾 **Above** *A Dusky dolphin performing an exuberant leap. After feeding on shoals of anchovy, Dusky dolphins habitually leap acrobatically and play together. This is perhaps the most important time for these highly social animals, since play reinforces the bonds between individuals that make them an effective hunting unit.*

🔾 **Left** *A group of Dusky dolphins in close formation. When hunting for anchovy, the dolphins will space themselves more widely apart, in order to sweep the maximum area of ocean with their echolocating capacity.*

# HOW DOLPHINS KEEP IN TOUCH

## Acoustic communication in the undersea environment

PLACE A HYDROPHONE IN THE SEA CLOSE TO A group of dolphins and you will almost certainly hear a rich variety of clicks, whistles, and cries. Dolphins are among the most vocal of mammals: they have a well-developed echolocation system for which they produce the high-frequency clicks, and they also communicate acoustically, primarily using tonal sounds such as whistles.

The importance of vocal communication for this group is explained by the animals' biology and by the physical characteristics of the medium in which they live. Most dolphins are highly social animals, interacting and coordinating their behavior with many different individuals as well as maintaining longterm relationships. They also spend their lives moving rapidly though an extensive, featureless environment that transmits light poorly – the visual range is typically of the order of tens of meters or less – but through which sound is conducted more efficiently than any other form of energy. To maintain the social organization that is so important for their survival, dolphins need to communicate over considerable distances, and sound is the only efficient means for them to achieve this.

Some of the most characteristic dolphin vocalizations are narrow-band whistles. All dolphins, with the exception of a few inshore species whose social organization is unknown, produce whistles. Some whistles have characteristic, distinctive patterns of frequency modulation that are unique to individual animals; they sweep up and down the frequency scale in a specific way. These are called "signature whistles," and they seem to serve as individual identification signals.

Signature whistles are usually produced by dolphins when they are out of visual contact with other members of their group, and they may function primarily as contact calls. Dolphins are adept at vocal learning, an ability that is relatively uncommon in mammals. A dolphin may imitate the signature whistles of other individuals in its group, perhaps as a way of gaining their attention. A dolphin establishes its own signature whistle by the time it is 2 years of age, and it then remains fixed. Males may copy the whistles of their mothers, which serves to prevent incest.

Acoustic identification by humans of individuals or groups has been possible in several dolphin species and seems to occur at the level that makes most sense biologically. For example, the smaller dolphins typically exhibit a complex fission–fusion type of social organization, with the composition of groups changing from day to day, which makes it important to develop an ability to recognize individuals and to behave appropriately to them, based on past experience. The social structure of the largest member of the dolphin family, the Killer whale, however, is quite different. It lives in extremely stable social groups, and in this species it is the groups, or pods, that have characteristic vocalizations. Each pod has a unique dialect (a particular repertoire of calls), and the degree of similarity in dialects between pods generally reflects their genetic relatedness and the extent to which they spend time together.

Relatively little has been discovered about the way that dolphins use sound to communicate in the wild. However, specific calls that may coordinate cooperative feeding have been identified in some species, and correlations have also been demonstrated between activity states and the sort of vocalizations that dolphin groups produce.

In captivity, dolphins have readily learned a variety of artificial languages. Controversially, some studies have suggested that they use rules of syntax and grammar to understand novel sentences. This capacity suggests they may have evolved a sophisticated communication system for use in the wild.

Another intriguing aspect of dolphin communication is that they seem able to eavesdrop on the echolocation calls of other dolphins. At the very least, dolphins can probably "hear" how successfully other individuals within auditory range (which may extend to 1km/0.6mi or more) are feeding. Recent work with captive animals has shown that at shorter ranges dolphins can actually "analyze" the echoes from the echolocation clicks of other individuals, using sonar in a bistatic mode. Dolphins can also produce sound by nonvocal means, for example when they slap the water with their flukes or crash back down after a leap.

Although acoustics is undoubtedly the dominant sense used by these animals, other senses, such as vision, touch, and taste, are also important. Vision, for example, may be useful for coordinating movements at short range, and this may be responsible for the bold patterns and coloration on the heads and flanks of many dolphins. Characteristic body postures and movements, signifying behavioral states such as threat or submissiveness, have also been identified in both captive and wild dolphins. Dolphins have no sense of smell, but they are able to taste chemicals in the seawater through which they and their companions swim. Chemicals released in urine and feces may be an important way of communicating breeding condition or feeding success.                    JG

◖ *Right* *Sociable and intelligent, dolphins have developed complex auditory signals to keep in touch in an undersea world in which sound is the best medium for long-distance communication.*

# River Dolphins

**d**OLPHINS ARE USUALLY THOUGHT OF AS *inhabiting the vastness of the oceans, so the idea of them navigating a narrow channel through the Amazonian rain forest, in a muddy, sunbaked watercourse crossing the countryside of Bangladesh, or in the clear, cool flow of a Himalayan foothill stream may be unexpected. And yet these are all circumstances to which river dolphins are adapted.*

The term "river dolphin" has conventionally been applied to a group of longbeaked, many-toothed small cetaceans: the Yangtze River dolphin; the Ganges and Indus river dolphins; the Amazon dolphin; and the La Plata dolphin. These dolphins may not have a common ancestry, but have converged due to their similar niches. All but the La Plata dolphin, which lives in the estuary of the River Plate and along the Atlantic coast of South America between northern Argentina and central Brazil, are confined to freshwater environments.

Several other small cetacean species have populations that inhabit both marine waters and freshwater systems, although they are not true river dolphins. The species in question are the tucuxi (*Sotalia fluviatilis*) of Central and South America, the Irrawaddy dolphin (*Orcaella brevirostris*) of Southeast Asia, and the Finless porpoise (*Neophocaena phocaenoides*) of the Far East. Although there is no conclusive proof, these populations of "facultative" river cetaceans probably remain permanently in fresh waters and do not regularly migrate into and out of the sea. Here, they are treated mainly in the entries on Dolphins and Porpoises, respectively.

## Flipper in Fresh Waters
### FORM AND FUNCTION

In addition to their long, narrow beaks and numerous teeth, river dolphins exhibit some extreme characteristics in their morphology and sensory systems. Amazon dolphins, for example, are the only modern cetaceans with differentiated teeth; those in the front half of the jaw are conical, typically for dolphins, but in the back they are flanged on the inside portion of the crown. Amazon dolphins have a diverse diet that includes not only many species of softbodied fish but also spiny and hardbodied prey like crabs, armored catfish, and even small turtles, so they probably use their modified rear teeth to crush and soften prey items. It is a misconception that all river dolphins are blind, but the atrophied eyes of the Ganges and Indus dolphins lack a lens, leaving

these species unable to resolve images. The most they can do is perceive the presence or absence of light. The other species within the group also have reduced vision, but not nearly to the same degree; in fact, the Amazon dolphin has quite good vision.

The sonar abilities of all the river dolphins are highly developed, enabling them to detect objects (including prey) in the murky conditions prevailing in much of their environment. The Ganges and Indus dolphins are known to be side swimmers; in other words, after surfacing to breathe, they immediately roll onto one side, "feeling" for the bottom with a flipper while scanning the area ahead of them with constant clicking sounds.

## Social or Solitary?
### SOCIAL BEHAVIOR

Groups of river dolphins rarely exceed 10 in number, and it is not unusual to encounter solitary individuals. The relationships of associated individuals have not been studied, so the composition, structure, and nature of river dolphin societies are completely unknown. Calves, of course, remain close to their mothers for several months. Although densities, or the numbers of animals present in a given area of water surface, can be a good deal higher for river dolphins than for most marine dolphins, this is probably due mainly to the differences of scale between rivers and the open sea. Small bands of Tucuxis or Irrawaddy dolphins will typically surface in synchrony and within one or two body lengths of one another.

In contrast, river dolphins proper will often appear to surface and dive independently, while also conveying the impression that animals across a wide area are engaged in similar activities and are somehow linked.

River dolphins are found mainly in confluences (where rivers or streams converge), at sharp bends, along sandbanks, and near the downstream ends of islands. Such areas offer both deep water and hydraulic refuge, the latter in the form of eddy countercurrent systems, where dolphins can reduce their energy expenditure but still avoid being swept downstream by the main current.

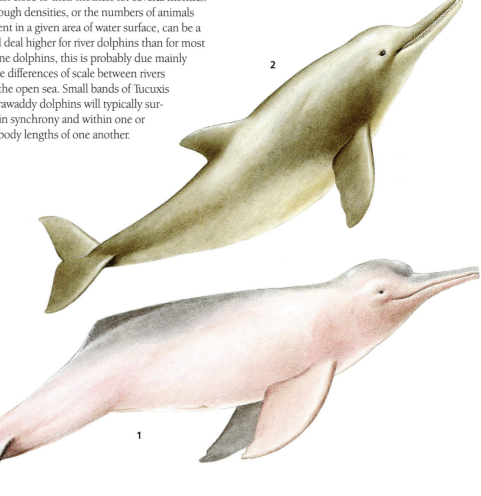

◐ **Below and left** *The five species of "true" river dolphins. Despite their widely separated habitats, they are very similar in appearance, differing primarily in skin color, length of beak, and number of teeth:*
*1 Amazon dolphin; 2 La Plata dolphin; 3 Ganges dolphin; 4 Indus dolphin; 5 Yangtze river dolphin.*

## A Lethal Proximity to Humans

CONSERVATION AND ENVIRONMENT

River dolphins everywhere live in danger of incidental capture in fishing gear (especially gill nets), and of the transformation and fragmentation of their habitat to serve human needs. Levels of toxic contaminants found in river dolphin tissue – for example, organochlorine pesticides, polychlorinated biphenyls (PCBs), and organotins – have raised concern about their implications for health and reproduction. The animals' close proximity to sources of pollution (such as sewage outfalls, factory discharge, and agricultural runoff) and their relative inability to metabolize contaminants make them especially vulnerable. Dams also impede their natural movements; subpopulations upriver of barrages have declined steadily, and some are already extinct. In Asia especially, much of the water impounded above barrages is diverted to irrigate fields and supply homes and businesses, thus directly reducing the dolphins' habitat.

The Yangtze river dolphin is the most critically endangered cetacean in the world. Discovered by Western science only in 1918, it was still common and widely distributed along the entire length of the Yangtze River in the 1950s. However, from the start of China's "Great Leap Forward" (the rapid industrialization of the state) in the autumn of 1958, the dolphins were hunted intensively to provide meat, oil, and leather. Today, although they are legally protected, they continue to be killed accidentally in fisheries, and to die from collisions with powered vessels and exposure to underwater blasting. Their figures are thought to number only in tens. The Finless porpoises that share much of the Yangtze river dolphin's historical range have also suffered a rapid decline, although several hundred of this species, possibly even a thousand and more, survive.

Perhaps only a few thousand Ganges dolphins survive, and fewer than 1,000 Indus dolphins. Tribal people in remote reaches of the Ganges and Brahmaputra rivers still hunt dolphins for food, and fishermen in the Subcontinent use their oil to lure a highly prized species of catfish. The Irrawaddy dolphins in the Mekong and Mahakam rivers are in grave danger of extinction. The situation is somewhat brighter in South America, where two river dolphins, the Amazon and the tucuxi, are still quite numerous and widely distributed.     RR

---

### RIVER DOLPHINS

Order: Cetacea

Families: Platanistidae, Lipotidae, Iniidae, Pontoporiidae

5 species in 4 genera

**DISTRIBUTION** SE Asia, S America

**GANGES DOLPHIN**
*Platanista gangetica*
Ganges dolphin or susu
India, Nepal, Bangladesh, in Ganges-Brahmaputra-Meghna river system. HTL 210–260cm (83–102in); WT 80–90kg (175–200lb). Skin: light grayish-brown, paler beneath. Gestation: 10 months. Longevity: over 28 years. Conservation status: Endangered.

**INDUS DOLPHIN** *Platanista minor*
Indus dolphin or bhulan
Pakistan, in Indus river. Size, coat, diet, gestation, and (probably) longevity: as Ganges dolphin. Conservation status: Endangered.

**YANGTZE RIVER DOLPHIN** *Lipotes vexillifer*
Yangtze River dolphin, Whitefin dolphin, or baiji
China, in Yangtze and lower Fuchunjian Rivers. HTL 230–250cm (91–98in); WT 135–230kg (300–510lb). Skin: bluish-gray, white underneath. Gestation: probably 10–12 months. Conservation status: Critically Endangered.

**AMAZON DOLPHIN** *Inia geoffrensis*
Amazon dolphin or boto
S America, in Amazon and Orinoco river systems. HTL 208–228cm (82–90in) (Orinoco), 224–247cm (88–97in) (Amazon); WT 85–130kg (190–285lb). Skin: dark bluish-gray above, pink beneath; darker in Orinoco. Gestation: probably 10–12 months. Conservation status: Vulnerable.

**LA PLATA DOLPHIN** *Pontoporia blainvillei*
La Plata dolphin or franciscana
Coast of E South America, from Ubatuba to Valdes Peninsula (not in La Plata river). HTL 155–175cm (61–69in); WT 32–52kg (70–115lb). Skin: light, warm brown, paler beneath. Gestation: 11 months. Longevity: more than 16 years.

Abbreviations HTL = head–tail length  WT = weight

# Beluga and Narwhal

**b**ELUGAS AND NARWHALS, THE so-called "white whales", are among the most social of all cetaceans. A large aggregation of brilliant white belugas in an Arctic bay makes an impressive enough sight, but a procession of hundreds or even thousands of narwhals moving along the coast is truly awe-inspiring. White whales are known to have lived in temperate seas in prehistoric times, but now exclusively occupy cold Arctic waters.

The narwhal's skin coloration is striking in itself: small patches of gray-green, cream, and black pigmentation seem painted onto its body by short strokes of a stiff brush. Even more astonishing, though, is the renowned spiraled tusk, thrust above the water as the male breaks the surface. Not only does this seem disproportionately long – 3m (10ft) of tusk on a 5m (15ft) whale – but it is also curiously off-center, protruding from the left upper lip at an awkward angle and pointing down. To crown these oddities, the tails of older males appear to be put on back-to-front!

## Fat for Insulation
### FORM AND FUNCTION

Narwhals and belugas are similarly shaped, though the beluga is slightly smaller. One feature that is peculiar to the beluga is its neck; unlike most whales, it can turn its head sideways to a near right-angle. The beluga has no dorsal fin – hence its scientific name, *Delphinapterus* or "dolphin-without-a-wing" – although there is a ridge along the back from mid-body to the tail; a true fin might lose body heat, and would be at risk of getting damaged in ice.

In both species, males are about 50cm (20in) longer than females, and their flippers increasingly turn upward at the tips with age. The flippers of belugas are capable of a wide range of movements, and appear to serve an important function in close-quarters maneuvering, including very slow reverse swimming. In aging male narwhals, the shape of the tail changes; the tips migrate forward, giving a concave leading edge when viewed from above or below. Both species have thick layers of blubber to provide insulation against the near-freezing water in which they live, but the beluga is so fat that the head (which of necessity is less well-endowed with blubber) always looks too small for its body.

⊙ **Below** From June to September, belugas congregate in hundreds and thousands at their traditional birthing grounds in wide river estuaries. The immense numbers involved in migratory patterns may be judged from this aerial view of belugas at the mouth of the Cunningham River, on Somerset Island.

◔ *Left* A beluga and its calf. Suckling may last for two years, during which time the mother and calf are almost inseparable. Newborn belugas are brown, and the skin gradually lightens through gray, as in this one-year-old, to white.

**FACTFILE**

## BELUGA AND NARWHAL

Order: Cetacea

Family: Monodontidae

2 species in 2 genera

**DISTRIBUTION** Northern circumpolar

**BELUGA** *Delphinapterus leucas*
Beluga or White whale
N Russia and N America, Greenland, Svalbard. Cold waters, usually near ice; offshore and coastal; estuaries in summer. HTL 300–500cm (10–16ft), WT 500–1,500kg (1,100–3,300lb). Adult males c.25 percent longer than females, and nearly double their mass. Skin: adults white or yellowish; young slate-gray, becoming medium gray at 2 years and white on maturity. Diet: mostly benthic; schooling fish, crustacea, worms, mollusks. Breeding: gestation probably 14–15 months. Longevity: 30–40 years. Conservation status: Vulnerable.

**NARWHAL**
*Monodon monoceros*
N Canada and Russia, Greenland, Svalbard. Cold waters, invariably in or near sea ice; mainly offshore, but often fjords and coasts in summer. HTL 400–500cm (13–16.5ft); WT 800–1,600kg (1,760–3,520lb); male tusk length 150–300cm (5–10ft); males larger than females. Skin: mottled gray-green, cream, and black, whitening with age, beginning with the belly; young dark gray. Diet: Arctic cod, flatfish, cephalopods, shrimps. Breeding: gestation probably 14–15 months. Longevity: 30–40 years.

Abbreviations HTL = head–tail length  WT = weight

The narwhal has only two teeth, both of which are non-functional. In the female, these grow to about 20cm (8in) in length but never emerge from the gums; in the male, the left tooth continues to grow to form the tusk. A tiny minority of males – less than 1 percent – produce twin tusks, while a similar proportion of females have single tusks. The purpose of the tusk has been the subject of various theories but it seems to be simply a secondary sexual characteristic that plays a role in establishing dominance in social life and breeding.

Belugas are capable of a wide range of bodily and facial expressions, including an impressive mouth gape displaying 32–40 peglike teeth that abut one another. The surfaces can be heavily worn – sometimes so much so that they cannot be effective for grasping prey. This – and the fact that the teeth do not fully emerge until well into the second or third year – suggests that their prime function may not be for feeding. Belugas commonly clap their jaws together to make drumming sounds, and the teeth may contribute to these; they are also used visually in showing-off displays.

In contrast to the narwhal, the beluga is a highly vocal animal, producing moos, chirps, whistles, and clangs that long ago earned it the nickname of "sea canary." Some of the sounds it makes are easily heard through the hulls of boats and even above water; underwater, the din from a herd is reminiscent of a barnyard. In addition to its vocal and echolocation skills, the beluga also uses vision for both communication and predation. The versatility of its expressions suggests the likelihood of subtle social communication.

◔ *Right* A pod of narwhals off the coast of Baffin Island, northern Canada. On migratory journeys such as this, pods may coalesce into schools of up to 2,000 animals, all swimming near the surface. However, when foraging for food, narwhals are capable of diving to great depths to reach the ocean floor.

◔ *Above* The development of facial features and expressions in the beluga. Adult belugas have a very pronounced forehead melon, but this is slow to develop: in newborn calves **a** it is almost absent; in yearlings **b** the melon is quite large but the beak undeveloped; maturity **c** is reached at 5–8 years. The beluga's mouth and neck are highly flexible; belugas communicate with each other a great deal by sound and facial expression; in repose the beluga seems to our eyes to be smiling. **1** Besides clicks and bell-like tones, belugas produce loud reports by clapping their jaws together. Belugas are versatile feeders and the pursed mouth **2** is believed to be used in bottom-feeding.

## Deep Feeders
### Diet

Both belugas and narwhals are diverse feeders: the beluga on a variety of schooling fish (including cod), as well as crustacea, worms, and sometimes mollusks, and the narwhal on cephalopods, arctic cod, flatfish, and shrimps. Belugas find most of their prey on the seabed at depths of up to 500m (1,650ft), and the narwhal similarly feeds at depth, though not necessarily on the bottom. Both species are capable of dives in excess of 1,000m (3,300ft), and are limited only by their breath-hold capacity, which is normally 10–20 minutes during deep dives but can exceed 20 minutes in exceptional circumstances. The highly flexible neck of belugas permits a wide visual or acoustic sweep of the bottom, and they can produce both suction and a jet of water to dislodge prey. The narwhal, with no functional teeth at all, can, like the beluga, probably suck up its dinner. The male and the tuskless female have similar diets, so the tusk appears to play no part in feeding – indeed, it can only be an impediment, obstructing the mouth of the whale as it approaches prey.

## Migrating Whales
### Social Behavior

The beluga and the narwhal are probably similar in their growth and reproduction, although more is known about the beluga. Females become sexually mature at around 5 years, males after 8, but there are differences between populations. Judging by the sexual dimorphism, dominant males probably mate with many females. Births mostly occur in early summer as the sea ice begins to break up. Many populations occupy estuaries in July, but this is probably not linked to breeding, for few calves are born in these sheltered areas. Single calves are the norm, with twinning an extremely rare event. A strong bond is established between mother and calf immediately after birth, and physical contact is maintained so closely that the calf seems attached to the mother's side or back. The mother may provide milk for more than two years, after which she will again be pregnant. The complete reproductive cycle of gestation and lactation takes three or more years.

Narwhals sometimes move from the offshore pack ice into fjords during mid-summer, but spend less time in shallow waters than do belugas. Both species are extremely social and sometimes appear in the same fjord together, but such co-occurrence seems coincidental and does not normally result in any obvious interaction. Animals are rarely seen alone or even in small groups, so the occasional beluga or narwhal observed in temperate European waters is abnormal socially as well as geographically.

Aggregations of hundreds or thousands of whales are common, often covering areas of many square kilometers. The aggregations behave as one entity, even though, when seen from the air, they clearly comprise many smaller, tightly-knit groups, usually containing whales of a similar size and/or sexual status. Females with calves come together, as do groups of large adult males. It is known that these male groups often stay together for several months, and maybe even longer.

Satellite telemetry has also revealed much about the migrations of belugas and narwhals. Both species spend most of the year offshore in areas dominated by sea ice, but sometimes in open areas within the pack ice called polynyas. Narwhals may remain offshore all year, or may enter fjords for brief periods in July or August. Most beluga populations frequent estuaries in summer, but individual whales do not remain in them for long. In the Canadian Beaufort Sea, belugas pause in their eastward migration in the immense Mackenzie Delta for a week or so, then continue on to deeper waters. The area can be likened to a highway service station; even though hunters and observers see hundreds of whales there every day for more than a month, there is in fact a continuous turnover of individuals, and tens of thousands of belugas visit during this period. In some areas such as Svalbard, estuaries are not available and belugas head for glacier fronts instead. What estuaries and glaciers have in common is that each is a source of fresh water. At this time of year, the belugas undergo a molt, in which their old yellow skin is shed to reveal the new, gleaming white skin underneath. Fresh water absorbed through the epidermis may hasten the shedding process, which certainly occurs very rapidly, aided by the whales rubbing themselves on the gravel of the seabed.

◐ *Above* The narwhal's extraordinary tusk results from its left tooth growing out into a counter-clockwise spiral. Like antlers in deer, the tusk's sheer size may serve to indicate an animal's prowess; it is also used as a weapon, as evidenced by the accumulation of scars on aging narwhals and the occasional tusk-tip found embedded in a skull.

**Above** The narwhal has long been hunted by the indigenous Eskimo peoples of the Arctic. Every part of the animal is used – its meat and skin (which is rich in vitamin C) are eaten, while its sinews are dried and turned into stout cord. Yet the high prices commanded by the narwhal's tusk have raised concerns about overexploitation of the species.

**Below** Belugas loom up like ghostly apparitions in the murky waters of Hudson Bay. The bulbous frontal "melon" is used for echolocation, in which the beluga sends out acoustic signals to judge its distance from objects by the frequency at which the sound waves bounce back. This is vital for navigating and finding prey in dark or muddy waters.

## Easy Pickings for Hunters
### CONSERVATION AND ENVIRONMENT

Belugas return faithfully to their summer grounds along migration routes that are probably learned in infancy. This fidelity can have unfortunate consequences, for the whales will go on returning to a given site even if overexploited by hunters until the population is extinguished. Furthermore, the 30 recognized populations of belugas are so inflexible in their preference for familiar routes and breeding grounds that they will not recolonize areas where the population has been wiped out. One such location is Ungava Bay in Labrador, where belugas were formerly abundant but are now rarely encountered.

The predictable migratory behavior of belugas has made the species particularly vulnerable to exploitation. In the 18th and 19th centuries American and European whalers would force mass strandings of hundreds of belugas in order to "top up" their cargo of whale oil rendered from their primary quarry, the Bowhead. Aboriginal peoples also hunted the whales, though historically they took relatively small harvests which were probably sustainable; today's Eskimo hunters are more mechanized (with high-velocity rifles, explosive harpoons, and motorboats) and serve greater human populations, and so have the potential seriously to deplete white whale stocks. Currently, belugas are thought to number in excess of 100,000 worldwide, but individual populations range from healthy (in the tens of thousands) to effectively extinct following excessive hunting. Combined annual catches are now in the hundreds or low thousands, with the precise number varying from year to year.

The beluga's seasonal affinity for shallow coastal areas also makes it vulnerable to more indirect modern-day threats. The pollution of prey, and habitat degradation through oil exploration and the building of hydroelectric dams, are presently of greatest concern, while global warming and its effects on sea ice may be a looming problem. Though belugas and narwhals have survived periodic fluctuations in Arctic ice extent within even the recent geological past, the currently predicted rate of change in this region is exceptional and will demand rapid adaptation if these pagophilic (ice-loving) species are to continue to thrive.

The most recent estimate of narwhal numbers is in the order of 25,000–30,000, consisting of three putative stocks. In contrast to the beluga, this species avoids nearshore waters for most of the year, thus reducing the threat from industrial development, but hunting occurs and is not evenly distributed. The narwhal's tusk has always been the prime cause of its persecution, from medieval times – when it was reputed to be the horn of the mythical unicorn, endowed with magical properties – up to the present day, when it is much in demand from private collectors and museums.                                    AM/PB

# Sperm Whales

**I**MMORTALIZED IN HERMAN MELVILLE'S NOVEL
*Moby Dick, Sperm whales run to extremes. They
are the largest of the toothed whales, have the
biggest brains on Earth, are very sexually dimorphic
(males weigh three times as much as females), and
make possibly the deepest and longest dives of any
creature in the animal kingdom.*

Long ago, sailors thought that the regularly-
spaced clicking noises they heard through the
hulls of their ships originated from what they
called "carpenter fish," because they sounded like
hammers tapping. They were in fact listening to
the sounds of Sperm whales. As for the name
"Sperm whale," it seems to have come from
whalers misinterpreting the nature of the oily substance known as spermaceti found in the whales'
massive foreheads.

## Sound in the Deep Ocean
### FORM AND FUNCTION

The ancient family of Physeteridae seems to have
separated from the main odontocete line early in
cetacean evolution, about 30 million years ago.
The single extant species, the Sperm whale –
*Physeter catadon* (*macrocephalus*) along with the far
smaller Dwarf and Pygmy sperm whales (family
Kogiidae) – all share a barrelshaped head, a long,
narrow, underslung lower jaw with uniform teeth,
paddleshaped flippers, and a blowhole which is
displaced to the left side. The *Kogia* genus
emerged much later, around 8 million years ago.

The Sperm whale's great, square forehead, situated above the upper jaw and in front of the skull,
makes up a quarter to a third of the animal's
length. It holds the spermaceti organ, an ellipsoid
structure contained within a sheath of connective
tissue. Both the organ itself and the tissue surrounding it are dense with spermaceti – a semi-
liquid, waxy oil. Air sacs bound both ends of the
spermaceti organ. The skull and air passages that
surround the organ are highly asymmetrical. The
two nasal passages have become very different in
both form and function: the left is used for breathing, the right for sound production.

Why the Sperm whale carries such large,
unwieldy headgear is not clear. One suggested reason is that it helps focus the clicks which serve in
echolocating food in the murky depths of the
deep sea. Sperm whales also use the clicks for
communication, being the most vocal of the three
Physeteridae species.

The rodlike lower jaw of the Sperm whale contains 20–26 pairs of large teeth, while the Dwarf

sperm whale may have 8–13 and the Pygmy
sperm whale 10–16 pairs. These teeth do not
seem to be required for feeding, as well-fed Sperm
whales have been caught lacking teeth or even
lower jaws. Moreover, the teeth do not erupt
(emerge) until the whales reach sexual maturity.
None of the species normally have teeth in the
upper jaw, and if they do, the teeth usually do not
erupt. *Kogia* teeth are thin, very sharp, curved,
and lack enamel.

Except for the head and tail flukes, the skin of
the Sperm whale is corrugated to create an irregular, undulating surface. The low dorsal fin may be
topped by a rough, whitish callus, especially in
mature females.

Sperm whales make repeated, deep foraging
dives, on average to about 400m (1,300ft) and for
about 35 minutes, though they can reach over
1,000m (3,300ft) and last for more than an hour.
Between dives, the whales surface to breathe, on
average for about 8 minutes. The whales descend
nearly vertically, raising their flukes straight out of
the water.

For both sexes, squid form the bulk of the diet.
Female Sperm whales spend about 75 percent of
their time foraging. Although they go for smaller
prey than the males, they will occasionally take on
Giant and Jumbo squid, and scars from the
squids' sucker marks on their heads bear testimo-
ny to their undersea battles. Prey items recovered
from male Sperm whales tend to be larger versions
of the same species eaten by and recovered from
females, though the males also eat rather more
fish, including sharks and rays.

In the Pygmy and Dwarf sperm whales, the
head is more conical and much shorter in relation
to the overall body length. The two *Kogia* species
look rather sharklike, with an underslung mouth
and sharp teeth, plus a bracket-shaped mark on
the side of the head resembling gill slits. While
they mainly eat squid and octopus, *Kogia* have a
flattened snout, and benthic fish and crabs have
been recovered from their stomachs, suggesting
that they may be bottom-feeders at least some of
the time. Their diet is otherwise not dissimilar to
that of the Sperm whale.

## Global Voyagers
### DISTRIBUTION PATTERNS

Few animals on earth are as widely distributed as Sperm whales. They occupy
waters from near both poles to the equator.
The two sexes seem to be geographically segregated for much of the year, with females and
juveniles inhabiting warmer waters at latitudes
of less than about 40°, while the males move on
to higher latitudes as they age and grow. The
largest males are found close to the edge of the
Arctic and Antarctic pack ice. In order to mate,
they must migrate to the tropics, where the
females abide.

Genetic studies indicate that all Sperm whale
populations are broadly similar. Mitochondrial
DNA, transmitted only through the mother,
shows no geographical structure at scales of less
than an ocean basin. Nuclear DNA, half of which
comes through the wide-ranging males, is even
more geographically homogeneous – there are no
significant differences between Sperm whale populations within oceans, and whatever differences

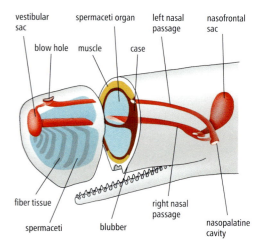

**⬧ Above** *Cutaway drawing of the head of a Sperm
whale, showing its anatomical features. The whale can
alter its buoyancy by cooling or warming the huge
volume of spermaceti in the upper part of its head.
It achieves this by regulating the flow of water
through its nasal passages.*

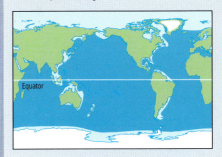

⬥ **Above** *The three species of Sperm whale:* **1** *Sperm whale (Physeter catodon)* diving for squid, which it sometimes catches at extraordinary depths near the ocean floor; **2** *Pygmy sperm whale (Kogia breviceps);* **3** *Dwarf sperm whale (Kogia simus).*

**FACTFILE**

## SPERM WHALES

Order: Cetacea

Families: Physeteridae and Kogiidae

3 species in 2 genera

**DISTRIBUTION** Worldwide in tropical and temperate waters to latitudes of about 40°; mature male Sperm whales to polar ice edge.

[map: Equator]

**HABITAT** Mainly deep waters (over 1,000m/3,300ft) off the edge of the continental shelf. Juvenile and immature *Kogia* may inhabit shallower, more inshore waters over the outer part of the continental shelf.

**SPERM WHALE** *Physeter catodon (macrocephalus)*
Cachalot, Spermacet whale, Pot whale, sea-guap
HTL male 16m (52.5ft), max. 18m (59ft); female 11m (36ft), max.12.5m (41ft). WT male 45 tonnes, max. 57 tonnes; female 15 tonnes, max. 24 tonnes. Skin dark gray, but often with white lining to mouth and white patches on belly; wrinkled, except for head and flukes. Breeding: females mature sexually around age 9; in males, puberty extends from ages 10–20, though they do not participate actively in breeding until roughly age 30. Single calves born in summer after 14–15 months' gestation; calf care is prolonged, with lactation lasting 2 years or more. Longevity: at least 60–70 years. Conservation status: Vulnerable.

**PYGMY SPERM WHALE** *Kogia breviceps*
Pygmy or Lesser sperm whale, Lesser cachalot
HTL male 4 m (13ft); female max. 3m (10ft). WT 318–408kg (700–900lb). Skin: bluish gray on back, shading to lighter gray on the sides, and white or pinkish on belly; lighter mark – the "bracket" or "false gill" – on side of head. Breeding: mating believed to occur in summer; gestation period 9–11 months, with births in the spring. Calves, which are about 1m (3.3ft) long at birth, are nursed for about a year; females may give birth two years in a row. Longevity: may be 17 years or more.

**DWARF SPERM WHALE** *Kogia simus*
Dwarf sperm whale or Owen's pygmy whale
HTL 2.1–2.7m (7–9ft). WT 136–272kg (300–600lb). Skin: bluish-gray on back, shading to lighter gray on the sides, and white or pinkish on the belly; lighter "bracket" or "false gill" on side of head. Breeding: calves are somewhat smaller at birth than those of *K. breviceps*. Longevity: unknown.

Abbreviations: HTL = head–tail length   WT = weight

do exist are between oceanic populations. They live in deep water, usually deeper than 1,000m (3,300ft) and far from land. The edges of the continental shelf seem to suit them well.

Pygmy and Dwarf sperm whales are also cosmopolitan. Pygmy sperm whales are found in deep waters of temperate, subtropical, and tropical seas. The Dwarf sperm whale occurs in somewhat warmer water.

The two *Kogia* species spend a substantial amount of time lying quietly on the surface exposing the back of their heads, with their tails hanging down limply. Pygmy sperm whales are timid and slowmoving. They will not swim toward boats themselves, but are easy to approach as they lie motionless at the surface. They come up to breathe in a slow and deliberate manner, and have an inconspicuous blow. When startled or distressed, *Kogia* may discharge a reddish-brown intestinal fluid that perhaps helps them to escape from predators such as large sharks and killer whales, in the manner of an octopus's ink. *Kogia* also have eyes adapted for functioning in the poor light of the deep sea.

Very little is known of the reproductive strategy of the Pygmy or Dwarf sperm whales. No sexual dimorphism is apparent in either species. This is in marked contrast to the Sperm whale, which is radically sexually dimorphic; the size of the mature male seems to confer a reproductive advantage. *Kogia* may therefore have a different mating system.

Female Sperm whales attain physical maturity at roughly 30 years of age, but males continue to grow until they are about 50 years old. Large, mature, male Sperm whales (late 20s or older) make the journey from pole to equator, where they roam between groups searching for receptive females with whom to mate. It is not known whether males return annually or biennially. The time spent with each group varies from a few minutes to several hours. Breeding males mostly avoid one another, much like bull elephants in the rutting condition known as "musth." Occasionally, though, they may fight, as evidenced by deep scars on the heads of some mature adults. The spacing of these scars leaves little doubt that they are produced by other males' teeth.

Pygmy sperm whales may bear a calf two years in succession, i.e. they can be pregnant and nursing simultaneously. In contrast, Sperm whales give birth roughly once every 5 years or so, following a gestation period that is not accurately known, but is within the range of 14–15 months. Reproductive rates in females decline with age.

⬤ **Right** *A family group comprising mother, daughter, and new calf swimming together near the Azores. Sperm whales are about 4m (13ft) long at birth and may weigh as much as 1,000kg (2,200lb). Sperm whale calves eat solid food by one year of age, but continue to suckle for several years.*

## Care in a Cetacean Community

SOCIAL BEHAVIOR

Female Sperm whales are exceedingly gregarious. Their social life is based on the family unit, which consists of about 12 permanently attached, closely related females and their young. Two or more units may join together for a period of several days, forming a cohesive group of about 20 whales, perhaps to enhance foraging efficiency or at least to reduce interference among different units foraging in the same area.

Male Sperm whales, in contrast, leave the natal unit when they are roughly 6 years old to form "bachelor schools." As males age, they are found in progressively smaller aggregations. Mature males' associations with other males rarely last longer than a day, although males have been found stranded together on beaches, suggesting social relationships are not entirely absent.

It is the potential of other whales to act as baby-sitters which seems to draw female Sperm whales to affiliate. Young calves are apparently unable to make prolonged dives with their mothers to the depths to feed. Left alone at the surface, they would be vulnerable to attacks by sharks or killer whales. Members of groups containing young

○ **Above** The power of the Sperm whale is dramatically apparent as this pod forges ahead in formation. The dorsal hump, slightly suggestive of a submarine, is prominent here, and the individual on the right is demonstrating its oblique blow.

○ **Right** The "marguerite" formation, in which members of a pod will encircle an injured Sperm whale while it remains alive. Such supportive behavior used to be disastrous for the whales, allowing them to be picked off one-by-one by whalers.

### CHAMPION DIVERS

Sperm whales may be considered to be the champion divers among all aquatic mammals. They have been accurately recorded by sonar as diving to 1,200m (3,936ft), and Sperm whale carcasses have been recovered entangled in cables from 1,140m (3,740ft), where they had probably been feeding on the bottom-dwelling squid that form the bulk of their diet. One of two bulls observed diving for one to nearly two hours each dive, was found – on capture – to have in its stomach two specimens of Scymodon, a small, bottom-living shark. The depth of water in the area was about 3,200m (10,500ft), suggesting an amazing diving ability. The fact that Sperm whales dive right to the seabed for food is borne out by the discovery of all manner of objects in their stomachs, from stones to tin cans, suggesting that they literally shovel up the bottom mud.

Bulls are the deepest and longest divers, although females may dive to 1,000m (3,280ft) for more than one hour. Juveniles and calves dive for only half this time, to about 700m (2,300ft). Females often accompany young whales, and this, rather than an inability to dive deeper, may be what limits their diving range. However, the gregariousness and caring behavior within the nursery school means that young calves may temporarily be adopted by other females, thus enabling the mother to dive deeper for food than she might otherwise be able to do.

If diving as a group, Sperm whales appear to remain close and do almost everything together. They recover quickly from a long, deep dive, and

dive again after only 2–5 minutes. After several long dives, they reach their physiological limit and recover by lolling on the surface for many minutes.

The descent and ascent rates are astonishing. The fastest recorded averaged 170m (550ft) per min in descent and 140m (450ft) per min in ascent. The adaptations that enable the Sperm whale to perform these prodigious feats are largely similar to those of other cetaceans but more efficient. For example, the muscle in Sperm whale can absorb up to 50 percent of the total oxygen store – at least double the proportion in land mammals, and significantly more than in baleen whales and seals.

A unique feature of the Sperm whale is the vast spermaceti organ, which fills most of the upper part of the head, and is thought to be an aid to buoyancy control. The theory is that the nasal passages and sinuses which permeate the organ can control the cooling and warming rate of the wax, which has a consistent melting point of 29°C (84.2°F). As the whale dives from warm surface waters to the colder depths, the flow of water into the head passages is controlled to quickly cool the head wax from the whale's normal body temperature of 33.5°C (92.3°F). As a result, the wax solidifies, shrinking as it does so, increasing the density of the head, and thus assisting the descent. On ascending, the blood flow to the capillaries in the head can be increased, so warming the wax slightly and increasing buoyancy to provide lift to the exhausted whale.　　　　　　　　　CL

calves seem therefore to stagger their dives, so that some adults are at the surface at all times. In addition to this communal care within family units, there is strong, though not definitive, evidence for females suckling calves who are not their own.

Communal group defense against predators extends to protecting other adults too. Clustering tightly together, the whales coordinate their efforts in a "marguerite" formation, with their heads together at the center and their bodies radiating out like the petals of a flower. Alternatively, they may adopt a "heads out" formation. The former strategy makes use of the whales' flukes as defense; the latter, their jaws.

On occasion, individual whales will even place themselves at risk to help others. In one well-observed incident off California, Sperm whales under attack by killer whales were seen to leave the comparative safety of the marguerite formation to "rescue" another whale which had become separated and was being badly mauled by the killers.

Female Sperm whales regularly gather at the

*Kogia* appear less sociable than Sperm whales. Pygmy sperm whales live either alone or in groups of up to six animals, while up to ten Dwarfs may coexist. In contrast to Sperm whales, male Dwarf sperm whales may associate in groups with females and their calves, and groups of immatures also form. All three species in the family Physeteridae are known to strand, but the Pygmy sperm whale is particularly prone, being one of the most commonly stranded cetacean species. In fact, much of what is known of *Kogia* comes from data collected at strandings.

## Past Exploitation, Present Risk
### CONSERVATION AND ENVIRONMENT

Estimates for the global population of Sperm whales range from 200,000 to 1.5 million. Sperm whales are listed as Vulnerable on the IUCN Red List, and the International Whaling Commission's 1988 moratorium has forbidden commercial whaling. *Kogia* are probably also rare, but their populations have not been properly censused.

Historically, however, the Sperm whale's contribution to human civilization has been prodigious. The huge animals' spermaceti oil and blubber largely fueled the Industrial Revolution. A second wave of whaling took place in the 20th century, using mechanized catcher vessels and explosive harpoons, resulting in the deaths of up to 30,000 Sperm whales each year. Due to their much greater size and proportionally larger spermaceti organs, large males were the main targets of the hunters, who by now marketed the oil as a high-grade industrial lubricant. This practice continues in the southeast Pacific, where large males are now rare and calving rates are so low as to put the longterm survival of this population in doubt.

According to the International Whaling Commission's Sperm whale model, populations grow at the tiny rate of less than one animal per year, even in ideal conditions. Sperm whales also die from entanglement in fishing gear, choking on plastic bags, and collision with ships. Chemical pollution is also evident in their blubber; levels of contaminants in Sperm whales are intermediate between inshore odontocetes – the highest – and baleen whales.

Because they rely so heavily on sound for all aspects of their lives, and because sound often carries further at depth, noise pollution is considered to be an additional threat. Shipping, underwater explosions, seismic exploration, oil drilling, military sonars and exercises, and oceanographic experiments all contribute to the increased undersea noise levels in the modern world. Sperm whales react markedly to such threats; for example, in response to sonar during the US invasion of Grenada in 1983, Sperm whales fell silent and presumably ceased foraging. They have also been seen to respond in a similar way to the sounds of a seismic vessel at work, even though it lay several hundred kilometers away.                    LW/HW

surface to rest or socialize for several hours a day. They may lie parallel to each other, in a behavior sometimes called "logging" (because of their resemblance to immobile logs), or twist and turn in the water, rolling and touching each other. The whales also perform breaches (leaps from the water), lobtails (hitting the water with their tail flukes), and spy-hops (raising the head vertically out of the water). Females and immatures breach or lobtail at an overall rate of about once an hour. However, breaches and lobtails are almost always clustered into bouts, which often coincide with the start or end of periods of surface socializing.

During these social times, Sperm whales often emit "codas" (stereotyped, patterned series of around 3–20 clicks). Reminiscent of our Morse code, codas last around 1–2 seconds, and can often be heard as exchanges, or "dialogs," between individuals. Codas are a form of communication. So, one whale may emit "click-click–pause–click," and another may respond with "click-click-click-click-click." Two whales can emit the same coda almost simultaneously, forming a duet that sounds like an echo. Groups of females have distinctive repertoires of roughly 12 commonly-used codas ("dialects"), and coda repertoires also vary geographically. Coda repertoire is probably culturally transmitted, passed down from mother and family unit to offspring.

More commonly, Sperm whales produce precisely-spaced echolocation clicks – called "usual" clicks – that are iterated at about two clicks per second. Also in the repertoire are streams of clicks, known as "creaks" because together they make a creaking sound. These are used in social situations among codas or in foraging, perhaps to home in on potential prey. Ringing "slow" clicks, produced around once every six seconds, are characteristic of large, breeding males. It is thought that slow clicks may advertise a breeding male's presence, size, and/or fitness, repel other males, attract females, or be bounced off other whales to aid the originator in his echolocation. Sperm whales are a notable exception to other social, toothed whales in that their sounds consist almost entirely of clicks (rather than whistles, as made by dolphins).

# Gray Whale

RAY WHALES ARE THE MOST COASTAL OF THE baleen whales, and are often found within one kilometer of shore. This preference for coastal waters, and the accessibility to humans of the breeding lagoons in Mexico, make them among the best-known cetaceans. Thousands of people watch the "Grays" swimming past the shores of California.

Each fall and spring, gray whales migrate along the western coast of North America on their yearly passage between summer feeding grounds in the Arctic and winter calving areas in the protected lagoons of Baja California, Mexico. Their migration can be the longest of any mammal; some individuals may swim as far as 20,400km (12,675mi) yearly from the Arctic ice-pack to the subtropics and back.

## Big and Barnacled
### FORM AND FUNCTION

The Gray whale averages about 12m (40ft) in length, but can reach up to 15m (50ft). The skin is a mottled dark to light gray in color, and is one of the most heavily parasitized among cetaceans. Both barnacles and whale lice (cyamids) live on it in great abundance, barnacles particularly on top of the whale's relatively short, bowed head, around the blowhole, and on the anterior part of the back; one barnacle and three whale lice species are unique to the Gray whale and have not – so far – been found anywhere else. Albino Grays have been sighted, though they would appear to be extremely rare.

Gray whales lack a dorsal fin, but do have a dorsal ridge of 8–9 humps along the last third of the back. The baleen is yellowish-white, and is much heavier and shorter than in other baleen whales, never exceeding 38cm (15in) in length, no doubt because Gray whales strain bottom sediments to get at their prey, whereas other whales merely strain the water column (see Deep Harvest box). Under the throat are two longitudinal grooves about 2m (6.6ft) long and 40cm (16in) apart. These grooves may stretch open and allow the mouth to expand during feeding, thus enabling the whale to take in more food.

While migrating, Gray whales swim at about 4.5 knots (8km/h), but they can attain speeds of 11 knots (20km/h) under stress. Migrating Grays swim steadily, surfacing every 3–4 minutes to blow 3–5 times. The spout is short and puffy, and is forked as it issues from both blowholes. The tail flukes often come out of the water on the last blow in a series as the whale dives.

🔺 **Above** *Gray whale mother and calf. The young Gray whales are smooth and sleek compared to their barnacled elders. Calves are usually born between late December and early February and at birth can weigh up to 500kg (1,100lb), at which point they still lack the blubber necessary to withstand the freezing temperatures of Arctic waters.*

🔻 **Below** *Like tiny, bejeweled grottoes, barnacle clusters surround the blowhole of a Gray whale. Most of the great whales are host to barnacles, but Gray whales are particularly heavily encrusted. It is in and around these clusters of barnacles that whale lice live – small, pale, spidery creatures usually about 2.5cm (1in) in length.*

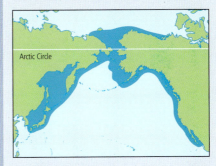

## GRAY WHALE

*Eschrichtius robustus*

Gray whale, California gray whale, or devilfish

Family: Eschrichtiidae

Sole member of genus

**DISTRIBUTION** Two stocks: E Pacific, or Californian, from Baja California along Pacific coast to Bering and Chukchi seas; W Pacific from S Korea to Okhotsk Sea.

Arctic Circle

**HABITAT** Usually in coastal waters less than 100m (330ft) deep.

**SIZE** Head–tail length male 11.9–14.3m (39–47ft), female 12.8–15.2m (42–50ft); **weight** male 16 tonnes, female (pregnant) 31–34 tonnes.

**SKIN** Mottled gray, usually covered with patches of barnacles and whale lice, no dorsal fin, but low ridge on rear half of back. Two throat grooves. White baleen. Spout paired, short, and bushy.

**DIET** Bottom-dwelling amphipods and a variety of planktonic invertebrates.

**BREEDING** Gestation 13 months; a single calf is born in alternate years.

**LONGEVITY** Sexually mature at 8 years, physically at 40; maximum recorded lifespan 77.

**CONSERVATION STATUS** Classified generally as Lower Risk: Conservation Dependent, though the Northwest Pacific stock is Critically Endangered.

◁ **Left** *Some characteristic attitudes of the Gray whale: **1** "spy-hopping," in which the whale's head protrudes from the water as it surveys its surroundings; **2** diving – tail flukes appear above the water before big dives, but not shallow ones; **3** blowing after a dive.*

The Gray whale's sound repertoire includes grunts, pulses, clicks, moans, and knocks; in the lagoons of Baja California calves also emit a low, resonant pulse that attracts their mothers. But in Gray whales sounds do not appear to have the complexity or social importance of those produced by other cetaceans. The exact significance of most of their communications is not known.

## Along the Pacific Coast
### DISTRIBUTION PATTERNS

At present there are only two stocks of Gray whales: the Californian, and the separate Western Pacific stock. Gray whales once inhabited the North Atlantic but disappeared in the early 1700s, probably due to whaling.

The Californian Gray whale calves during the winter in lagoons, such as Laguna Ojo de Liebre and Laguna San Ignacio, on the desert peninsula of Baja California, Mexico. They summer in the northern Bering Sea near Saint Lawrence Island and north through the Bering Straits into the Chukchi Sea, almost to the edge of the Arctic pack ice. A small portion of the population summers along the North American coast from northern California to Alaska. The only known current summer ground of the Western Pacific stock is near Sakhalin Island in the Okhotsk Sea. This population, numbering as few as 100 animals, migrates southward each fall past the east and west shores of Japan to unknown calving grounds.

## Calving Grounds to Feeding Grounds
### SOCIAL BEHAVIOR

Gray whales reach puberty at about 8 years of age (range 5–11 years), when the mean length is 11.1m (36ft) for males and 11.7m (38ft) for females; they attain full physical maturity at about 40. Like the other baleen whales, females of the species are larger than males, probably to satisfy the greater physical demands of bearing and nursing young. Females give birth in alternate years to a single calf about 4.9m (16ft) long, after a gestation period of just over a year.

Gray whales are adapted to migration, and many aspects of their life history and ecology reflect this yearly movement from the Arctic to the subtropics. The majority of the Eastern Pacific, or Californian, population spends from May through November in Arctic waters.

At the start of the Arctic winter their feeding grounds begin to freeze over. The whales then migrate to the protected lagoons, where the females calve. The calves are born within a period of 5–6 weeks, with a peak occurring about 10th January. At birth the calves have coats of blubber that would be too thin for them to withstand cold Arctic water, though they thrive in the warm lagoons. For the first few hours after birth the breathing and swimming of the calf are uncoordinated and labored, and the mother sometimes has to help the calf to breathe by holding it to the surface with her back or tail flukes. The calves are nursed for about seven months, beginning in the confined shallow lagoons, where they gain motor coordination and perhaps establish the mother–young bond necessary to keep together on the migration north to the summering grounds where they are weaned. By the time the calves have arrived in the Arctic, they have built up thick insulating blubber coats from the milk of the nursing females. In the lagoons and off southern California, the calves stay close to and almost touching their mothers; but by the time they reach the Bering Sea in late May and June they are good swimmers and may be seen breaching energetically away from their mothers.

Since the migration route follows the coast closely, the whales may navigate simply by staying in shallow water and keeping the land on their right or left side, depending on whether they are migrating north or south. At points along the migration route Gray whales are often seen "spy-hopping." To spy-hop, a whale thrusts its head straight up out of the water and then slowly sinks back down along its horizontal axis. This contrasts with the breach, where a whale leaps half way or more out of the water and then falls back on its side, creating a large splash. It is possible that Gray whales spy-hop to view the adjacent shore and thus orient their migration.

Mating and other sexual behavior have been observed throughout the range at all times of year, but most conceptions occur within a three-week period during the southward migration, with a peak around mid-December. Gray whale sex may involve as many as five or more individuals rolling and milling together, but when conception occurs is unknown. Some authors have speculated that the extra animals are necessary to hold the mating

○ **Above** *As part of the mating ritual, male and female Gray whales caress one another as they swim along. Provided that the female does not rebuff the male's advances, a fleeting congress will occur; although this only lasts between 10–30 seconds, it will occur repeatedly.*

○ **Right** *Pinkish in color, the Gray whale's penis, which is pliable, is some 2m (6ft) in length and approximately 20cm (8in) broad at the base. When the penis is flaccid, it folds up in an "S" shape into an abdominal groove.*

pair together; if so this would class as an extreme example of cooperation.

The migration off California occurs in a sequence according to reproductive status, sex, and age-group. Heading south, the migration is led by females in the late stages of pregnancy, presumably responding to a physiological imperative to give birth in warm water; all other whales probably make the migration for social purposes connected with mating. Next come the recently impregnated females who have weaned their calves the previous summer. Then come immature females and adult males and finally the immature males. The migration north is led by the newly

pregnant females, perhaps hurrying to spend the maximum length of time feeding in the Arctic to nurture the fetus developing inside them. The adult males and nonbreeding females follow, then immature whales of both sexes, and finally, meandering slowly, come females with newborn calves.

Observers have noticed changes in the sizes of groups as the migration progresses. In the early part of the southward migration, single whales predominate, presumably mostly females carrying near-term fetuses, and almost no whales are in groups of more than six. These leading whales swim steadily, seldom deviating from the migratory path, which suggests that they are hurrying

south to give birth. During the remainder of the migration, groups of two predominate, but there may be as many as 11 in one group in the middle of the procession. These later whales seem to have a tendency to loiter more en route, particularly toward the end of the migration.

In the calving grounds, the males and subadults are concentrated in the areas around the lagoon mouths where much rolling, milling, and sexual play can be seen, while the mothers and calves seem to use the shallower portions deep inside the lagoons. In the Arctic, 100 or more Gray whales may gather to feed in roughly the same area.

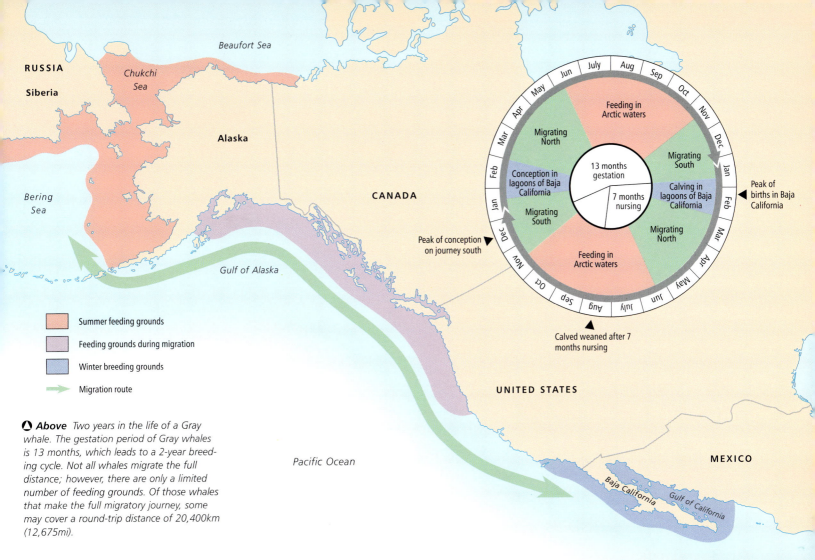

RUSSIA

Siberia

Chukchi
Sea

Beaufort Sea

Alaska

CANADA

Bering
Sea

Gulf of Alaska

**Circular diagram (two-year life cycle):**

13 months gestation / 7 months nursing

- Feeding in Arctic waters
- Migrating North
- Migrating South
- Conception in lagoons of Baja California
- Calving in lagoons of Baja California
- Migrating South
- Migrating North
- Feeding in Arctic waters

Months around outer ring: Jun, July, Aug, Sep, Oct, Nov, Dec, Jan, Feb, Mar, Apr, May (repeating)

Peak of births in Baja California

Peak of conception on journey south

Calved weaned after 7 months nursing

UNITED STATES

Summer feeding grounds

Feeding grounds during migration

Winter breeding grounds

Migration route

Pacific Ocean

MEXICO

Baja California

Gulf of California

⬯ *Above* Two years in the life of a Gray whale. The gestation period of Gray whales is 13 months, which leads to a 2-year breeding cycle. Not all whales migrate the full distance; however, there are only a limited number of feeding grounds. Of those whales that make the full migratory journey, some may cover a round-trip distance of 20,400km (12,675mi).

Some individuals do not make the entire migration north. For example, off the coast of British Columbia some individuals stay in the same area feeding for the eight or nine months between north and southbound migration, and some individual whales have been recorded returning to the same location each summer. Similar small, summer resident populations occur from northern California to Alaska. These residents seem to include both sexes and all age groups, including females with calves. This is perhaps an alternative feeding strategy to making the full migration, but it is one that only a few whales can afford, since feeding areas south of the northern Bering Sea are probably rare and can, therefore, only support a fraction of the population.

The only known nonhuman predator on the Gray whale is the Killer whale. Several attacks have been observed, most often on cows with calves, presumably in an attempt to get at the relatively defenseless calf. Killer whales seem to attack particularly the lips, tongue, and flukes of the Grays, the areas that may most readily be grasped. Adult Grays accompanying calves will place themselves protectively between the attackers and the calves. When under attack, Grays swim toward shallow water and kelp beds near shore, where Killer whales seem hesitant to enter. Gray whales respond to underwater playback of recordings of Killer whale sounds by swimming rapidly away or by taking refuge in thick kelp beds.

⬮ *Below* When young Gray whales are first born they are not especially coordinated and sometimes the mother will hold the calf to the surface on her back to help it breathe; however, as the calf gets a little older swimming onto its mother's back becomes a game.

## Hostages to the Hunt
### CONSERVATION AND ENVIRONMENT

The Western Pacific Gray whale currently exists in very small numbers, and is one of the most endangered whales. Heavy whaling pressures in the first third of the 20th century, and sporadic whaling since, are undoubtedly responsible for this sad decline.

For thousands of years, Eskimo, Aleut, and Native American whaling tribes took Gray whales from the Californian stock in the northern part of its range. In the 1850s Yankee whalers began killing Gray whales, both in the calving lagoons and along the migration route, in such numbers that by 1874 one whaling captain, Charles Scammon, was predicting that the Californian Gray would soon be extinct. By 1900, with the Californian stock reduced to a tiny remnant population, whaling virtually ceased. It resumed in 1913, continuing sporadically until 1946, when the International Whaling Commission (IWC) was formed. This body prohibited a commercial take of Gray whales, although the Soviet Union was permitted an aboriginal catch for the Eskimo people living on the Chukchi peninsula. At present Russia has an annual quota of 140 Gray whales. The United States also has a hunt quota of five whales a year, taken by the Makah people of Washington State.

Since the decline of whaling, the Eastern Pacific, or Californian, stock has made a steady recovery. The present population is estimated at approximately 25,000, with some indications that its growth is beginning to level off.     JD/AT

> ❖ **Right** A Gray whale calf breaching. Not to be confused with the "spy-hop," in which the head is thrust out of the water, a breach occurs when a whale leaps half-way – or more – out of the water and then falls back onto its side.

## DEEP HARVEST

Gray whales are adapted to exploiting the tremendous seasonal abundance of food that results as the Arctic pack ice retreats in spring, exposing the sea to the polar summer's 24-hour daylight and thus triggering an enormous bloom of micro-organisms in the water from the surface down to the sea floor. While present in the Arctic from May to November, Gray whales store enough fat to sustain them virtually without feeding through the rest of the year, when they migrate to calve in warm waters while their summer feeding grounds are covered with ice. By the time they return to the feeding grounds, they may have lost up to one-third of their body weight.

The whales feed in shallow waters between 5–100m (15–330ft) deep; the diet comprises amphipods and isopods (both orders of crustaceans), polychaete worms, and mollusks that live on the ocean floor or a few centimeters into the bottom sediment. The gammarid amphipod *Ampelisca nacrocephala* is probably the species that is most commonly taken. To feed, Gray whales dive to the sea floor, turn on their side (usually the right), and plant the side of their head on the bottom. By suction they obtain a mouthful of invertebrate prey along with sand and mud sediments. They filter out the food by forcing the mixture through their baleen, trailing long plumes of sand and mud behind as they surface. The food items are swallowed; they take a few breaths, and dive again. As Gray whales feed, they leave pits, or bites, in the ocean floor. Some scientists have speculated that they may thus effectively plow the sea floor, possibly increasing its productivity in subsequent years.

Although Gray whales are primarily known as bottom-feeders, they may also prey on a variety of small planktonic organisms present in the water column, such as mysids and crab larvae, herring eggs, and even small fish. Most feeding occurs on the summer grounds, but if the opportunity arises, it may also occur during migrations, or even on the winter grounds.

Several species of sea bird associate with feeding Gray whales, including Horned puffins, Glaucous gulls, and Arctic terns. These birds apparently feed on crustaceans that escape through the baleen during the straining process while the whales are surfacing. The discovery of this association answered the perplexing question of how large numbers of bottom-dwelling invertebrates, from beyond the birds' diving depth, got into their digestive tracts.

# Rorquals

ITHIN THIS GROUP OF WHALES IS THE largest animal that has ever lived: the giant Blue whale, which weighs up to 150 tonnes, the weight of 25 six-tonne male African elephants. The rorquals also include one of the most tuneful and agile whales, the Humpback, which not only produces eerie and wide-ranging sounds but also performs remarkable acrobatics, leaping from the water, sometimes upside down.

The name "rorqual" comes from the Norwegian, and literally means "furrow whale" – a reference to the longitudinal folds of skin below and behind the mouth that are a distinctive feature of these species. Many rorquals travel great distances across the world's oceans on annual migrations to and from breeding grounds in the tropics and feeding grounds in the polar regions. The larger species have been hunted intensively over the past 100 years, and their numbers have consequently been severely reduced.

## Giants of the Deep
### FORM AND FUNCTION

Sleek and streamlined in form, rorquals have a series of grooves or folds of skin that, in all species except the Sei whale, extend from the chin backward under the belly to the navel. During feeding these grooves expand, allowing the mouth to increase considerably in volume. Photos of dead whales show the throats sagging, contributing in the past to a falsely clumsy picture of these creatures that was a grotesque distortion of their sleek underwater reality.

Animals in the southern hemisphere are a little bigger than those in the northern, and in all species the female grows to be slightly bigger than the male. The head occupies up to a quarter of the body length and, except in the Humpback whale, has a distinct central ridge running forward from the blowhole to the snout; the Bryde's whale also has additional ridges on either side of this one. In all species, the lower jaw is bowed and protrudes beyond the end of the snout.

 **Below** This Southern minke whale swimming in the waters around Australia's Great Barrier Reef belongs to the dwarf form of the species, which averages just 7m (23ft) in length. Its dimensions are modest in comparison with the gigantic size of the Blue whale; one female Blue taken in Antarctic waters early in the 20th century measured 33.58m (110ft).

**RORQUALS**

Order: Cetacea

Family: Balaenopteridae

8 species in 2 genera: *Balaenoptera* (7 species), including the **Blue whale** (*B. musculus*) and **Fin whale** (*B. physalus*); and *Megaptera* (1 species), the **Humpback whale** (*M. novaeangliae*).

**DISTRIBUTION**  All major oceans

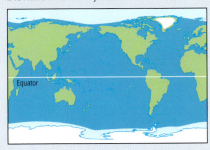

**HABITAT**  All species but *B. edeni* and *B. brydei* migrate between summer feeding grounds in the polar regions and winter breeding grounds in temperate waters.

**SIZE**  Head–tail length ranges from 9m (30ft) in the Northern minke whale to 27m (90ft) in the Blue whale, the world's largest animal. **Weight** ranges from 9 tonnes to 150 tonnes in the same 2 species. In all species, females grow slightly larger than males.

**FORM**  Streamlined appearance, with black or gray coloration above, often lighter on belly and lower surface of flippers. Filter-feeders, with 250–400 baleen plates growing down from either side of roof of mouth; a series of folds or grooves that expand during feeding extend from the chin back under the belly. Tail flukes are broad and conspicuously indented in the middle.

**DIET**  Krill, copepods, and fish, in varying proportions; Bryde's whale eats mainly fish, the Blue whale almost exclusively krill.

**BREEDING**  Single calf born 10–12 months after mating. In most species, there is a 2-year gap between pregnancies.

**LONGEVITY**  From 45 years in the minkes up to 100 or more in the bigger species.

See species table ▷

○ **Above** *Silhouetted against the setting sun in Alaskan waters, a Humpback whale dives in search of fish, the main component of northern Humpbacks' diets; those in southern oceans are predominantly krill-eaters. The tail flukes are so distinctive in shape and coloration that they can be used to identify individual whales.*

The flippers are lancetlike and narrow in all but the Humpback whale, where they are scalloped on at least the leading edge and form almost a third of the body length. The dorsal fin is set far back. The tail flukes are broad, with a conspicuous indentation in the middle, spreading especially widely in the Humpback whale. The blow as the whale exhales consists of a single spout from a double blowhole on the top of the head; the height and shape vary between species.

## Across the Seven Seas
### DISTRIBUTION PATTERNS

Blue, Fin, Sei, Minke, and Humpback whales are found in all the world's major oceans. They spend the summer months in polar feeding grounds and the winter in more temperate breeding grounds. Humpback whales swim close to coasts during their migrations, but the other rorquals tend to be more oceanic. Bryde's whale occurs only in temperate and warm waters, generally near shore in the Atlantic, Pacific, and Indian Oceans.

In the southern hemisphere, Blue whales start to migrate ahead of the Fin and Humpback whales, with Sei whales following some two months later. Within each species, age and sex determine the distribution of individuals. Older animals and pregnant females tend to migrate in advance of the other classes, with sexually immature whales at the rear of the stream. In all species, the bigger, older animals tend to travel closer to the poles than the younger whales.

In contrast to the other rorqual species, Blue and Minke whales occur right up to the ice-edge. Fin whales do not go quite that far, while Sei whales are much more sub-Antarctic in their distribution. This succession is not so clearly apparent in the northern hemisphere, where a more complex pattern of land masses and water currents has a distorting effect.

The various species of rorquals are thought to be divided across the world's oceans into different populations that do not generally interbreed. Yet genetic evidence, and the recovery of marked whales, indicate some interchange, at least between the northern and southern hemispheres. Most populations tend to be spread widely across the oceans, though the Humpback, which breeds in coastal waters, tends also to be more concentrated around feeding grounds.

## A Life of Great Migrations
### SOCIAL BEHAVIOR

The life cycles of the Blue, Fin, Sei, Minke, and Humpback whales are very closely related to the pattern of seasonal migrations. In both hemispheres the whales mate in low-latitude warm waters during the winter months, and then migrate to their respective polar feeding grounds, where they spend 3–4 months feeding on the rich plankton that constitutes their diet. After this period of intensive feeding, they migrate back to the temperate zone once again, where females give birth to a single calf 10–12 months after mating. Conceptions and births may occur at almost any time of the year, but the greatest reproductive activity is confined to relatively short peak periods of 3–4 months.

The newborn calf is about a third of the mother's length and 4–5 percent of her weight. It accompanies its mother on the spring migration,

swimming 3,200km (2,000mi) or more towards the polar seas. During this time it lives on its mother's rich milk, which has a fat content of up to 46 percent, as compared to the 3–5 percent in human and cows' milk. The mother squirts the milk into the mouth of the calf with the aid of the muscles surrounding her mammary glands as the baby holds on to one of her two nipples. The young grow quickly on this high-energy diet, gaining as much as 90kg (200lb) a day, so that in six to seven months a Blue whale calf will add about

17 tonnes to its 2.5–tonne birth weight. Calves are weaned at 7–8 months, when they are about 10m (33ft) long.

The age at which rorquals start to reproduce has changed over recent years due to a fascinating interaction between whale biology and human predation. Fin whales born before 1930 became sexually mature at around 10 years, but the mean age has subsequently declined to about 6 years. Sei whales caught before 1935 did not reproduce until around 11 years, but they are now ready at just 7 in some areas. As for the southern Minke whales, their age of maturity has dropped by a massive 8 years, from 14 to 6.

The most likely explanation for these changes is that individual whales now have access to increased amounts of food because of the massive reductions in whale stocks, permitting the survivors to grow more quickly. Because the start of reproduction is closely related to body size, faster growth means that the whales reach the critical size at a younger age.

◁ **Left** Seen from behind, a Blue whale exhibits the twin "nostrils" that jointly form the blowhole in this as in the other rorqual species. When the whale exhales, a single jet of spray emerges from both orifices. The size and shape of the spout varies between species; experienced whale-watchers use this clue to distinguish different types of rorqual from a distance.

▷ **Right** Five different rorqual species, drawn to scale, illustrate the wide range of size in the family: **1** Fin whale (Balaenoptera physalus); **2** Bryde's whale (B. edeni); **3** Blue whale (B. musculus); **4** Northern minke whale (B. acutorostrata); and **5** Humpback whale (Megaptera novaeangliae), shown surfacing belly uppermost.

## Fin whale   En
*Balaenoptera physalus*

Polar to tropical seas. 2 subspecies: *B. p. physalus*, N Atlantic and N Pacific, HTL 24m (80ft); WT 70 tonnes; and *B. p. quoyi*, S Hemisphere, HTL 27m (90ft), WT 80 tonnes.
FORM: skin gray above, white below, asymmetrical on jaw; flipper and flukes white below; baleen plates: 260–470, blue-gray with whitish fringes, but left front white; throat grooves: 56–100.

## Sei whale   En
*Balaenoptera borealis*

Polar to tropical seas. 2 subspecies: *B. b. borealis*, N Atlantic and N Pacific oceans, HTL 19m (60ft), WT 30 tonnes; and *B. b. schlegellii*, S.Hemisphere, HTL 21m (70ft), WT 35 tonnes.
FORM: skin dark steely-gray, white grooves on belly; baleen plates: 320–400, gray-black with pale fringes; throat grooves: 32–62.

## Bryde's whale
*Balaenoptera edeni*

Coastal waters of E Indian Ocean and W Pacific.
HTL 11m (36ft); WT 20 tonnes.
FORM: skin dark gray; baleen plates: 250–370, gray with dark fringes; throat grooves: 47–70.

## *Balaenoptera brydei*

Offshore tropical and warm temperate waters worldwide.
HTL 15m (50ft); WT 26 tonnes.
FORM: as for *B. edeni*, of which *B. brydei* was formerly regarded as a subspecies.

## Blue whale   En
*Balaenoptera musculus*

Polar to tropical seas. 3 subspecies: Northern blue whale (*B. m. musculus*), N Atlantic and N Pacific, HTL 24–27m (80–90ft), WT 130–150 tonnes; Southern blue whale (*B. m. indica*), S hemisphere, HTL 27m (90ft), WT 150 tonnes; and the Pygmy blue whale (*B. m. brevicauda*), S hemisphere, particularly in the southern Indian Ocean and South Pacific, HTL 24m (80ft), WT 70 tonnes. FORM: skin mottled bluish-gray (silvery-gray in *B. m. brevicauda*), flippers pale beneath; baleen plates: 270–395, blue-black; throat grooves: 55–88 (76–94 in *B. m. brevicauda*).

## Northern minke whale   LR
*Balaenoptera acutorostrata*

Polar to tropical seas. 2 subspecies: *B. a. acutorostrata*, N Atlantic, and *B. a. scammoni*, N Pacific.
HTL 9m (30ft); WT 9 tonnes.
FORM: skin dark gray above, belly and flippers white below; white or pale band on flippers; pale streaks behind head. Baleen plates: 230–350, yellowish-white, some black. Throat grooves: 50–70.
CONSERVATION STATUS: LR Near Threatened.

## Southern minke whale   LR
*Balaenoptera bonaerensis*

Polar to tropical seas of the S hemisphere.
HTL 11m (36ft); WT 10 tonnes.
FORM: as for *B. acutorostrata*, though often without pale band on flippers. There also appears to be a "Dwarf" minke whale in the lower latitudes of the S hemisphere, resembling the N Pacific population.
CONSERVATION STATUS: LR Conservation Dependent.

## Humpback whale   Vu
*Megaptera novaeangliae*

Polar to tropical seas.
HTL 16m (50ft); WT 65 tonnes.
FORM: skin black above, grooves white, flukes with variable white pattern below; baleen plates: 270–400, dark gray; throat grooves: 14–24.

Abbreviations   HTL = head–tail length   WT = weight   En   Endangered   Vu   Vulnerable   LR   Lower Risk

a   b

◁ **Left** Sei whales (*Balaenoptera borealis*), not shown below, are similar in appearance to Bryde's whales. The two are most easily distinguished by the ridges on the head; there are three in Bryde's whale **a**, only one in the Sei **b**.

4

5

3

## Behemoths at Risk
### CONSERVATION AND ENVIRONMENT

The future of the rorquals now depends largely on the success of the measures taken in recent years to protect them from overhunting. There is evidence of increasing numbers in some species, but because of their very low birthrates it will be decades before there is full recovery. Left to themselves, whale populations may double in size in 10–20 years, depending on reproduction rates; but the Antarctic Blue whale still probably numbers only 5–10 percent of its original abundance, and it does not reproduce very quickly.

There is also increasing concern about alterations in, and degradation of, the marine environment due to climate change and pollution. While it is unlikely that increases in water temperature would have a direct effect on whales, which are insulated from their immediate environment by their blubber, the food organisms on which they depend, such as krill and fish, may well move in response to these environmental alterations and to changes in the ocean currents. Similarly, it is possible that depletion of the ozone layer over the polar regions will allow more ultraviolet radiation to enter the surface waters, changing the productivity of the areas of the oceans that have long been frequented as feeding grounds by the whales. Direct pollution in the form of harmful chemicals, as well as of nondegradable objects such as plastic bags, bottles, and other waste that can be swallowed and block the whales' food tracts, is a cause for growing concern, as is sound pollution, which impinges on their sensing and communication capacity. To these hazards must be added the risks of entrapment in fishing gear and collisions with vessels in increasingly busy shipping lanes.                                    RG

○ **Right** *Showing one of its two flippers – the longest of any cetacean species – a Humpback whale breaches majestically before returning to the water with a resounding splash. As with other species, breaching seems to serve two main functions: stunning or panicking fish shoals and communicating information to other herd members.*

### BIG APPETITES, SMALL PREY

· The biggest animals in the world keep themselves alive by eating some of the smallest. Rorquals are filter-feeders. They have huge, sievelike baleen plates growing from the roofs of their mouths, which gather the tiny plants and animals in the marine water column. The whale opens its mouth widely, engulfing the plankton in a large volume of water **a**. The water is then sieved through the spaces between the baleen plates as the mouth closes; the previously expanded throat region tightens up and the tongue is raised. The food material is held back on the bristles lining the inner edges of the baleen plates before being swallowed **b**.

Sei whales can also feed by skimming through patches of plankton-rich water with their mouths half open. The head is normally raised a little above the surface, so that water and food are sieved continuously through the baleen plates. When enough has been collected, the whale closes its mouth and swallows the food.

The bristles fringing the baleen plates vary in texture between the species, as do the shapes and sizes of the plates, thus determining which food organisms each different species can capture. The Blue whale has rather coarse baleen bristles, and feeds almost exclusively on shrimplike food, especially krill. This organism is the basic sustenance for all the baleen whales in the Antarctic, but a wider range of nutriment appears in other areas, especially in the northern hemisphere.

Fin whales, with their medium-texture baleen bristles, eat mainly krill and copepods, with fish third in importance, but there is considerable variation by area and season. Sei whales, which have much finer baleen fringes, are primarily copepod feeders, but krill and other crustaceans are also consumed. Minke and Humpback whales feed mainly on fish in the northern hemisphere and krill in the south, while Bryde's whales are more exclusively fish eaters, with only a few crustacea in their diet.

The fish taken by these whales are generally schooling species, and include herring, cod, mackerel, capelin, and sardines. The Humpback and Minke whales have a characteristic lunging action which may serve to scare and concentrate the prey fish as the whale circles them before shooting up vertically with its mouth open to engulf the food. Humpback whales may also "herd" their prey by releasing a circle of bubbles that whirl to the surface around them.

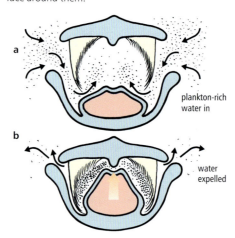

a — plankton-rich water in

b — water expelled

It is estimated that a large Blue whale weighing 100 tonnes has to eat 4 tonnes of krill every day during the summer feeding season. The first chamber of the three-part stomach can hold about one tonne at a time, so the whale has to fill this about four times a day. The stored energy represented by the oil and fat laid down in blubber under the skin and around the internal organs fuels the animal during the rest of the year when very little food is consumed. Over the course of the whole year the whale eats roughly 1.5–2 percent of its own body weight daily.

# NEW LIGHT ON THE SINGING WHALE

## What fresh research techniques have shown about the Humpback

THE 1990S WITNESSED GREAT ADVANCES IN scientific research on cetaceans in general, and on the Humpback whale in particular. The new techniques that have been applied to studying the fascinating behavior of this leviathan fall into three main categories: genetic analysis of its DNA; electronic tagging for satellite tracking; and acoustic monitoring by deep-sea hydrophone arrays.

Increasingly sophisticated techniques of genetic analysis have had a profound influence on several different fields of research. In broad-based studies of populations, they can be used both to determine their structure and to assess the long-term consequences of particular behavioral patterns across different populations over evolutionary time. More narrowly, DNA analysis can confirm the sex of whales and throw new light on paternity and matrilineal relationships. During the early 1990s, biologists photoidentified and biopsied several thousand Humpbacks in the North Atlantic, a significant percentage of the entire population. From these samples, an accurate picture is emerging of which calves are likely to have been sired by which males. Formerly, whale paternity was shrouded in mystery and conjecture, as no scientist had ever managed to observe Humpback copulation at first hand!

One particular line of genetic research has confirmed and deepened our awareness of Humpbacks' migratory patterns. This has been achieved by taking samples of mitochondrial DNA. Mitochondria are tiny energy-processing structures that occur inside cells of the body. They are present in eggs but not in sperm, so they are inherited only from mother to offspring, never coming down the male line. Mitochondria contain DNA, and the mitochondrial DNA of whales from different feeding grounds is distinct enough to suggest that there is low gene flow across these subpopulations. Nuclear DNA, which is inherited from the father as well as the mother, does not show the same specificity to feeding ground. Therefore, the genetic analyses corroborate evidence from sightings, which indicates matrilineal fidelity to feeding areas; but while sighting data are limited to time scales of a decade or two, the genetic data show that the pattern has prevailed for thousands of years. This result is especially striking, since Humpback whales from the same tropical breeding grounds only migrate once with their mother; even so, the genetic data suggest that they then continue to travel thousands of kilometers to the same feeding ground annually for the rest of their life.

Modern methods of satellite tracking have proved invaluable in plotting the movement of Humpbacks over thousands of kilometers of ocean.

Fitting whales with electronic tags not only allows scientists to follow their migratory routes over vast distances and protracted periods, but also to gather information on such features as dive profiles. Tagging has also yielded a mass of data on local movements within feeding and breeding grounds.

The seismic shift in superpower relations in the 1990s brought an added bonus to researchers tracking Humpback whales. During the Cold War, the US Navy secretly installed an extensive array of hydrophones on many ocean basins to follow the movement of Soviet submarines. Data collected by these listening devices were telemetered back to central sites, enabling sound sources to be monitored over enormous ranges. This system, which was called SOSUS (SOund SUrveillance System), was declassified and made available to biologists in the 1990s. With its aid, the sounds of Humpbacks and other whales can be picked up at a distance of hundreds of kilometers.

What these diverse research methods have all served to emphasize is the far-reaching effects of the annual migratory cycle on baleen whales. It influences every aspect of Humpback life and behavior, beginning most fundamentally with their biology; the annual cycle actually selects for large size in the whales. In the summer Humpbacks feed intensely, and then must live off their energy stores for the rest of the year as they migrate thousands of kilometers to breed and calve. Not only can large whales store more energy; they can also swim long distances more efficiently, and they have lower metabolic costs of thermoregulation. The extra energetic demands of pregnancy and lactation in females mean that they must store even more energy, and this has selected for adult females to grow larger than adult males.

The ability to lactate after months of fasting is very unusual among mammals, and is a critical feature of the baleen whale reproductive cycle. A pregnant female must bring her calf to term while fasting during migration. After she gives birth in the tropics, she must suckle the calf on her energy reserves for up to half a year before she returns to the feeding area the next summer. The calf grows rapidly during this period in order to wean at a length of 8–9m (26–30ft) within a year.

Two further key areas of research interest – also intimately linked with the migratory cycle – are feeding and mating. In the North Atlantic, Humpback whales return to discrete feeding areas such as Iceland or Norway, though within each of these the whales may shift their distribution to match the changing distribution of prey. Over the years, resighting data of naturally marked whales has suggested that Humpbacks from many feeding

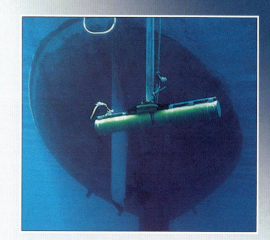

⬥ **Above** *Most Humpback recordings are made from small inshore boats, but the songs can also be tracked by deep-sea SOSUS arrays. Research shows that the whales sing over large expanses of ocean and that their songs can be heard at great ranges.*

grounds mix and interbreed on the tropical breeding grounds, but then reliably migrate back to their mother's feeding area.

During the winter, Humpback whales migrate to tropical waters where they mate and give birth. Female humpbacks seek out calm, protected waters in the lee of an island or in a shallow bank. Males congregate near these areas to mate with the females. One mating strategy is to compete directly with other males for access to a female; this involves one male humpback escorting a female, trying to prevent rivals from approaching her, while the other males swim close by, mounting challenges. Such intense competition usually only lasts for a few hours at most, during which time challengers may change roles with principal escorts several times. The winner does not seem to stay with the female for long, for females have been seen with other males on the very next day;

◑ **Above** *A Humpback mother and calf. Modern genetic analysis has proved that offspring return to the mother's feeding ground for their entire lives.*

as on the feeding grounds, associations between individuals other than mother and calf are brief. Genetic analyses of successive calves of the same female have proved that females mate with different males in different breeding seasons.

The other male mating strategy is to sing. During the breeding season, lone males repeat long, complex songs, each lasting for about 10 minutes, in an unbroken series. They can sing incessantly for over 24 hours. Analysis of the songs reveals that the sound sequences of which they are composed are generated by a hierarchical model. Each song consists of a series of themes repeated in a specific order; the themes in turn are made up of phrases repeated a variable number of times.

Most males within a single population perform very similar songs. However, the song changes gradually but continuously over time, so that songs from different years are quite distinct from

one another, and there are no common sounds in songs recorded a decade apart. Usually the songs from different populations of Humpbacks are independent, though biologists noted a fascinating exception to this rule off the east coast of Australia, the site of long-running song research. One year, several whales were recorded singing a song totally different from that of the rest – yet very like songs heard off Australia's west coast. It appeared that one or two west-coast Humpbacks had migrated east, a rare but not unknown phenomenon. The west-coast song gradually gained ascendancy and eclipsed the original east-coast song within two years. Both the gradual evolution of songs and this sudden adoption of a new one show that Humpback males learn the detailed acoustic structure of their songs, and that whales from different populations do not sing different songs because of different genotypes, but rather because they

imitate what they hear. In other words, Humpback song is a form of culture.

Once singing Humpbacks join with others, their song ends. When a singer joins a female, behaviors associated with mating (e.g. rolling and flippering) have been seen. Yet when another male is met, aggressive interactions often ensue, after which the original singer or the joiner will resume singing once the whales have split up again. These sightings suggest that males sing to attract females, and that other males compete with singers. Humpback males do not appear to compete over territory, for daily photo-ID of whales in the same area shows a very low incidence of resightings; rather, the whales move on, borne on ocean currents. Unlike terrestrial animals, many of which defend a specific geographic location, Humpbacks seem to maintain more coordination with respect to one another than to any particular place.    PLT

# Right Whales

t HE RIGHT WHALE OWES ITS NAME TO WHALERS. *It was so called because it was the "right" whale to hunt – it swam slowly, floated when killed, and had a high yield of baleen and oil. No other whale was hunted to such precariously low levels as this species. Even today, after decades of protection from industrial whaling, the North Atlantic and North Pacific populations both number less than a few hundred animals.*

Right whales worldwide are at risk from humans. They share with us a preference for coastal waters, where they give birth to their young. This leads the most vulnerable members of their populations into the most crowded habitats in the world's oceans. In the North Atlantic, these habitats are filled with ships and fishing gear, which kill Right whales at a rate that threatens their survival. Due to human-induced mortality and declining birth rates, this population appears to be in a state of decline, and recent population models predict extinction within two centuries. In the North Pacific, insufficient information is available to make any assessment of either population size or growth rate. Southern hemisphere Right whales, however, appear to be doing relatively well, numbering perhaps 6,000 animals and growing at a rate of 6–7 percent per year.

## Big Heads and Curved Jaws
### FORM AND FUNCTION

Right whales, Bowhead whales, and Pygmy right whales share certain characteristics that distinguish them from the rorquals. These include an arched rostrum (upper jaw), giving a deeply curved jawline in profile in contrast to the nearly straight line of the rorqual mouth; this trait is most pronounced in the Bowhead whale, in which the head may make up as much as 40 percent of total body length. Other distinctive features include long, slender baleen plates instead of relatively short ones, and a complete absence of throat grooves in the large species (the Pygmy has two), compared to many in all the rorquals. There are also a number of marked differences in cranial features: in particular, the upper jawbone is narrow in Right whales and broad in rorquals. In all three Right whale species, the head is large in proportion to the rest of the body. While the two large species are exceptionally bulky in comparison to the rorquals, the Pygmy right whale is relatively small and slim; unlike the other two species, it has a small, triangular dorsal fin.

Right whales are uniquely identifiable from Bowheads as well as other cetacean species through the patches of thickened skin, called "callosities," that form along the rostrum, above the eyes, and along the lower jaw. The largest patch, found on the snout, was called the "bonnet" by old-time whalers. Colonies of whale lice (species of the genus *Cyamus*) live within these outgrowths. Callosities are slightly larger in males than females, and may be employed in competition for females. They are also useful to scientific observers, for they form unique patterns that can be used to identify individual whales without the need to capture or contact them. Thanks to them, identification catalogues have been drawn up for every Right whale population currently being studied; from these it is possible to tell such facts as how long each animals lives, when it reproduces, and how it migrates.

Right whales make low-frequency sounds, and studies have shown that they have at least two types of call – contact calls between widely separated individuals, and calls used by females to attract mates – though in practice their repertoire is probably much broader. Unlike humpbacks,

○ **Below** *Male Northern right whales gather round a female in estrus during the breeding season. While there have been reports of inter-male aggression at this time, there are also reliable accounts of reproductive cooperation, with one male supporting a female while another male mates with her.*

## RIGHT WHALES

Order: Cetacea

Families: Balaenidae and Neobalaenidae

4 species in 3 genera, *Eubalaena*, *Balaena*, and *Caperea*; some authorities, though, include the **Right whales** and the **Bowhead** within a single genus, *Balaena*. The **Pygmy right whale** (genus *Caperea*) is sometimes treated as a subfamily, but here we consider it as the sole representative of its own family, the Neobalaenidae.

**DISTRIBUTION** Arctic and temperate waters

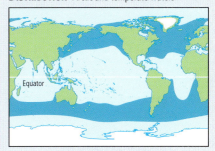

Equator

**NORTHERN RIGHT WHALE** *Eubalaena glacialis*
Temperate waters of N hemisphere; in the Atlantic, recorded as far S as Florida. HTL Up to 18m (59ft), average adult about 15m (49ft); WT 50–56 tonnes; N Pacific animals larger than other species by 5–10 percent. Form: body black, with white patches on the chin and belly, sometimes extensive; head and jaws characteristically bear individually distinctive patterns of rough, thickened skin patches called callosities that are heavily infested with crustacean parasites known as cyamids; baleen is black, and up to 2.5m (8ft) in length. Breeding: gestation 12–13 months. Longevity: one known female lived at least 65 years. Conservation status: Endangered.

**SOUTHERN RIGHT WHALE** *Eubalaena australis*
Temperate waters of S hemisphere; in the Atlantic, recorded as far N as S Brazil. Length, Form, Breeding, and Longevity: as for Northern right whale. Conservation status: Lower Risk – Conservation Dependent.

**BOWHEAD WHALE** *Balaena mysticetus*
Arctic Basin, with winter migration into Bering and Labrador Seas. HTL 3.5–20m (11–66ft), average adult about 17m (56ft); WT probably 60–80 tonnes. Form: body black, except for white or ocherous chin patch; no callosities; baleen narrow, dark gray to blackish, up to 4m (13ft) in length. Breeding: gestation 10–11 months. Longevity: evidence (e.g. old harpoon heads) points to extreme age. Conservation status: Lower Risk – Conservation Dependent, though the Svalbard–Barents Sea stock is Critically Endangered, while the Okhotsk Sea and Baffin Bay subpopulations are Endangered.

**PYGMY RIGHT WHALE** *Caperea marginata*
Circumpolar in S temperate and sub-Antarctic waters; not a true Antarctic species. HTL 2–6.5m (7–21ft), average adult about 5m (16ft); WT about 3–3.5 tonnes. Form: body gray, darker above and lighter below, with some variable pale streaks on the back and shoulders, and dark streaks from eye to flipper; baleen plates relatively long for its size, whitish with dark outer borders. Breeding: gestation probably 10–11 months.

Abbreviations HTL = head–tail length  WT = weight

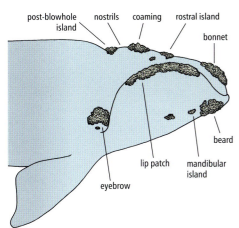

post-blowhole island  nostrils  coaming  rostral island
bonnet
beard
lip patch  mandibular island
eyebrow

⬤ **Above** *Surfacing off Argentina's Valdez Peninsula, a Southern right whale mother and calf display the "bonnets" that are among the species' most distinctive features. Consisting of layers of hardened skin protruding from the upper jaw, the bonnets are usually infested with barnacles and other parasites.*

⬤ **Left** *The bonnet is in fact only one of several groups of callosities displayed by most Right whales. They are present from birth, but their exact function is still unknown. Observers have noted that males have more of them than females, leading some people to suggest that they might serve as weapons used to graze other males' skin during breeding contests.*

which produce repeated "song" sequences, Right whales make many single and grouped sounds in the 50–500Hz range. Feeding whales also make a variable 2–4kHz low-amplitude noise that has been traced to water rattling across their partially-exposed baleen plates. Nothing is known of vocalizations in the Pygmy right whale, whereas those of the Bowhead are simple and change over time.

## A Long-Distance Annual Round

DISTRIBUTION PATTERNS

The migratory habits of the Right whale are not fully known. In the North Atlantic, the coastal waters of Florida and Georgia are the primary winter calving ground, but the distribution of non-calving animals at this time is unknown. About two-thirds of the North Atlantic population is regularly seen in the spring, summer, and fall in the Gulf of Maine, but genetic and sightings data suggest the existence of a second, as-yet unidentified summering habitat for this subspecies.

In the southern hemisphere, Right whales are known to congregate in winter for calving in the coastal waters of South Africa, Argentina, Australia,

and New Zealand's sub-Antarctic islands. Exactly where they feed or spend the summer is only partly known, although Right whales have been spotted occasionally around the Antarctic.

In the north Pacific, scattered sightings suggest that remnant populations of Right whales occur seasonally in the Gulf of Alaska and the Sea of Okhotsk. Although rare winter sightings of Right whales along the west coast of the USA and in Hawaii have been reported, no information on wintering habitats, calving grounds, or migratory routes is available. Combined data suggest that calves are born in the winter and that mating, leading to conception, occurs during late fall to early winter in the respective hemispheres. Therefore, the "mating activity" observed in all areas during the rest of the year may be more related to social behavior than actual reproduction.

The annual migratory cycle of the Bowhead is best seen in the Bering Sea–Beaufort Sea population, which is by far the largest surviving stock of this species, and the best-known in the Arctic. Distributions are closely connected with seasonal changes in the position and extent of ice-free

areas. The route and timing of migration each year are dictated by the development of open channels (leads) between the ice floes from the northern Bering Sea eastward to the Amundsen Gulf in spring and summer.

Bowheads winter in the Bering Sea, particularly around St. Lawrence and St. Matthew Islands, and it is here that the calves are born. Mating occurs in the spring during the first stage of the migration. Aerial and satellite photographs reveal that the ice in the northern Bering and southern Chukchi Seas develops fractures in April, which first open to Cape Lisburne and then Point Barrow. The leads are relatively close to shore, so that most of the population passes Barrow on their way into the Beaufort Sea. Beyond Barrow, however, the winds and current circulation open large offshore leads, and the eastward migration shifts further from land. Whales reach Cape Bathurst and the Amundsen Gulf as early as May. The slow breakup of coastal ice east of Alaska normally prevents Bowheads utilizing the Mackenzie Delta and Yukon shore in any numbers until the second half of July.

Eskimo hunters state that there is segregation by age and sex during this migration (as in Australian Humpback whales). The migration certainly takes place in "pulses," with animals during May and June straggling in a column along the whole length of the route from Barrow to southwestern Banks Island. The return migration to the Bering Sea in late summer–early fall tends not only to be rather rapid (according to old whaling records) but also further offshore, and hence less easy to observe.

### Skimming the Plankton Swarms
DIET

Right whales, Bowheads, and Pygmy right whales all feed primarily on copepods, but the North Atlantic Right whale also takes juvenile krill, and occasionally other swarming planktonic larvae. The Southern Ocean population appears to eat adult krill regularly as well.

Bowhead feeding is usually associated with restricted belts of high productivity in arctic areas, such as the edge of the plume from the Mackenzie River, where nutrient enrichment and water clarity

are both optimal for active photosynthesis by phytoplankton, resulting in turn in relatively high zooplankton production. Both Bowhead and Right whales generally feed by skimming with their mouths open through concentrations of zooplankton; this is in contrast to the feeding methods of most rorquals (other than Sei whales), which tend to gulp patches of highly concentrated fish or krill and filter the food through their baleen plates. In most northern hemisphere feeding grounds, Right whales usually feed at depth, diving for 8–12 minutes at a time, though they will occasionally feed at the surface when prey concentrations are dense. Right whales have occasionally been observed to feed side by side.

Right whales and Bowheads probably need 1,000–2,500kg (2,200–5,500lb) of food per day, and the Pygmy right whale perhaps 50–100kg (110–220lb); little is known of its feeding habits, except that two animals taken by the Russians had stomachs full of copepods.

### Seeking Company in the Ocean Wastes
SOCIAL BEHAVIOR

Right whale social structure is poorly understood. Recognizable individuals may be seen alone at some times of day, and with one or more groups later that day or on other days. When large groups of whales are seen within a few kilometers of each other, however, it is most likely merely in response to concentrations of food. These groups are probably not behaviorally comparable to pods of dolphins or toothed whales.

The most tightly-linked social pairing is that between mother and calf. These two can remain within one bodylength for the first 6 months of the calf's life. Weaning occurs at 10–12 months, and mothers and their offspring are rarely seen together again. Breaching behavior (leaping from the surface) and lobtailing (slapping the water with the flukes) occur frequently in this species; these behaviors may allow the whales to indicate their location, especially when surface noise

1

**Above** *Different Right whale species have quite distinct body forms. The Northern right (Eubalaena glacialis) **1** is distinguished by its huge baleen and tongue, its deeply arched lower jaw, and its callosities. Bowheads (Balaena mysticetus) **2** have an even more pronounced curve to the lower jaw, but no callosities. The Pygmy right whale (Caperea marginata) **3** has a dorsal fin and only moderate bowing of the lower jaw.*

**Below** *A Southern right whale calf (Eubalaena australis) accompanies its mother in surface waters off Patagonia. The mother–calf pair are inseparable for the first six months after birth, but rarely link up again once the infant has been weaned, at about 1 year.*

means that vocalizations cannot be heard.

The long reproductive cycle (3 years or more between births) means that less than one-third of the adult females in a given area may be receptive to males each year. Females appear to solicit males acoustically, and then make mating difficult, either by swimming away or by lying on their back with both flippers in the air so that the genital region is inaccessible. Males compete for access to the female through active pushing and by displacing one another, and it appears that females mate with many males. Males also probably employ sperm competition – male testes are both the

largest in the world (over 800kg) and the largest relative to body size in the baleen whales.

A single 4–5m (13–16ft) calf is born to a Right whale mother in the winter months. Cows give birth every 3–5 years after a 12–13 month gestation, and suckle the young for 10–12 (or sometimes as long as 17) months. By the time it is 1 year old, the rapidly-growing calf is already 8–9m (26–30ft) long. Young females reach sexual maturity around 9 years of age, although unusually precocious whales have been observed with their first calf as early as age 6.

The number of calves born to each mature North Atlantic Right whale female has declined significantly from 1980–99. Since the mid-1990s, the interval between calves for an individual female has increased from 3.67 years (1980–92) to over 5 years. The population growth rate appears to be substantially lower than among southern Right whale populations off Argentina and South Africa. Many factors may be reducing success rates, including inbreeding depression, competition for food from other species, climatic changes resulting in reduced food availability, disease, biotoxins, and the harmful (but not lethal) effects of toxic contaminants.

Natural mortality rates in the North Atlantic animals have been estimated at 17 percent for the first year of life, and about 3 percent for the next 3 years. Adult mortality rates are apparently very low – only three adults are known to have died of natural causes in this population since 1970. Longevity remains unknown, although at least one North Atlantic female has been sighted since 1935 (making her over 60 years old). About 7 percent of the North Atlantic population have scars from Killer whale attacks, but while this may cause some deaths, anecdotal reports of orca/Right whale encounters suggest that Right whales are more than adequately capable of defending themselves. No fatal diseases or epizootics have been reported for this species, although lesions thought to be related to illness have been reported. Three species of cyamid lice have been found on northern Right whales, *Cyamus ovalis*, *C. gracilis*, and *C. erraticus*. None of these appear to have a long-term effect upon the whales, even though they apparently live on the animals' sloughing skin.

Approximately 38 percent of all mortality in this species is due to collisions with large ships, with an additional 8 percent due to entanglements in fishing gear. Almost 60 percent of all Right whales in the North Atlantic display scars from entanglement in fishing gear at some time in their lives. Vertical lines from lobster and crab pots and groundfish gill-nets appear to be primarily responsible. Extensive efforts are underway in the US to develop alternative fishing methods to reduce kills of Right whales.

The Pygmy right whale resembles the Right whale in its preference for relatively shallow water at some times of year, and there is speculation that mating occurs during this inshore phase. Nevertheless, Pygmy right whales have been seen during most months of the year in all the regions from which the species has been reported, so it may be that there are localized populations and limited migrations. There, however, the resemblance to their larger distant cousins ends; no deep diving for long periods has been noted, despite an earlier suggestion that the peculiar flattening of the underside of the ribcage might indicate that Pygmy right whales spent long periods on the bottom. In addition, there is none of the exuberant tail-fluking or lobtailing and breaching characteristic of the larger species.

The Pygmy right swims relatively slowly, often without its dorsal fin breaking the surface, and the whole snout usually breaks clear of the water at surfacing – behavior similar to that of the Minke whale, with which it is easily confused. The respiratory rhythm of undisturbed animals is regular,

with rather less than one blow per minute in a sequence of about five ventilations with dives of 3–4 minutes between them. The Pygmy right's general behavior has been characterized as "unspectacular" – another feature, coupled with its small size, that has contributed to the lack of recorded observations of the species. It appears to be present in sub-Antarctic and southern temperate zones right around the globe – areas of low population density and relatively little land mass where there are few researchers on hand to note the whales' behavior or attributes.

◗ **Above** Shedding rivulets of water, a Southern right whale leaps from the South Atlantic within sight of the Argentinian coast. The whales breach more often in inshore waters than in the open ocean, perhaps as a way of communicating in areas where human-induced disturbance makes acoustic signaling difficult.

◗ **Below** A Bowhead from America's eastern population basks on the surface off Baffin Island during the annual southward migration. Each spring the whales travel north from waters off the Gulf of St. Lawrence to feeding grounds in the high Arctic, returning in the fall to spend winter in slightly more temperate climes.

## Saving the Survivors
### CONSERVATION AND ENVIRONMENT

All remaining Bowhead and Right whales stocks are remnants of much larger populations. The earliest Right whale hunting, by the Basques, began over a thousand years ago, and the methods developed then provided the basis for much of the worldwide whaling industry up until the factory-ship technology of the 20th century. The last Right whaling by Europeans and Americans took place in the early 1900s in the Atlantic. Right whales were finally given international protection in 1935, although illegal Soviet whaling in the 1960s is now known to have resulted in the deaths of a few thousand Right whales in the South Atlantic, Indian, and Pacific Oceans.

Historically, much of the hunting was carried out in southern-hemisphere calving grounds and bays. Traditionally, whalers would attempt to take a calf first, to draw the mother in for an easy kill. The carcasses were hauled ashore, or into the shallows, and the baleen cut out. If the oil was taken, the blubber was stripped and cut into pieces to be "rendered down" in large cast iron "try pots."

The future outlook for Right whales is mixed. Southern-hemisphere populations appear to be increasing, and marine parks and regulations are in place to protect the animals around South Africa, Argentina, New Zealand, and Australia. The North Pacific population is currently unknown, but new studies should provide more information soon. Since this population does not appear to have a particular coastal calving ground, and the known summer areas are mostly offshore, these whales may be less vulnerable than other populations to conflicts with human activities. In the North Atlantic, increasing human-induced deaths and decreasing calving rates are driving the population to extinction. Even so, most researchers and conservationists believe that, if deaths from shipping and fishing gear can be stopped, the North Atlantic Right whales could over time make a comeback.                SDK/DEG

### THE ALASKA BOWHEAD HUNT

For thousands of years the Eskimo peoples of Alaska have hunted the Bowhead whales that follow the inshore lead in the pack ice eastward each spring, traditionally using ivory or stone-tipped harpoons and sealskin floats as their weapons. For much of that time the whale population in the region numbered 10,000–20,000 or more, and the effect of the hunt was negligible. In the 19th century, however, American and European commercial whalers reduced eastern Bowhead populations to a few hundreds, and the Bering Sea population as a whole to perhaps a few thousands, in a matter of decades.

Commercial whaling ceased in 1915, although a low-level Eskimo hunt persisted. Yet the eastern population did not regain its former levels. Factors such as predation by Killer whales, inbreeding depression, and (rarely) suffocation under ice may all have been implicated in the failure. But it was also suggested that changes in Eskimo hunting methods – since the 1880s, grenade-tipped darting guns have been in use – may have played their part.

In 1977, the Scientific Committee of the International Whaling Commission (IWC) recommended that the hunt cease. The Eskimos vehemently insisted that it was materially and culturally necessary for their own welfare, and a small quota was allowed by the IWC, to be administered by the Alaska Eskimo Whaling Commission. Improvements in hunting methods – for example the replacement of black-powder grenades by a modern explosive, penthrite – have also greatly increased the efficiency (and hence humaneness) of whale killing.

Studies have subsequently shown that the western (Bering/Chukchi/Beaufort Sea) population of Bowheads is increasing at an annual rate of 3 percent even with the Eskimo harvest, leading biologists to conclude recently that the present population (8,200 in 1993) can permit the nutritional needs of the Eskimo people for approximately 56 whales annually to be met comfortably. So, the situation looks bright both for the Eskimo hunters and for the Bowheads.                CG

# WHALEHUNTING TO WHALEWATCHING
### The role of ecotourism in sustainable whale management

THE INTERNATIONAL WHALING COMMISSION (IWC) decided in 1982 that all commercial whaling should be suspended from 1986. In 1983 the Convention on International Trade in Endangered Species (CITES) listed the great whales on Appendix 1, thus prohibiting international trade and bringing CITES into line with the IWC. Despite these decisions, however, both Norway and Japan continue whaling for primarily commercial purposes. Norway filed a formal objection to the IWC moratorium decision, and is therefore not bound by it; Japan uses the loophole of scientific research to kill whales in the Southern Ocean and North Pacific. The moratorium was adopted in part because it was recognized that the existing regulatory mechanisms were inadequate. The IWC needed breathing space to design a better system for managing any future whaling, should the moratorium be lifted.

The whaling issue is unique in that whales have a special status in international law, both as highly migratory species and specifically as whales. All nations can contribute to decisions regarding their future by joining the IWC, which is a global intergovernmental convention. The IWC was set up to ensure that any use of whales should be sustainable, both to ensure the "proper conservation of whale stocks" and for the "orderly development of the whaling industry." In reality, "sustainable" has proved a very difficult term to pin down, and the IWC has been pivotal as a forum for deciding what is needed to ensure sustainability in practice.

No single group of mammals has been exploited as ruthlessly as the great whales. To take one example, only a few hundred of an original population of 250,000 Blue whales now remain in the Southern Ocean. Most populations of great whales have shown no signs of recovery, partly because there is insufficient data to detect trends in abundance and partly because insufficient time has elapsed since they were protected. As early as 1946, at its inception, the IWC recognized that "the history of whaling has seen overfishing of one area after another and of one species of whale after another to such a degree that it is essential to protect all species of whale from further overfishing." However, the Commission has so far largely failed to achieve this objective.

The world is at odds over whaling. Some countries, such as Australia and the United Kingdom, have argued that commercial whaling meets no pressing human need, and therefore oppose it on the grounds that it is cruel and unnecessary. A number of other nonwhaling countries are instead pressing for the IWC to develop means to ensure that any future whaling, if permitted, would be strictly managed. As a first step, catch limits would be calculated under IWC supervision and not just by the whaling nations themselves. Then a mechanism to prevent illegal whaling, provisionally known as the Revised Management Scheme, would need to be agreed and implemented.

🔵 **Above** As ecotourism continues to grow in popularity, the financial worth of wildlife can change dramatically – causing communities that previously hunted a resource to have an interest in conserving it. Here tourists watch a Gray whale.

🔵 **Left** The crew of a Norwegian vessel haul aboard the carcass of a Minke whale in the Barents Sea. Despite assurances to the contrary from nations still active in whaling, there is evidence that protected species of whale are still culled.

Meanwhile, Norway and Japan avoid IWC decisions and are pressing to take more whales without international regulation.

The mechanism for calculating catch quotas, known as the Revised Management Procedure, is a good example of sustainability in practice. Permitted catch sizes depend on the quality of the data on whale numbers and the level of depletion of the population. Thus, if the population has already been reduced by whaling, catches are set at zero until that population recovers. If there is poor data on the size of a population, the catch limits are lowered, under the precautionary principle that it is better to err on the side of safety. The burden of proof is put on those who wish to exploit the resource.

Whaling's sorry history demonstrates that strict measures would be required to prevent past mis-

takes from being repeated. More often than not in earlier days, IWC catch limits were not respected. In the 1960s and 1970s, the whaling ships of the former Soviet Union broke every rule in the book, catching protected species and supplying false data to the international community. The falsification of records, which continued for almost 30 years, has only recently come to light, thanks to research by Russian scientists, some of whom were themselves involved in whaling operations when younger. So, for instance, it is now known that in the 1960s a Soviet factory ship illegally killed several hundred Right whales in the Okhotsk Sea, despite the fact that the species had been protected since 1935. It is known too that Japan's whaling ships also falsified data, and it is likely that other countries did the same.

Nations that want to continue whaling argue that such problems are now past history. However, DNA analyses of whale meat recently on sale in Japan has shown that the scientific culling of Minke whales is in fact providing a cover for the sale of meat from other species, including such protected ones as the Gray, Humpback, Sei, and Sperm whales. It is impossible, however, to determine where exactly the meat is coming from because of insufficiencies in Japan's regulation of its internal market. It is also unclear how much whale meat is being smuggled around the world.

The fact is that, without proper regulation, any whaling, even of abundant species, also puts endangered species at risk. Both Norway and Japan argue against the international supervision that could be provided by DNA monitoring of markets and fully international inspection and observation schemes, stating that the industry can be regulated nationally instead. Despite the present lack of an agreed scheme to regulate whaling, both Norway and Japan submitted proposals to the CITES meetings in 1994, 1997, and again in 2000 to allow international trade in some populations of whale, all of which failed. In that respect, the present discussions within the IWC mirror those of 30 years ago. It is clear that if commercial whaling were ever to be conducted on a genuinely sustainable basis, the costs of preventing overfishing would be substantial.

One option for commercially exploiting whales that has much more potential for sustainability involves watching rather than killing them. By 1998, whalewatching was an activity conducted for profit in 87 countries, with over 9 million participants and an annual turnover of more than US$1 billion. In many countries whalewatching has become a substantial source of foreign currency: many isolated communities, such as Husavik, a small fishing town in northern Iceland, and Kaikoura in New Zealand, have seen their fortunes

transformed by it. One of the advantages of whalewatching is that it allows money to circulate widely within local communities, unlike the whaling industry, which concentrates profits in the hands of a few.

Even so, whalewatching itself has the potential to cause problems; for instance, there are concerns that whales could be disturbed if boats approach them too closely or too fast, and there is a risk of collisions. The rapid growth of the industry has resulted in concerns that it should be conducted in a sustainable, humane, and equitable manner, and the IWC has produced a framework to assist in the establishment of rules and guidelines. While recognizing that the rules have to be developed on a case-by-case basis, a number of general principles have been put forward: thus, the whales should be allowed to control the nature and the duration of the interactions; whalewatchers' boats should be designed and maintained to minimize risks; and the industry as a whole needs to be managed, for example to limit approach distances and numbers of vessels.

Whatever turn the whaling debate takes, and regardless of whether the IWC moratorium is eventually lifted, it is likely that the issues of defining genuine sustainability, ensuring appropriate regulation, and agreeing mechanisms to enforce compliance will remain hotly debated. VP

# DUGONG & MANATEES

**a**LTHOUGH SIRENIANS HAVE STREAMLINED *body forms like those of other marine mammals that never leave the water, they are the only ones that feed primarily on plants. This unique feeding niche is the key to understanding the evolution of the order's form and life history, and possibly explains why it contains so few species.*

Sirenians are descended from terrestrial mammals that once browsed the shallow, grassy swamps of the Paleocene, some 60 million years ago. These herbivores gradually became more aquatic, yet their closest modern relative remains a land mammal, the elephant.

Current theories suggest that, during the relatively warm Eocene period (55–34 million years ago), a sea cow (*Protosiren*) that was the ancestor of the modern dugong and manatees fed on the vast seagrass meadows found in shallow tropical waters of the west Atlantic and Caribbean. After the global climate cooled during the Oligocene (34–24 million years ago), the seagrass beds retreated. The manatees (family Trichechidae) appeared during the Miocene (24–5 million years ago), a geological period that favored the growth of freshwater plants in nutrient-rich rivers along the coast of South America. Unlike the seagrasses, these floating mats of river grass contained silica, an abrasive defense against herbivores, which causes rapid wearing of the teeth. To counter this deterrent, manatees have an unusual adaptation that minimizes the impact of wear: throughout their lives, worn teeth are shed at the front and are replaced at the back (see box opposite).

Today, there are only four sirenian species: one dugong and three manatees. A fifth, Steller's sea cow, was exterminated by humans in the mid-1700s. Adapted to the cold temperatures of the northern Pacific, Steller's sea cow was a specialist, feeding on kelp, the dense marine algae that became abundant after the retreat of the seagrass beds (see An Extinct Giant box).

## ▌ Large, Slow, and Docile
### FORM AND FUNCTION

Sirenians are non-ruminant herbivores, like the horse and elephant but unlike sheep and cows, and they do not have a chambered or compartmentalized stomach. The intestines are extremely long – over 45m (150ft) in manatees – and between the large and small intestines there is a large mid-gut cecum, with paired, blind-ending branches. Bacterial digestion of cellulose occurs in this hind part of the digestive tract and enables the four species to process the large volume of relatively low-quality forage they require to obtain adequate energy and nutrients; this amounts to 8–15 percent of their body weight daily.

Sirenians expend little energy: for manatees, about one-third that of a typical mammal of the same weight. Their slow, languid movements are said to have reminded early mariners of mermaids – sirens of the sea. Although capable of rapid movement when pursued, they have little need for speed in an environment without humans, having few other predators. Living in tropical waters, sirenians can afford to have a low metabolic rate, because they expend little energy on regulating body temperature. Sirenians also conserve energy by virtue of their relatively large body size.

Manatees have the typical sirenian body form and are distinguished from the dugong mainly by their large, horizontal, paddle-shaped tails, which move up and down when they swim. They have only six neck vertebrae; all other mammals have seven. The lips are covered with stiff bristles, and there are two muscular projections that grasp and

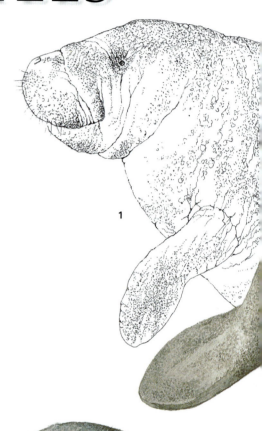

1

## SKULLS AND DENTITION OF SIRENIANS

Adult dugongs of both sexes have only a few, peglike molar teeth, located at the back of the jaws. Juveniles also have premolars, but these are lost in the first years of life. Adult males also have a pair of "tusks": incisor teeth that project through the upper lip a short distance in front of the mouth and behind the disk. The uses to which these stubby tusks are put are not clear, but it is thought that the males may use them to guide their slippery mates during courtship.

A unique feature of manatees is a constant horizontal replacement of the molar teeth. When a manatee is born, it has both premolars and molars. As the calf is weaned and begins to eat vegetable matter, the mechanical stimulation involved in chewing starts a forward movement of the whole tooth row. New teeth entering at the back of the jaw push each row forward through the jawbone until the roots are eaten away and the tooth falls out. This type of replacement is unique to manatees.

4

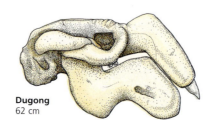

**Dugong**
62 cm

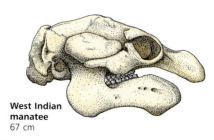

**West Indian manatee**
67 cm

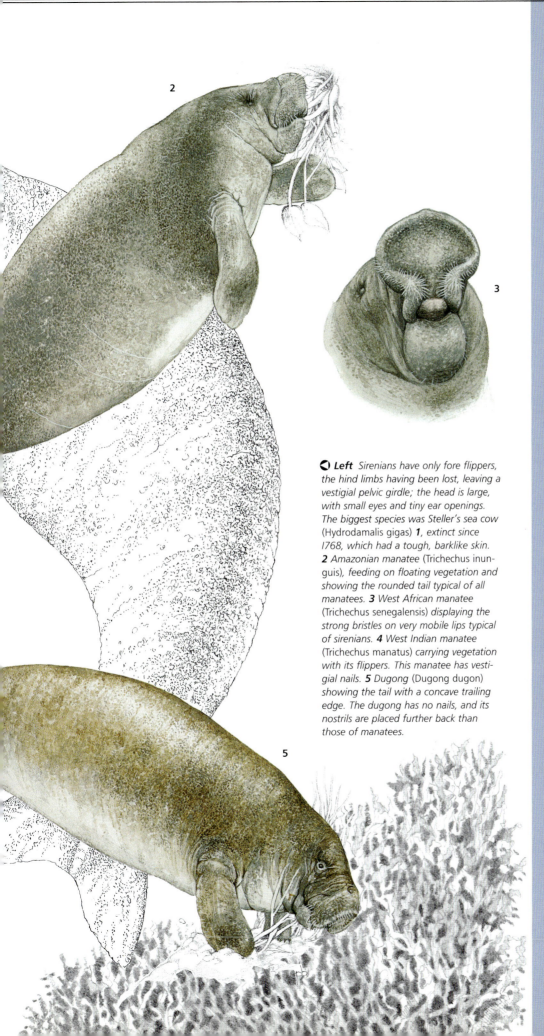

## ORDER: SIRENIA
2 families; 2 genera; 4 species

**Distribution** Tropical coasts of E Africa, Asia, Australia, and New Guinea; SE North America, Caribbean, and N South America; River Amazon; W African coast (Senegal to Angola).

**Habitat** Coastal shallows and river estuaries.

**Size** **Head–tail length** from 1–4m (3.3–13ft) in the dugong, 2.5–4.6m (7.7–15ft) in manatees; **weight** 230–900kg (500–2,000lb) in the dugong, 350–1,600kg (770–3,550lb) in manatees.

**Diet** Water plants – sirenians are the only mammals that have evolved to exploit plant life in coastal waters. The dugong is a seabed grazer, feeding primarily on sea grasses and some algae. The manatees browse on a variety of submerged and floating plants, including large quantities of water hyacinths in Florida and of mangroves in W Africa, where manatees are said also to depend heavily on riverbank growth. They also ingest some crustaceans along with the vegetation, and have been reported to eat fish entangled in nets.

### WEST INDIAN MANATEE *Trichechus manatus*

West Indian or Caribbean manatee
SE North America (Florida), Caribbean, and N South America on Atlantic coast to C Brazil. Shallow coastal waters, estuaries, and rivers. 2 subspecies – *T. m. manatus* and *T. m. latirostris* – have been proposed for the North and South American coastal population and the Caribbean populations respectively, but such a division is probably not justified because detailed comparative studies of the two groups have not yet been made. Head–tail length 3.7–4.6m (12.1–15.1ft); weight 1,600kg (3,500lb). Skin: gray-brownish and hairless; rudimentary nails on fore flippers. Breeding: gestation approximately 12 months. Longevity: 28 years in captivity, probably longer in the wild. Conservation status: Vulnerable.

### WEST AFRICAN MANATEE *Trichechus senegalensis*

West African or Senegal manatee
W Africa (Senegal to Angola). Other details, where known, are similar to those of the West Indian manatee. Conservation status: Vulnerable

### AMAZONIAN MANATEE *Trichechus inunguis*

Amazonian or South American manatee
Amazon river drainage basin in floodplain lakes, rivers, and channels. Head–tail length 2.5–3m (8–10ft); weight 350–500kg (770–1,100lb). Skin: lead-gray with variable pink belly patch (white when dead); no nails on fore flippers. Breeding: gestation not known, but probably similar to that of the West Indian manatee. Longevity: greater than 30 years. Conservation status: Vulnerable.

### DUGONG *Dugong dugon*

Dugong or Sea cow or Sea Pig
SW Pacific Ocean from New Caledonia, W Micronesia, and the Philippines to Taiwan, Vietnam, Indonesia, New Guinea, and the N coasts of Australia; Indian Ocean from Australia and Indonesia to Sri Lanka and India, the Red Sea, and S along the African coast to Mozambique. Coastal shallows. Head–tail length 1–4m (3.3–13ft); weight 230–900kg (500–2,000lb). Skin: smooth, brown to gray, with short sensory bristles at intervals of 2–3cm (0.8–1.2in). Breeding: gestation 13 months (estimated). Longevity: to around 60 years. Conservation status: Vulnerable.

◁ **Left** Sirenians have only fore flippers, the hind limbs having been lost, leaving a vestigial pelvic girdle; the head is large, with small eyes and tiny ear openings. The biggest species was Steller's sea cow (Hydrodamalis gigas) **1**, extinct since 1768, which had a tough, barklike skin. **2** Amazonian manatee (Trichechus inunguis), feeding on floating vegetation and showing the rounded tail typical of all manatees. **3** West African manatee (Trichechus senegalensis) displaying the strong bristles on very mobile lips typical of sirenians. **4** West Indian manatee (Trichechus manatus) carrying vegetation with its flippers. This manatee has vestigial nails. **5** Dugong (Dugong dugon) showing the tail with a concave trailing edge. The dugong has no nails, and its nostrils are placed further back than those of manatees.

pass the grasses and aquatic plants that they feed on into the mouth.

The eyes of manatees are not particularly well-adapted to the aquatic environment, but their hearing is good, despite the tiny external ear openings. They seem particularly sensitive to high-frequency noises, which may be an adaptation to shallow water, where the propagation of low-frequency sound is limited. The hearing abilities of manatees and other marine mammals may have also been shaped by ambient and thermal noise curves in the sea.

Being unable to hear low-frequency noises may be a contributing factor to the manatees' inability to effectively detect boat noise and therefore avoid collisions. They do not use echolocation or sonar,

and may bump into objects in murky waters; nor do they possess vocal cords. Even so, they do communicate by vocalizations, which may be high-pitched chirps or squeaks; how these sounds are produced is a mystery.

Taste buds are present on the tongue, and are apparently used in the selection of food plants; manatees can also recognize other individuals by "tasting" the scent marks left on prominent objects. Unlike toothed whales, they still possess the brain organs involved in smell, but since they spend most of their time underwater with the nose valves closed, this sense may not be used.

Manatees explore their environment by touch, using their highly-developed muzzles and muscular lips. The tactile resolving power of their bristle-

like hairs is lower than that of pinnipeds, but compares well with that of the trunk of Asian elephants. This increases grazing and browsing efficiency and maximizes the potential of the manatee as a generalist feeder.

Manatees can store large amounts of fat as blubber beneath the skin and around the intestines, which affords some degree of thermal protection from the environment. Despite this, manatees in the Atlantic Ocean generally avoid areas where temperatures drop below 20°C (68°F). The blubber also helps them to endure long periods of fasting – up to six months in the Amazonian manatee during the dry season, when aquatic plants are unavailable.

The dugong grows to a length of 3m (10ft) and

summer feeding grounds and their choicest food plants. After a migration of over 160km (100mi) to the warmer waters of the western bay, they feed during the winter months by browsing the terminal leaves of *Amphibolis antarctica*, a tough-stemmed, bushlike seagrass.

In both feeding modes, the dugong's foraging apparatus is the highly mobile, horseshoe-shaped disk at the end of its snout. In the disk, laterally-moving waves of muscular contraction sweep away overlying sediments, while stiffer bristles scoop up exposed rhizomes and any leaves that may remain attached. A meandering, flat-bottomed furrow is left behind on the seabed as evidence of a dugong's passage. Foraging dugongs rise to the surface to breathe every 40–400 seconds; the deeper the water, the longer the intervals become.

### Isolated Survivors
DISTRIBUTION PATTERNS

The four sirenian species are geographically isolated. The dugong's range spans 40 countries from east Africa to Vanuatu, including tropical and subtropical coastal and island waters between about 26° and 27° north and south of the Equator. Their historical distribution broadly coincides with the tropical Indo-Pacific distribution of seagrasses. Outside Australia, the dugong probably survives through most of its range only in relict populations separated by large areas where it is close to extinction or even extinct. The degree to which dugong numbers have dwindled and their range has fragmented is unknown.

The West African and West Indian manatees have been isolated for long enough to become

◐ **Above** An Amazonian manatee displaying its rubbery, almost seal-like skin. The Amazonian is the smallest of the three manatee species and is the only one that occurs exclusively in freshwater environments. Other distinctive features are flippers that usually lack nails and an elongated snout.

◁ **Left** Fearlessly approaching the photographer, a West Indian manatee demonstrates the curiosity that is a feature of all sirenian species. One reason why they may wish to explore unfamiliar newcomers from close up is that their eyesight is poor; touch and hearing are more important weapons in their sensory arsenal.

◑ **Below** A dugong cruises the Pacific shallows in search of seagrass to graze on. Dugongs are less bulky than manatees, and can most easily be distinguished from them by the shape of the tail; this is rounded or fan-shaped in the manatee, but in the dugong is indented to form a shallow V.

a weight of 400kg (880lb). In contrast to the three manatee species, all of which spend time in fresh water to varying degrees, it is the only extant plant-eating mammal that spends all its life at sea. Unlike those of manatees, its tail has a straight or slightly concave trailing edge. A short, broad, trunklike snout ends in a downward-facing flexible disk and a slitlike mouth.

Dugongs appear to "chew" vegetation, mainly with rough, horny pads located in the roof and floor of the mouth. While their preferred feeding mode is piglike, rooting out carbohydrate-rich rhizomes (underground storage roots) from the seabed, the name "sea cow" is not always a misnomer. At Shark Bay, Western Australia, low winter temperatures drive the herds from their

🔽 **Below** *The mother–child bond, exhibited here by a West Indian manatee and her calf, is easily the strongest social tie in the sirenian world. Cows give birth to a single offspring once every other year, and the young stay with them for 12–18 months, learning about choice feeding areas and annual migration routes.*

distinct since their supposed common ancestor migrated to Africa across the Atlantic Ocean. Each can occupy both saltwater and freshwater habitats. The Amazonian manatee apparently became isolated when the Andes mountain range was uplifted in the Pliocene 5–1.8 million years ago, changing the river drainage out of the Amazon basin from the Pacific to the Atlantic Ocean. Amazonian manatees are not tolerant of salt water and occupy only the Amazon River and its tributaries.

Despite the manatee's ability to move thousands of kilometers along continental margins, genetic studies have revealed strong population separations between most locations. These findings are consistent with tagging studies which indicate that stretches of open water and unsuitable coastal habitats constitute substantial barriers to gene flow and colonization. Conversely, within Florida and Brazil, manatees are genetically more similar than might be expected, which may be explained by recent colonization into high latitudes or bottleneck effects. Adult survival probabilities in these areas appear high enough to maintain growing populations if other traits such as reproductive rates and juvenile survival are also sufficiently high. Lower and variable survival rates on the Atlantic coast are a cause for concern.

## Grazing the Shallows
### DIET

Sirenians have few competitors for food. In terrestrial grasslands there are many grazers and browsers, requiring a complex division of resources; but the only large herbivores in seagrass meadows are sirenians and sea turtles. Marine plant communities are low in diversity compared with terrestrial communities and lack species with high-energy seeds, which facilitate niche subdivision among herbivores in terrestrial systems. It is not surprising that dugongs and manatees dig into the sediments when they feed on rooted aquatics; over half of the mass of seagrasses is found in the rhizomes, which concentrate carbohydrates. In contrast, the cold-blooded sea turtles subsist by grazing on the blades of seagrasses without disturbing the rhizomes, and appear to feed in deeper water. Thus even the herbivorous sea turtles probably do not compete significantly for food taken by the sirenians.

As aquatic herbivores, manatees are restricted to feeding on plants in, or very near, the water. Occasionally, they feed with their head and shoulders out of water, but normally they consume floating or submerged grasses and other vascular plants. They may eat algae, but this does not form an important part of the diet. The coastal West Indian and West African manatees feed on seagrasses growing in relatively shallow, clear marine waters, and also enter inland waterways to feed on freshwater plants. Amazonian manatees are surface feeders, browsing floating grasses (the murky

○ **Above** *The sensitive vibrissae (whiskers) on a manatee's protruding upper lip play an essential part in feeding. With their aid, an animal can feel its way through clumps of floating vegetation or root for nutrients on the seabed, much as pigs do on land.*

◐ **Left** *A West Indian manatee feeds on aquatic plants off Florida. As the downward-pointing snout might suggest, this species spends some of its time grazing on the seabed, in contrast to the Amazonian manatee, which is almost entirely a surface feeder.*

Amazon waters inhibit the growth of submerged aquatic plants). The habit of surface feeding may explain why the downward deflection in the snout of Amazonian manatees is much less pronounced than in bottom-feeding West Indian and African species. Some 44 species of plants and 10 species of algae have been recorded as foods of West Indian manatees, but only 24 for Amazonian manatees.

Many food plants on which the manatees graze have evolved anti-herbivore protective mechanisms – spicules of silica in the grasses, and tannins, nitrates, and oxalates in other aquatics – that reduce their digestibility and lower their food value. Microbes in the manatees' digestive tract may be able to detoxify some of these chemical defenses.

Dugongs feed on seagrasses – marine flowering plants that sometimes resemble terrestrial grasses and are distinct from seaweeds. Seagrasses grow on the bottom in coastal shallows, and dugongs generally feed at depths of 2–6m (6–20ft), though characteristic rooting scars have been observed in seagrass beds at a depth of 23m (75ft). The food they most prefer is the carbohydrate-rich rhizomes of the smaller seagrass species.

## The Cow–Calf Bond
### SOCIAL BEHAVIOR

The large sirenian body size, dictated by the requirements of nutrition and temperature regulation, is associated with traits seen in other large mammalian herbivores as well as large marine mammals. The life span is long – ages of 30 or more have been recorded in captivity – and the reproductive rate is low. Females give birth to a single calf after about a year's gestation, calves stay with the mother for 1–2 years, and sexual maturity is delayed for 4–8 years. Consequently, the potential rate of population increase is low. It is possible that rapid reproduction brings no advantage where the renewability of food resources is slow and there are few predators.

Manatees are extremely slow breeders: at most they produce only a single calf every two years, and calves may be weaned from 12–18 months. Although young calves may feed on plants within weeks of being born, the long nursing period probably allows them to learn the necessary migration routes, foods, and preferred feeding areas from their mother.

In highly seasonal environments such as the Amazon, and probably also at the northern and southern limits of their distribution, the availability of food dictates when the majority of manatee females are ready to mate, and this, in turn, results in a seasonal peak in calving. The reproductive biology of male manatees is poorly known, but it is not uncommon for a receptive female to be accompanied by 6–8 males and to mate with several of these within a short time. Direct observation and radio-tracking studies have shown that manatees are essentially solitary, but occasionally form groups of a dozen or more.

Little is known about the behavior and ecology of dugongs, for they are not easily studied. The waters where they are found are generally turbid, and their shyness frustrates close observation. When disturbed, their flight is rapid and furtive; only the top of the head and nostrils are exposed as they rise to breathe. When underwater visibility is adequate and they are approached cautiously, they will come from 100m (330ft) or more to investigate a diver or a small boat, probably alerted by their extremely keen underwater hearing. Normal behavior stops until their curiosity is satisfied; then they swim off, frequently on a zig-zag course that keeps the intruder in view with alternate eyes.

The dugongs' curiosity suggests that, as adults at least, they have few predators, although attacks by Killer whales and sharks have been recorded. Dugongs have smaller and less complexly structured brains than whales and dolphins, and their greater tendency to approach and investigate objects visually is consistent with a lack of echolocation apparatus. Known dugong calls include

355

**Left** *A manatee raises its nostrils to the water's surface to take in air. Manatees normally breathe at intervals of less than a minute, though dives of more than 15 minutes have been recorded.*

chirps, trills, and whistles, which may signal danger and maintain mother–young contact. Large size, tough skin, dense bone structure, and blood that clots very rapidly to close wounds seem to be an adult dugong's main means of defense.

Dugongs sometimes form large herds, but are more often found in groups of less than a dozen; many individuals may be solitary. Sexing is difficult in the wild, but the groups generally appear to include one or more females with calves. In some habitats, herds 60–100 strong may gather to exploit rich seagrass resources; "cultivating" the beds cooperatively with their grazing.

Radio tagging has shown that dugongs are mostly quite sedentary, inhabiting home ranges of a few dozen square kilometers. Sometimes, however, for reasons unknown, they make excursions of hundreds of kilometers.

Tropical environments make long mating seasons possible, and dugongs may mate over a period of 4–5 months. In at least one area males gather at a traditional "lek" site where they patrol and vocalize. Territorial males perform "situps" that appear to serve a display function. The dugong is the only marine mammal that displays this classic lekking pattern. Females become sexually mature at 10–17 years, and give birth to a single calf after a gestation of about 13 months. Few births have been observed, but it seems that the females seek out shallows at the water's edge. The calf keeps close contact with its mother for up to 2 years, suckling from a single teat in the axilla of each flipper while lying beside her and taking refuge behind her back in the presence of danger. Although females can become pregnant while lactating, inter-birth intervals average from 3–7 years. Females may live to over 60 years.

**Right** *In Florida, a pair of manatees share a snack at a favorite feeding spot. Although the big animals are not highly social, they tolerate one another's company without showing aggression, and enjoy apparent play activities that include nuzzling and "kissing."*

## Lambs to the Slaughter

CONSERVATION AND ENVIRONMENT

Docility, delicious flesh, and a low reproductive capacity are not auspicious characteristics for animals in the modern world. The dugong and manatees have all three, and are consequently among the most threatened of aquatic mammals.

All three species of manatees are considered by the IUCN to be vulnerable as a result of both historic and modern overhunting for their meat and skins; they are also at risk from more recent threats such as pollution and high-speed pleasure craft. One study estimated that a 10 percent increase in adult mortality or reproduction would drive the Florida population to extinction over a 1,000-year time scale, whereas a 10 percent decrease in adult mortality would allow slow population growth. They are protected under the Convention on International Trade in Endangered Species of Fauna and Flora (CITES), and legally in most countries where they exist.

In Costa Rica, local residents blame an apparent decline in their numbers on illegal hunting, high levels of toxicants in coastal waters, ingestion of plastic banana bags, and increased motorboat traffic. Badly managed "eco-tourism," and environmental degradation have also played a part. A study of manatee carcasses in Florida revealed that most deaths there were due to human interaction, especially captures and watercraft collisions. When a manatee does die of natural causes, it is usually a dependent calf.

Amazonian manatees have been commercially exploited for their meat and hide since 1542, and

### AN EXTINCT GIANT

The only close relative of the dugong to survive into historic times was Steller's sea cow. This giant marine grazer was the largest sirenian of all, with a body length of up to 7.5m (25ft) and a weight of 4.5–5.9 tonnes. The sea cow was unique among mammals in having no phalanges. The pectoral flipper had a stumpy, densely bristled termination described by the biologist Steller as "hoof-like." Sea cows were apparently unable to submerge, and instead used these appendages to support themselves against rocks while they fed on kelp. Fossil evidence suggests that 100,000 years ago their range extended along northern Pacific coasts from Baja California up through the Aleutian Islands as far as Japan.

Its inshore feeding habits made Steller's sea cow vulnerable to hunters in small boats. Native peoples almost certainly hunted it, so, even before the arrival of Western explorers, the population had probably already been severely reduced to as few as 1,000–2,000 animals. When shipwrecked Russian sailors first sighted it in 1741, it was restricted to two subarctic Pacific islands, each 50–100km (30–60mi) long. The survivors killed and ate the sea cows out of dire necessity, and thereafter fur-hunting parties overwintered on the islands to exploit this ready food supply. Moreover, by slaughtering sea otters the hunters caused a boom in the urchin population, which stripped the kelp beds, the sea cows' main food. By 1768 the sea cows were extinct.

In later times, several isolated dugong populations seem to have suffered similar fates. Even though there are still a few surviving herds as numerous as those of Steller's sea cow were at the time of its discovery, the story of the extinction of the species' huge relative nevertheless has an obvious moral for the present day.                                    PKA

Below *A fanciful 18th-century illustration of Steller's sea cows.*

they are now considered an endangered species. Although they have been legally protected since 1973, exploitation for meat has in fact continued without any practical restrictions. Manatees are also hunted in Peru, and are sometimes taken incidentally in fishing gear.

Another important factor in manatee deaths are blooms of toxic algae that may be exacerbated by pollution. During a period of several weeks in the spring of 1996, over 200 manatees were found dead or dying in Florida's coastal waters or on the beaches of the west coast. At the same time, high densities of a dinoflagellate which produces a potent neurotoxin that binds to manatee brain cells were observed in the same coastal areas. Yet another threat is morbillivirus, which may cause fatal infections and possibly also more insidious effects on the immune system or reproduction.

Improving the manatee's lot will require proactive management. Scientific research, rescue, and rehabilitation also have their place. Boat-free zones provide sanctuaries for manatees in Florida, and are an effective management tool. If speed and boating regulations are effectively enforced in 13 key coastal counties, Florida's manatees should be able to coexist indefinitely with human recreational requirements, whereas if regulation is

◑ **Above** *In Florida's Homosassa Springs State Wildlife Park, a conservation worker feeds vitamin supplements to an eager clutch of manatees. The species' long-term survival in the state now depends on the effectiveness of management programs.*

unsuccessful, the population is likely to decline slowly toward extinction. Control of hunting and management of tourism may also make the manatee's future more certain elsewhere.

In recent times, people have found a non-lethal employment for manatees that they seem only too happy to fulfill: that of clearing weeds from irrigation canals and the dams of hydroelectric power stations. It is thus possible that the animals' gentle, herbivorous lifestyle might yet help them to survive in an aggressive world.

As a marine creature, the dugong has had less direct contact with people than the riverine manatees, but even so the relationship has not been a happy one. Dugongs have traditionally been hunted by coastal peoples in most of their range. In recent times, the increase in human populations and the growing availability of nylon gill-nets and boats with outboard motors have led to the decimation of dugong populations outside of Australia and the Persian Gulf.          PKA/JMP/GBR/DPD/RB

◑ **Above** *Caught in a fish-trap off Sulawesi (Indonesia), a young dugong uses its sensitive snout to investigate its prison. Over the centuries hunting has driven the dugong from much of its former range.*

# GRAZING THE SEAGRASS MEADOWS

## Feeding strategy of the Dugong

A PERSON WANDERING THE INTERTIDAL SEAGRASS meadows of northern Australia will likely notice long, serpentine furrows devoid of all vegetation. These are the feeding trails of the dugong, a large marine mammal that uproots whole seagrass plants, including their roots and rhizomes. Dugongs prefer small, delicate, "weedy" seagrasses that are low in fiber, yet high in available nutrients and easily digested – mainly species from the genera *Halophila* and *Halodule*. Experiments simulating dugong grazing indicate that their feeding alters both the species composition and nutrient qualities of seagrass communities, causing them to become lower in fiber and higher in nitrogen. In effect, dugongs are like farmers cultivating their crops. If these animals were to become locally extinct, the seagrass meadows would, in turn, deteriorate as dugong habitat.

Over most of its range, the dugong is known only from incidental sightings, accidental drownings, and the anecdotal reports of fishermen. However, within Australia, intensive aerial surveys have produced a more comprehensive picture of dugong distribution, which is now known to extend from Moreton Bay in Queensland, on the east coast, around to Shark Bay in Western Australia. These same surveys show dugongs to be the most abundant marine mammal in the inshore waters of northern Australia, numbering some 85,000 individuals. What is more, this figure is probably an underestimate, since some areas of suitable habitat have not been surveyed and the mathematical correction for animals that cannot be seen in turbid water is conservative. In other words, Australia is the dugong's last stronghold.

More than 60 individual dugongs have been tracked using satellite transmitters. Most of their movements have been localized to the vicinity of seagrass beds and are dictated by the tide. At localities where the tidal range is large, dugongs can gain access to their inshore feeding areas only when the water depth is at least one meter (3.3ft). In areas with low tidal amplitude or where seagrass grows subtidally, dugongs can generally feed without making significant local movements. However, at the high-latitude limits of their range, dugongs make seasonal movements to warmer waters. While overwintering in Moreton Bay, many dugongs frequently make round trips of 15–40km (9–25mi) between their foraging grounds inside the bay and oceanic waters, which are, on average, up to 5°C warmer. Dugongs also apparently relocate within Shark Bay itself, moving from east to west, where the water is warmer. Some travel for long distances; for example, in the Great Barrier Reef region and the Gulf of Carpentaria, several

◑ ◐ **Above and Right** *Seagrasses grow abundantly in the shallow waters that surround northern Australia. This plentiful supply of vegetation attracts great numbers of dugongs. Stirring up the substrate as they browse, these sedate marine grazers appear when seen from the air almost like combine harvesters moving slowly across a field of crops.*

dugongs have been recorded making trips of 100–600km (62–372mi) over just a few days. Many of these movements were return trips. One plausible explanation for such long journeys is that dugongs are checking the status of the seagrass beds in their region. Many seagrass meadows arise and promptly disappear again, for no apparent reason. Sometimes hundreds of kilometers of seagrass may be lost after storms or flooding.

Dugongs are long-lived, with a low reproductive rate, long generation time, and a high investment in each offspring. On the basis of annual growth rings in its tusks, the oldest dugong was estimated to be 73 years old when she died. Females give birth aged 10–17, and the period between successive births varies from three to seven years. The gestation period is around 13 months, and the (almost always single) calf suckles for at least 18 months. Dugongs start eating seagrasses soon after they are born and grow rapidly during the suckling period. Population simulations indicate that a dugong population is unlikely to be able to increase by more than 5 percent annually. This makes the dugong highly susceptible to overexploitation by indigenous hunters or to incidental drowning in fishing nets. Consequently, they are classified as Vulnerable to global extinction.    HM

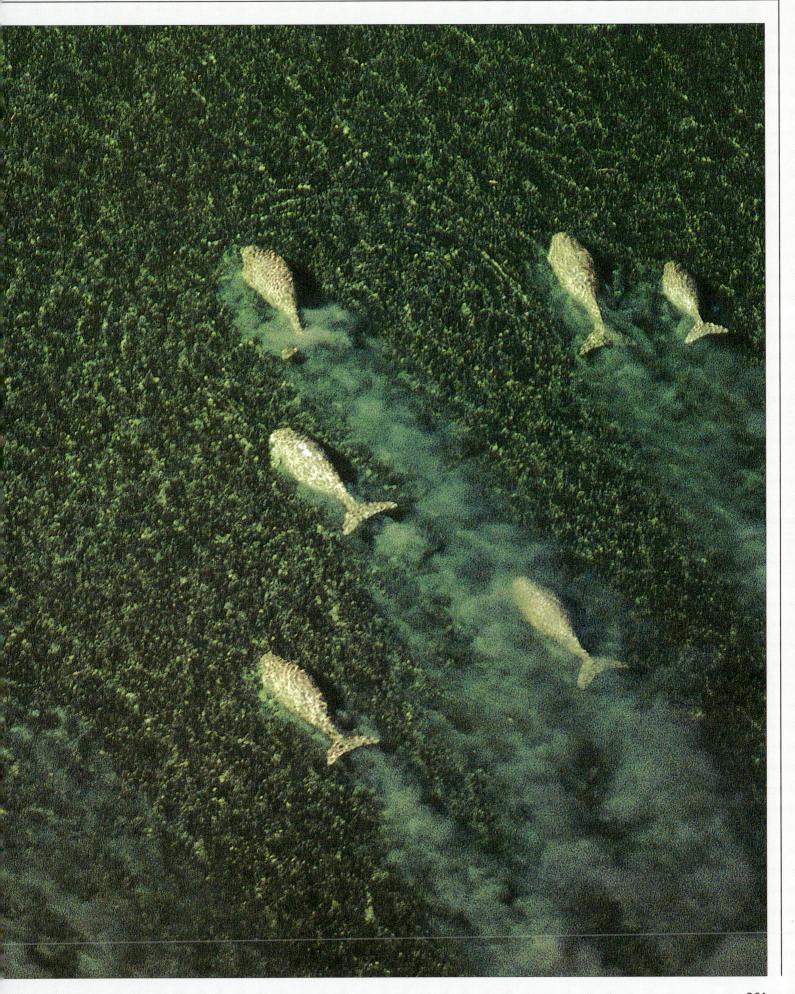

# Glossary

## FISHES

**Adaptation** features of an animal which adjust it to its environment. Adaptations may be genetic, i.e. produced by evolution and hence not alterable within the animal's lifetime, or they maybe phenotypic, i.e. produced by adjustment on the behalf of the individual and may be reversible within its lifetime.

**Adipose fin** a fatty fin behind the rayed DORSAL FIN, normally rayless (exceptionally provided with a spine or pseudorays in some catfish).

**Adult** a fully developed and mature individual, capable of breeding but not necessarily doing so until social and/or ecological conditions allow.

**Air bladder** see SWIM BLADDER.

**Algae** very primitive plants, e.g. epilithic algae, algae growing on liths (i.e. stones).

**Ammocoetes** the larval stage of the lamprey.

**Anadromous** of fish that run up from the sea to spawn in fresh water.

**Brood sac or pouch** a protective device made from fins or plates of one or other parent fish in which the fertilized eggs are placed to hatch in safety.

**Cartilage** gristle.

**Caudal fin** the "tail" fin.

**Caudal peduncle** a narrowing of the body in front of the caudal fin.

**Cerebellum** a part of the brain.

**Cilia** tiny hair-like protrusions.

**Class** a taxonomic level. The main levels (in descending order) are Phylum, Class, Order, Family, Genus, Species.

**Cogener** a member of the same genus.

**Colonial** living together in a colony.

**Colony** a group of animals gathered together for breeding.

**Conspecific** a member of the same species.

**Cryptic** camouflaged and difficult to see.

**Ctenoid** scales scales of "advanced" fishes which have a comb-like posterior edge, thereby giving a rough feeling.

**Cutaneous respiration** breathing through the skin.

**Cycloid** scales with a smooth posterior (exposed) edge.

**Denticle** literally a "small tooth"; used of dermal denticles, i.e. tooth-like scales (all denticles are dermal in origin).

**Diatoms** small planktonic plants with silicaceous tests (shells).

**Dimorphism** the existence of two distinctive forms.

**Disjunct** distribution geographical distribution of taxons that is marked by gaps. Many factors may cause it.

**Display** any relatively conspicuous pattern of behavior that conveys specific information to others, usually to members of the same species; often associated with courtship but also e.g. "threat displays."

**Dorsal fin** the fin on the back.

**Endostyle** a complex hairy (ciliated) groove that forms part of the feeding mechanism of the larval lamprey.

**Epigean** living on the surface. See also HYPOGEAN.

**Esca** the luminous lure at the end of the ILLICIUM (the fishing rod) of the angler fishes.

**Family** either a group of closely related species or a pair of animals and their offspring.

**Feces** excrement from the digestive system passed out through the anus.

**Fin** in fishes the equivalent of a leg, arm, or wing.

**Fin girdles** bony internal supports for paired fins.

**Ganoid scales** a primitive type of thick scale.

**Gape** the width of the open mouth.

**Genus** the lowest taxonomic grouping.

**Gills** the primary respiratory organs of fish. Basically a vascularized series of slits in the PHARYNX allowing water to pass and effect gas exchange. The gills are the bars that separate the gill slits.

**Gill slits** the slits between the gills that allow water through.

**Gular plates** bony plates lying in the skin of the "throat" between the two halves of the lower jaw in many primitive and a few living bony fishes.

**Heterocercal** a tail shape in which the upper lobe is longer than the lower and into which the upturned backbone continues for a short distance.

**Hypogean** living below the surface of the ground, e.g. in caves.

**Illicium** a modified dorsal fin ray in angler fishes which is mobile and acts as a lure to attract prey.

**Introduced** of a species which has been brought from lands where it occurs naturally to lands where it has not previously occurred. Some introductions are natural but some are made on purpose for biological control, farming or other economic reasons.

**Invertebrate** animals lacking backbones, e.g. insects, crustacea, coelenterates, "worms" of all varieties, echinoderms etc.

**Krill** small shrimplike marine crustaceans which are an important food for certain species of seabirds, whales, and fishes.

**Lamellae** plate-like serial structures (e.g. gill lamellae) usually of an absorbent or semi-permeable nature.

**Larva** a pre-adult form unlike its parent in appearance.

**Lateral-line organs** pressure-sensitive organs lying in a perforated canal along the side of the fish and on the head.

**Maxillary bone** the posterior bone of the upper jaw. Tooth-bearing in primitive fish, it acts as a lever to protrude the tooth-bearing anterior bone (premaxilla) in advanced fish.

**Metamorphosis** a dramatic change of shape during the course of ontogeny (growing up). Usually occurs where the adult condition is assumed.

**Mollusk** a shellfish.

**Monotypic** the sole member of its genus.

**Natural selection** the process whereby individuals with the most appropriate ADAPTATIONS are more successful than other individuals, and hence survive to produce more offspring. To the extent that the successful traits are heritable (genetic) they will therefore spread in the population.

**Neoteny** a condition in which a species becomes sexually mature and breeds whilst still in the larval body form, i.e. the ancestral adult body stage is never reached.

**Niche** the position of a species within the community, defined in terms of all aspects of its lifestyle (e.g. food, competitors, predators and other resource requirements).

**Olfactory** sac the sac below the-nostrils containing the olfactory organ.

**Opercular bones** the series of bones including the operculum (gill flap) and its supports.

**Operculum** the correct name for the bone forming the gill flap.

**Order** a level of taxonomic ranking. See CLASS and Introduction.

**Osmosis** the tendency for ions to flow through a semipermeable membrane from the side with the greatest concentration to the side with the least. This means that in the sea fish fluids pick up ions and have to get rid of them whereas in fresh water retention of vital ions is essential.

**Oviparous** egg-laying.

**Ovipositor** a tube by which eggs are inserted into small openings and cracks.

**Ovoviviparity** the retention of eggs and hatching within the body of the mother.

**Pelvic girdle** the bones forming the support for the pelvic fins.

**Perianal organ** an organ around the anus.

**pH** a measure of the acidity or alkalinity of water: pH7 is neutral; the lower the number the more acid the water and vice versa.

**Pharyngeal teeth** teeth borne on modified bones of the gill arches in the "throat" of the fish.

**Pharynx** that part of the alimentary tract that has the gill arches.

**Photophore** an organ emitting light.

**Piscivore** fish-eater.

**Plankton** very small organisms and larvae that drift largely passively in the water.

**Predator** an animal that forages for live prey; hence "anti-predator behavior" describes the evasive actions of prey.

**Prehensile** capable of being bent and/or moved.

**Rostrum** snout.

**Scale** a small flat plate forming part of the external covering of a fish; hence deciduous scale, a scale that easily falls off the fish.

**Scutes** bony plates on or in the skin of a fish.

**Spawning** the laying and fertilizing of eggs, sometimes done in a spawning ground.

**Specialist** an animal whose lifestyle involves highly specialized strategems, e.g. feeding with one technique on a particular food.

**Species** a population, or series of populations which interbreed freely, but not with others.

**Spiracle** a now largely relict GILL SLIT lying in front of the more functional gill slits.

**Subcutaneous canal** a canal passing beneath the skin.

**Swimbladder or air bladder** A gas- or air-filled bladder lying between the gut and the backbone. It may be open via a duct to the PHARYNX so that changes of pressure can be accommodated by exhalation or inhalation of atmospheric air. If closed, gas is secreted or excreted by special glands. Its main function is buoyancy but it can also be used, in some species, for respiration, sound reception, or sound production.

**Teleosts** a group of fishes, defined by particular characters. The fishes most familiar to us are almost all teleosts.

**Temperate zone** an area of climatic zones in mid latitude, warmer than the northerly areas, but cooler than subtropical areas.

**Territory** area that a fish considers its own and defends against intruders.

**Tropics** strictly an area lying between 22.5°N and 22.50°S. Often, because of local geography, animals' habitats do not match this area precisely.

**Tubercles** small keratinized protrusions of unknown and doubtless different functions which are either permanent or seasonally or irregularly present on the skin of fishes.

**Type** the species on which the definition of a genus depends.

**Vascularized** possessed of many small, usually thin-walled, blood vessels.

**Velum** a hood around the mouth of larval lampreys (ammocoetes) that is a feeding adaptation.

**Vertebrate** an animal with a backbone. primitively consisting of rigidly articulating bones.

**Villi** small hair-like processes that often have an absorptive function.

**Viviparous** producing live offspring from within the body of the mother.

**Vomerine teeth** teeth carried on the vomer, a median bone near the roof of the mouth.

**Weberian apparatus** a modification of the anterior few vertebrae in ostariophysan fishes (carps, catfish, characins etc) that transmit sound waves as compression impulses from the SWIMBLADDER to the inner ear, thereby enabling the fish to hear.

# AQUATIC INVERTEBRATES

**Abdomen** a group of up to 10 similar segments, situated behind the THORAX of crustaceans and insects, which in the former group may possess appendages.

**Abyss, abyssal** the part, or concerning the part, of the ocean, including the ocean floor, that extends downward from some 4,000m (13,000ft).

**Acoelomate** having no COELOM (main body cavity).

**Acrorhagi** groups of NEMATOCYSTS.

**Adaptation** a characteristic which enhances an organism's chances of survival in the environment in which it lives, in comparison with the chances of a similar organism lacking the same characteristic.

**Adult** a fully developed and mature individual capable of breeding, but not necessarily doing so until social and/or ecological conditions allow.

**Americ** having a body not divided into SEGMENTS.

**Ampulla** a small contractile fluid reservoir associated with the tube-feet of some echinoderms.

**Anabiosis** suspended animation, with a low metabolic rate enabling an animal to survive adverse environmental conditions, particularly desiccation.

**Ancestral stock** a group of animals usually showing primitive characteristics, which is believed to have given rise to later more specialized forms.

**Anisogamous** of reproduction, involving gametes of the same species that are unalike in size or in form.

**Antennae** the first pair of head appendages of uniramians and the second pair of crustaceans.

**Antennules** the first pair of head appendages of crustaceans.

**Apophysis** an outgrowth or process on an organ or bone.

**Aquatic** associated with, or living in water.

**Arthropod** an invertebrate, such as an insect, spider or crustacean, which is TRIPLOBLASTIC and COELOMATE, with a chitinous, jointed EXOSKELETON, paired, jointed limbs and a lack of NEPHRIDIA and CILIA; in some classifications, a member of the phylum Arthropoda; here includes the members of the phyla Crustacea, Chelicerata, Uniramia, Tardigrada, Pentastomida, Onychophora.

**Arachnid** a member of the Arachnida, a class of the phylum Chelicerata, which includes spiders, scorpions, mites and ticks.

**Asexual reproduction** reproduction that does not include fertilization (exchange Of GAMETES) or MEIOSIS. See BINARY FISSION: BUDDING; GEMMULE; PARTHENOGENESIS.

**Asymmetrical** having no plane of symmetry, e.g. an animal of indeterminate shape that cannot be divided into two halves which are mirror images.

**Atrium** the volume enclosed by the tentacles of an endoproct; also the chamber through which the water current passes before leaving the body of a sea squirt or lancelet.

**Autrotrophy** the synthesis, by an organism, of its own organic constituents from inorganic material, i.e. independent of organic sources; autrotrophic organisms may synthesize food phototrophically (e.g. green plants) or chemotrophically (e.g. bacteria) via inorganic oxidations.

**Axon** a long process of a nerve cell, normally conducting impulses away from nerve cell body.

**Axopodium** a stiff filament or pseudopodium which radiates outward from the body of a heliozoan or radiolarian.

**Bacterium** member of a division of uni-cellular or multi-cellular microscopic PROKARYOTIC organisms, lacking CHLOROPHYLL. Distinct from both plants and animals, rod-like, spherical or spiral in shape, occasionally forming a mycelium.

**Benthic** associated with the bottom of seas or lakes.

**Bilateral symmetry** a bilaterally symmetrical animal can be halved in one plane only to give two halves which are mirror images of each other. Most multi-cellular animals are bilaterally symmetrical, a form of symmetry generally associated with a mobile, free-living lifestyle.

**Binary fission** a form of ASEXUAL REPRODUCTION of a cell in which the nucleus divides, and then the CYTOPLASM divides into two approximately equal parts.

**Biomass** a measure of the abundance of a life form in terms of its mass.

**Bipectinate** comb-like, of structures with two branches, particularly the OSPHRADIUM and/or CTENIDIUM in some mollusks.

**Biramous** of those ARTHROPODS (e.g. crustaceans) with forked ("two-branched") appendages.

**Bivalve** a shell or protective covering composed of two parts hinged together and which usually encases the body; also, a member of the molluskan class Bivalvia, which includes most bivalved animals.

**Bothria** long, narrow grooves of weak muscularity found in Pseudophyllidea (an order of tapeworm); form an efficient sucking organ.

**Branchial hearts** contractile hearts near the base of each CTENIDIUM in certain mollusks.

**Brood sac** a thoracic pouch of certain crustaceans into which fertilized eggs are deposited and where they develop.

**Buccal mass** a muscular structure surrounding the RADULA, horny jaw and ODONTOPHORE of a mollusk (not a bivalve).

**Budding** a form of ASEXUAL REPRODUCTION in which a new individual develops as a direct growth from the parent's body.

**Calcareous** composed of, or containing, calcium carbonate as in the spicules of certain sponges or the shells of mollusks.

**Cambrian** a geological period some 543–490 million years ago, also the oldest system of rocks in which fossils can be used for dating, containing the first shelled fossil remains.

**Carapace** the dorsal shield of the exoskeleton covering part of the body (mainly anterior) of most crustaceans; particularly large in e.g. crabs, it protects the animal from both predation and water loss.

**Carboniferous** a geological period some 354–290 million years ago.

**Carnivore** an animal that feeds on other animals.

**Catabolic** of processes involving breakdown of complex organic molecules by living organisms, typically animals, resulting in the liberation of energy.

**Caudal** relating to the tail or to the rearmost SEGMENT of an invertebrate.

**Cecum** a blindly-ending branch of the gut or other hollow organ.

**Cellulose** the tough, fibrous fundamental constituent of the cell walls of all green plants and some algae and fungi.

**Cephalization** development of the head during evolution, different organisms show different degrees of cephalization, generally according to their "level of evolution".

**Cephalothorax** the fusion of head and anterior thoracic segments in certain crustaceans to form a single body region which may be covered by a protective CARAPACE.

**Cerata** (sing. ceras) projections on the back of some shell-less sea slugs, often brightly colored, which may bear NEMATOCYSTS from cnidarians and may act as secondary respiratory organs.

**Cercaria** a swimming larval form of flukes; produced asexually by REDIA larvae while parasitic in snails; cercaria infects a new final or intermediate host via food or the skin.

**Chaetae** the chitinous bristles characteristic of annelid worms.

**Chela** the pincer-like tip of limbs in some arthropods.

**Chelicera** one of the first pair of append-ages behind the mouth of a chelicerate.

**Chelicerate** a member of the phylum Chelicerata.

**Chitin** a complex nitrogen-containing polysaccharide which forms a material of considerable mechanical strength and resistance to chemicals; forms the external "shell" or CUTICLE of arthropods.

**Chloroplast** a small granule (plastid) found in cells and containing the green pigment chlorophyll, site of PHOTOSYNTHESIS.

**Chordate** a member or characteristic of the phylum Chordata, animals which possess a NOTOCHORD.

**Chromatophore** a cell with pigment in its CYTOPLASM.

**Cilia** (sing. cilium) the only differences between FLAGELLA and cilia is in the former's greater length and the greater number of cilia found on a cell; flagella measure up to 22μm, cilia up to 10μm. Ciliary feeding feeding by filtering minute organisms from a current of water drawn through or toward the animal by CILIA.

**Ciliated** having a number of cilia on a surface which beat in a coordinated rhythm; ciliary action is a common method of moving fluids within an animal body or over body surfaces, employed in CILIARY FEEDING, and a common means of locomotion in microscopic and small animals. The ciliated ciliates are a major class (Ciliata) of protozoans.

**Cirri** (sing. cirrus) in barnacles, paired thoracic feeding appendages; in protozoans, short, spine-like projections in tufts called CILIA; in annelids, broad flattened projections situated dorsally on segments; in flukes and some turbellarian flatworms the cirrus is the male copulatory apparatus.

**Class** a rank used in the classification of organisms; consists of a number of similar ORDERS (in some cases only one order may be distinguished); similar classes are grouped into a PHYLUM.

**Cleavage** see RADIAL CLEAVAGE: SPIRAL CLEAVAGE.

**Clitellum** the saddle-like region of earthworms which is prominent in sexually mature worms.

**Coelom** the main body cavity of many TRIPLOBLASTIC animals, situated in the middle layer of cells or MESODERM and lined by EPITHELIUM. In many organisms the coelom contains the internal organs of the body and plays an important part in collecting excretions which are removed via NEPHRIDIA or coelomoducts.

**Coelomate** having a COELOM.

**Coelomocyte** a free cell in the coelom of some invertebrates which appears to be involved with the excretion of waste material, wound healing and regeneration.

**Colony** an organism consisting of a number of individual members in a permanent colonial association.

**Commensalism** a relationship between members of different species in which one species benefits from the relationship, often by access to food; the other species neither benefits nor is harmed.

**Community** a naturally occurring group of different organisms inhabiting a common environment, sometimes named for one of its members, e.g. the *Donax* community of sandy beaches named for a genus of bivalve mollusks.

**Compound eyes** the type of eyes possessed by most crustaceans and insects, composed of many long, cylindrical units (ommatidia) each of which is capable of light reception and image formation.

**Conjugation** the union of GAMETES, or two cells (in certain bacteria); or the process of sexual reproduction in most ciliates.

**Convergent evolution** the evolution of two organisms with some increasingly similar characteristics but different ancestry.

**Copulation** the process by which internal fertilization is accomplished, the transfer of sperm from one member of a species to another via specialized organs.

**Corona** the characteristic, ciliated, wheel-like organ at the anterior end of rotifers.

**Coxa** the basal segment of an arthropod appendage which joins the limb to the body.

**Cretaceous** a geological period extending from some 144 to 65 million years ago.

**Cross-fertilization** the fusion of male and female GAMETES produced by different individuals of the same species.

**Cryptobiosis** a form of suspended animation enabling an organism to survive adverse environmental conditions.

**Ctenidium** one of the pair of gills within the MANTLE CAVITY of some mollusks.

**Cuticle** the external layer covering certain multicellular animals (e.g. arthropods), formed from a collagen-like protein or

CHITIN, which is secreted by the EPIDERMIS. It acts as a physiological barrier between the animal and its external environment, may reduce water loss, acts as a barrier to the entry of microorganisms and in arthropods acts as an EXOSKELETON.

**Cyst** a thick-walled protective membrane enclosing a cell, larva or organism.

**Cytoplasm** all the living matter of a cell excluding the nucleus.

**Dactylozooid** the specialized defensive polyp of colonial hydrozoans.

**Desiccation** loss of water, or drying out.

**Detritivore** an animal that feeds on dead or decaying organic matter.

**Detritus** organic debris derived from decomposing organisms which provides a food source for a large number of organisms.

**Deuterostome** a member of a major branch of multicellular animals (the others are PROTOSTOMES). The mouth is formed as a secondary opening and the original embryonic blastopore becomes the anus. The embryo undergoes radial cleavage, the body cavity (ENTEROCOEL) arises as a pouch from the ENDODERM, and the central nervous system is dorsal.

**Devonian** a geological period from some 417 to 354 million years ago.

**Dextral** of spirally coiled gastropod shells in which, as is usual, the whorls rise to the right and the aperture is on the right where the shell is viewed from the side.

**Diatom** a single-celled alga, a component of the PHYTOPLANKTON.

**Dimorphism** the presence of two distinct forms, e.g. in color or size, in a species or population.

**Dioecious** having separate sexes.

**Diploblastic** a multicellular animal having a body composed of two distinct cellular layers, the ECTODERM and ENDODERM.

**Dispersal** the movement of individuals away from their previous home range, often as they approach maturity.

**Display** a relatively conspicuous pattern of behavior that conveys specific information to others, usually involving visual elements.

**Dinoflagellate** a unicellular member of the PHYTOPLANKTON characterized by the possession of two FLAGELLA, one directed posteriorly, the other lying at right angles to the posterior flagellum.

**Diverticulum** (plural -ae) a blind-ending tube forming a side branch of a cavity or passage.

**DNA** deoxyribonucleic acid, a complex molecule, found almost exclusively in chromosomes of plants and animals, whose "double helix" structure contains the hereditary information necessary for an organism to replicate itself.

**Dorsal** situated at or related to, the back of an animal, i.e. the side which is generally directed upwards.

**Dorso-ventral** a plane running from the top to the bottom of an animal, as in a dorso-ventrally flattened horseshoe crab or sea slater.

**Ecology** the study of animal and plant communities in relation to each other and their natural surroundings.

**Ecosystem** an intricate community of organisms within a particular environment,

interacting with one another and with the environment in which they live.

**Ectoderm (is)** the superficial or outer germ layer of a multicellular embryo which mainly develops into the skin, nervous tissue and excretory organs.

**Ectoparasite** a parasite which lives on the outside of its host and may be permanently attached or only come into contact with the host when feeding or reproducing.

**Elongate** relatively long in comparison with width.

**Endemic** confined to a given region, such as an island or country.

**Endocuticle** the inner layer of the crustacean CUTICLE which is composed of CHITIN.

**Endoderm (is)** the innermost of the three germ layers in the early embryo of most animals, developing into, for example, in jellyfishes the lining of the ENTERON or, in many animals, the GUT lining.

**Endoparasite** a parasite that lives permanently within its host's tissues (except for some reproductive or larval stages). Often there are primary and SECONDARY HOSTS for different stages of the life cycle. Endo-parasites are typically highly specialized.

**Endoskeleton** an internal skeleton, as in echinoderms and vertebrates.

**Enterocoelom** a COELOM that is thought to have arisen from cavities in the sacs of the MESODERM of the embryo.

**Enteron** the body cavity of cnidarians which is lined with ENDODERM and opens to the exterior via a single opening, the mouth.

**Epibenthic** living on the seabed between low water mark and some 200m (670ft) depth.

**Epicuticle** the outer layer of the crustacean CUTICLE, a thin, non-chitinous protective layer.

**Epidermis** the outer tissue layer of the epithelium.

**Epithelium** a sheet or tube of cells lining cavities and vessels and covering exposed body surfaces.

**Epizoic** a sedentary animal which is attached to the exterior of another animal but is not parasitic, i.e. is epizoic.

**Esophagus** part of the foregut of certain invertebrates connecting the pharynx with the stomach or crop and concerned with the passage of food along the gut.

**Eukaryote** a cell, or organism possessing cells, in which the nuclear material is separated from the CYTOPLASM by a nuclear membrane and the genetic material is borne on a number of chromosomes consisting of DNA and protein; the unit of structure in all organisms except bacteria and blue-green algae.

**Exoskeleton** the skeleton covering the outside of the body, or situated in the skin.

**Extracellular digestion** digestion of food within an organism but not within its constituent cells.

**Family** a rank used in the classification of organisms, consisting of a number of similar GENERA (or sometimes only one). Similar families are grouped into an ORDER. In zoological classifications the name of the family usually ends in -idae.

**Fibril** a small fiber, or subdivision of a fiber; used as contractile ORGANELLES in protozoans.

**Filamentous** a type of structure, e.g. a crustacean GILL, in which the branches are thread-like, but not sub-branched, and are arranged in several series along the central axis.

**Filter feeding** a form of SUSPENSION FEEDING in which food particles are extracted from the surrounding water by filtering. Filtering requires the setting up of a water current usually by means of CILIA, with mucus being used to trap particles and sometimes to filter them from the surrounding water.

**Fission** see BINARY FISSION. Flagellum (plural flagella) a fine, long thread, moving in a lashing or undulating fashion, projecting from a cell.

**Flame cell** the hollow, cup-shaped cell lying at the inner end of a protonephridium, important in the excretory system of some invertebrates. The inner end bears FLAGELLA whose beating causes body fluids to enter the NEPHRIDIUM.

**Fragmentation** a form of SEXUAL REPRODUCTION in which an organism produces eggs in SEGMENTS of its body, which then break off and themselves split after leaving the host body, allowing the eggs to develop eventually into new organisms.

**Free-living** having an independent lifestyle, not directly dependent on another organism for survival.

**Funnel** part of the molluskan "foot" in cephalopods responsible for respiratory currents to the CTENIDIA and for jet propulsion.

**Gamete** a female (ovum) or male (spermatozoan) reproductive cell whose nucleus and often CYTOPLASM fuses with another gamete, so constituting fertilization.

**Gametocyte** a cell which undergoes MEIOSIS to form GAMETES; an oocyte forms an ovum (female gamete) and a spermatocyte forms a spermatozoan (male gamete).

**Ganglion** a small discrete collection of nervous tissue containing numerous cell bodies. The nervous system of most invertebrates consists largely of such ganglia connected by nerve cords and which may be concentrated into a cerebral ganglion constituting the "brain."

**Gastrozooid** a type of individual POLYP in colonial hydrozoans which captures and ingests prey.

**Gemmule** a mass of sponge cells which acts as a resting stage under adverse conditions and is composed of amoebocytes surrounded by two membranes in which SPICULES are embedded.

**Gene** the unit of the material of inheritance, a short length of chromosome and the set of characters which it influences in a particular way.

**Generalist** an animal not specialized, not adapted to a particular niche; may be found in a variety of habitats.

**Genus** a rank used in classifying organisms, consisting of similar SPECIES (in some cases only one species). Similar genera are grouped into FAMILIES.

**Gill** the respiratory organ of aquatic animals.

**Gill book** a type of gill, possessed by e.g. horseshoe crabs, formed by the five posterior pairs of appendages on the OPISTHOSOMA.

**Gizzard** part of the alimentary canal where food is broken up, preceding main digestion. In crustaceans its walls bear hard "teeth."

**Gonoduct** the duct through which sperm and eggs are released into the surrounding water.

**Gut** the alimentary canal -a tube concerned with digestion and absorption of food. In most animals there are two openings (cnidarians and flatworms have only one), the mouth into which food is taken and the anus from which material is ejected.

**Hemal system** a tubular system of undecided function found in echinoderms.

**Hemocoel** the major secondary body cavity of arthropods and mollusks which is filled with blood. Unlike the COELOM it does not communicate with the exterior and does not contain germ cells. However, body organs lie within or are suspended in the hemocoel. It functions in the transport and storage of many essential materials.

**Herbivore** animal that feeds on plants.

**Hermaphrodite** an animal producing both male and female GAMETES; among unisexual animals hermaphrodites may occur as aberrations.

**Hermatypic** of corals, reef-building corals with commensal zooanthellae.

**Heterotrophic** heterotrophic organisms are unable to synthesize their own food substances from inorganic material, therefore they require a supply of organic material as a food source. They include all animals, all fungi, most bacteria and a few flowering plants.

**Hibernation** dormancy in winter.

**Holoplankton** organisms in which the whole life cycle is spent in the PLANKTON.

**Host** see INTERMEDIATE HOST; PRIMARY HOST: SECONDARY HOST.

**Hybrid** a plant or animal resulting from a cross between parents that are genetically different, usually from two different species.

**Hydrostatic skeleton** a fluid-filled cavity enclosed by a body wall which acts as a skeleton against which the muscles can act.

**Hyperparasite** (verb hyperparasitize) an organism which is a parasite upon another parasite.

**Infusariiform** a larval stage of mesozoans produced in members of the order Dicyemida by the hermaphrodite RHOMBOGEN generation, and in the order Orthonectida by free-living males and females and reinfecting the host.

**Inorganic material** material not derived from living or dead animals or plants, carbon atoms being absent from the molecular structure.

**Intermediate host** an organism that plays host to parasitic larvae before they mature sexually in the final or definitive host.

**Interstitial** living in the spaces between SUBSTRATE particles.

**Intracellular digestion** digestion of food within the cell.

**Introduction** a species which has settled in lands where it does not occur naturally as a result of human activities.

**Invertebrate** an animal which is not a member of the subphylum vertebrata of the Chordata, i.e. it lacks a skull surrounding a well-developed brain and does not have a skeleton of bone or cartilage.

**Isogamy** (adjective isogamous) a condition in which the GAMETES produced by a species are similar, i.e. not differentiated into male and female.

**Jurassic** a geological period that extended from about 206 to 144 million years ago.

**Keratin** a tough, fibrous protein rich in sulfur, the outer layer of the CUTICLE of nematode worms is keratinized.

**Kinety** in ciliate protozoans, a row of kinetosomes and FIBRILS; from kinetosomes arise CILIA, the fibrils linking each kinetosome in a longitudinal row.

**Kingdom** the uppermost rank of classification dividing bacteria and blue-green algae, algae, plants, fungi, protista and animals into their respective kingdoms.

**Lacunae** minute spaces in invertebrate tissue containing fluid.

**Larva** a general term for a distinct pre-adult form into which most invertebrates hatch from the egg and which may develop directly into adult form or into another larval form.

**Lymph** an intercellular body fluid drained by lymph vessels; contains all the constituents of blood plasma except the protein, and varying numbers of cells.

**Macronucleus** one of two nuclei found in ciliate protozoans.

**Macrophagous** diet of pieces which are large relative to the size of animal; feeding usually occurs at intervals

**Madreporite** a delicate, perforated sieve plate through which seawater may be drawn into the WATER VASCULAR SYSTEM of echinoderms: may be internal (e.g. sea cucumbers) or prominent external convex disk (starfishes).

**Malpighian tubule/gland** a tubular excretory gland which opens into the front of the hindgut of insects, arachnids, myriapods, and water bears.

**Mandible** the paired appendages behind the mouth of crustaceans and uniramians, used in biting and chewing, and having grinding and biting surfaces.

**Mantle** a fold of skin covering all or part of the body of mollusks; its outer edge secretes the shell.

**Mantle cavity** the cavity between the body and MANTLE of a mollusk, containing the feeding and/or respiratory organs.

**Maxilla** paired head appendages of crustaceans and uniramians which are located behind the MANDIBLES on the fifth segment. They act as accessory feeding appendages.

**Maxilliped** the first one, two or three pairs of thoracic limbs of malocostracan crustaceans which have turned forward and become adapted as accessory feeding appendages rather than being involved in locomotion.

**Maxillule** paired head appendages of crustaceans and uniramians which are located on segment six behind the MAXILLAE. They also function in the manipulation of food.

**Medusa** the free-swimming sexual stage of the cnidarian life cycle, produced by the asexual BUDDING POLYPS.

**Megalopa** a postlarval stage of brachyuran crustaceans in which, unlike the adult (e.g. crab), the abdomen is large, unflexed and bears the full number of appendages.

**Meiosis** cell division whereby the DNA complement is halved in the daughter cells. Compare MITOSIS.

**Meroplankton** organisms passing part of their life cycle in the PLANKTON, usually the larval forms of BENTHIC animals. Compare HOLOPLANKTON.

**Merozoite** a stage in the life cycle of some parasitic protozoans which enters red blood corpuscles of the host.

**Mesenchyme** embryonic connective tissue consisting of scattered, irregularly branching cells in a jelly-like matrix; gives rise to connective tissue, bone, cartilage, blood.

**Mesoderm** the cell layer of TRIPLO-BLASTIC animals that develops into tissues lying between the ENDODERM and ECTODERM.

**Mesogloea** the layer of jelly-like material between the ECTODERM and ENDODERM of cnidarians (Jellyfishes etc.)

**Mesozoic** a geological era ranging from 248 to 65 million years ago, comprising the TRIASSIC, JURASSIC, and CRETACEOUS systems.

**Metabolic rate** the rate at which the chemical processes within an organism take place.

**Metameric** having many similar SEGMENTS constituting the body.

**Metamorphosis** the period of rapid transformation of an animal from larval to adult form, often involving destruction of larval tissues and major changes in morphology.

**Metazoan** an animal, as in the vast majority of invertebrates, whose body consists of many cells in contrast to PROTOZOANS which are unicellular; a member of the subkingdom Metazoa.

**Microfilaria** the larval form of filaroid nematode worm parasites found in the SECONDARY HOST, usually mosquitoes.

**Microflora** microscopic bacteria occurring in the soil.

**Microhabitat** the particular parts of the habitat that are encountered by an individual in the course of its activities.

**Micronucleus** one of two nuclei found in the protozoan ciliates, the smaller micronucleus provides the gametes during conjugation. See MACRONUCLEUS.

**Microphagous diet** a diet of pieces of food which are minute relative to the animal's own size; feeding occurs continually.

**Microtubule** a very small long, hollow cylindrical vessel conveying liquids within a cell.

**Miracidium** a ciliated larva of flukes which emerges from eggs passed out with the feces of the vertebrate host and parasitizes snails, where it reproduces asexually.

**Mitosis** cell division in which daughter cells replicate exactly the chromosome pattern of the parent cell, unlike meiosis.

**Molt** periodic shedding of the arthropod EXOSKELETON. Possession of a hardened

exoskeleton prevents continuous growth until the adult stage is reached. Molting occurs under hormonal control after the secretion of a new and larger CUTICLE. An increase in size occurs during the short period prior to the hardening of the new cuticle, involving water or air uptake into the internal spaces. New tissue then grows into these spaces after the hardening of the new cuticle, i.e. between molts.

**Monoblastic** organisms having a single cell layer (e.g. sponges).

**Monophyletic** descended from a common ancestor. Some scientists hold a monophyletic view of arthropods, while others recognize several phyla of jointed-limbed invertebrates with separate evolutionary origins.

**Morphology** the structure and shape of an organism.

**Multicellular** composed of a large number of cells.

**Myotome** a block of muscle, one of a series along the body of a lancelet, sea squirt larva, or vertebrate.

**Natural selection** the mechanism of evolutionary change suggested by Charles Darwin, whereby organisms with character-istics which enhance the chance of survival in the environment in which they live are more likely to survive and produce more offspring with the same characteristics than organisms without those characteristics, or with other less advantageous characteristics.

**Nauplius** the first larval stage of some crustaceans which is divided into three segments each possessing a pair of jointed limbs that develop into the adult's two pairs of antennae and the mandibles. The nauplius uses its limbs in feeding and locomotion.

**Nekton** aquatic organisms, such as fish, which, unlike the smaller PLANKTON, can maintain their position in the water column and move against local currents.

**Nematocyst** the characteristic stinging ORGANELLE of cnidarians (e.g. jellyfishes) located particularly on the tentacles. A short process at one end of the ovoid cell (cnido-blast) containing the nematocyst acts as a trigger opening the lid-like OPERCULUM. Water entering the cnidoblast swells the nematocyst, a long thread-like tube coiled up inside. The nematocyst discharges, ensnaring prey in its barbed coils or releasing poison down the tube into the victim.

**Nematogen** the first and subsequent early generations of certain mesozoans (order Dicyemida), parasites of immature cephalopods.

**Nephridiopore** the pore by which a NEPHRIDIUM opens into the external environment.

**Nephridium** an excretory tubule opening to the exterior via a pore (nephridiopore). The inner end of the tubule may be blind, ending in FLAME CELLS or it may open into the COELOM via a ciliated funnel.

**Nerve cord** a solid strand of nervous tissue forming part of the central nervous system of invertebrates

**Niche** the position of a species within the community, defined in terms of all aspects of its lifestyle.

**Nocturnal** awake and active by night,

particularly of animals which hunt for food by night.

**Notochord** a row of vacuolated cells forming a skeletal rod lying lengthwise between the central nervous system and gut of all CHORDATES.

**Oligomeric/ous** having a few segments constituting the body.

**Omnivore** an animal that feeds on both plant and animal tissue.

**Operculate** the condition of gastropods having an OPERCULUM.

**Operculum** a lid-like structure; the calcareous plate on the top surface of the foot of some gastropods, serving to close the aperture when the animal withdraws into the shell.

**Opisthosoma** the posterior body region of chelicerates which may be segmented in primitive forms but generally has the segments fused.

**Order** a group used in classifying organisms, consisting of a number of similar FAMILIES (sometimes only one family). Similar orders are grouped into a CLASS.

**Ordovician** a geological period extending from about 490 to 443 million years ago.

**Organ** part of an animal or plant which forms a structural and functional unit, e.g. spore, lung.

**Organelle** a persistent structure forming part of a cell, with a specialized function within it analogous to an ORGAN within the whole organism.

**Organic material** material derived from living or dead animals and plants, molecules making up the organisms being based on carbon, the other principle elements being oxygen and hydrogen.

**Osmotic pressure and regulation** osmotic pressure is the force that tends to move water in an osmotic system, i.e. the pressure exerted by a more concentrated solution on one of a lower concentration. The body fluids of a freshwater animal will exert an osmotic pressure on the surrounding aqueous medium, causing water to enter the animal. Osmoregulation is the maintenance of the internal body fluids at a different osmotic pressure from that of the external aqueous environment.

**Osphradium** a patch of sensory EPITHELIUM located on gill membranes of mollusks.

**Paleozoic** a geological era ranging from 543–248 million years ago, comprising the CAMBRIAN, ORDOVICIAN and SILURIAN systems in the older or lower Paleozoic sub-era and the DEVONIAN, CARBONIF-EROUS and PERMIAN systems in the newer or Upper Paleozoic sub-era.

**Palp** an appendage, usually near the mouth, which may be sensory, aid in feeding, or be used in locomotion.

**Papilla** a small protuberance ("little nipple") above a surface

**Parapodium** one of a pair of appendages extending from the sides of the segments of polychaete worms.

**Parthenogenesis** the development of a new individual from an unfertilized egg. It occurs when rapid colonization is important under adverse environmental conditions, or when there is an absence or only a small number of males in the population.

**Pathogen** an agent which causes disease, always parasitic.

**Pedicellariae** minute, pincer-like grooming and defensive structures on the body of sea urchins and starfishes.

**Pedipalp** an appendage borne on the third prosomal segment of chelicerates, sensory or prehensile in horseshoe crabs, adapted for seizing prey in scorpions, and sensory or used by the male in reproduction in spiders.

**Peduncle** a narrow part supporting a longer part, e.g. the muscular stalk by which the body of an endoproct is attached to the SUBSTRATE.

**Pelagic** of organisms or life-styles in the water column, as opposed to the bottom SUBSTRATE.

**Pentamerism** the fivefold RADIAL SYMMETRY typical of echinoderms.

**Pericardial cavity** the cavity within the body containing the heart. In vertebrates a hemococtic space, which is an expanded part of the blood system, supplying blood to the heart.

**Peristalsis** rhythmic waves of contraction passing along tubular organs, particularly the GUT, produced by a layer of smooth muscle.

**Permian** a geological period from 290 to 248 million years ago, marking the end of the PALEOZOIC era.

**Pharynx** part of the alimentary tract or gut behind the mouth, often muscular.

**Pheromone** a chemical substance which when released by an animal influences the behavior or development of other individuals of the same species.

**Photosynthesis** the synthesis of organic compounds, primarily sugars, from carbon dioxide and water using sunlight as a source of energy and chlorophyll or some other related pigment for trapping the light energy.

**Phyletic** concerning evolutionary descent.

**Phylogeny** the evolutionary history or ancestry of a group of organisms.

**Phylum** a major group used in the classification of animals. Consists of one or more CLASSES. Several (sometimes one) phyla make up a KINGDOM.

**Physiology** the study of the processes that occur within living organisms.

**Phytoplankton** microscopic algae that are suspended in surface waters of seas and lakes where there is sufficient light for PHOTOSYNTHESIS to take place.

**Pinnate** of tentacles, GILLS, resembling a feather or compound leaf in structure, with similar parts arranged either side of a central axis.

**Pinnule** a jointed appendage found in large numbers on the arms of crinoids giving a feather-like appearance, hence the name feather star.

**Plankton** drifting or swimming animals and plants, many minute or microscopic, which live freely in the water and are borne by water currents due to their limited powers of locomotion.

**Planula** the free-swimming ciliated larva of cnidarians (Jellyfishes and allies).

**Plasma** the fluid medium of the blood in which highly specialized cells are suspended; mainly water, containing a variety of dissolved substances which are transported from one part of the body to another.

**Plasmodium** the asexual stage of orthonectid mesozoans, resembling the protozoan plasmodium, which divide repeatedly by FISSION, filling the hosts' tissue spaces.

**Pneumostome** the aperture to the lung-like MANTLE CAVITY of pulmonates.

**Polyp** the stage, the most important in the life cycle of most cnidarians, in which the body is typically tubular or cylindrical, the oral end bearing the mouth and tentacles and the opposite end being attached to the SUBSTRATE.

**Polysaccharide** a carbohydrate produced by a combination of many simple sugar or monosaccharide molecules, e.g. starch and CELLULOSE.

**Primary host** the main host of a parasite in which the adult parasite or the sexually mature form is present.

**Proboscis** a tubular organ that may be extended from the mouth of many invertebrates such as moths and butterflies; in ribbon worms, the proboscis can be everted.

**Proglottides** (sing. proglottis) the segments that make up the "body" of a tapeworm. When mature, each proglottis will contain at least one set of reproductive organs.

**Prokaryote** cell having, or organism made of cells having, genetic material in the form of simple filaments of DNA, not separated from the CYTOPLASM by a nuclear membrane (cf. EUKARYOTE). Bacteria and blue-green algae have cells of this type.

**Prosoma** the anterior body region of CHELICERATES, composed of eight SEGMENTS, analogous to the head and THORAX of other arthropods, or the CEPHALOTHORAX of chelicerates. The segments are generally fused and are only distinguishable in the embryo.

**Prostomium** the anterior non-segmental region of annelid worms, bearing the eyes, ANTENNAE and a pair of PALPS; comparable to the head of other phyla.

**Protein** a complex organic compound composed of numerous amino acids joined together by peptide linkages, forming one or more folded chains. The sequence of amino acids is peculiar to a particular protein.

**Protoconch** the first shell of a gastropod which is laid down by the larva.

**Protonephridium** a type of excretory organ in which the tubule usually ends in a FLAME CELL.

**Protostome** a member of one major branch of the multicellular animals (the other, complementary, branch is the DEUTEROSTOMES). The mouth is formed from the embryonic blastopore, the embryo undergoes SPIRAL CLEAVAGE, the body cavity is formed by the MESODERM splitting into two, and the central nervous system is ventral.

**Protozoan** an organism of the phylum Protozoa, Kingdom Protista, differing from animals of the Kingdom Animalia in consisting of one cell only, but resembling them and plants and differing from bacteria in having at least one well-defined nucleus.

**Pseudocoel** the secondary body cavity of roundworms, rotifers, gastrotrichs and endoprocts, between an inner MESODERM layer of the body wall and the ENDODERM of the gut, i.e. it is not a true COELOM.

**Pseudopodium** (plural: -a) a temporary projection of the cell when the fluid endoplasm flows forward inside the stiffer ectoplasm. Occurs during locomotion and feeding.

**Pseudotrachea** a branched TUBULE resulting from intuckings of the CUTICLE of certain terrestrial isopods which acts as a specialized respiratory surface. Pseudo-tracheae resemble the TRACHEAE of uniramians and certain arachnids, although they have evolved independently.

**Pulmonate** having a lung, e.g. certain snails and slugs.

**Pygidium** the terminal, non-segmental region of some invertebrates which bears the anus.

**Radial symmetry** a form of symmetry in which the body consists of a central axis around which similar parts are symmetrically arranged.

**Radula** the "toothed tongue" of mollusks, a horny strip with ridges or "teeth" on its surface which rasp food. Absent in members of the class Bivalvia.

**Ray** a radial division of an echinoderm, e.g. a starfish "arm."

**Redia** a larval type produced asexually by a previous larval stage of flukes (Trematoda). Lives parasitically in snails and reproduces asexually, giving rise to more rediae or to CERCARIAE.

**Reticulopodium** a type of PSEUDO-PODIUM characteristic of the foraminiferans; reticulopodia are thread-like, branched and interconnected.

**Rhombogen** an hermaphrodite form of dicyenid mesozoan derived from a NEMATOGEN when the cephalopod host has reached maturity. It resembles the nematogen morphologically and gives rise to INFUSARIIFORM larvae.

**Rostrum** the anterior plate of the crustacean CARAPACE, present in malacostracans, which extends toward the head and ends in a point.

**Sclerotization** hardening of the arthropod CUTICLE by TANNING.

**Scolex** the head region of a tapeworm, which attaches to the wall of the host's gut by suckers and/or hooks.

**Secondary host** the host in which the larval or resting stages of a parasite are present.

**Sedentary** sedentary organisms, or stages in the life cycle of certain organisms, are permanently attached to a SUBSTRATE; as opposed to FREE-LIVING.

**Segment** a repeating unit of the body which has a structure fundamentally similar to other segments, although certain segments may be grouped together into TAGMATA to perform certain functions, as in the head, THORAX or ABDOMEN.

**Segmentation** the repetition of a pattern of segments along the length of the body, or along an appendage. The similarity between different segments of an animal may be imperfect, particularly the segments forming the head.

**Septum** a portion dividing a tissue or organ into a number of compartments.

**Seta** (plural setae) a bristle-like projection on the invertebrate EPIDERMIS.

**Sexual reproduction** reproduction involving MEIOSIS and fertilization, usually fusion of two GAMETES, one female and one male. See also COPULATION, CONJUGATION, FRAGMENTATION.

**Siliceous** composed of or containing silicate, as in the skeleton of glass sponges (see SPICULES).

**Silurian** a geological era, 443–417 million years ago.

**Sinistral** of gastropod shells, with whorls rising to the left and not as usual to the right (compare DEXTRAL).

**Sinus** a space or cavity in an animal's body.

**Siphon** a tube through which water enters and/or leaves a cavity within the body of an animal, e.g. in mollusks and in sea squirts.

**Solitary** a lifestyle in which an organism exists by itself and not in permanent association with others of the same species.

**Specialist** an organism having special adaptations to a particular habitat or mode of life; its range of habitats or variety of modes of life may thus be limited and, as a result, its evolutionary flexibility also.

**Speciation** the origin of species, the diverging of two like organisms into different forms resulting in new species.

**Species** a taxonomic rank, the lowest commonly used; reproductively an isolated group of interbreeding organisms. Similar species make up a GENUS.

**Spermatophore** a package of sperm produced by males, usually of species in which fertilization is internal but does not involve direct COPULATION. Spermatotheca an organ, usually one of a pair, in a female or hermaphrodite that receives and stores sperm from the male.

**Spicule** a mineral secretion (calcium carbonate or silica) of sponges which forms part of the skeleton of most species and whose structure is of importance in sponge classification.

**Spiral cleavage** a form of embryonic division which occurs in PROTOSTOMES; in the spiral arrangement of cells any one cell is located between the two cells above or below it. In all other many-celled animals, i.e. DEUTEROSTOMES, there is radial CLEAVAGE.

**Spore** a single- or multi-celled reproductive body that becomes detached from its parent and gives rise directly or indirectly to a new individual.

**Sporocyst** a sac-like body formed by the MIRACIDIUM larva of a blood fluke while within the snail, the intermediate host; produces numerous CERCARIAE, over 3,000 per day from a single sporocyst.

**Sporozoite** SPORE produced in certain protozoans which then develops into gametes.

**Statocyst** the balancing organ of a number of invertebrates consisting of a vesicle containing granules of sand or calcium carbonate. These granules move within the vesicle and stimulate sensory cells as the animal moves, so providing information on its position in relation to gravity.

**Stolon** the tubular structure of colonial cnidarian POLYPS that anchors them to the SUBSTRATE and from which the polyps arise.

**Stomodeum** a region of unfolding ECTODERM from which derive the mouth cavity and foregut in many invertebrates.

**Strobila** the "body" of a tapeworm, consisting of a string of segments, through which food is absorbed from the gut of the host.

**Stylet** a small, sharp appendage, for example in water bears used to pierce plant cells.

**Suborder** members of an ORDER forming a group of organisms which differ in some way from the other members but also resemble them in many characteristics.

**Substrate** the surface or sediment on or in which an organism lives.

**Superfamily** a division containing a number of families or a single family differing in some way from other families which are included in the same ORDER.

**Suspension feeding** a feeding mechanism in which small organisms and other matter suspended in the water are removed and consumed.

**Symbiosis** a close and mutually beneficial relationship between individuals of two species.

**Synapse** the site at which one nerve cell is connected to another.

**Tagmata** (sing. tagma) functional body regions of arthropods and annelids consisting of a number of segments; e.g. the head, THORAX and ABDOMEN of crustaceans.

**Tanning** hardening of the arthropod CUTICLE achieved by the cross-linking of the protein chains by arthoquinones, involving also polyphenol and polyphenoloxidase catalysts.

**Taxon** a taxonomic grouping of organisms or the name applied to it.

**Taxonomy** the study of the classification of organisms according to resemblances and differences.

**Tegumental gland** a gland below the EPIDERMIS of the crustacean cuticle. Ducts from the glands convey the constituents of the EPICUTICLE to the cuticle surface during molting, when the new epicuticle is formed.

**Telson** the posterior segment of the arthropod abdomen which is present only embryonically in insects. In certain crustaceans the telson is flattened to form a tail fin which is used in swimming.

**Terrestrial** associated with, or living on the earth or ground.

**Tertiary** the geological period of time from the end of the CRETACEOUS era 65 million years ago to the present time, divided into a number of epochs, the last 1.8 million years sometimes distinguished as the Quaternary Period.

**Test** an external covering or "shell" of an invertebrate, especially sea squirts (tunicates), sea urchins etc; is in fact an internal skeleton just below the EPIDERMIS.

**Thorax** the segmented body region of insects and crustaceans which lies behind the head and which typically bears locomotory appendages. Up to 11 segments are present in crustaceans but only 3 in insects.

**Tissue** a region consisting mainly of cells of the same sort and performing the same function, associated in large numbers and bound together by cell walls (plants) or by intercellular material (animals).

**Torsion** the process of twisting of the body in the larval stage of gastropods.

**Trachea** a cuticle-lined respiratory tubule of uniramians and certain arachnids which is involved in gas exchange. Tracheae open to the exterior via a spiracle which can often be sealed to reduce desiccation. The tracheae are branched and ramify into the tissues, they end in thin-walled, blind-ending tracheoles within the cells.

**Triassic** a geological period extending from 248 to 206 million years ago, marking the beginning of the MESOZOIC era.

**Trichocyst** rod-like or oval ORGANELLE in the ECTODERM of protozoans which may discharge a long thread on contact with prey.

**Trochophore** an oval or pear-shaped, free-swimming, planktonic larval form of organisms from different phyla, including segmented worms and mollusks.

**Tube feet or podia** hollow, extensive appendages of echinoderins connected to the WATER VASCULAR SYSTEM that may have suckers, or serve as stilt-like limbs or be ciliated to waft food particles toward the mouth.

**Tubule** long hollow cylinder within a cell, normally for conveying or holding liquids.

**Tunicin, tunic** a form of CELLULOSE, the main constituent in the fibrous matrix forming the tunic or TEST of sea squirts.

**Unicellular** an organism composed of only a single cell.

**Uniramian** a member of the phylum Uniramia which includes the insects, centipedes and millipedes. They possess a single pair of antennae, and mandibles. The appendages are basically unbranched or UNIRAMOUS in contrast to those of crustaceans.

**Uniramous** condition describing an arthropod limb which is not branched and is found in insects and myripods (hence the Uniramia) and chelicerates. Some crustacean limbs are secondarily uniramous where one of the branches of the BIRAMOUS limb has been lost.

**Urogenital tract** ducts and tubules common to the genital and urinary systems voiding via a common aperture.

**Uropod** flattened extension of the sixth abdominal appendage of malacostracan crustaceans which together with the flattened TELSON form a tail fin used in swimming.

**Vacuole** a fluid-filled space within the CYTOPLASM of a cell, bounded by a membrane.

**Valve** in bivalves, one half of the two-valved shell.

**Vascular** containing vessels which conduct fluid – in animals usually blood, as in the vasculariized MANTLE CAVITY of pulmonate snails.

**Veliger** a free-swimming larval form of mollusks possessing a VELUM; develops from a TROCHOPHORE; foot, mantle, shell and other adult organs are present.

**Velum** the veil-like ciliated lobe of the VELIGER larva, used in swimming; also the inward-projecting margin of the umbrella in most hydrozoan medusae.

**Ventral** situated at, or related to, the lower bottom side or surface.

**Vermiform** a worm-like larval stage of dicyenid mesozoans formed within the axial cells of the NEMATOGEN generation, or generally meaning worm-like.

**Vertebrate** an organism which belongs to the subphylum Vertebrata (Craniata) of the phylum Chordata; differs from other chordates and invertebrates in having a skull which surrounds a well-developed brain, and a skeleton of cartilage and bone.

**Water vascular system** or **ambulacral system** a system of canals and appendages of the body wall that is unique to echinoderms, derived from the coelom and used, e.g. in locomotion in starfishes.

**Zoea** a planktonic larval form of some decapod crustaceans which possesses a segmented THORAX, a CARAPACE and at least three pairs of BIRAMOUS thoracic appendages. In contrast to the antennal propulsion of the NAUPLIUS these thoracic appendages are used in locomotion. The abdominal pleopods appear but are not functional until the postlarval stage.

**Zoochlorella** a symbiotic green alga of the Chloroplyceae which occurs in the amoebocytes of certain freshwater sponges, the gastrodermal cells of some hydra species and the jelly-like connective tissue (parenchyme) of certain turbellarian flatworms.

**Zooid** a member of a colony of animals which are joined together; may be specialized for certain functions.

**Zoospore** a motile spore which swims by means of a flagellum, is produced by some unicellular animals and algae, and is a means of ASEXUAL REPRODUCTION.

**Zooplankton** small or minute animals that live freely in the water column of seas and lakes and consists of adult PELAGIC animals or the larval forms of pelagic and some BENTHIC animals; most are motile, but the water movements determine their position in the water column.

**Zygote** a fertilized ovum before it undergoes cleavage.

## SEA MAMMALS

**Adaptive radiation** the pattern in which different species develop from a common ancestor (as distinct from convergent evolution process whereby species from different origins become similar in response to the same SELECTIVE PRESSURES).

**Amphipod** a CRUSTACEAN of the invertebrate order amphipoda. Includes many freshwater and marine shrimps.

**Antarctic** Convergence the region between 50–55°S where the antarctic surface water slides beneath the less-dense southward-flowing subantarctic water.

**Aquatic** living chiefly in water.

**Baleen** a horny substance, commonly known as whalebone, growing as plates from the upper jaws of whales of the suborder Mysticeti, and forming a fringe-like sieve for extraction of plankton from seawater

**Bends** the colloquial name for caisson disease, a condition produced by pressure changes in the blood as a diving mammal surfaces. Too rapid an ascent results in nitrogen dissolved in the blood forming bubbles which cause excruciating pain.

**Benthic** the bottom layer of the marine environment.

**Biotic community** a naturally occurring group of plants and animals in the same environment.

**Blowhole** the opening of the nostril(s) of a whale, situated on the animal's head, from which the "spout" or "blow" is produced.

**Blubber** a layer of fat beneath the skin, well developed in whales.

**Breaching** leaping clear of the water.

**Cecum** a blind sac in the digestive tract of a mammal, at the junction between the small and large intestines.

**Cephalopod** a member of an order of mollusks including such marine invertebrates as squid, octopus, and cuttlefish.

**Cerebral cortex** the surface layer of cells (gray matter) covering the main part of the brain, consisting of the cerebral hemispheres.

**Cetacea** mammalian order comprising whales, dolphins and porpoises.

**Chromatin** materials in the chromosomes of living cells containing the genes and proteins.

**Clavicle** the collar-bone

**Copepod** a small marine CRUSTACEAN of the invertebrate order Copepoda.

**Crustaceans** members of a class within the phylum Arthropoda typified by five pairs of legs, two pairs of antennae, head and thorax joined, and calcareous deposits in the exoskeleton, e.g. crayfish, crabs, shrimps.

**Cyamids** amphipod CRUSTACEANS of the family Cyamidae that parasitize the skin of the whales; hence the popular name "whale lice."

**Dentition** the arrangement of teeth characteristic of a particular species.

**Discontinuous distribution** geographical distribution of a species that is marked by gaps.

**Dispersal** the movements of animals, often as they reach maturity, away from their previous home range (equivalent to EMIGRATION). Distinct from dispersion, that is, the pattern in which things (perhaps animals, food supplies, nest sites) are distributed or scattered.

**Display** any relatively conspicuous pattern of behavior that conveys specific information to others, usually to members of the same species; can involve visual and/or vocal elements, as in threat, courtship or "greeting" displays.

**Dominant** see HIERARCHY.

**Dorsal** on the upper or top side or surface (e.g. dorsal fin).

**Echolocation** the process of perception, often direction finding, based upon reaction to the pattern of reflected sound waves (echoes).

**Ecology** the study of plants and animals in relation to their natural environmental setting. Each species may be said to occupy a distinctive ecological NICHE.

**Ecosystem** a unit of the environment within which living and non-living elements interact.

**Emigration** departure of animal(s), usually at or about the time of reaching adulthood, from the group or place of birth.

**Esophagus** the gullet connecting the mouth with the stomach.

**Estrus** the period in the estrous cycle of female mammals at which they are often attractive to males and receptive to mating. The period coincides with the maturation of eggs and ovulation (the release of mature eggs from the ovaries). Animals in estrus are often said to be "on heat" or "in heat."

**Family** a taxonomic division subordinate to an order and superior to a genus (see TAXONOMY).

**Fast ice** sea ice which forms in polar regions along the coast, and remains fast, being attached to the shore, to an ice wall, an ice front, or over shoals, generally in the position where it originally formed.

**Fin** an organ projecting from the body of aquatic animals and generally used in steering and propulsion.

**Flense** to strip blubber from a whale or seal.

**Flipper** a limb adapted for swimming.

**Floe** a sheet of floating ice.

**Fluke** one of the lobes of a whale's tail; the name refers to their broad triangular shape.

**Generalist** an animal whose lifestyle does not involve highly specialized stratagems (cf. SPECIALIST); for example, feeding on a variety of foods which may require different foraging techniques.

**Genus** (plural genera) a taxonomic division superior to species and subordinate to family (see TAXONOMY).

**Gestation** the period of development within the uterus.

**Glands** (marking) specialized glandular areas of the skin, used in depositing SCENT MARKS.

**Harem group** a social group consisting of a single adult male, at least two adult females and immature animals; the most common pattern of social organization among mammals.

**Hemoglobin** an iron-containing protein in the red corpuscles which plays a crucial role in oxygen exchange between blood and tissues in mammals.

**Herbivore** an animal eating mainly plants or parts of plants.

**Hierarchy** (social or dominance) the existence of divisions within society, based on the outcome of interactions which show some individuals to be consistently dominant to others. Higher-ranking individuals thus have control of aspects (e.g. access to food or mates) of the life and behavior of low-ranking ones. Hierarchies may be branching, but simple linear ones are often called peck orders (after the behavior of farmyard chickens).

**Home range** the area in which an animal normally lives (generally excluding rare excursions or migrations), irrespective of whether or not the area is defended from other animals (cf. TERRITORY).

**Hydrophone** a water-proof microphone held in position under the sea surface and used to detect the sounds emitted by sea mammals.

**Juvenile** no longer possessing the characteristics of an infant, but not yet fully adult.

**Krill** shrimp-like CRUSTACEANS of the genera Euphausia, Meganyctiphanes etc. occurring in very great numbers in polar seas, particularly of Antarctica, where they form the principal prey of baleen whales.

**Lactation** (verb: lactate) the secretion of milk from MAMMARY GLANDS.

**Laminar flow** streamline flow in a viscous fluid near a solid boundary : the flow of water over the surface of whales is laminar.

**Lead** a channel of open water between ice floes.

**Lob-tailing** a whale beating the water with its tail FLUKES, perhaps to communicate with other whales.

**Lumbar** a term locating anatomical features in the loin region, e.g. lumbar vertebrae are at the base of the spine.

**Mammal** a member of a CLASS of VERTEBRATE animals having MAMMARY GLANDS producing milk with which they nurse their young (properly: Mammalia).

**Mammary glands** glands of female mammals that secrete milk.

**Marine** living in the sea.

**Metabolic rate** the rate at which the chemical processes of the body occur.

**Migration** movement, usually seasonal, from one region or climate to another for purposes of feeding or breeding.

**Monogamy** a mating system in which individuals have only one mate per breeding season.

**Myoglobin** a protein related to HEMOGLOBIN, found in the muscles of vertebrates; like hemoglobin, it is involved in the oxygen exchange processes of respiration.

**Mysticete** a member of the suborder Mysticeti, whales with baleen plates rather than teeth as their feeding apparatus.

**Natural selection** the process whereby individuals with the most appropriate ADAPTATIONS are more successful than other individuals, and hence survive to produce more offspring. To the extent that the successful traits are heritable (genetic), they will therefore spread in the population.

**Niche** the role of a species within the community, defined in terms of all aspects of its lifestyle (e.g. food, competitors, predators, and other resource requirements).

**Odontocete** a member of the suborder Odontoceti, the toothed whales.

**Olfaction, olfactory** the olfactory sense is the sense of smell, depending on receptors located in the epithelium (surface membrane) lining the nasal cavity.

**Opportunist** (of feeding) flexible behavior of exploiting circumstances to take a wide range of food items. See GENERALIST; SPECIALIST.

**Order** a taxonomic division subordinate to class and superior to family (see TAXONOMY).

**Pack ice** large blocks of ice formed on the surface of the sea when an ice field has been broken up by wind and waves, and drifted from its original position.

**Pelagic** the upper part of the open sea, above the BENTHIC zone.

**Pelvis** a girdle of bones that supports the hindlimbs of vertebrates.

**Phytoplankton** minute plants floating near the surface of aquatic environments (cf. ZOOPLANKTON).

**Pod** a group of individuals, usually applied to whales, with some, at least temporary, cohesive social structure.

**Polygamous** a mating system wherein an individual has more than one mate per breeding season.

**Polygynous** a mating system in which a male mates with several females during one breeding season (as opposed to polyandrous, where one female mates with several males).

**Population** a more or less separate (discrete) group of animals of the same species within a given BIOTIC COMMUNITY.

**Predator** an animal which forages for live prey; hence "anti-predator behavior" describes the evasive actions of the prey.

**Promiscuous** a mating system wherein an individual mates more or less indiscriminately.

**Purse seine** a fishing net, the bottom of which can be closed by cords, operated usually from boats (cf. SEINE).

**Radio-tracking** a technique used for monitoring an individual's movements remotely; it involves affixing a radio transmitter to the animal and thereafter receiving a signal through directional antennae, which enables the subject's position to be plotted. The transmitter is often attached to a collar, hence "radio-collar."

**Receptive** state of a female mammal ready to mate or in ESTRUS.

**Reduced** (anatomical) of relatively small dimension (e.g. of certain bones, by comparison with those of an ancestor or related animals).

**Reproductive rate** the rate of production of offspring; the net productive rate may be defined as the average number of female offspring produced by each female during her entire lifetime.

**Rorqual** one of the six species of baleen whales of the genus Balaenoptera.

**Rostrum** a forward-directed process at the front of the skull of some whales and dolphins, forming a beak.

**Scent gland** an organ secreting odorous material with communicative properties: see SCENT MARK.

**Scent mark** a site where the secretions of scent glands or urine or feces are deposited and which has communicative significance. Often left regularly at traditional sites which are also visually conspicuous. Also the "chemical message" left by this means; and (verb) to leave such a deposit.

**Seasonality** (of births) the restriction of births to a particular time of the year.

**Seine** a fishing net with floats at the top and weights at the bottom, used for encircling fish.

**Selective pressure** a factor affecting the reproductive success of individuals (whose success will depend on their fitness, i.e. the extent to which they are adapted to thrive under that selective pressure).

**Sinus** a cavity in bone or tissue.

**Sirenia** an order of herbivorous aquatic mammals, comprising the manatees and dugong.

**Solitary** living on its own, as opposed to social or group-living in lifestyle.

**Sonar** sound used in connection with navigation (SOund NAvigation Ranging).

**Specialist** an animal whose lifestyle involves highly specialized stratagems: e.g. feeding with one technique on a particular food.

**Species** a taxonomic division subordinate to genus and superior to subspecies. In general a species is a group of animals similar in structure and which are able to breed and produce viable offspring. See TAXONOMY.

**Subfamily** a division of a FAMILY.

**Suborder** a subdivision of an order.

**Subordinate** see HIERARCHY.

**Subspecies** a recognizable subpopulation of a single species, typically with a distinct geographical distribution.

**Taxonomy** the science of classifying organisms. It is very convenient to group together animals which share common features and are thought to have common descent. Each individual is thus a member of a series of ever-broader categories (individual–species–genus–family–order–class–phylum) and each of these can be further divided where it is convenient (e.g. subspecies, superfamily or infraorder). The SPECIES is a convenient unit in that it links animals according to an obvious criterion, namely that they interbreed successfully. However, the unit on which NATURAL SELECTION operates is the individual: it is by the differential reproductive success of individuals bearing different characteristics that evolutionary change proceeds.

**Territory** an area defended from intruders by an individual or group. Originally the term was used where ranges were exclusive and obviously defended at their borders. A more general definition of territoriality allows some overlap between neighbors by defining territoriality as a system of spacing wherein home ranges do not overlap randomly – that is, the location of one individual, or group's home range influences that of others.

**Ungulate** a hoofed mammal, e.g. deer, cattle, horses, elephants.

**Upwelling** an upward movement of ocean currents, resulting from convection, causing an upward movement of nutrients and hence an increase in plankton populations.

**Ventral** on the lower or bottom side or surface: thus ventral or abdominal glands occur on the underside of the abdomen.

**Vertebrate** an animal with a backbone; a division of the phylum Chordata which includes animals with notochords (as distinct from invertebrates).

**Vestigial** a characteristic with little or no contemporary use, but derived from one which was useful and well-developed in an ancestral form.

**Zooplankton** minute animals living near the surface of the sea (cf. PHYTOPLANKTON).

# Bibliography

The following list of titles indicates key reference works used in the preparation of this volume, and those recommended for further reading.

Adouette, A., Balavoine, G., Lartillot, N., Lespinet, O., Prud'homme, B. and de Rosa, R. (2000) The new animal phylogeny: Reliability and implications. In: *PNAS* 97, 9 (25 April), pp. 4453–4456.

Alexander, R. McN. (1979) *The Invertebrates.* Cambridge University Press, Cambridge.

Allen, T. B. (2001) *Shark Attacks: Their Causes and Avoidance.* Lyons Press, New York.

Amlacher, E (1970) *A Textbook of Fish Diseases.* T.F.H. Publications, Inc., Neptune City, New Jersey.

Anon (1986) *Sharks: Silent Hunters of the Deep.* Reader's Digest.

Baker, M. L. (1987) *Whales, Dolphins and Porpoises of the World.* Garden City, New York.

Banister, K. and Campbell, A. (eds.) (1985) *The Encyclopedia of Underwater Life.* George Allen & Unwin.

Barnes, R. S. K., Calow, P. and Olive, P. J. W. (1993) *The Invertebrates – a New Synthesis* (2nd edition). Blackwell Scientific Publications, Oxford.

Barrington, E. J. W. (1982) *The Invertebrate Structure and Function*, Van Nostrand Reinhold, New York.

Berta, A. and Sumich, J. L. (1999) *Marine Mammals: Evolutionary Biology.* Academic Press, London.

Bliss, D. E. (ed.) (1982) *The Biology of the Crustacea, vols 1–10.* Academic Press, London and New York.

Bond, C. E. (1979) *Biology of Fishes.* Saunders College Publishing.

Bonner, W. N. and Berry, R. J. (eds.) (1981) *Ecology in the Antarctic.* Academic Press, London.

Boyd, I. L. (ed.) (1979) *Marine Mammals: Advances in Behavioural and Population Biology.* Oxford University Press, Oxford.

Bright, M. (2002) *Sharks.* Natural History Museum, London.

Bryden, M. M., Marsh, H. & Shaughnessy, P (1999) *Dugongs, Whales, Dolphins, and Seals: A Guide to the Sea Mammals of Australasia.* Allen & Unwin, Sydney.

Brusca, R.C. and Brusca, P. J. (2002) *Invertebrates* (2nd edition) Sinauer Associates, Inc., Sunderland, Massachusetts.

Campbell, A. C. (1982) *The Hamlyn Guide to the Flora and Fauna of the Mediterranean Sea*, Hamlyn, London.

Campbell, A. C. (1984) *The Country Life Guide to the Sea Shores and Shallow Seas of Britain and Europe*, Country Life Books, London.

Carwardine, M. (1998) *Whales and Dolphins.* HarperCollins, New York.

Carwardine, M., Harrison, P. & Bryden, M. (eds.) (1999) *Whales, Dolphins and Porpoises* (2nd edition). Checkmark Books, New York.

Compagno, L. J. V. (1989) *FAO Species Catalogue Vol. 4: Sharks of the World. Part 1: Hexanchiformes to Lamniformes.* FAO, Rome, Italy.

Compagno, L. J. V. (1984) *FAO Species Catalogue Vol. 4: Sharks of the World. Part 2: Carcharhiniformes.* FAO, Rome, Italy,

Corbera, J., Sabetés, A. and García-Rubies, A. (1996) *Peces de Mar de la Península Ibérica.* Planeta, S.A., Madrid.

Dawes, J., (1991) *Livebearing Fishes: A Guide to Their Aquarium Care, Biology and Classification.* Blandford, London.

Dawes, J., Lim, L. L., and Cheong, L. (eds.) (1999) *The Dragon Fish.* Kingdom Books.

Ellis, R. (1989) *The Book of Sharks.* Grosset and Dunlap.

Evans, P. G. H. (1987) *The Natural History of Whales and Dolphins.* Christopher Helm, London.

Fontaine, P.-H. (1998) *Whales of the North Atlantic: Biology and Ecology.* Editions MultiMondes, Sainte-Foy, Quebec.

Fretter, V. and Graham, A. (1976) *A Functional Anatomy of Invertebrates*, Academic Press, London, New York, San Francisco.

Gaskin, D.E. (1982) *Whales, Dolphins and Seals.* Heinemann Educational Books, London.

Harrison Matthews, L. (1978) *The Natural History of the Whale.* Weidenfeld & Nicolson, London.

Helfman, G. S. , Collette B. B., and Facey, D. E. (1997) *The Diversity of Fishes.* Blackwell Scientific Publications, Oxford.

Hennemann, R. M. (2001) *Sharks & Rays - Elasomobranch Guide of the World.* IKAN Unterwasserarchiv.

Herman, L. M (1980) *Cetacean Behavior: Mechanisms and Functions.* John Wiley & Sons, Chichester.

Hieronimus, H. (2002) *All Rainbows and Related Families.*Verlag A.C.S. GmbH.

Kedera, H., Igarashi, T., Kuroiwa N., Maeda, H., Mitani, S., Mori, E., and Yamasaki, K., (1994) *Jurassic Fishes.* T.F.H. Publications, Inc., Neptune City, New Jersey.

Kempkes, M. and Schäfer, F. (1998) *All Livebearers and Halfbeaks: Guppys, Platys, Mollys* (Verlag A.C.S. GmbH, 1998)

Lawrence, J. (1987) *A Functional Biology of Echinoderms.*Croom Helm, London and Sydney.

Lever, C. (1996) *Naturalized Fishes of the World.* Academic Press

Mann, A. J. and Williams W. D. (19 82) *Textbook of Zoology: Invertebrates*, Macmillan, London.

Mann, J., Connor, R. C., Tyack, P. L. & Whitehead, H. (1999) *Cetacean Socities: Field Studies of Dolphins and Whales.* Chicago University Press, Chicago.

Meffe, G. K. and Snelson, F. F., Jr. (eds.) (1989) *Ecology and Evolution of Livebearing Fishes (Poeciliidae).* Prentice Hall.

Moyle, P. B. and Cech, J. J. (Jr.) (2000) *Fishes: An Introduction to Ichthyology* (4th edition) Prentice-Hall, Inc.

*National Audubon Field Guide to Fishes (North America)* (2nd edition, 2002). Alfred A. Knopf, New York.

*National Audubon Field Guide to North American Fishes, Whales, and Dolphins* (1983). Alfred A Knopf, New York.

*National Audubon Field Guide to North American Seashore Creatures* (1981). Alfred A. Knopf, New York.

Nelson, J.R. (1994) *Fishes of the World* (3rd edition). John Wiley and Sons, Inc., New York and Chichester.

Neilsen, C. (1995) *Animal Evolution: Interrelationships of the Living Phyla* Oxford University Press, Oxford.

Neilsen, C. (1998) Origin and evolution of animal life cycles. In: *Biological Reviews*, 73, pp. 125–155.

Ono, R. D. Williams, J. D., and Wagner A., (1983) *Vanishing Fishes of North America.* Stone Wall Press, Inc.

Owen, W. (1999) *Whales, Dolphins and Porpoises.* Checkmark Books, New York.

Page, L. M. and Burr, B. M. (1991) *A Field Guide to Freshwater Fishes (North America, North of Mexico).* Peterson Field Guide Series, Houghton Mifflin Co., Boston.

Paxton, J. R. and Eschmeyer, W. N. (1998) *Encyclopedia of Fishes* (2nd edition). Academic Press, New York and London.

Pryor, K. and Norris, K. S. (1998) *Dolphin Societies: Discoveries and Puzzles.* University of California Press, Berkeley.

Quinn, J. R. (1992) *Piranhas – Fact and Fiction.* T.F.H. Publications, Inc., Neptune City, New Jersey.

Reynolds, J. E. and Rommel, S. A. (1999) *Biology of Marine Mammals.* Smithsonian Institution Press, Washington, D.C.

Reynolds, J. E. (2000) *The Bottlenose Dolphin: Biology and Conservation.* Florida University Press, Gainesville.

Rice, D. W. (1998) *Marine Mammals of the World: Systematics and Distribution.* Allen Press, Lawrence, Kansas.

Ridgeway, S. H. and Harrison, R. J. (eds.) (1981–1998) *The Handbook of Marine Mammals: Vols 1-VI.* Academic Press, London.

Ripple, J. and Perrine, D. (1999) *Manatees and Dugongs of the World.* Voyageur Press, Stillwater, Maine.

Ross, R. A. and Schäfer, F. (2000) *Freshwater Rays.* Verlag A.C.S. GmbH.

Schäfer, F. (1997) *All Labyrinths – Bettas, Gouramis, Snakeheads, Nandids.* Verlag A.C.S. GmbH.

Scheel, J. J. (1998) *Atlas of Killifishes of the Old World.* T.F.H. Publications, Inc., Neptune City, New Jersey.

Schraml, E. (1998) *African Cichlids: I– Malawi Mbuna.* Verlag A.C.S. GmbH.

Spotte, S. (1992) *Captive Seawater Fishes (Science and Technology.* John Wiley and Sons, Inc., New York and Chichester.

Stevens, J. (ed) (1987) *Sharks.* Facts On File, New York.

Taylor, L. R. (ed.) (1997) *Sharks & Rays - The Ultimate Guide to Underwater Predators.* Harper Collins Publishers.

Thompson, T. E. (1976) *Biology of the Opisthobranch Molluscs 1*, Ray Society, London.

Thompson, T. E. and Brown, G. H. (1984) *Biology of the Opisthobranch Molluscs 2.* Ray Society, London.

Thompson, K. S. (1991) *Living Fossil – The Story of the Coelacanth.* Hutchinson Radius.

Warner, G. F. (1977) *The Biology of Crabs*, Elek, London.

Watson, L. (1981) *Sea Guide to Whales of the World.* Hutchinson, London.

Watson, R. (1999) *Salmon, Trout and Charr of the World – A Fisherman's Natural History.* Simon Hall Press.

Würsig, B., Jefferson, T. A. & Schmidly, D. J. (2000) *The Marine Mammals of the Gulf of Mexico.* Texas A&M University Press, College Station.

Wishnath, L. (1993) *Atlas of Livebearers of the World.* T.F.H. Publications, Inc., Neptune City, New Jersey.

Yonge, C. M. and Thompson, T. E. (1976) *Living Marine Molluscs.* Collins, London.

# Index

## Picture Credits

Prelims Vol 1: OSF: Daniel Cox ii; Prelims Vol 2: Doug Perrine: ii

Ardea: 119, Kurt Amsler 245, Kev Deacon 246-7, Jean-Paul Ferrero 51, JM Labat 253, Ken Lucas 32b, 82, 226-7, P. Morris 160-1, 164-5, Mark Spencer 262, Ron & Valerie Taylor 261b 29, 261b, Ron Taylor 279t; Alissa Arp/ San Francisco State University: 110; Beverly Factor: 21; Biophotos Associates: 115; Bruce Coleman Collection: Franco Banfi 211b, Sven Halling 42, Malcolm Hey 35, 244t, C & S Hood 260, Pacific Stock 4/5, 234-5, Kim Taylor 252c; Coral Reef Research Institute : 38; Corbis: Hal Beral 46, Lester V Bergman 17, Jonathan Blair 145, Brandeon D. Cole 57, Mimmo Jodice 148/9, Jeffrey L. Rotman 155, Stuart Westmorland 78; Corbis Sygma: Thierry Prat 63; Dr G.L. Baron: 71b; Mark Erdmann: 273c; Frank Lane Picture Library: F. Bavendam/Minden Pictures 101, Susan Dewinsky 109, Foto Natura Stock 224-5, W.T. Miller 82 insert, Flip Nicklin/Minden Pictures 47b; Imagequestmarine.com: 142t, Peter Herring 190, 204-5, 208t, 208b, 209t; Natural Visions: Peter David 239, Heather Angel 67; Nature Picture Library: Dan Burton 182-3, Brandon Cole 142b, 152b, Georgette Douwma 32c, 244b, 256-7, 259t, Jeff Foott 241, Jurgen Freund 22, 282t, David Hall 284-5, Alan James 201, Reijo Juurinen 156-7, Avi Klapfer & Jeff Rotamn 254-5, 281, Conrad Maufe 275c, John Downer Productions 152bl, Fabio Liverani 49, 152t, Naturbild 187, Michael Pitts 6b, 141, Jeff Rotman 256, 275b, 278-9, 282b, 283, John Sparks 153, Sinclair Stammers 70; NHPA: A.N.T 195b, ANT Photo Library 266, 289, Pete Atkinson 34, 56b, Anthony Bannister 56t, Bill Coster 64, Daniel Heuclin 263, Image Quest 3D 37b, Scott Johnson 95t, B. Jones & M. Shimlock 32t, 33, 65, 72, 108, 138/9, 140, 211t, Lutra 188-9, 220-1, Trevor McDonald 23t, 58b, 286-7, Ashod Francis Papazian 265, Peter Parks 11, 121t, Tom & Theresa Stack 28t, MI Walker 25, Nobert Wu 28b, 37t, 238, 251, 264-5; Oxford Scientific Films: 3, 4, 10, 12/13, 20, 39, 74-75, 111b, 117t, 132/3, 160, 175, 178, 196t, Doug Allan 230, Kathie Atkinson 52b, 84, 104, 137t, Tobias Bernhard 86/7, 128b, 259b, 274-5, Waina Cheng 8, Paulo De Oliveira 170, 181, 279b, Mark Deeble & Victoria Stone 83b, Dr F. Ehrenstrom & L. Beyer 121b, 220t, 233,

235b, David Fleetham 2, 9, 50b, 52t, 79, 83t, 90/1, 123, 174, 176, 210, 247b, 261t, 278b, Stephen Foote 117b, Jeff Foote/Okapia 202t, 203t, 203b, David Fox 60b, Gary Gaugler 77, Max Gibbs 176/7, Lawrence Gould 177, Karen Gowlett-Holmes 7, 23b, 24, 27, 86t, 92, 94t, 102, 103, 118-9, 126-7, 126b, 126l, 128/9, 134/5, 134b, 258, Green Cape PTY Ltd 50t, Howard Hall 48/9, 167, Mark Hamblin 47t, Richard Hermann 98/9, 100, 122, Frank Huber 202b, Rodger Jackman 128t, 171, Paul Kay 30/1, 130b, Breck P. Kent 186, Richard Kirby 60t, Rudie Kuiter 85, 96/7, 101t, 131, 194, 195t, 213, Zig Leszczynski 180, Alastair MacEwen 18/9, Victoria A. McCornick 198/9, Prof H. Melhhorn/ Okapia 75, Colin Milikins 48, 54/5, 166, Patrick Morris 191, Tammy Peluso 130t, Michael Pitss 172/3, Science Pictures Ltd 196b, Sue Scott 198, 231, Frithjof Skibbe 87, Gerard Soury 85b, 274, 288, Survival Anglia, Harold Taylor 58t, 92/3, Konrad Wothe 6t, Norbert Wu 94/5, 154, 252t; PA Photos: EPA 150; Photomax: Max Gibbs 204, 214, 216/7, 220b, 224, 232, 235d, 240, 241b, 252b, 268; Premaphotos Wildlife: Ken Preston-Mafham 41t, 68, 105, Dr Rod Preston-Mafham 134t; SAIAB: 272c, 272b; Seaphot: John Lythgoe 99; Seapics: Shedd Aquar/Ceisel 209b; Science Photo Library: 273t, Martin Dohrn 111t, Eye of Science 16, 69, Claude Nuridsany & Marie Perennou 271, David Scharf 71t, Andrew Syred 40, John Walsh 112; Still Pictures: Roland Birke 14/15; Welcome Trust Medical Photographic Library : Graham Budd 137b.

**Diagrams by:** Martin Anderson, Simon Driver

All artwork ©Brown Reference Group plc.

While every effort has been made to trace the copyright holders of illustrations reproduced in this book, the publishers will be pleased to rectify any omissions or inaccuracies.